Feminist Narrative and the Supernatural

CRITICAL EXPLORATIONS IN SCIENCE FICTION AND FANTASY
(a series edited by Donald E. Palumbo and C.W. Sullivan III)

1. *Worlds Apart?
Dualism and Transgression in Contemporary Female Dystopias*
(Dunja M. Mohr, 2005)

2. *Tolkien and Shakespeare:
Essays on Shared Themes and Language*
(edited by Janet Brennan Croft, 2007)

3. *Culture, Identities and Technology in the Star Wars Films:
Essays on the Two Trilogies*
(edited by Carl Silvio and Tony M. Vinci, 2007)

4. *The Influence of Star Trek on Television, Film and Culture*
(edited by Lincoln Geraghty, 2008)

5. *Hugo Gernsback and the Century of Science Fiction* (Gary Westfahl, 2007)

6. *One Earth, One People: The Mythopoeic Fantasy Series
of Ursula K. Le Guin, Lloyd Alexander, Madeleine L'Engle and Orson Scott Card*
(Marek Oziewicz, 2008)

7. *The Evolution of Tolkien's Mythology:
A Study of the History of Middle-earth*
(Elizabeth A. Whittingham, 2008)

8. *H. Beam Piper: A Biography*
(John F. Carr, 2008)

9. *Dreams and Nightmares:
Science and Technology in Myth and Fiction*
(Mordecai Roshwald, 2008)

10. *Lilith in a New Light:
Essays on the George MacDonald Fantasy Novel*
(edited by Lucas H. Harriman, 2008)

11. *Feminist Narrative and the Supernatural:
The Function of Fantastic Devices in Seven Recent Novels*
(Katherine J. Weese, 2008)

Feminist Narrative and the Supernatural

The Function of Fantastic Devices in Seven Recent Novels

KATHERINE J. WEESE

CRITICAL EXPLORATIONS IN
SCIENCE FICTION AND FANTASY, 11

Donald E. Palumbo *and* C.W. Sullivan III, *series editors*

McFarland & Company, Inc., Publishers
Jefferson, North Carolina, and London

LIBRARY OF CONGRESS CATALOGUING-IN-PUBLICATION DATA

Weese, Katherine J.
  Feminist narrative and the supernatural : the function of
fantastic devices in seven recent novels / Katherine J. Weese.
    p. cm. — (Critical explorations in science fiction and fantasy ; 11)
  Includes bibliographical references and index.

  ISBN 978-0-7864-3615-6
  softcover : 50# alkaline paper ∞

  1. American literature—Women authors—History and criticism—
Theory, etc.   2. English literature—Women authors—History and
criticism—Theory, etc.   3. Fantasy in literature.   4. Feminism and
literature—English-speaking countries—History—20th century.
5. Women and literature—English-speaking countries—History—
20th century.   6. Feminist fiction—History and criticism—Theory, etc.
7. Supernatural in literature.   8. Gender identity in literature. I. Title.
  PS147.W44 2008
  823'.914093522—dc22   2008010941

British Library cataloguing data are available

©2008 Katherine J. Weese. All rights reserved

*No part of this book may be reproduced or transmitted in any form
or by any means, electronic or mechanical, including photocopying
or recording, or by any information storage and retrieval system,
without permission in writing from the publisher.*

Cover art ©2008 Shutterstock

Manufactured in the United States of America

*McFarland & Company, Inc., Publishers
  Box 611, Jefferson, North Carolina 28640
  www.mcfarlandpub.com*

For Jane Acomb Leake,
feminist activist and scholar role model

Contents

Acknowledgments	xi
Preface	1
Introduction: Theories of the Fantastic and Feminist Narrative Theory—An Intersection	5

PART I. GOTHIC FICTIONS AND THE FANTASTIC

1. The Novel Weapon: Gender and Genre in Iris Murdoch's *The Sea, the Sea* — 31
2. From "The Lady of Shalott" to "Lady Lazarus": Margaret Atwood's *Lady Oracle* — 48

PART II. GHOSTLY NARRATORS AND NARRATIVE VOICE

3. Narration from Beyond the Grave in Marilynne Robinson's *Housekeeping* — 71
4. The "Invisible" Woman: Narrative Strategies in Carol Shields's *The Stone Diaries* — 87

PART III. THE HISTORICAL NOVEL AND THE FANTASTIC

5. "The Eyes in the Trees": Transculturation and Magic Realism in Barbara Kingsolver's *The Poisonwood Bible* — 109
6. Telling Beloved's Story — 125
7. The Gospel According to Consolata: Alternative Christianities and Toni Morrison's *Paradise* — 146

Chapter Notes	175
Bibliography	203
Index	217

Acknowledgments

I could not have written this book without the support and encouragement of many individuals. My research on the fantastic began at the University of Wisconsin-Madison, where I wrote a doctoral dissertation under the direction of Thomas Schaub, completed in 1993. Almost none of that dissertation survives in this book, which includes readings of five novels that I did not consider as a graduate student (several of them had not yet been published) and which employs a different theoretical framework than I did in my early work. (I was not then interested in feminist theory.) Nonetheless, I'm indebted to Tom for encouraging me to pursue my interest in recent literature of the fantastic and for his careful commentary on my chapters, the chapter on Iris Murdoch, especially, since that one alone appears in this book in a form similar to what I wrote while studying with him.

More recently, numerous of my colleagues at Hampden-Sydney College read portions of the manuscript and provided invaluable responses and suggestions, among them Elizabeth Deis, Sarah Hardy, Lizabeth Rand, Susan Robbins, and Mary Saunders. I am grateful to them for their ongoing interest in my work on the fantastic, an interest that provided me with much motivation to keep working on the project over the years, and for the time they took to comment on various chapters. Mary Saunders was kind enough periodically to request to read portions of the manuscript without my even having to ask for her assistance; Sarah Hardy was present at numerous conferences where I presented portions of this project and always asked probing questions in that capacity. I would also like to thank other audience members at the conferences of the Society for the Study of Narrative Literature and the Society for the Study of American Woman Writers, the Twentieth Century Literature Conference (now the Louisville Conference on Literature and Culture since 1900), and the 1997 Conference on Borders and Foundations in Literature and the Visual Arts, all venues where I have presented papers that eventually evolved into chapters of this book.

Gerry Randall, head of circulation at the Hampden-Sydney College library, is due many thanks for her tireless efforts in obtaining books and articles for me through interlibrary loan, making it possible for me to find countless sources not otherwise available and without which I could not have completed this project. Elizabeth Kocevar-Weidinger at Longwood University's Greenwood Library was also very helpful to me in obtaining sources available there. In addition, I am grateful to the Hampden-Sydney women's book club for introducing me to Carol Shields's *The Stone Diaries* and for inviting me to lead discussions of *Beloved, Housekeeping,* and *The Poisonwood Bible.* As always, my appreciation for these fictions was enhanced by the lively response of the book club members.

Earlier versions of three chapters were published previously as articles, and I am indebted to the editors of the journals in which they appeared for allowing me to print those essays in revised form. An earlier version of Chapter Two appeared as "Feminist Uses of the Fantastic in Iris Murdoch's *The Sea, the Sea*" in *Modern Fiction Studies* 47.3 (Autumn 2001): 630–656 and is included with permission of the Johns Hopkins University Press, Journals Publishing Division (© 2001 by the Purdue Research Foundation). The original version of Chapter Five appeared as "The 'Invisible' Woman: Narrative Strategies in *The Stone Diaries*" in the *Journal of Narrative Theory* 36.1 (Winter 2006): 90–120 and is included with permission of *JNT* and Eastern Michigan University (© 2006 *JNT: Journal of Narrative Theory*). Finally, a version of Chapter Six, on Barbara Kingsolver's *The Poisonwood Bible,* appeared under the same title in *Journal of the Fantastic in the Arts* 17.1 (Spring 2006): 4–20 and is included with permission of *JFA* and IAFA (© 2006 International Association for the Fantastic in the Arts).

Finally, I am indebted to Hampden-Sydney College's Committee on Professional Development for providing numerous faculty summer development grants to support my work on many sections of this book, and for granting a sabbatical leave in 2006 and 2007 that allowed me to bring the project to completion.

Preface

More than twenty years ago, a special issue of *Women's Studies: An Interdisciplinary Journal*, edited by Patrick D. Murphy and Marleen Barr and titled "Feminism Faces the Fantastic," made a call for feminist theory to engage more thoroughly with literature of the fantastic. In the introduction, Murphy observed that "still too often, feminist critics in treating an author like Marge Piercy or Margaret Atwood ignore or downplay the fantastic element of the fiction in the course of emphasizing the feminist thematics" (83); and in the afterword, Barr called for feminist critics to devote more attention to "contemporary feminist fabulation" (190). An interesting feature of the *Women's Studies* special issue, however, is that the articles therein dealt almost exclusively with science fiction and utopian/dystopian fiction, rather than with works that I would term "fantastic." The body of fiction that interests me is one that does not lend itself easily to generic classifications: the works incorporate moments of the fantastic—events that are perhaps supernatural—within narratives otherwise steeped in realistic detail about the historical circumstances of women's lives. The fantastic moments may constitute a relatively small portion of the narrative, with the effect that in the critical literature, the works might be construed primarily as domestic or historical fictions rather than as fictions of the fantastic. Yet in each case, the fantastic element affects the narrative and narration in crucial ways. Such novels include Iris Murdoch's *The Sea, the Sea*, Margaret Atwood's *Lady Oracle*, Marilynne Robinson's *Housekeeping*, Carol Shields's *The Stone Diaries*, Barbara Kingsolver's *The Poisonwood Bible*, and Toni Morrison's *Beloved* and *Paradise*. In undertaking research on these novels, I have observed the same phenomenon that Murphy described in 1987: even when many of these novels have received a great deal of critical attention from theorists interested in the feminist issues raised, the fantastic elements have often gone unexamined, sometimes even unremarked upon altogether, and have never been systematically explored through the lens of theories of the fantastic.

My own interest in literature of the fantastic emerged at about the same time as the special issue of *Women's Studies* was published, although my focus then was not a feminist one. Writing a dissertation on the postmodern fantastic and focusing on more novels written by men than by women, I encountered

Tzvetan Todorov's structuralist approach to the fantastic, my first introduction to theories of this literary mode. I also encountered several then-current studies of postmodern fiction, mostly written about male authors, that seemed to apply Todorov's ideas in ways that simply didn't account for the moments of the fantastic that I was increasingly finding in contemporary novels. As my own interests shifted toward women writers in particular, there seemed to be an even greater divide between feminist fiction that employed the fantastic and theories of the fantastic as a literary mode.

Todorov's study of the fantastic—indeed, his work in general—addresses questions of narrative structure as they pertain to the fantastic; my own emerging interest in seemingly supernatural moments in fiction written by contemporary women novelists and in narrative theory led me to investigate the relationship between the fantastic and feminist storytelling practices. Several important studies of women authors' narrative practice emerged in the late 1980s and early 1990s, but these studies did not reconsider theories of the fantastic from a feminist perspective, even when they analyzed feminist fictions that employed the fantastic. The purpose of this book, then, is to explore the ways in which theories of the fantastic and feminist narrative theories intersect, bringing together two theoretical discourses that have not adequately engaged one another in order to illuminate an important body of recent fiction that blends the supernatural and the real.

While critics have been slow to answer Murphy and Barr's injunction, there have been some notable exceptions. Of particular importance is Anne Koenen's *Visions of Doom, Plots of Power: The Fantastic in Anglo-American Women's Literature* (1999), which thoroughly grounds the study of the fantastic in feminist theory. Some of the literary works that Koenen analyzes overlap with those that I consider; however, the body of fiction she examines differs insofar as many of the works tend more toward fantasy than the fantastic, and several novels and stories that she includes precede the postmodern period on which I focus in this study. In addition, my study focuses more intensely than does Koenen's on feminist narrative theory in particular, with close attention to narrative voice as well as to narrative form. In this endeavor, I have been greatly aided by Susan Snaider Lanser's *Fictions of Authority: Women Writers and Narrative Voice*, a work of feminist narrative theory that, although it does not engage with theories of the fantastic, has provided many useful ways to consider the unusual narrative perspectives employed in the novels I examine. Finally, I am indebted to the recent work of Anne Hegerfeldt, *Lies that Tell the Truth: Magic Realism Seen through Contemporary Fiction from Britain*. Theories of magic realism that coincide with critical interest in postcolonial fiction offer a counterpoint to the theories of the fantastic in postmodern literature that fail to account for feminist uses of the fantastic. Hegerfeldt does not approach magic realism from a feminist perspective, but nonetheless many of her ideas are well-suited to a feminist study of the fantastic, and many of the tenets of magic realist theory that she identifies illuminate the novels I consider here, even when those novels do not quite fit definitions of magic realism. Especially useful is Hegerfeldt's focus on the phenomenon of hesitation in the reader's encounter with the magic realist text: I posit that her account of the relationship between hesitation and the reader's confrontation with social constructions of reality, a dynamic that she finds in the magic realist tale but not necessarily in the fantastic tale as theorized by Todorov, can be extended to a feminist reading of the novels of the fantastic in a manner that recuperates Todorov's structuralist approach by extending it to an ideological context.

Considering new approaches to the study of narrative specifically within a feminist framework, narrative theorist Robyn Warhol points out that feminist narratologists have generally been more attuned to close readings of individual texts than classical, structuralist narratologists, while still finding general "patterns among narrative forms of story and discourse" (340). In answering the question central to feminist considerations of narrative—"'How does this text construct masculinity or femininity in and for its reader?'"—Warhol argues that "any attempt at a complete answer for such a question requires a close reading of that text" (343).[1] In keeping, then, with the feminist concern to elucidate texts fully and coherently, this study is organized around readings of individual novels rather than around particular functions or forms of the fantastic as illustrated cursorily in a large group of novels. Connections among the various novels are pointed out, and novels are grouped in ways that emphasize those similarities, but ultimately structural similarities are subordinated to full considerations of the context and function of the fantastic devices and these devices' relationship to feminist narrative practice in each individual novel.

This group of seven novels illustrates a significant but often overlooked trend in fiction written by women in the last three decades of the twentieth century, incorporating moments of the fantastic within otherwise realistic narratives concerned with patriarchal constructions of femininity. The novels' fantastic devices highlight various feminist narrative concerns such as the authority of the female voice, the implications of narrative form for gender construction, revisions to traditional genre conventions by women writers, and the recovery of alternative versions of stories suppressed by dominant historical narratives. The fantastic thus provides a valuable framework for illuminating feminist narrative praxis. Exploring the intersection of feminist narrative theory and theories of the fantastic allows literary critics to answer Murphy and Barr's 1987 call for feminism to face the fantastic.

Introduction: Theories of the Fantastic and Feminist Narrative Theory— An Intersection

> Women splitting the world open by writing their improbable interpretations of "reality" [...] deconstruct a misogynist tradition and challenge androcentric literary paradigms, exposing ideological premises and violating patriarchal order.
> —Anne Koenen, *Visions of Doom, Plots of Power* [38]

In Iris Murdoch's *The Sea, the Sea*, a man seemingly transforms himself into a lizard-like creature to rescue his cousin from drowning in a dangerous tidal pool. In Margaret Atwood's *Lady Oracle*, a woman writer is visited by the astral spirit of her dead mother and participates in automatic writing sessions over which she has no conscious control. Marilynne Robinson's *Housekeeping* is narrated by an adolescent girl who might possibly have drowned at the end of the novel, but who continues her autobiographical narrative past the moment of her death, speaking of how she haunts the living. Similarly, Carol Shields employs in *The Stone Diaries* a highly complex narrative perspective that, it can be argued, originates from a typical housewife who recounts the moment of her own death seemingly from a point beyond the grave, her ghostly voice expressing dissatisfaction with her conventional existence. Likewise, a voice that perhaps emanates from a dead child narrates the final chapter of Barbara Kingsolver's *The Poisonwood Bible*, the child having been transformed into snake that hides in the trees and observes the living members of her family. In Toni Morrison's *Beloved*, a murdered child perhaps returns from the dead and moves into the house where her mother and sister reside, a strange visitor whose identity is only gradually revealed—and never definitively confirmed. In Morrison's *Paradise*, five women are shot by a group of men, but their bodies disappear from the site of the massacre, and they seem to then inhabit an afterlife realm where they devote themselves to enacting social change.

Although these novels do not conform to the conventions of classic literary realism, they portray the social realities of women's lives and are often considered to be primarily historical or domestic fictions. In varying degrees, however, they incorporate supernatural or seemingly impossible events, ranging, for example, from a brief moment in Carol Shields's *The Stone Diaries* when the first-person narrator claims to have died but seems to continue telling her story from beyond the grave, to the much more prominent and prolonged presence of a character often assumed to be a ghost in Toni Morrison's *Beloved*.

These novels comprise a body of fiction that can be illuminated by reconsidering theories of the fantastic through the lens of feminist narrative theory, since the presence of the fantastic enables feminist narrative strategies. Though many of these fictions have received a great deal of critical attention, theorists of the fantastic and feminist narrative theorists have generally failed to account systematically for the hybrid nature of these texts that blend the impossible with the real, largely because the two theoretical discussions fail to engage one another. And yet these two discourses—discussions of how the fantastic functions in narrative to disrupt conventional reality and discussions of how feminist writers' narrative techniques challenge patriarchal ideology—prove mutually illuminating when considered in conjunction with one another. As Anne Koenen points out of women's fiction, "writing from the position of the other and challenging dominant values [...] coincides with definitions of the fantastic" (38). By exploring the intersections of these theories, critics can develop a better understanding of the fantastic as it relates to the social and historical concerns of contemporary women authors.[1]

Why have theorists of the fantastic and feminist theorists been relatively reluctant to explore the mutually illuminating facets of their particular projects? Perhaps it is in part because of the potential danger, noted by Maria Clark, of defining the "feminine fantastic as the expression of what is essentially feminine, namely irrational, mad, imaginary, and everything else that takes a negative position in a hierarchical polar opposition" (239). Drawing on the work of Mary Ann Doane, Clark goes on to caution that considering the coincidence of the feminine and the supernatural might simply reinforce "a tendency identified by feminist theorists to 'further dematerialize and derealize 'woman'" (Doane et al. 12), a tendency certainly anathema to the feminist project.[2] Yet as we will see, feminist narrative theory provides a way to ground a discussion of the fantastic elements of these novels firmly in the social and historical realms, avoiding the pitfalls of essentializing women; the fantastic works precisely to "realize" the female experience against socially constructed, patriarchal realities.

Many theories of the fantastic also do little to encourage feminist scholarship of the hybrid fictions considered in this study. Though some of these novels—chiefly *Beloved*—have been examined as magic realist novels or novels of the fantastic by critics interested in these types of narratives, many of them have not, perhaps in part because the novels are difficult to classify according to reigning theories of these modes. Feminist studies of novels that do not wholly conform to realism have tended to focus instead on genre fiction, novels easily identifiable as second-world fantasy, science fiction, or utopian/dystopian fictions. Armitt and Koenen, two critics who have more thoroughly than others addressed the call for feminism to face the fantastic, make similar points about how women's genre fiction has been more thoroughly examined than other works that employ fantastic devices (Armitt, *Theorizing* 12; Koenen 2). Theories of the fantastic, as distinct from science fiction or fantasy, more often than not are concerned primarily with matters of classification that do not readily lend themselves to feminist analysis, and women's fictions of the fantastic often cannot be readily fitted into the classifications that the theories propose. This is especially true of theories of the postmodern fantastic that dominated the discussion of the fantastic in the 1980s: they fail adequately to account for how women authors employ postmodern devices; these theories and contemporary women's fiction seem worlds apart.

Many theorists have relied heavily on structuralist premises, in particular on the work of Tzevetan Todorov in his seminal study, *The Fantastic: A Structural Approach to a Literary Genre*, a work that might seem at first glance theoretically outmoded and of little use to feminist critics. As Rosemary Jackson points out, critics must acknowledge the importance of Todorov's work (5) but also need to extend Todorov's "investigation from one being limited to the *poetics* of the fantastic into one aware of the *politics* of its forms" (6).[3] Todorov's largely structural approach to the fantastic often gestures toward "the social function" of this body of literature (*The Fantastic* 158), a point that he of course does not consider within a feminist context but that does pave the way for feminist applications of his theory. Reconsidering several of Todorov's important observations through the lens of feminist narrative theory in particular provides a means for feminist critics to develop theories of feminist narrative praxis that both move critical discussion beyond issues of classification and avoid the pitfalls of essentializing the feminine fantastic, given feminist narrative theory's focus on the role of social construction on discursive practices. In general, this book revises and extends Todorov's work in the spirit described by David Herman in *Narratologies: New Perspectives on Narrative Analysis*: Historicist critical methods have allowed literary scholars to evolve new theories about stories, new modes of narrative analysis, which "stand in a more or less critical and reflexive relation to the structuralist tradition, borrowing more or less extensively from the analytic heritage they aim to surpass" (1). In what Herman calls a "root transformation" of the "narratological landscape," there has been "a shift from text-centered or formal models to models that are jointly formal and functional—models attentive both to the text and to the context of stories," including issues such as "ways of living out or contesting more or less implicitly gendered response to certain kinds of narrative structure; modes of resisting or acceding to ideological interpellations encoded in the way a story is recounted; or ethical responses to the values represented, assumed, undercut, ironized, complicated, or reinforced, as the case might be, through various kinds of narrative techniques" (8-9). These issues are of great interest to feminist critics concerned with narrative theory, and they are all highly relevant to a study of the fantastic in feminist novels.

Approaches to defining the fantastic, from the publication of Todorov's theory in 1970 (translated 1973) to the present, have been thoroughly rehearsed elsewhere, most recently by Martin Horstkotte (2004) and Anne Hegerfeldt (2005) in their examinations of the fantastic and of magic realism, respectively.[4] Rather than cover this ground in detail again, this introduction touches on only a few key points of definition, in part to illustrate how the works considered in this book defy easy classification, even though they all clearly employ fantastic moments. Distinctions made between the fantastic and magic realism do not always hold true in these novels, and frequently critical/theoretical observations about magic realism prove very useful for the body of novels examined, even when the novels are not themselves magic realist. Likewise, Todorov's crucial concept of hesitation in the fantastic tale, a point of definition that is often used to distinguish the fantastic from magic realism, can also be applied to magic realist texts. The introduction then turns to a discussion of how the fantastic devices depicted in these novels illustrate tenets of feminist narrative theory insofar as these devices call attention to social constructions of gender and provide a means by which authors overturn these constructions.

All of the works considered share the following six interrelated features and functions. The fiction introduces an event that defies explanation according to scientific, empirical, post–Enlightenment means of understanding the world. The event challenges the way that women's realities have been constructed in a masculinist society and offers alternative feminist understandings of women's experience. The narrative as a whole is constructed in such a way that it includes realistic details of the historical world—indeed may be dominated by such details—but does not conform to the standards of conventional literary realism; it is non-mimetic both in its inclusion of a seemingly impossible event and in its narrative technique, even when the realistic detail dominates the work. The work employs narrative strategies that fracture teleology, defy closure, and highlight ambiguities of meaning. The narrative exhibits self-consciousness about narratives in general and/or about its own status as a narrative; the fantastic device facilitates this self-consciousness about storytelling practices.[5] The narrative revises conventional literary genres from a feminist perspective, introducing new versions of, for example, the gothic novel, the quest novel, the *Kunstlerroman*, the autobiographical novel, and the historical novel. These features and functions recall two of Todorov's chief concerns that provide useful points of departure for this book: first, the complex relationship between the fantastic and the real, and the concomitant hesitation evoked in the text about the reality status of a seemingly supernatural event; and second, the coincidence of the fantastic with *narrative* literature.

DEFINING TERMS

In spite of frequent complaints about the narrowness of Todorov's definition of the fantastic, critics nonetheless return to his seminal work as a starting place for revised definitions of the mode.[6] Todorov defines the "pure" fantastic in literature as the moment of hesitation a reader experiences when he or she attempts to resolve a seemingly supernatural event in a text "so that the event is acknowledged as reality, or so that the event is identified as the fruit of the imagination or the result of an illusion; in other words, we may decide that the event *is* or *is not*" (157). Once a reader decides that such an event actually occurs within the fictional world depicted, the work ceases to be "fantastic" and becomes "marvelous," which Todorov defines as a genre in which mysterious events are presented as probable and supernatural. If, on the other hand, the reader determines that the event is either the result of some illusion or that it never took place (was purely imaginary, a psychological effect), the work may be considered "uncanny," in that it provides an improbable but essentially rational explanation for the event (25). The pure fantastic exists, then, only when the reader cannot decide between these two solutions to the problem: it exists only in the reader's and/or one or more characters' uncertainty. The fantastic is thus for the most part only a transitory state: in few works does it persist throughout the entire work (Henry James's *The Turn of the Screw* provides one such instance); usually it is resolved into either the marvelous or uncanny.[7]

Todorov's focus on hesitation proves essential for other theorists, whether those theorists be primarily interested in taxonomies of fantastic narratives or in the social uses to which the fantastic is put. The perceived absence of hesitation becomes a crucial defining feature for those interested in distinguishing the fantastic from both fantasy and from magic realism. The fantastic and fantasy can be defined differently insofar as the former introduces a seemingly supernatural or logically impossible event into a world that operates according to the laws of empirical, scientific reality, a world recognizably the historical world that readers inhabit, whereas the latter creates in essence its own world that operates according to its own set of laws, where there is no distinction between the real and the supernatural: the created world is "unidimensional," to borrow Amaryll Chanady's term. In fantastic literature, hesitation plays a key role, while in fantasy literature, it does not: encountering fantasy, readers suspend disbelief and accept that the world depicted operates according to a different set of laws than the laws by which they generally understand the world they inhabit. This distinction between fantasy and the fantastic is important because the novels considered in this book are so thoroughly set in the historical world, and because this fact is crucial to reading them through the lens of feminist narrative theory.[8] But the distinction between the fantastic and magic realism that many theorists maintain in their classifications of these modes seems less crucial—perhaps even counterproductive—for the body of novels considered in this book.

In contrast to fantasy, both literature of the fantastic and magic realism are "bidimensional" insofar as they contain elements both of the recognizable, historical world and of the supernatural. Todorov does not himself use the term magic realism, but theorists of this mode often employ Todorov's focus on hesitation, or some variation of it, to define magic realism in contradistinction to the fantastic. Chanady, for example, broadens Todorov's concept of hesitation by using the term "antimony, or the simultaneous presence of two conflicting codes in the text," neither of which "can be accepted in the presence of the other" so that the "apparently supernatural phenomenon remains inexplicable" (12). Antimony, like hesitation, involves the response of the reader, producing "disorientation" about the ambiguous reality presented in the text (13-14). Chanady distinguishes between the fantastic and magic realism, however, by describing the fantastic as a mode that necessarily renders problematic the appearance of two codes of reality (14). Magical realism, on the other hand, results when "the supernatural is not presented as problematic" (23) and thus, unlike its presentation in the mode of the fantastic, "the supernatural in magical realism does not disconcert the reader," a fact that for Chanady constitutes "the fundamental difference between the two modes" (24). Summing up her theory, she writes,

> Although [both] the fantastic and magic realism are characterized by the presence of coherently developed codes of the natural and the supernatural, and are therefore structurally similar, the manner in which these two codes interact in the text distinguishes the two modes from each other. Whereas the antimony appears to be resolved in magic realism, the contradictions between different conceptions of reality are placed in the foreground by the author of a fantastic text. In fact, the emphasis on conflicting world views which cannot be resolved according to the laws posited by the text itself is the most important distinguishing characteristic of the fantastic [69].

More recently, Horstkotte sums up the differences among fantasy, the fantastic, and magic realism, coming to a conclusion similar to Chanady's in distinguishing between the latter two: "magic realism [...] does not elicit any hesitancy or wonder in the reader" (41).[9]

What some critics describe as magic realism—in essence a literary work that combines a representation of the historical world with the supernatural while removing the hesitation experienced by character, narrator, and/or reader in the classic fantastic tale—Todorov himself describes as marking the end of the fantastic as a genre, using Kafka's *The Metamorphosis* as the central text to illustrate the shift away from the fantastic in literary history.[10] Quite apart from theorists of magic realism (who tended until recently to focus on Latin American fiction that presents the supernatural as real, without any hesitation on the part of characters and narrators), there emerged a group of theorists who essentially followed Todorov in his conclusion about the disappearance of the real, and hence of the fantastic, to account for the absence of hesitation in twentieth-century fantastic literature. Before returning to recent developments in magic realist theory that restore the concept of hesitation to magic realist fiction, we need to examine theories of the so-called "generalized fantastic," which seemed to dominate discussions of twentieth-century fantastic literature in the 1980s.

Central to Todorov's theory of the fantastic is the relationship between the fantastic and the real; as we have seen, Todorov's definition of the fantastic depends upon the concept of hesitation about the status of the reality of an event. Once hesitation is eliminated, a work is resolved into either the uncanny or the marvelous. Kafka's *The Metamorphosis*, the work that signals for Todorov the demise of the fantastic as a genre, employs both the marvelous and the uncanny, an impossible contradiction according to the rules of Todorov's schema. First, Gregor Samsa's transformation is not accompanied, as it would be in a traditional uncanny tale, by a gradual building from a semblance of normalcy to an abnormal or supernatural aura. Rather, Kafka presents the transformation in the work's first sentence as though he were reporting something as mundane as the weather. Second, *The Metamorphosis* does not fit the category of the marvelous either, which, according to Todorov, "implies that we are plunged into a world whose laws are totally different from what they are in our own and in consequence that the supernatural events which occur are in no way disturbing" (171-2). Instead, Kafka's tale is set within an otherwise realistic setting, clearly the historical world of everyday reality. *The Metamorphosis* presents, then, "indeed a shocking, impossible event which concerns us, but it is an event which ends by becoming possible, paradoxically enough. In this sense, Kafka's narratives relate both to the marvelous and to the uncanny; they are the coincidence of two apparently incompatible genres. The supernatural is given, and yet it does not cease to seem inadmissible to us" (172).[11]

According to Todorov, pre-modern fantastic literature maintains an explicit relation with the real. However, he continues,

> today, we can no longer believe in an immutable, external reality, nor in a literature which is merely the transcription of such a reality. Words have gained an autonomy which things have lost. [...] Fantastic literature itself—which on every page subverts linguistic categorizations—has received a fatal blow from these very categorizations. [...] The literature of the twentieth century is, in a certain sense, more purely "literature" than any other [168].

That is, fantastic literature, by virtue of the loss of the real that surrounds the fantastic in pre-modern literature, has become extinct in the modern era, a genre no longer possible, because the fantastic cannot exist independent of some sense of the real against which it defines itself; twentieth-century fantastic literature is "more purely 'literature' than any other" because it "no longer has anything to do with the real" (173), having been replaced by "a generalized fantastic which swallows up the entire world of the book and the reader along with it" (174).

Many other theorists have followed Todorov in this conclusion, and their heavy reliance on Todorov's final chapter of *The Fantastic* accounts for their theories' failure to describe the project of contemporary women authors who employ the fantastic. Until recently, most studies of twentieth-century literature and the fantastic have concluded that postmodern works employ what Gerhard Hoffman, like Todorov, terms a "generalized fantastic" and what Christine Brooke-Rose terms a "displaced fantastic": works call into question the status of all reality and meaning, deconstructing these categories without reconstructing anything in their place. The novels on which these critics of the fantastic focus—mostly metafictions written by male authors of the 1960s and 1970s—need not employ supernatural devices of any kind; indeed, the generalized fantastic is the self-referential world these fictions create, where character, self, history, reality, and truth are all presented simply as textual constructions and hence are "unreal."

As Brooke-Rose points out in *A Rhetoric of the Unreal*, Todorov's emphasis on the moment of ambiguity or hesitation can, if one does not emphasize that this moment surrounds a supernatural event, lead to the conclusion that all ambiguous texts, even ones that do not hint at any supernatural devices, fall under the rubric of the fantastic. Brooke-Rose concludes that we "must treat such other non-'fantastic' texts as a displaced form of the fantastic" (65), since Todorov's pure fantastic in fact historically "prefigur[es] many modern (non-fantastic) texts which can be read on several and often paradoxically contradictory levels" (71). In Brooke-Rose's chapter on postmodernism, consideration of the fantastic as a potentially supernatural occurrence drops out of the discussion altogether, as though the supernatural ceased to be a force in postmodern texts, which seem to have gone over wholly to what she calls the displaced fantastic.

Hoffmann's long article "The Fantastic in Fiction: Its 'Reality' Status, its Historical Development and its Transformation in Postmodern Narration" (1982) develops a related concept, arguing that the fantastic should include not only the supernatural, but also the "active play, creativity, the imaginative construct" that characterizes fictions by Barth, Barthelme, Coover, Pynchon, and Hawkes. According to Hoffman's theory, in works by these and other authors, Todorov's concept of the fantastic (hesitation) is replaced by a radical negation of the recognizability or explainability and even of the need to recognize or explain. Not only the concepts of essence and authenticity but also of relevance (and coherence) are abandoned in favor of non-relevance and non-meaning which the human being, accustomed to and constituted by meaning-building processes, must conceive as "irreal," as fantastic [320].

Hoffman traces the manner in which all narrative conventions such as character, plot, and action gradually fall under this definition of the fantastic during the evolution of narrative forms through history, until finally narrative itself becomes a "fantastic irrelevance" (320). By the time we reach the postmodern era, then, fiction has "no thematic coherence and no reference to a recognizable world 'outside'"; rather, its "significance lies in the surface of narrative situations" (314).[12]

Brian McHale reaches a similar conclusion in his chapter on the fantastic in *Postmodernist Fiction*, "A World Next Door." McHale, who focuses upon ontological (as opposed to epistemological) uncertainty in all postmodern fiction, concludes that "postmodernist fiction has close affinities with the genre of the fantastic [… b]ecause the fantastic genre, […] like postmodern fiction itself, is governed by the ontological dominant" (74). McHale notes that some form of Todorov's fantastic does persist in postmodernist writing, but he also partially concurs with Todorov's point about the genre's demise by naming postmodern fiction (in very much the same vein as Brooke-Rose) a "displaced fantastic": "a generalized fantastic effect or 'charge' seems to be diffused throughout postmodernist writing, making its presence felt in displaced forms in the texts that are not formally fantastic at all" (81). McHale, despite his prior claim that representation is still alive and well in the postmodern text (75), goes on to assert further that in the displaced fantastic, often "it looks as if hesitation has been transferred from ontological structure to *language* […]" (81). Drawing on texts by William Gass and Maurice Blanchot, McHale concludes that these instances of the displaced fantastic turn out to be not "the haunted house or 'gothic enclosure'" of the classic fantastic tale but "haunted houses of fiction or even haunted prison-houses of language" (81-2). Like other theorists following Todorov, McHale stresses "the anti-representational foregrounding of *language for its own sake*" (83) that the postmodern fantastic exploits.[13] Likewise Lance Olsen's *Ellipse of Uncertainty: An Introduction to Postmodern Fantasy* (1987) states that "contemporary fantasy may be thought of as the literary equivalent of deconstructionism" (3). Olsen furthermore adopts the frequently made claim that "the fantastic becomes the realism our culture understands" (14), thereby draining the fantastic of its defamiliarizing potential.[14]

Writing much more recently and revisiting theories of the generalized fantastic, Martin Horstkotte objects, as do I, to the narrow range of authors to which these definitions apply (works by Borges, Calvino, the French new novelists and American metafictionists), as well as taking issue with the conclusion that "postmodernism *is* fantastic" (61-62). Horstkotte makes a case for the inclusion of British authors in his definition of the postmodern fantastic, which combines elements of the traditional fantastic as defined by Todorov and elements of postmodernism (62-63). But later in his work he seems to contradict himself, writing that "metafiction [...] has traits that mark it as inherently fantastic" even in the absence of "other non-mimetic moments" (140). In addition, his study of what he terms "the totalisation of the fantastic" (64) in postmodern British literature includes only fiction written by men.

These theories of the fantastic, like the theorists' choice of exemplary authors suggests, are far better suited to male metafictionists' experiments than to works by most contemporary women authors. The discussions set forth by feminist critics of women's experimental narratives—to which we will turn shortly—make clear that women authors do not by and large subscribe to the brand of postmodernism embraced by many male authors of the time since women seek to reestablish a connection with the real. Instead, women's fiction of recent years moves beyond the generalized fantastic of the male metafictionists while still retaining metafictional elements. Certainly Todorov's observations about the impossibility of accessing some stable truth in the twentieth century are true—many feminist fictions explicitly address this problem—but this same body of literature allows critics to draw a very different set of conclusions about the continued existence of fantastic literature and about the relationship of that literature to what we call the "real" than do Todorov and those subscribing to the theory of the generalized fantastic in the postmodern age. Literature of the fantastic does indeed still exist—and nowhere more vibrantly than in contemporary women's fiction in which instances of the unreal highlight the authors' social and historical concerns.

Most of these women's fictions seem to accept, to one degree or another, the presence of the supernatural, but, just as Todorov suggests about *The Metamorphosis,* these works place these events squarely within our world, rather than within a marvelous, unreal world,[15] and hence the texts occupy a both/and rather than an either/or position within Todorov's schema. In these works, the supernatural and the real intersect, without being resolved into either Todorov's marvelous or uncanny, in such a way that these novels allow us to understand the historical world more deeply, rather than simply inviting us to eschew reality as a meaningful category. As Koenen points out, "Women's fantastic literature does not reduce postmodernism to the aspect of aesthetics where 'anything goes,' but connects to postmodernism as a social and political phenomenon in which marginalized groups question the hegemony of white male supremacy, while at the same time pointing to strategies of resistance and subversion and exposing the limits and mechanizations of hegemony" (309). In other words, the presence of the supernatural disrupts conventional narrative practice and forces the reader to confront alternative realities to official histories; the fantastic "scrutinizes the categories of the patriarchal real" (Cranny-Francis 77).[16]

In essence, recent women writers' uses of the fantastic demonstrate that Todorov is wrong on two counts: first, diegetic hesitation has not entirely disappeared from the workings of the fantastic text, since we can see many examples of recent fictions that do in fact contain this feature of the traditional fantastic tale; and second, its absence within the diegesis or in the comments of an extradiegetic narrator does not in fact cut off the text from any relationship to extra-textual reality. Magic realist theory, which develops quite a different response to the absence of diegetic hesitation in contemporary narratives than do theories of the generalized fantastic, proves much more useful to illuminate the feminist novels explored in this book than do theories of the generalized fantastic.[17]

As magic realist theorists demonstrate in analyzing works that structurally resemble *The Metamorphosis*, such works indeed engage with the real by highlighting historical clashes about the nature of reality and the efforts of a dominant group to impose its world view on a marginal group. A key difference, then, between magic realist theory and Todorov's theory of the end of the fantastic lies precisely in the issue of the relationship between the fantastic elements and the realistic elements of these fictions. While Todorov concludes that the real in essence disappears, those theorizing magic realism claim quite the opposite: Wendy Faris, for example, observes that because the magical elements are presented not as strange or surprising to the characters or the narrator, they have the effect that "the element of surprise is redirected onto the history we are about to witness, which constitutes the nasty shock" (*Ordinary Enchantments* 14). In other words, the presence of the fantastic in effect calls attention to the fantastical or unreal nature of the conqueror's version of history. It is both impossible and undesirable to consider magic realist works apart from the historical real. Faris's comment implicitly recognizes reader hesitation and belies Chanady's distinction between the fantastic and magic realism insofar as the latter does indeed foreground conflicting codes of reality and does render problematic the distinction between the real and the not-real. Thus one can argue that even those texts that dispense with hesitation at the level of character and narrator do not necessarily eliminate the reader's experience of hesitation about the relationship between two incompatible codes or ways of knowing represented in texts that blend the natural and the supernatural. Critic Anne Hegerfeldt likewise disagrees with the argument that one can distinguish between the fantastic and magic realist text by asserting that the former evokes hesitation but the latter does not. While magic realism does not thematize hesitation like the fantastic does by exploring a character's attempts to come to terms with a supernatural occurrence or by expressing any narrative surprise about events that would seem to be surprising, still "magic realist texts do in fact engender a moment of hesitation—it merely has been relocated to the level of the reader" (55).[18] Hegerfeldt, revising Chanady's theory, writes that magic realism's bidimensionality arises from its evocation and subsequent transgression of the narrative conventions of literary realism. The matter-of-fact manner of narration, combined with a realistic setting, calls to mind the realist mode, only to immediately come into conflict with the non-realistic events narrated. While the narrator's attitude indicates that a certain event is to be accepted as an empirically real and often not even particularly astonishing occurrence, the conventions of the realist mode point in the opposite direction, designating the event as impossible. [...] The uncertainty over which set of conventions to apply in reading draws attention to these conventions as cultural constructs [54-55].

All of the novels considered in this book involve reader hesitation that functions precisely as Hegerfeldt describes, inviting the reader to rethink conventions of realism and recognize them as constructs.[19] Because feminist narrative theory has quite a similar project in demonstrating how narrative conventions have served patriarchal ends in the construction of dominant versions of reality, this formulation of hesitation in both the fantastic and the magical realist novel can be productively explored in conjunction with theories of feminist narrative practice.

Some of the novels explored in this book, in accordance with the definition of the classic fantastic tale, thematize character hesitation as well as reader hesitation: Murdoch's *The Sea, the Sea* more so than the others fits Todorov's definition of the pure fantastic, and both Morrison's *Beloved* and *Paradise* thematize character hesitation over a fantastic event: in the former, characters and the reader wonder if Sethe's murdered child has returned incarnate, and the novel holds in tension a supernatural and a naturalistic explanation of the presence of the young woman called Beloved; in the latter, characters wonder what has happened to the bodies of five women assumed to be shot and killed, and the novel holds in tension supernatural and naturalistic explanations of the women's disappearance. But at the same time, Morrison's novels blend the hesitation characteristic of the fantastic tale with the narrators' unfazed presentation of the impossible: the baby ghost in *Beloved* is introduced in the novel's opening lines matter-of-factly with no sense of astonishment from either the narrator or the characters, and in *Paradise* fantastic events other than the disappearance of the women are presented in the same blasé manner, such as the ability of one character to raise the dead and to prolong human life, or the spiritual presence of another woman's two dead children. Morrison's two novels, then, seem to employ both the fantastic and magic realism as they have been commonly defined. Atwood's *Lady Oracle* likewise combines elements of a fantastic and magic realist presentation of the supernatural: while the first-person narrator and main character expresses hesitation over the first seemingly supernatural occurrence in the novel, she later presents subsequent strange events in a matter-of-fact manner. Yet there develops a tension between male characters' tendency to naturalize or not even to register the supernatural while the female characters accept it, and from this tension there results an interrogation of masculinist constructions of "reality."

No character hesitation about the status of what I am calling a supernatural event exists in either Robinson's *Housekeeping*, Shields's *The Stone Diaries*, or Kingsolver's *The Poisonwood Bible* for the simple reason that the supernatural moment exists only in the relationship between the first-person narrator who claims to be dead and the reader—no other character in the novels ever witnesses or becomes privy to the fact that the narrative or some part of it seems to emanate from a narrator who has already died prior to the point in time from which the narrative is generated. Because the character-narrators state matter-of-factly that they have died, they do not exhibit any hesitation, either. But hesitation certainly exists for the reader, who might wonder if the narrators of *The Stone Diaries* and *Housekeeping* really are dead at the time of narration, and who might, based on cues in the text, conclude either yes or no, opting for either a supernatural or a naturalistic explanation of the seemingly impossible narrative perspective. (Alternatively, the reader might decide the narrator's ontological status is undecidable, an instance of the pure fantastic.) In the case of the third novel, *The Poisonwood Bible*, the reader will hesitate initially about who is narrating the final section of the novel and about whether the dead child Ruth May has indeed been transformed into a snake or spirit, but the narrative cues seem to invite readers to conclude that this is in fact what has transpired in the narrative world.[20] Because it takes place in a colonial and postcolonial setting even if the author is an American and not postcolonial writer, because its fantastic event relates to the colonizeds' belief system, and because the fantastic is conveyed without surprise, this novel perhaps more than the others in the study fits definitions of magic realism. Morrison's novels, of course, also partake of magic realist narrative techniques and fit the category along with Kingsolver's novel if one adopts the stance that magic realism is not confined to postcolonial fictions. (The novels by Murdoch, Shields, and Robinson do not fit definitions of magic realism.)

But the degree to which the fantastic in *The Poisonwood Bible* is held up alongside the realistic, historical world of the novel (through most of which African spiritual beliefs are presented as just that, beliefs as opposed to realities) sets it apart from other novels often considered to be representatives of the magic realist mode, in which the fantastic is a much more prominent, integral part of the whole narrative. The much more muted presence of Ruth May's narrative and her transformation in the last several pages of the novel is a far cry from the presence of the fantastic throughout such novels as Garcia Marquez's *One Hundred Years of Solitude* or Rushdie's *Midnight's Children* or Carter's *Nights at the Circus*. Of the novels I consider, only *Lady Oracle*, *Beloved*, and *The Sea, the Sea* thoroughly integrate fantastical events, whether in a manner that one calls fantastic or magical realist, throughout the entire narrative. The other novels—*The Poisonwood Bible*, *Paradise*, *Housekeeping*, and *The Stone Diaries*—do not satisfy Chanady's criterion that a fantastic or magic realist work must thoroughly integrate the supernatural element to be considered as belonging to those categories: the element cannot be cursorily introduced at the beginning or end and must be "maintained throughout the book" so that the reader is "constantly reminded of the antinomy between the natural and the supernatural" (58).[21] All four of these novels introduce the central supernatural (or possibly supernatural) element only at or near the end, and *The Stone Diaries* only very, very briefly, though I would argue that in spite of the brevity of the fantastic moment, it is not simply tacked on or extraneous to the work as a whole but is in fact integral to it insofar as the narrative perspective throughout the entire novel is impossible, right from the first page, and the claim at the end that the narrator has died provides one way of reading the impossible perspective as a feminist narrative strategy linked to the fantastic. Even in Morrison's *Paradise*, part of the oeuvre of an author widely considered to employ the supernatural (unlike Shields or Robinson or Kingsolver), the actual instances of the fantastic are confined to a handful of pages in the narrative; most of the story proceeds without any reference to supernatural events, and yet the way in which the instances of the fantastic situate the novel amidst both African spiritual traditions and the discourse on suppressed Christianities is absolutely crucial to the project of the narrative as a whole.

Endings are highly privileged moments in narratives: readers must reread a novel in light of the ending, especially a contemporary novel that makes closure both thematic and problematic, to appreciate fully the impact of that ending and the way it is anticipated throughout the narrative. In the case of these novels in which the supernatural or impossible is introduced only or primarily at the end, that element is privileged enough that readers must consider the novel as belonging to the fantastic or the magically real. Readers cannot but help to recast the historical and/or realistic aspects of the rest of the novel against the other reality or other code that the ending poses. Again, classifying these novels is problematic, and perhaps some of them have been neglected in the critical discourse on fantastic literature because they fail to meet the so-called degree requirement. The novels, however, should cause readers to realize and move beyond the limitations of classificatory schemas.

Moreover, it would seem to be increasingly difficult to distinguish definitively between the fantastic and magic realism. Hegerfeldt's work illustrates convincingly that hesitation, crucial to defining the fantastic but often not considered an element of the magic realist text, is in fact central to magic realism, encoded in the reader's response to that text. Hegerfeldt, along with Faris, D'Haen, and Rawdon Wilson, also argues convincingly against applying the term magic realist only to Latin American works or more generally postcolonial literary works. Perhaps it is ultimately unimportant and even counter-productive to insist upon a clear-cut distinction: it matters less what we call works incorporating impossible events that defy the conventions of an empirical, scientific world view than how we understand what these works *do*, how they *function*.[22]

For the purpose of this book, I do want to preserve a sense that fantasy, with its unidimensional portrayal of a fabulous world that is not the historical world, remains distinct from the fantastic and from magic realism, but I am less concerned about blurring the bounds between the latter two categories by grouping contemporary women's novels that in some cases might fit more closely definitions of the fantastic, and in other cases might fit more closely definitions of magic realism (and in some cases seem to fit both to some degree, or neither very precisely), but that nonetheless share in common several interrelated features and functions. In referring to the narratives' supernatural elements, I will generally use the term "fantastic" rather than "magic realist" for several reasons. First, for simplicity's sake, there needs to be a consistent terminology. Second, discourse on magic realism frequently uses the term "fantastic" to describe the seemingly impossible events incorporated in magic realist fiction, while the reverse is not true. And if reader hesitation is considered crucial to our understanding of how magic realism functions, then it might be fair to consider magic realism one type of fantastic narration, whereas we cannot consider the fantastic to be a subset of magic realism since the fantastic might involve character and/or narrator hesitation, an element specifically excluded from definitions of magic realism.[23] Finally, I use the term "fantastic" in part because I, like many other critics, take Todorov's study of the fantastic as a starting point. I will continue to draw on the insights of theorists who consider themselves to be theorists of magic realism as opposed to the fantastic, however, because these theories usefully describe many aspects of the body of works that I consider, where the two modes often blend into one another and always function in similar ways.[24]

FEMINIST NARRATIVE STRATEGIES AND THE FANTASTIC

In the group of novels considered in this book, the fantastic's relationship to the real is thoroughly interconnected with the second of Todorov's concerns that I use as a point of departure: the fantastic's relationship to narrative practices. It is to this matter, and to the work of feminist narrative theorists, that we must now turn. Todorov suggests that "there exists a curious coincidence between authors who cultivate the supernatural and those who, within their works, are especially concerned with the development of the action, or to put it another way, those who seek above all to tell *stories*" (162-163). He goes on to describe one of the basic principles of narrative structure itself: "*all narrative is a movement between two equilibriums, which are similar but not identical*" (163), concluding that the fantastic mode is particularly appropriate to the narrative model, since "what could better disturb the subtle situation of the beginning [...] if not precisely an event external not only to the situation but to the world itself?" (165). Todorov does not theorize that the fantastic creates new narrative forms—merely that it is especially suited to established, general narrative patterns. But by coupling these claims with feminist theories of narrative, we can see how the fantastic would be especially suited to disrupting not just stable situations but also traditional narrative patterns, and we can begin to account for the prevalence of fantastic devices in the novels written by contemporary women authors who seek to revise narrative forms.

Central to recent feminist narrative theory is the critical commonplace that narrative forms are ideological. The methods by which feminist narrative disrupts the teleology of traditional narrative, the various experimental formal strategies which suggest social change and ways of liberating women from dominant constructions of Womanhood, literary and historical, have received a great deal of critical attention in recent years. As Margaret Homans points out, many critics agree that traditional "the structure of narrative itself is gendered and that narrative structure is cognate with social structure" ("Feminist Fictions" 5). These critics find that traditional linear narrative cannot adequately portray women's experience and suggest that alternative, nonlinear narrative forms, even nonnarrative forms, "can have emancipatory effects for women" (6).[25]

At the same time, many feminist critics, including those who embrace the idea that traditional narrative forms must be subverted, also comment on women's reliance upon narrative structures and the act of storytelling in order to reclaim their lives from masculinist constructions of women's stories. Homans, then, goes on to point out that other critics do not view narrative as inherently phallic and hence value "the social uses that can be made of [narrative]"; they argue that narratives of the self are crucial for women who seek the ability to tell their own stories (7). In recognizing the important theoretical contributions made by both groups—the psychoanalytic critics who see narrative form as gendered and post–Marxian critics interested in the positive social function of women's narrative—Homans proposes a middle ground whereby the act of narration can lead to new narrative forms (9). In a similar vein, Sally Robinson, who uses narrative as a means to "ground [her] theorizing about the articulation of gendered subjectivity" because "narrative is one arena in which gender and subjectivity are produced in powerful ways," concludes that although "it is through narrative that women most often become Woman, [...] that process can be fractured through women's self-representation" (10). Critics agree that it is important to avoid essentializing narrative forms: as Sally Robinson puts it, women's subject positions "are not guaranteed and consolidated by the gender of writers and readers, prior to the text's reading. [...] These subjectivities are not products, but rather effects that emerge in the process of reading" (12-13). Susan Snaider Lanser makes a very similar point in her study of women writers' narrative voice (5). The fantastic elements of contemporary feminist fiction are not addressed by these critics but can certainly be construed in similar, non-essentialist terms, thus avoiding the potential pitfall identified by Maria Clark of identifying "the feminine fantastic as [...] essentially [...] irrational, mad, imaginary" (239). Rather, the uses of the fantastic in these narratives, like the narrative strategies, stem from particular socio-historical circumstances and redress shortcomings in patriarchal constructions of womanhood.

In exploring recent women writers' experiments in narrative technique, most feminist critics also agree that most women's narratives are more grounded in history, social concerns, and the day-to-day realities of their characters' experience than are the experimental, metafictional narratives produced by male authors. Like Homans, most of these critics also locate contemporary women writers' narrative praxis in a "middle ground."[26] In addressing the balance between experimental narrative and reliance on traditional narrative premises, Molly Hite, for example, finds that

> a number of the most eminent and influential women writing in the contemporary period are attempting innovations in narrative form that are *more* radical in their implications than the dominant modes of fictional experiment, and more radical precisely inasmuch as the context for innovation is a critique of a culture and a literary tradition apprehended as profoundly masculinist. [...] In particular, experimental fictions by women seem to share the decentering and disseminating strategies of postmodernist narratives, but they also seem to arrive at these strategies by an entirely different route, which involves emphasizing conventionally marginal characters and themes, in this way *re*-centering the value structure of the narrative [2].

Similarly, Joanne Frye contends that feminist novelists, like modernist and postmodernist writers, experiment with the form of the novel, overthrowing old conventions that "have been demonstrably problematic [...] for characterizing female experience outside the assumptions of male dominance," but that "much of the postmodernist movement toward self-contained structures of verbal play or Robbe-Grillet's object-centered texts will not in itself meet the feminist need for a redefined capacity to represent" (37-38). Finally, the authors whom Gayle Greene examines "reaffirm a knowable reality" in conjunction with their metafiction: "Women writers enlist metafictional devices not as gamesmanship or self-display [...]; language is, rather, critiqued as 'social fact,' and thereby reestablishes the connection Graff urges 'with recognizably central patterns of individual and social experience'" (19-20).[27] The fiction Greene examines "bridges this gap between naive realism and esoteric experimentalism, enlisting realism while also employing self-conscious devices that interrogate the assumptions of realism" (22).

These comments sound quite similar to those made by Theo D'Haen about magic realism's contestatory relationship to the "privileged" discourse of "central" postmodernism (203). According to D'Haen, we need to understand "*what* part [magic realism] plays in this larger current or movement [i.e. postmodernism], and where, and why" (194). He concludes that the particular subset of postmodernism that is magic realism challenges "central" narrative forms from realism to modernism to strains of postmodernism that contest the conventions of realism but that nonetheless themselves belong to a central tradition because the authors—those penning the French *nouveau roman*, for example, or the American male metafictionists—are not "marginalized—geographically, socially, economically." In contrast, magic realist postmodern authors, who need not be Latin American, write from an "ex-centric" position in order to "displace[e]" central line literary traditions from realism to postmodernism. D'Haen argues that these authors accomplish this goal by employing conventional postmodern literary techniques in order to subvert them by using them not

> "realistically," that is, to duplicate existing reality as perceived by the theoretical or philosophical tenets underlying said movements, but rather to create an alternative world *correcting* so-called existing reality, and thus to right the wrongs this "reality" depends upon. Magic realism thus reveals itself as a *ruse* to invade and take over dominant discourse(s) [195].[28]

D'Haen's formulation for magic realist writers is quite apropos to the fictions of the fantastic written by the feminist writers considered in this book, insofar as those authors write from a socially marginal position and offer a corrective to their male counterparts' experimental fictions that challenge realism by calling into question the idea of reality itself, that embrace a version of postmodernism positing that the only reality is that there is no reality. Women writers who employ the narrative strategies described by feminist theorists in conjunction with fantastic or magic realist devices that also interrogate assumptions about socially constructed realities thus enlist two powerful and interrelated tools in creating narratives that lay bare patriarchal ideologies and craft new stories, in new forms, to represent reality more fully, more democratically.

Sally Robinson captures well the manner in which the writers considered in this study interrogate the assumptions of realism in their narrative form, though she treats an entirely different group of writers (Angela Carter, Gayle Jones, Doris Lessing):

> Contemporary women's fiction *strategically* engages with official narratives—of history, of sexual difference, subjectivity—in order to deconstruct them and to forge new narratives. These official or "master" narratives range from the traditional male-centered quest story, to discourses of colonialism, to philosophical and psychological discourses which posit Woman either as a metaphor for difference in man, or as an a priori lack. These discourses construct gendered positions, for writers and readers, and are all mobilized by the desire for coherence or closure—a systematic accounting of difference in relation to hegemonic perspectives that very often leads to the recuperation of that difference [17].

The feminist novels considered in this study, while not always heavily plotted in the sense that Todorov means when he speaks of narrative, are nonetheless profoundly and explicitly concerned with plots, with the ways that narrative has shaped cultural constructions of gender, and with the ways that women writers can develop alternative discourses and narrative techniques. I give a great deal of attention to the ways these narratives resist closure, a move that can be further explored when studied in conjunction with the fantastic, a device that often coincides with feminist strategies such as "writing beyond the ending" and works against forms of closure that restrict women's choices to either marriage or death, as Rachel Blau DuPlessis points out (3-4).[29] Carol Shields, for example, writes beyond the ending of marriage and death for her character Daisy Goodwill Flett in *The Stone Diaries* by creating a fantastic narrative perspective in which Daisy seems to reflect on the limitations of her marriage(s) from beyond the grave, rather than simply to die silenced by the male stories that surround and construct her. Her narrative voice ultimately lays bare these constructions and employs a variety of feminist narrative voices so that she lives "outside her story as well as inside it" (*Stone* 123). Toni Morrison provides another example in depicting the mysterious realm in which the murdered women of *Paradise* appear following their deaths, a world that challenges in its very construction the narratives of intolerance and closure that prompted the women's slaughter by the neighboring townsmen.

Robinson and DuPlessis and a host of other critics argue that since closure recuperates difference, challenging the ideology of closure through the use of an open ending is a common strategy in feminist narrative, though of course it is not unique to feminist fictions. The fantastic, a mode which itself challenges closure through the hesitation it involves, is frequently employed in feminist fictions. Yet nowhere in their discussions of various feminist novels do feminist narrative theorists draw on theories of the fantastic to elucidate the women writers' narrative projects. In many cases, novels that employ the fantastic are simply overlooked (in the case of Murdoch's oeuvre, for example), or they post-date the criticism (in the case of Kingsolver's *Poisonwood Bible*), but oftentimes, the feminist narrative theorists analyze fictions that do in fact fall into the category of the fantastic without engaging the relevant theory.[30] Sally Robinson, for instance, provides an insightful reading of two of Angela Carter's novels without mentioning the fantastic or magic realism per se; Greene and Hite both offer brilliant, detailed readings of Atwood's *Lady Oracle* that draw on theories of the female gothic but never on theories of the fantastic; and Lanser, pointing out the "unspeakable voice" in Toni Morrison's oeuvre, zeroes in on Morrison's use of the spirit world and the "rationally unknowable" as a challenge to "realist authority" (134-5) without ever mentioning the fantastic or drawing upon the work of Todorov and his successors, in spite of Lanser's considerable debt to structuralist narratology in her feminist revision of it. Conversely, as we have seen, some recent theorists of the fantastic fail to consider contemporary women's fiction at all, while others who do explore these novels fail to draw on the important observations of feminist narratology to enrich the theoretical underpinnings of their revisions to Todorov's study and other studies. It is not that these reading strategies are inadequate in themselves without the theoretical framework of the fantastic on the one hand and the lens of feminist narratology on the other, but it is somewhat surprising that these two discourses fail to engage one another explicitly when they share common goals and when an important body of recent literature seems to invite the merging of these perspectives.

In addition to focusing on issues of closure, I also focus on issues of narrative voice and narrative perspective that are often central both to feminist narrative theory and to theories of the fantastic. In particular, Lanser's work on the authority of various forms of the female narrating voice illuminates the way in which the fantastic functions in these novels, although Lanser herself does not explicitly address the fantastic. Most of the novels included in this book are narrated from the perspective of a homodiegetic first-person narrator. Murdoch's and Atwood's novels employ such a voice in a relatively straightforward manner, with Atwood's work addressing more so than does Murdoch's the question of authority for a female narrator. Robinson's and Shields's novels complicate first-person narration, experimenting with voice in ways facilitated by the presence of the fantastic in these novels. Kingsolver's novel, narrated by several homodiegetic first-person narrators, likewise complicates personal narration by approaching Lanser's definition of communal narration in the way that it employs several narrators, and by blurring bounds among personal, authorial, and communal narration in its final chapter, the chapter in which the novel in fact becomes fantastic. Morrison's two novels, unlike the others, employ an authorial narrative voice that frequently becomes figural rather than a personal voice, though *Beloved* does contain several chapters narrated in the first person. These novels' self-consciousness about narrative forms derives not from the narrators' self-reflexive commentary on the storytelling process as in the case of the other novels, but from the way that the novels thematize the telling of history, using the fantastic to challenge narrative conventions and dominant versions of historical events. Morrison's novels, like all the works included in this book, employ the fantastic also to revise the conventions of various novelistic subgenres, a project in which the narrative voice and narrative perspective are as central as the narrative form.

CHAPTER SUMMARIES

This book is divided into three parts, with the first part examining the connection between gender and genre, using a pair of novels written in the mid 1970s that revise gothic conventions. Both novels employ self-conscious, first-person narrators engaged in writing fictions that first participate in, and then later challenge, the classic gothic tale and its assumptions about gender. Chapter 1, "The Novel Weapon: Gender and Genre in Iris Murdoch's *The Sea, the Sea*," analyzes Charles Arrowby's preoccupations with novelistic form. Because this novel comments more overtly on its own form than do novels explored in subsequent chapters, it provides a useful initial example of a strategy developed in more implicit ways in other of the works examined. Writing a conventional novel about his first love, Charles eventually realizes the connections between his narrative form and acts of violence he commits toward Hartley. She represents a feminine force in the novel that defies definition and encapsulation in narrative. The novel employs various fantastic devices, some of which have naturalized explanations but some of which do not, that eventually cause Charles to recognize his patriarchal impulses and to adopt in his writings a new narrative form consonant with feminist theories of narrative structure. In creating hesitation on the part of the character and reader about the reality status of fantastic events, this novel fits Todorov's definition of the pure fantastic, employing that fantastic element for its feminist narrative ends.

Chapter 2, "From 'The Lady of Shalott' to 'Lady Lazarus': Margaret Atwood's *Lady Oracle*," explores how Atwood's comic gothic novel also lays bare the implications of genre conventions for the social construction of femininity. Like Charles Arrowby, Atwood's narrator Joan Foster is extremely self-conscious about narrative form and eventually rejects for her own stories conventional novelistic forms, revising the gothic for the twentieth century. Seemingly supernatural events occur in the novel that help the protagonist confront the constructedness of gender and to challenge rather than fulfill those social conventions. These events, such as experiments with automatic writing and the appearance of the astral body of the narrator's dead mother, defy conventional closure and disrupt the narrative forms linked with the construction of female subjectivity in the gothic. This novel, unlike Murdoch's, employs a female narrator and raises questions about woman's narrative voice and narrative authority.

In Part II of this book, the third and fourth chapters examine another pair of novels that employ first-person narrators, this time focusing on narrative strategies that challenge traditional autobiographical narrative voice and narrative form. In both cases, it is suggested that the women narrators have died and generate their stories from an impossible narrative perspective, but this perspective can be illuminated by theories of feminist narrative voice, so that the fantastic becomes a means by which to generate a feminist narrative. These fictions, written in the 1980s and 1990s, employ more muted fantastic devices than Atwood's and Murdoch's novels, but these subtle uses of the fantastic generate a complicated treatment of female narrative authority.

Chapter 3, "Narration from Beyond the Grave in Marilynne Robinson's *Housekeeping*," examines the way in which *Housekeeping* employs a ghostly narrator who returns after death to "haunt" the conventional world and to narrate her story with new perspective from "the other side." Critics disagree about the feminist status of the novel's ending. But an examination of this debate through the lens of theories of the fantastic allows readers a framework by which to interpret the characters' ghostly status as a means of feminist resistance to patriarchal narratives. In the course of the novel, the trope of ghostliness is doubled and transferred from the dead women characters Ruth and Sylvie at the novel's end to other living characters who are ghostly because they lack identity. Thus the living women are revealed to be hollow social constructions while the "fantastic" characters take on more life and become more "real" than their conventional counterparts. In its narrative strategy, *Housekeeping*, like *The Stone Diaries*, counterbalances what might be termed semiotic modes of discourse with an insistence that the narrator achieves a high degree of narrative authority in storytelling situations and thus makes her narrative socially symbolic. The authority of women's different narrating voices is examined in more detail in the next chapter.

Chapter 4, "The 'Invisible' Woman: Narrative Strategies in Carol Shields's *The Stone Diaries*," treats the novel that is the most tangentially fantastic of the novels in this book but which does suggest, if only momentarily, that the narrator, Daisy Goodwill Flett, continues to narrate the story of her life even after her death has occurred. The chapter considers how this impossible narrative moment extends to the narrative voice throughout the fictional autobiography, the whole of which is generated from a seemingly impossible perspective. While many of the novel's critics have postulated that the main character is not a sophisticated enough presence to be the sole narrating voice, I posit instead that the different voices all belong to Daisy Goodwill Flett. Examining the novel through the lenses of feminist narrative theories and theories of women's autobiography allows readers to explore how the notion of writing beyond the ending—literally and metaphorically—can challenge socially constructed narratives about women. While many critics also argue that the novel belongs to what Theo D'haen would term a "central" version of postmodern play in its narrative experimentation, I illustrate that reconsidering Daisy as the sole narrator allows the reader to see the novel's postmodern quality as a feminist postmodernism that gives voice to suppressed stories, not simply as a self-referential strategy that calls into question the reader's ability to access reality. The chapter explores the novel through different theories of women's narrative voice, especially Joanne Frye's and Susan Lanser's, centering on the question of authority in first- and third-person narration.

The next three chapters of the book, comprising Part III, analyze hybrid novels that fuse the historical and the fantastic. The fantastic is used in these three novels to probe historical knowledge generated from the oppressors' standpoint and to restore alternative versions of the past to the historical record. All three novels involve discussions of race as well as gender, either in the context of American missionary imperialism in Africa, or in the context of slavery and its aftermath in America. All three employ, as part of their treatment of the fantastic, spiritual practices that challenge orthodox Christian beliefs. It is important to note, however, that when these novels employ fantastic devices that are clearly linked to spiritual beliefs, they do so not to embrace a particular religious outlook but rather to suggest the presence of alternative realities, to evoke a very real history of religious intolerance, and to point out the ways that orthodox Christianity has been interpreted to justify racial and gender discrimination.

Chapter 5, "'The Eyes in the Trees': Transculturation and Magic Realism in Barbara Kingsolver's *The Poisonwood Bible*," illustrates how the novel employs the fantastic in a postcolonial context to counter both racism and patriarchy. The novel's communal feminist narrative counters the single-voiced discourse of the white male racist patriarch, Nathan Price, and the Christian missionary project in Africa. The novel debunks official history as the various female characters tell their versions of the colonial project in ways that recognize the other's story that Nathan Price's discourse does not recognize. While *The Poisonwood Bible* has been critically examined as an historical novel, a postcolonial novel, a neo-domestic novel, and a disability novel, it has not been considered as a novel of the fantastic. But through the character of the youngest daughter in particular, Ruth May, Kingsolver employs fantastic devices to illustrate transculturation, discussed by Mary Louise Pratt as the process not only by which the colonizer influences the colonized, but also by which the colonized reciprocally influences the colonizer, an influence that often manifests itself in linguistic and narrative practices (*Imperial Eyes* 6). Ruth May, who dies from a poisonous snake bite but who is apparently transformed into a snake and narrates the last section of the novel from this fantastic position, literally embodies the transculturation process and transforms her father's traditional Christian discourse. Like the novels studied in Wendy Faris's consideration of the coincidence of magic realism and postcolonialism, *The Poisonwood Bible*, which shares some characteristics of the postcolonial magic realist novel, "radically modifies and replenishes the dominant mode of realism in the West, challenging its basis of representation from within" (*Ordinary Enchantments* 1) through its use of the fantastic that offers a counterdiscourse to imperial missionary discourse.

In Chapter 6, "Telling Beloved's Story," we see how Toni Morrison employs the fantastic to recover suppressed versions of history and to reveal the "fantastic" nature of official histories. Like the first two novels considered in this book, *Beloved* employs conventions of the gothic in order to modify them. Beloved's presence—rendered ultimately uninterpretable in the novel—deconstructs ways of knowing constructed by rational scientific and historical discourses. An examination of the different versions of the novel's central event—Sethe's killing Beloved—reveals that the different narrative forms of Schoolteacher's and Sethe's accounts reflect different ways of knowing suggested by Beloved's presence in the novel. In its treatment of Beloved, the novel employs an aesthetic that is both magic realist (the presence of the baby ghost is presented straightforwardly, as an uncontested and unsurprising fact) and fantastic in Todorov's terms (there is a high degree of hesitation on the part of characters and readers about the supernatural/marvelous or real/uncanny status of the young woman Beloved), but in both cases Beloved's function is the same: disrupting "told" stories, restoring/restorying the "untold" story.

The seventh chapter, "The Gospel According to Consolata: Alternative Christianities and Toni Morrison's *Paradise*," offers a new reading of *Paradise* by exploring the ways in which Morrison employs and revises elements of Gnosticism to counter Orthodox Christianity and the canonization of the four gospels that form the New Testament, an historical process that excluded many other gospels. Employing Gnosticism in such a way as to invoke early Christian history, Morrison provides an alternative to the monological storytelling practices that inform the Ruby, Oklahoma town elders' world view and cause them to scapegoat the women who inhabit the Convent on the outskirts of town, brutally slaughtering them. In the novel's most prominent fantastic moment, the slaughtered women's bodies disappear, and the characters apparently return after death to this world to interact with their still-living family members, as well as appearing in an "other-earthly" realm described in the novel's final passage. The alternative spirituality practiced at the Convent and initiated by the soteriological figure Consolata Sosa encompasses aspects of Christian Gnositicsm, elements of contemporary feminist Christianity, and elements of African religion, suggesting an inclusive vision of paradise itself. Examining the novel's fantastic devices within this historicized context counters charges that the novel's salvific ending is simply compensatory and evades real world concerns. Rather, the novel directly engages in a historical way with racism, classism, sexism, and religious intolerance and offers a vision of a non-exclusionary, paradisiacal earthly realm through its use of the fantastic.

Part I

Gothic Fictions and the Fantastic

1

The Novel Weapon: Gender and Genre in Iris Murdoch's The Sea, the Sea

> We can no longer take language for granted as a medium of communication. Its transparency has gone. We are like people who for a long time looked out of a window without noticing the glass—and then one day began to notice this too.
> —Iris Murdoch, *Sartre, Romantic Rationalist [64]*

> Whatever bondage we may be held in by [dark powers], however they may confine and cripple us, is a function of the moment in which we live. The Gothic heroine is in bondage to her society's conception of feminine identity, and the Gothic hero tears himself to bits in pursuit of an unattainable ideal of masculinity. The Gothic reveals that monsters of fantasy come, not from deep within our minds, but from the forms of identity and selfhood shaped by our conventional reality.
> —William Patrick Day, *In the Circles of Fear and Desire [192]*

INTRODUCTION

Of the novels included in this book, Iris Murdoch's Booker Prize-winning *The Sea, the Sea* represents the clearest example of a twentieth-century version of what Todorov terms the pure fantastic tale—so classic an example, in fact, that it is surprising that theorists of the fantastic have tended to overlooked this work. Murdoch's own critics recognize its fantastic dimension, yet none has systematically explored her work in conjunction with theories of the fantastic.[1] The narrator Charles Arrowby witnesses numerous strange events, all of which he tries to naturalize through rational explanations, but both he and the reader experience a high degree of hesitation about these events. Charles inhabits a classic gothic haunted house; in keeping with the setting, he finds objects broken by a mysterious hand, and he discovers a hidden room that comes to be associated with mystery and perhaps the supernatural. Most striking, however, are the appearances made by a sea monster, which Charles attempts to account for as an hallucination, the after-effect of an experience with LSD (21), but which always create a nagging doubt that he really has witnessed the impossible, and in whose existence he sometimes believes even late in the novel. Elizabeth Dipple argues that the reader is "gradually led to see that [the monster] is a projection of the subconscious" (278)—that the sightings are, to use Todorov's terms, resolved into the uncanny. But toward the end of the novel, Charles's cousin James undertakes a miraculous rescue of Charles from a dangerous whirlpool-like place in the sea, an event that is decidedly *not* resolved into the uncanny, either for Charles or for the reader. Charles suggests that James has metamorphosed into a creature capable of sticking to rocks, and as the novel comes to a close, questions persist in reader's mind about exactly how Charles was rescued from the sea.

The hesitation invoked in the reader, as well as Charles's own hesitation about the reality of various mysterious happenings that take place in the novel, is ultimately linked with issues of gender. Charles is in the process of writing the story of his life from his sea-side retreat. His writings exhibit extreme self-consciousness about form and a preoccupation with closure, and because Murdoch explicitly links his constant comments on the form of the text that he produces to his preoccupation with power over women, the novel provides an excellent example of feminist narrative theorists' argument that narrative form has social implications for women, an excellent example of the kind of text that might interest a feminist critic analyzing women writers' narrative experiments. But just as critics of the fantastic have paid scant attention to Murdoch's novel, so too other critics have overlooked its experimental dimensions, and feminist critics have undervalued the novel's treatment of gender. Gayle Greene, for example, recognizes that Murdoch is a contemporary woman writer who employs metafictional elements in her novels, but she argues that Murdoch does not do so within the context of feminism and hence deliberately excludes Murdoch from her study of contemporary metafictional feminist novels (25). *The Sea, the Sea*, however, as well as Murdoch's earlier and similar novel *The Black Prince*, does indeed employ metafiction in the service of feminist ideals. By examining this novel at the intersection of feminist narrative theories and theories of the fantastic, we can place Murdoch's work within a body of recent women writers' fiction that employs some degree of postmodern experiment in narrative form, but that nonetheless retains strong ties to a realist tradition.[2]

In an interview that took place ten years prior to *The Sea, the Sea*'s publication, Murdoch disdained contemporary experimental writing: "I would like to be thought of as a realistic writer [...]. I want to talk about ordinary life and what things are like and people are like [...]. Whether one could use experiment in the interests of this is something I have wondered about" (Rose 73). *The Sea, the Sea* takes up precisely this project as Murdoch not only explores the lives of real people but uses experiment—including narrative self-consciousness and fantastic devices—to interrogate commonplace assumptions about the nature of gender. As Gary Goshgarian puts it, "Murdoch is directly concerned with [...] the artificial mystiques and myths of womanhood that deny women recognition as free, independent, and contingent human beings" (519). Though, as we have seen, feminist theorists do not necessarily deal with literature of the fantastic in their discussions of contemporary women writers' novels, nonetheless their insights have a great deal of bearing on this body of literature since the function of the fantastic in these works coincides with the function of narrative experiment. That is, while many authors carry the critique of representation to an extreme in metafictions that fall into that category of the generalized fantastic, most contemporary women authors reject the idea of the generalized fantastic, instead employing fantastic devices that recuperate the relationship between the fantastic and the real that Todorov considers central to the classic fantastic tale. Contrary to the claims of many critics of the fantastic, then, the fantastic has not become synonymous with the most extreme kinds of narrative experimentation but does continue to exist in a middle ground between experimentation and realism. Murdoch, in her revision of the gothic novel, employs the fantastic to disrupt conventional narrative practice in a manner that calls attention to patriarchal constructions of reality, forcing her main character to recognize the way that the formal characteristics of his writing enact an ideology of domination, and ultimately to revise them.

At the same time that she was working on this novel, Murdoch also published *The Fire and the Sun: Why Plato Banished the Artists* (1977), in which she writes that Plato's "criticism of art extends and illuminates the conception of the shadow-bound consciousness"(5). For Plato,

> form in art is for illusion and hides the true cosmic beauty and the hard real forms of necessity and causality, and blurs with fantasy the thought-provoking paradox. Enjoyment of art deludes even the decent man by giving him a false self-knowledge based on a healthy egoism: the fire in the cave, which is mistaken for the sun, and where one may comfortably linger, imagining oneself to be enlightened.[...] The artist deceives the saving Eros by producing magical objects which feed the fantasy life of the ego and its desire for omnipotence[3] [66–7].

Though Murdoch sees art in more positive terms than does Plato, she agrees that "[m]agic in its unregenerate form as the fantastic doctoring of the real for consumption by the private ego is the bane of art [...]" (79). Rather, life should be "a pilgrimage from appearance to reality" (80). *The Sea, the Sea* conjures up Plato's allegory of the cave: the main character Charles speaks frequently of "the world of shadows" (57) and of being chained. He writes early on that Shruff End is his "cave" (4). Once Charles begins to tell his tale, the reader will envision him as a prisoner—handcuffed, able to see only the images and shadows of reality thrown in relief on the cavern wall of his mind, fully believing that he sees the real thing in the shadows, ghosts, or phantoms he perceives. It is through his journey out of the cave, as it were, toward a definition of femininity not bound by the conventions of the classic gothic plot, that Murdoch employs the fantastic to dismantle the patriarchal real.

NARRATIVE FORM, THE FEMALE GOTHIC, AND THE FANTASTIC

Patrick William Day reminds us that the gothic genre is not a universal one but one which reveals "the historicity of the imagination" (192). In the hands of Iris Murdoch, the gothic self-consciously explores the connection between the romance plot and the social construction of both masculinity and femininity. Published in 1978, *The Sea, the Sea* situates itself at the moment of the women's movement (at one point the narrator Charles Arrowby refers to "Women's Lib." [316]), but unlike many contemporary gothic novels that focus upon the heroine's development, Murdoch's work focuses upon the change in consciousness of her central male character, the prototypical gothic antagonist.[4] Central to this change are the fantastic devices that Murdoch employs throughout the novel, devices that, while serving as part of the novel's gothic machinery, simultaneously subvert the conventions of the genre, in particular its narrative of patriarchal domination, its story of rescue and control.

Throughout *The Sea, the Sea*, the narrator's self-conscious ruminations on narrative form provide fertile ground for exploring the connections between the novel's narrative strategies and its representation of gender roles. *The Sea, the Sea* opens with a section called "Prehistory" that both introduces the supernatural elements of the novel and establishes Charles's preoccupation with aesthetic form. Charles, a London director and actor, records in a diary his decision to leave the city and to move to his current location, an eerie old house called Shruff End. In this setting, perched precariously on a bluff overlooking the sea, he plans to write something of his life—exactly what, he isn't sure, but he is confident that he will eventually "discover [his] 'literary form'" (2). He goes to Shruff End to withdraw from the world he has known, promising that he will become a hermit, and like Shakespeare's Prospero, "repent of egoism" (3) and "abjure magic" (2), "drown[ing his] book" (39). Charles is unable to escape his past, however; it revisits him in various forms as figures from the past disrupt his solitude by the sea. Two former actors with whom he has worked, Gilbert and Peregrine, intrude upon him at Shruff End, as do two actresses and former lovers, Lizzie and Rosina. (Rosina performs several acts that seem supernatural to Charles—in effect she haunts his house as a means of gaining revenge, breaking objects mysteriously in the middle of the night and the like, but these instances are all naturalized when Charles realizes that Rosina, not a poltergeist, has been responsible.) James, a cousin whom Charles has not seen in some years, also makes surprise visits. Finally, one day Charles believes he also sees his former love Hartley, a figure from his past who preceded Charles's London theater days and who is now married to Ben, with whom she has adopted a son, Titus. Convinced that in Hartley he can find a way to recapture the innocence of his youth, he becomes obsessed with her, and with the idea of rescuing her from the husband whom he considers to be abusive. His writings about and treatment of Hartley reveal that far from abjuring magic and egoism, Charles is still deeply embroiled in both, a fact that becomes clear from his preoccupation with literary form.

Throughout the first section of the novel, Charles exhibits an extraordinary self-consciousness about his writing, calling it a diary, a chronicle, and a memoir; his writings in this section, up until the point when he begins to obsess about Hartley, are loose and rambling observations. But when he turns to consider Hartley, he muses, "if one had time to write the whole of one's life thus bit by bit as a novel how rewarding this would be" (99). Thick into his new subject matter, he finally admits "So I am writing my life, after all, as a novel! Why not? It was a matter of finding a form, and somehow history, my history, has found the form for me" (153). Though Charles quickly supplants history in general with his personal history, Murdoch, who titles the long middle section of her novel "History," suggests not only a collusion between narrativized historical accounts and traditional novelistic form, but also a collusion between the personal and the political, particularly where the social construction of femininity is concerned.[5] The story Charles tells is the larger story of society's patriarchy, its subordination of women to male authority and its circumscription of female identity to the domestic realm. As Michelle Massé points out in her work on the gothic, "history, both individual and societal, is the nightmare from which the [female] protagonist cannot awaken and whose inexorable logic must be followed" (12).[6] Charles's novel is conventional both in its story line and in its linear structure: Hartley is his "alpha and omega" (77); life with her "would connect [Charles's] end with [his] beginning in a way that was destined and proper" (371). In thus constructing his story according to the principles of teleology, Charles adopts precisely the narrative form that many feminist critics have identified as masculinist, while Murdoch's self-consciousness about history, individual and societal, undermines the novel that Charles writes and critiques the ideology on which it is based.

Charles's role as a director in the London theater provides a revealing commentary on the link between his formal self-consciousness and his treatment of women. Charles writes, for example, that "actors regard audiences as enemies, to be deceived, drugged, incarcerated, stupefied" (33), and that drama captivates and even "imprison[s] the spectator in it" (36). The images of incarceration and assault that he uses to describe the theater characterize as well Charles's dealings with Hartley. In classic gothic fashion, he locks her in the secret room in his house, imprisoning her literally just as he imprisons her metaphorically in his story, his house of fiction. Thus his conception of art as a means of power and magic surfaces in his "novelization" of Hartley, in the aggression of his narrative form itself. Until the end of the novel when he abandons his "history," nothing enables him to see that his relationship with Hartley is based less on love than on power, or that his narrativizing impulse, his attempt to force Hartley to become the heroine of a traditional love story, is an act not of tenderness but of aggression. As Steven Cohan points out, "the narrator's egocentric attempt to impose form onto experience through his fantasy of love actually manifests a predatory attack on woman" (236).

Charles's compulsion to narrativize his history with Hartley is critiqued through the fantastic devices of Murdoch's novel. Thus, according to Dipple, "The smooth elegance of form is projected whenever Charles can mold, shape and all too often belie his material, but the interruptions illustrate disorder and a breaking of control [...]" (277). These interruptions consist precisely in the strange events that perturb Charles, especially the mysterious appearance of a horrible sea monster and mysterious happenings associated with a secret inner room at Shruff end. As we have seen, Todorov posits a special affiliation between narrative and the fantastic, concluding that the fantastic mode is particularly appropriate to the narrative model, since supernatural episodes disturb the stable situation that one encounters at the beginning of a narrative and require resolution in order for equilibrium to be reestablished (162–5). *The Sea, the Sea* is profoundly and self-consciously concerned with the ideological implications of plots, with the ways that narrative has shaped cultural constructions of gender, and with the ways that alternative discourses and narrative techniques can disrupt dominant constructions of femininity, literary and historical. Such disruptions are accomplished in large part through the novel's fantastic devices. The instances of the fantastic raise questions for Charles regarding the reality status of his story and offer a counter-narrative that eventually returns Charles from his social withdrawal at Shruff End to the world of messy, contingent reality.[7] The fantastic elements that disrupt the continuity of his narrative—especially the gruesome sea monster—cannot readily be fitted into his reductive world where everything constitutes part of the artistic pattern he imposes on events. In this capacity, the ghosts and monsters that haunt his mansion are by-products of his world view that haunt him and reveal the error of his ways, eventually forcing him to acknowledge a different kind of reality. That is, the fantastic elements of the novel that cause Charles to hesitate, in Todorov's terms, over what is real and what is not, eventually cause him to question the "reality" of his novelistic version of the Hartley romance, to question his use of genre—in particular the gothic romance plot—to construct gender.

Theories of the female gothic illuminate Murdoch's project in *The Sea, the Sea*. Karen Stein points out that in the traditional gothic, "Males are portrayed as heroes struggling to define themselves and working for personal power and success in all aspects of human endeavor while females, according to Joanna Russ, have only one role, 'the protagonist of a Love Story'" (Stein 125–6).[8] This model certainly accounts for the way in which Charles views both himself and Hartley. Furthermore, according to Stein, monsters appear frequently in the female gothic, a commentary on the perceived monstrosity of female strength, independence, and sexuality (123). While jealousy is the most straightforward of the sea monster's significations,[9] all of the scenes in which Charles describes it or the monstrous qualities he sees in others also reveal, in keeping with Stein's comments, Charles's fear of female sexuality. The monster's open mouth recurs as a key terrifying image, with its fearsome teeth and "pink interior" (19) upon which Charles fixates. Later Charles sees in Rosina's face a vision of the monster's mouth (104–5) and also recalls his Aunt Estelle's singing from his childhood, commenting, in language that echoes almost exactly his initial description of the monster's mouth, that the gaping mouths of singing women have always frightened him (60). He notes later that "singing is of course a form of aggression" and even compares singers to predatory animals whose mouths are like the monster's (312). In addition to recalling quite explicitly the description of the sea monster, Charles's comments about singing also endow the women in the novel with siren-like qualities, suggesting the danger of their sexual allure.[10] In the conventional gothic novel, feminine sexuality is often portrayed as something monstrous and unacceptable; in *The Sea, the Sea*, female sexuality, in any form other than traditional submission, terrifies Charles.[11]

Charles, then, divides women into binary opposites, virgin and whore, in a manner that resonates with what Stein identifies as men's inability to accept female sexuality that commonly marks the genre of the female gothic (124). Charles distinguishes Hartley from the other women in his life because he considers her asexual, wanting always to describe their relationship in terms of its purity, to exclude Hartley from monstrous female sexuality. Writing of their relationship in the past, he claims, "[W]e were chaste, and respected each other absolutely and worshiped each other chastely" (80). Fantasizing about their future, he speculates that they will live alone together, and he will regain a lost innocence (371). Yet when Hartley rejects him, she, too, becomes monstrous: Charles exhibits a fear of her inner self and projects the sea serpent's qualities onto her. That is, while she struggles against him in a scene in which he has grasped her, he is both struck by the force with which she resists him and horrified to catch "a glimpse of her open mouth and of her glistening frothy teeth" (232). In the same scene, Charles "sh[ies] away in horror from the *interior* of [Ben and Hartley's house] and of that marriage" (237–8; emphasis added), because in that marriage, Hartley is a sexual being, fallen and impure. Only very late in the novel does Charles begin to accept Hartley's sexuality and to wonder incredulously to himself if "*sexual attraction*" could possibly characterize her relationship with Ben (436, emphasis in original). Yet Murdoch ultimately subverts the conventions of the female gothic: it is not the female self that becomes monstrous, but the male self who casts woman as nothing other than the protagonist of a love story. Indeed, when Charles describes the monster, he is "vague about its exact distance away from" him (21): Murdoch offers the monstrous as a metaphor for Arrowby's own patriarchal project.

While Charles is repeatedly drawn to other women's surfaces, finding their "insides" repulsive,[12] he claims that he wants desperately to "have access to [...Hartley's] interior being" (295), which he assumes to be purer, more submissive than the other women's interior selves. Murdoch constructs an elaborate metaphor around Charles's assumptions about Hartley's sexuality and his attempts to penetrate to Hartley's interior: the mysterious "inner room" at Shruff End, which Charles describes as "the chief peculiarity of the house, and one for which I can produce no rational explanation [...]" (14).[13] He writes at one point that Hartley is "a pale partly disembodied being, her face hanging always just above my field of vision like an elusive moon" (170). This description is woven in with a string of related images throughout the novel. Charles envisions early in the narrative "a face looking at me through the glass of the inner room" (68). He considers three possible explanations: first, he saw his own face reflected in the room's window; second, someone very tall or someone standing on something did peer out at him; or third, he saw simply a reflection of the moon in the window (69). At first he settles on the third explanation (his preference being to privilege surface, not to wish to acknowledge depth, to admit of something in the inner room), but after he learns that Rosina has been "haunting" his house, he favors the second. The novel, however, never confirms or discomfirms that this is the case; given what we know of Rosina's activities, it seems a logical enough explanation, but the possibility persists that Charles did see a ghostly Hartley in the inner room, an image that troubles the rational explanations of his vision, the inner room itself being associated with the irrational since as Charles notes, there seems to be no reason for its existence.

Charles's drive is, of course, to recuperate Hartley to his world view, to strip her of her "truth" by making her conform to his, by making her tellable or representable. Thus he tries desperately to narrativize the events that take place in the inner room and to contain the threat or excess that Hartley herself might be seen to represent. While he might ultimately be unsuccessful in this endeavor, nonetheless his attempts and Hartley's passive responses to them invite a second reading of the function of her character in the novel, as a critique of the stereotypical gothic heroine. Thus, when Charles has disturbing dreams about Hartley's death, the mysterious face in the inner room takes on for him a new significance, the language of the novel linking Charles's description of the mysterious face explicitly with Hartley's elusive "moon" face. At one point he dreams that Hartley is carried away by a black prince (a playful allusion to Murdoch's earlier novel of that title, whose narrator resembles Charles), and that "her head hung back over his shoulder as if her neck was broken" (147); next he dreams that he discovers another secret room in the house, containing the body of a dead woman (199). Finally, after he captures Hartley and actually locks her in the inner room to keep her from returning to Ben, he dreams that he sees Hartley there and that she is very tall, or that she is standing on something, but then he realizes "that she was suspended from the lamp bracket. She had hanged herself" (309). When he wakes from the dream, he reluctantly goes to look through the window into the inner room and connects in his mind the image from this dream to his earlier vision of a face peering at him from the inner room, realizing that the "face was *too high up*. It could not have been the face of someone standing on the floor. It was just at the level at which Hartley's face would have been if she had really hanged herself" (309–310). In his mind, Hartley is a model of "true" femininity according to traditional Gothic representations of womanhood, while the reader will interpret the inner room motif and its accompanying imagery as suggestive of Charles's inability really to see into women's interiors or inner beings, of his continuing tendency to see only surfaces or socially constructed ideals of femininity, since the Hartley he envisions in the inner room is the stereotypical masochistic gothic heroine.

Michelle Massé's *In the Name of Love: Women, Masochism, and the Gothic* provides a way to read masochism not as a personal weakness but as both a symptom of social trauma and, in psychoanalytic terms, as an attempt to bring to the surface a recognition of oppression. Through Freud's account of the repetition compulsion, Massé accounts for the gothic pattern of a woman's moving from her domineering father's house to a husband's house that is supposed to grant her freedom but in actuality turns out to be simply a version of the same. In *The Sea, the Sea*, Hartley's repetition compulsion manifests itself not in the move from a father's house to a husband's, but in the shuttling back and forth she does (or is forced to do) between a husband and a suitor who are doubles of one another.[14] Massé "reconsider[s] the erased, retrospectively trivialized heroine's text and the trauma and repetition that give it shape" (11), arguing that "repetition in the Gothic functions as it does for certain other traumas: the reactivation of trauma is an attempt to recognize, not relish, the incredible and unspeakable that nonetheless happened.[...] The originating trauma that prompts such repetition is the prohibition of female autonomy in the Gothic, in the families that people it, and in the society that reads it" (12). Rather than locate the source of gothic heroines' suffering in those heroines' "faults," Massé suggests "looking instead at the encapsulating social systems that engender repeated trauma" (19). These social systems give rise to what she identifies as the genre's most "ominous" implication: "the refusal of the heroine's existence as subject" (11, n. 2).

Yet in spite of Charles's attempts to contain Hartley by narrativizing her and by locking her in the inner room, both Hartley and the inner room become almost like excesses that cannot be wholly contained by his love story. The difficulty of rationalizing what Charles sees in the inner room simultaneously points to his construction of Hartley as passive gothic heroine and also calls forth hesitation in the reader about the possible supernatural status of this mysterious face in the window. Charles, as his cousin James points out, has turned Hartley from a real person into a ghost: "Some kind of fruitless preoccupations with the past can create such simulacra [...]. She is real [...] but what reality she has is elsewhere" (352–53). Hartley ultimately defies representation, her reality remaining elsewhere.[15] Upon first beginning to remember her, Charles terms their story "untellable" (78); upon looking for her likeness in the museum, Charles comments, "She was a vast absence" (170), and in his final impression of her, she appears to him, as she will to the reader, as someone whose face is "strangely blank" (493). Her very blankness itself might be construed in Kristevan terms as a disruptive force. Kristeva writes, for example, of how the principal of the feminine in the text constitutes a "truth" which has no self and which is found "in the gaps of identity," existing in "negativity" as a force that disrupts the symbolic (150–3), in this case the patriarchal order of discourse that Charles represents. Hartley's "truth," defined by negativity, opposes the patriarchal "truth" that Charles wants to impose upon her in his socially constructed definition of femininity.

As Deborah Johnson argues, it is possible to construe Murdoch's adopting a male narrative voice in terms of Irigaray's concept of "'male mimicry' [which], can be seen as a potential means of undoing the repressive (patriarchal) structures encoded in language itself (Lacan's 'symbolic order'), as way of 'exposing through imitation.' As such, it can point the way forward to a possible recovery of the operation of the 'feminine' in language" (9).[16] Although, as Johnson points out, the use of a male narrator "decentres the female point of view," Murdoch's self-consciousness about and playfulness with narrative conventions "exaggerate this decentring effect" (8), with the result that the erasure of the female point of view doubles back on itself and compels through its very negation the construction of a female perspective. This feminist narrative strategy works in concert with the novel's use of the fantastic: Rosemary Jackson suggests that literature of the fantastic

> [...] exists alongside the "real," on either side of the dominant cultural axis, as a muted presence, a silenced imaginary other. Structurally and semantically, the fantastic aims at dissolution of an order experienced as oppressive and insufficient. [...] By attempting to transform the relations between the imaginary and the sym-

bolic, fantasy hollows out the "real," revealing its absence, its "great Other," its unspoken and its unseen [180].

The exaggerated decentering of the female point of view and the fantastic have the effect of making the reader imagine this other Hartley. Murdoch's emphasis, however, lies less in developing voice and visibility in the "unspoken and unseen" woman character—a maneuver accomplished more thoroughly in Marilynne Robinson's *Housekeeping* and Carol Shields's *The Stone Diaries*, novels that employ women narrators as their chief characters—than in illustrating the transformation of her male narrator's conception of masculinity, an essential corollary to the construction by negation of the female subject.

CHARLES AND JAMES: REFORMING GOTHIC MASCULINITY

Murdoch explores in her "love" triangle the destructive underside of gender roles assigned not only to the female gothic protagonist but also those assigned to the male gothic antagonist. Her use of the surface/depth trope comments not only upon Hartley but also upon Charles and ultimately challenges social constructions of masculinity. He himself is all "surface"; his identity—of which he says he has "very little sense" (3)—stems from popular portrayals of the male gothic hero in which he becomes trapped. Charles evinces a perverse fascination with the antique mirror at Shruff End, to which he is "especially attached" (15), and which gives him the illusion that he has become someone he can at last represent to the reader. He describes the mirror in some detail and then writes, "Since I have just spent a while gazing at myself in this mirror it is perhaps time to attempt to describe my appearance" (32). The mirror provides him with a "source of light" (32) into his self, by providing the illusion of a coherent whole, like the ego formation the mirror provides according to Lacan's theory of the mirror phase. Murdoch suggests, however, that the self Charles sees there is not only narcissistic but illusory, an image, like his other visions of "reality."[17] As Lindsey Tucker points out, Charles is both "the enchanter and enchanted" ("Released from Bonds" 382): he is locked in his own devices, as much the prisoner of his delusions of power as anyone around him, trapped by gothic conventions and social constructions of masculinity. Though he locks Hartley up in the inner room, it is Charles himself who behaves like a caged animal (199).

If we extend Massé's observations to pertain to the male antagonist(s), as Murdoch's novel invites us to do, we can apply her theories of gothic repetition to illuminate Charles's situation. His initial efforts to remake himself merely replicate the same old formulas, a tendency most evident in Charles's insistence that he has gone to Shruff End to retire from the theater, believing that he has given up power and magic (39), while in truth he replicates his theatrical powers by subjugating Hartley and writing another book of magic that constitutes precisely what Murdoch terms "a fantastic doctoring of the real" (*Fire & Sun* 79). Toward the end of the novel, Charles becomes aware of his own repetition compulsion: "[O]ne surrenders power in one form, and grasps it in another" (500). Hartley, caught in her own repetitive horror, partially allows Charles finally to recognize his own perpetuation of the gothic plot, to acknowledge his participation in patriarchy and the denial of female subjectivity, and at last—and with great difficulty—to abandon his "history," with all its implications of the link between his personal history and the socio-historical reality of male domination and female submission.

This recognition on Charles's part depends ultimately on his interactions with his cousin James. While Charles has constructed a masculinist story of rescue and control, it is ultimately he who winds up being rescued by James. In a twist on the conventional gothic plot, Murdoch offers an alternative model of masculinity, introducing through the character of James another instance of the fantastic, which, like the other fantastic devices she employs, disrupts Charles's fantasy version of his "history." James's miraculous rescue of Charles, which is never fully explained, in effect challenges and changes the reality of male domination and prompts Charles to reconsider his patriarchal version of the "real."[18]

James, a practicing Tibetan Buddhist, believes that "every tiny action has its consequences" (384). Like Charles, James participates in magic and performs powerful tricks of his own. James, however, fully recognizes the danger of power, whereas Charles is seduced by it. The difference in the cousins' use of magic is that James "understands [his tricks'] meaning and their consequences" (Tucker "Released from Bonds" 387) and is willing to take responsibility for them. For example, he recounts to Charles the story of how, when he was in Tibet, he tried to practice a certain trick, using mental powers to maintain bodily warmth in freezing conditions, because he thought that he could generate enough heat to keep both himself and his companion warm enough to survive a cold night in a mountain pass. But, James laments, "there wasn't enough heat for two. Milarepa died in the night. [...] He trusted me…It was my vanity that killed him" (447). James exercises his powers again, with more success, in the final fantastic instance of the novel. Peregrine, in a fit of jealousy, pushes Charles into a dangerous part of the sea called Minn's Cauldron, where the waters are so rough and the rocks so steep that it is impossible for him to climb out. And yet, miraculously, he is saved. Weak, feverish, and with no memory of who pushed him or how he survived, Charles at first believes that the sea monster was in the ocean pool with him and saved him by lifting him out. But after Charles has recovered from the fever that follows his near-death experience, he suddenly recalls that he wrote down something about the event and hid it in his room. The piece of paper he finds reveals "a memory of an impossibility" (468): Charles has written that James saved him from drowning "by coming down like some animal [into the cauldron.... H]e was not climbing down with footholds and handholds like a man, he was creeping down on the smooth surface like some sort of beast.[...] Then James, as he crept right down into the churning whirlpool, detached himself from the rock like a caterpillar. There was an effect as of something sticky and adhesive deliberately unsticking itself" when James effortlessly lifts Charles from the water (468–9). Charles, who has earlier noted James's peculiarly deformed "feet like hands" (330), concludes that this memory of James's transformation must be accurate, "no hallucination" (569), even if the sea monster itself was not real. James's metamorphosis helps trigger Charles's own more mundane transformation from a romantic, solipsistic individual to a more socially responsible one.

In this particular fantastic instance, Murdoch's novel works against the commonplace claim that metamorphosis has become meaningless in postmodern literature. Thus while Jackson, for example, argues that in twentieth-century literature, transformation happens "without the will or desire of the subject" (81) and further that "metamorphosis in the modern fantastic suggests that the slipping of object into subject is no longer redemptive and that "perverse" images of mutilation/ horror/ monstrosity have taken precedence over utopian dreams of superhuman or magical transformation of the subject" (*Fantasy* 82), we see in Murdoch's novel that the fantastic maintains its redemptive function: James wills his metamorphosis into the strange creature capable of rescuing Charles, using his powers for good, turning the monstrous into the miraculous. In this light, James resembles the heroines of recent feminist fictions who, according to Koenen, choose their metamorphoses. Unlike classic fantastic tales written by men in which metamorphosis is "either punishment or elevation," and unlike postmodern fantastic tales by men in which metamorphosis "signifies alienation, the loss of identity and control," Koenen explains that "[i]n contemporary women's literature [...] the heroines are not victims of metamorphoses, they choose it deliberately" (228). They do so as a means to overcome "their powerlessness, their status as objects of male desire and violence [...]" (231), and, in the case of Margaret Atwood's *Lady Oracle*, for example, as a means to wrest "narrative control over writing women's lives" (232). The manner in which gothic devices are subverted in Atwood's novel is the subject of the next chapter; in Murdoch's novel, we do not see a female character literally transformed, but the metamorphosis of the character James functions in a manner very similar to what Koenen describes, revealing to Charles the limitations of his narrative control over Hartley.

"What finally does lay Gothic horror to rest," writes Michelle Massé, "is the refusal of masculinist authority as the only reality to which one can turn and return" (39). Massé also observes that "in the interpersonal realm of the Gothic, both the beaten *and* the beater must change" (265). Though traces of

Charles's old self and his delusions remain throughout the last section of the novel, "Postscript: Life Goes on," he adopts many of James's wise attitudes toward his obsession with Hartley, at last admitting that she was "a phantom Helen" (492), a creation of his own mind (491), recognizing his "acts and thoughts as those of madman" (491). The concluding postscript demonstrates, in its random form as well as in its themes, how the contingency of history disrupts the surface of Charles's novelistic endeavor. Charles comes to recognize what Peregrine tells him: "You've made it into a story, and stories are false" (335). As he approaches the end of his book, he abandons the part called "History" and begins the postscript with a comment on the nature of closure. Watching several playful seals frolicking in the sea, a sight that contrasts with the frightening vision of the sea monster that opened Charles's meditations, he imagines that the seals are "beneficent beings" coming to bestow their blessing on him (476). When he wakes the next morning, on the opening page of the novel's postscript, he ruminates that this peaceful moment constitutes a perfect moment of closure, and hence he ought to end his narrative here, with the "higher significance" of this moment of "explanation, resignation, reconciliation." But he goes on to note that "life, unlike art, has an irritating way of bumping and limping on [...]," a fact that prompts him to continue, in DuPlessis' terms, writing beyond this novelistic ending with a diary-like account that will conclude shortly, "arbitrarily enough" (*Sea* 477)—just as Hayden White notes that unlike narrativized history, the chronicle simply ends without any formal moment of closure. Indeed, as Dipple points out, Charles "rejects the novelistic shape of an ending which his morning visitation by four seals had given him and which earlier he would have seized on as artistically apropos, and accepts the formless, anti-artistic, shapeless reality of life instead" (298). Charles writes, "If this diary is 'waiting' for some final clarificatory statement which I am to make about Hartley it may have to wait forever" (490).

James might be said to represent a feminine principle in the novel, or the feminine side of the masculine self, one whose qualities oppose those of the gothic male. But while James provides welcome relief to Charles's unrelenting and violent egotism, James's character is not wholly unproblematic.[19] In fact, James, who tells Charles that "we must practice dying" (445), offers a "solution" to the problem of violence that proves rather limited and ineffective. His discourse on this matter resembles closely certain ideas presented in Derridean thinking, namely the idea of pure difference, which Murdoch finally rejects just as she rejects Charles's attempt to construct a reality based on a naive view of language's ability to make things present. For James, because "the good are unimaginable" (445), dying would seem to be the only way to be truly good, the path James finally chooses in the end. The letter that Charles receives about James's death near the novel's end reveals that his cousin simply willed his own death, which came peacefully, with no harm to James's body (473). Though James believes that his act, the surrender of power through death, constitutes the only available act of goodness, this withdrawal might be read simply as another version of Charles's withdrawal to Shruff End.

James has explained to Charles that in Buddhist thinking, most souls, after death, enter a state called *bardo*, although some souls are able to grasp a truer reality at the moment of death, becoming free of "attachments, cravings, desires, what chains us to an unreal world" (385). Though James is often viewed as the voice of wisdom in the novel, here the obtuse Charles's objections to his philosophy in a subsequent, similar conversation actually prove insightful. Charles counters that he believes goodness derives not from shedding all attachments but from loving people; he objects that James's talk of shedding attachments sounds more like death than freedom (445). Of course Charles's means of creating an attachment with Hartley is, as we have seen, violent and destructive, but the novel suggests that the impulse he has toward loving people is not in itself something to be viewed negatively, merely that it must shift from a relationship of dominator and dominated to a relationship of social equality. Instead of embracing James as Charles's wholly "good" double, Murdoch proposes a merger of the cousins' characters; she suggests that one needs to affect the world positively, not negatively, but she suggests that one must affect it positively in a different manner than Charles has attempted to do at Shruff End. In this regard, Murdoch's vision resembles that of John McGowan in *Postmodernism and Its Critics*: McGowan distinguishes between "negative" and "positive" versions of freedom, describing the former as the freedom the individual can achieve only apart from any involvement in the social context which he or she opposes, and the latter as the freedom "possible within the terms of membership in a society" (15). Instead of withdrawing from the world or giving up all attachments, even love, Charles continues to live very much in the world, but with the recognition that he must put an end to the historical reality of male domination by facing the fact that his concept of femininity is not a true one.

In the last image of the novel, Murdoch suggests the possibilities that the world holds for Charles. We have seen how Charles has a problematic relation to interiors, which Murdoch treats in two different ways: on the one hand, he is trapped in a cave, chained to the world of shadows and images, without access to the world of reality outside the cave; on the other hand, he fears women's "inner beings" and projects monstrous qualities onto women that actually reflect his own interior qualities. Both sets of images demonstrate Charles's inability to face what is real. As Charles ends his "History," however, when he is lying on the rocks by the sea, he sees "into the vast soft interior of the universe which was slowly and gently turning itself inside out. I went to sleep, and in my sleep I seemed to hear the sound of singing" (475). This passage illustrates Charles's progress out of the entrapping house at Shruff End, as the world turns itself "inside out." The sound of singing here contrasts with the terror Charles has previously associated with women's singing; in conjunction with his peaceful vision of the world turning inside out, the image further suggests that the novel's gothic horrors have been laid to rest. Indeed, Charles's last entry in the book furthers shows that Charles has resolved the interior/exterior conflict. He tells us that the demon casket in James's flat, one of James's relics of which Charles has been very protective, "fell off its bracket. The lid has come off and whatever was inside it has certainly got out. Upon the demon-ridden pilgrimage of human life, what next, I wonder?" (502). The novel thus ends with a suggestion of the supernatural—"demons appear to have an external reality" (Dipple 297)—that Charles does *not* try to naturalize; rather, he exuberantly embraces it. This incident has a distinctly comic, rather than horrific, tone and seems to open the way for many possibilities to follow, suggesting not only that Charles himself has escaped entrapment but also that he will no longer attempt to trap others in secret inner rooms. In his demon-ridden pilgrimage, he has put to rest his particular demon: monstrous masculinity, his patriarchal world view.

Conclusion

While Charles abandons his attempts to force Hartley into the role of protagonist of a love story, the classic gothic masochistic heroine, and while Hartley implicitly resists these attempts insofar as she remains "untellable" (78) and thus can be construed in a feminist light, still her very blankness and absence threaten to reinforce the very stereotypes about women that the novel works to undermine. Yet Murdoch presents as well a positive female alternative to Hartley's ghostliness, to her ultimate absence from the text: she depicts the transformation of Rosina from one who plays at being poltergeist, haunting Charles in his mansion, to one who gives up that role and enters the real world by taking political action. Once Hartley has disappeared from the text, much of Charles's final commentary concerns the fate of Rosina, who "had the fierce charm of the rather nasty girl in the fairy-tale who fails to get the prince, but is more interesting than the girl who does, and has better lines too" (73). Rosina and Peregrine reconcile when they have killed off the demon of jealousy that stood between them. Rosina, once "black, a black witch" (345), gives up that "nasty" role; she announces that she and Perry are "going to bring theatre to the people" in Ireland (435). Perry has earlier denounced Ireland quite vehemently as a hopeless cause (164) but has changed his mind, taking positive action to intervene in the colonial situation. Because the novel also highlights colonialism by drawing heavily upon *The Tempest*, a drama that raises issues of both colonial and patriarchal domination, Murdoch suggests a connection between Perry's using the medium of theater to affect a difficult political situation and Charles's revising his own conception of art, abandoning his novelist endeavor, an action that has political implications for reductive social constructions of femininity.[20] Charles learns later that Peregrine's work for peace through his theatrical productions has been effective, and that "Rosina is equally enthusiastic and is rumoured to have become politically conscious and power-mad" (482). This socially symbolic power is quite distinct not only from Charles's version of power but also from the power Rosina employed to haunt Charles at Shruff End and to prevent him from being with Lizzie. Rosina, who serves as an alternative to James by choosing activism over withdrawal, fights domination on behalf of others. Through the character of Hartley, the dominated, Murdoch both critiques the patriarchal society that perpetuates gothic plots and subtly suggests ways in which Hartley's ghostliness or negativity subverts Charles's project; through the character of Rosina, Murdoch creates a woman who in a positive fashion resists domination and awakens from the gothic nightmare in which she has been trapped.

Rosina, however, like all the women in the novel, is a minor character represented only through Charles's narration about her: *The Sea, the Sea* overtly challenges male representations of women, employing the fantastic to critique masculinist narrative forms that deny women's complexity and attempt to contain them in a severely circumscribed role, but it simply does not tackle the complicated question of a woman's authority to narrate her own story or explore what form that story might take. Those explorations take place in three women's novels of the fantastic that employ a female central consciousness as the first-person narrator: Atwood's *Lady Oracle*, Robinson's *Housekeeping*, and Shields's *The Stone Diaries*. Like *The Sea, the Sea*, *Lady Oracle* challenges gothic conventions in particular. The two novels dovetail extremely well, though they have not been paired in the critical literature produced about them. Both overturn the association of femininity with monstrosity, each in its unique way, and both portray a narrator/author whose self-consciousness about narrative form ultimately overturns the gendered assumptions inherent in the classic gothic text, subverting those conventions for feminist purposes. But unlike *The Sea, the Sea*, Atwood's *Lady Oracle* provides a means to explore the ways in which the fantastic enables a woman character to narrate her own story, to wrest control of her narrative from patriarchal forces that would silence and contain her.

2
From "The Lady of Shalott" to "Lady Lazarus": Margaret Atwood's Lady Oracle

> Two seemingly contradictory impulses are evident in recent Canadian literature. One is toward sociology; the other is toward the supernatural.
> —Susan J. Rosowski, "Margaret Atwood's *Lady Oracle: Social Mythology and the Gothic Novel*" [87]

> The body of the Fat Lady, like the "astral body" of Joan's mother, is a figure for the other "selves" that Joan—and other women as well—inhabit because the social definition of "woman" is too constricted to accommodate them. Such bodies are also surplus that the realist narrative cannot accommodate, representations of "woman" that exceed the patriarchal gesture whereby the real is defined and contained.
> —Molly Hite, *The Other Side of the Story: Structures and Strategies of Contemporary Feminist Narrative* [141]

INTRODUCTION

Lady Oracle, like the other novels examined in this book, employs a seemingly "unlikely mixture" (Rosowski 87) of realism and the fantastic. Indeed, the novel incorporates elements of social realism such as family and gender dynamics of the mid-twentieth century that recall, for example, Betty Friedan's *The Feminine Mystique* and Stephanie Coontz's *The Way We Never Were: American Families and the Nostalgia Trap*. Atwood's depiction of Frances Foster illustrates Friedan's comment that "there was a strange discrepancy between the reality of our lives as women and the image to which we were trying to conform, the image that I came to call the feminine mystique" (9).[1] Similarly,

Coonz writes that she "hope[s] to expose many of our 'memories' of traditional family life as myths" (2). In addition to recalling these historical and sociological accounts of family life, elements of *Lady Oracle* invoke other historical realities for women in the mid twentieth century. In the heroine Joan Foster's staged suicide, for example, the novel implicitly invokes—but also overcomes—the plight of women writers of this period, including Anne Sexton and Sylvia Plath.[2] In the fictional male community's sexist responses to Joan's writing, *Lady Oracle* captures the general dismissal of women's writing prevalent in the culture of the time in which the novel is set. Atwood's novel also invites analysis in terms of its realistic portrayal of the role of the romance novel in the lives of a female reading audience.[3] It devotes a good deal of attention as well to beauty myths and to idealist images of the female body perpetuated by a society preoccupied with appearances and with thinness, and it, like *The Sea, The Sea* specifically references "Women's Lib" (*LO* 248) and the "women's movement" (*LO* 226) that emerged in response to various of the social problems that the novel addresses.

At the same time, however, the novel comments on women's body image through repeated unrealistic appearances of a circus fat lady; it employs the occult device of Joan's mother's so-called "astral body" to interrogate cultural assumptions about gender roles and the family; and it couches discussions of Joan's most serious writing in terms of "automatic writing," an occult experiment by which one writes by voyaging into a mirror with a candle in front of it, composing in a kind of trance. The very integration of these seemingly opposed trends toward the real on the one hand and the supernatural on the other locates this novel within an important body of women's fiction that employs the fantastic to overturn conventional constructions of reality.

As Molly Hite points out in her insightful reading of *Lady Oracle*, several tropes in the novel—many of which appear in the guise of the fantastic—suggest that Joan's person exceeds the limits imposed upon her by normative definitions of femininity. Atwood's use of the fantastic resembles Murdoch's in this regard, though the ways in which Joan exceeds the culture's attempts to circumscribe her are developed much more fully than the ways in which Hartley resists Charles's interpretation of her. Although Joan seems at times to remain confined and contained by convention, these fantastic devices ultimately allow her to write beyond the ending typically experienced by the conventional gothic heroine. Though Hite herself does not do so, many of her observations can be couched in terms of theories of the fantastic, with its tendency to disrupt social norms and to call attention to distinctions between the real and the not real, functions highlighted by various theorists of both the fantastic and magic realism. Commenting on the novel's representation of reality and fantasy, Hite notes that the very images from which Joan creates herself are themselves "fantastic" insofar as they are unrealistic: "it is not 'reality' that dictates a radical split between female eroticism and daily life, but the whole of a consumer culture that relegates women's sexual desire to the domain of the fantastic and so curtails 'woman' as she is 'realistically' represented" (133). This is a strategy that resembles the dynamic Hegerfeldt describes in magic realist fiction—that of calling attention to the element of fantasy inherent in the historically real, or "the presentation of the realistic as fantastic" (59). Like other contemporary women's novels of the fantastic, *Lady Oracle* employs fantastic devices to curtail the unrealistic social expectations through which women in the novel are defined, and to return Joan and the reader to the "reality" of the limitations of those expectations. The novel's self-consciousness and its anti-realistic elements locate it within the realm of women's experimental fictions that Hite differentiates from male postmodernism and to which she accords greater "radical potential" for cultural change (2); these same features also locate Atwood's novel within the framework of the feminine fantastic, within "an interpretation of the fantastic as a discourse of the repressed and marginalized" that is, for example, Anne Koenen's project (303). As Koenen observes, "the introduction of a different, fantastic 'reality' and frame of reference [...] always points to the repressions, arbitrary character and constructedness of the 'real;' [...T]he fantastic points to the gaps and fissures in hegemonic discourse as locations from which the marginalized can speak" (307–308).[4]

This chapter, then, focuses on three interrelated elements of the novel: its two chief fantastic devices—the frequent appearances of the "astral body" of Joan's mother and Joan's experiments with "automatic writing"—and the impact of these devices on narrative strategy, especially on the moment of closure. Like Murdoch, Atwood is profoundly concerned with generic definitions and literary form, drawing not so much on ways of writing history but on the various conventions of different sub-genres of the novel, especially the gothic romance, whose rules her zany narrator alternately adopts and rejects.[5] The fantastic disrupts closure both in Atwood's *Lady Oracle* itself and in Joan's *Stalked by Love*, the embedded gothic novel, as well as in her prose-poem, "Lady Oracle." While many critics read the mother figure, even in her "astral" appearances, as being wholly consonant with social constructions of womanhood, and while many, including Hite, view the writing produced by Joan's automatic writing sessions in the same vein, as a repetition of the classic gothic conventions that characterize Joan's pulp Costume Gothics, I read both fantastic elements as being dissonant with cultural constructions. The astral body is a device that ultimately warns of the dangers of the marriage plot that has trapped Frances Foster in the 1940s and 1950s, and Joan's automatic writing ultimately interrogates rather than repeats the conventions of her gothic novels. The two devices, in fact, are thematically linked and cannot be analyzed independently of one another. When the two devices in effect merge near the novel's end, together they facilitate feminist narrative strategies that enable Joan to overturn the gothic conventions in the novel she is writing and to subvert reductive constructions of femininity.

Frances Foster's "Astral Body" and the Fantastic

Hite, whose reading of *Lady Oracle* comes closest to exploring the novel in terms of the fantastic, helpfully reviews prior analyses of the novel to distance her own interpretation from those readings that locate the novel's conflicts within the protagonist's psyche, specifically in her failure to separate from her mother (129). As Hite points out, this reading is reductive of both Joan's character and of the novel itself, since it in effect requires that the reader distinguish among different narrative strands, identifying them as "'real'" events within the diegesis, as "'fictions' embedded within the fiction," or false events, namely "Joan's dreams, hallucinations, or fantasies out of control" (129–30).[6] Thus not only does "this psychologizing of the plot" constitute "a familiar strategy for translating the political issues of gender oppression into the realm of self help" by blaming Joan for all her gender troubles, but also, by naturalizing the unrealistic/ fantastic elements of the novel, this reading becomes "far too congruent with the dominant construction of 'woman' within Western culture, in that woman's essential otherness is conventionally manifested in her culpability, her extravagance, and her need of constant control" (Hite 130–131). In other words, such a reading requires the reader to naturalize the novel's supernatural occurrences. Though Hite does not draw on Todorov's work or on other theories of the fantastic, one could say that, according to many of the novel's critics, the fantastic becomes resolved into the uncanny. Moreover, one could say that to perform such a move in the interpretation of this particular novel is to maintain the status quo of patriarchy.

In fact the fantastic devices are not naturalized and remain a source of puzzlement throughout the novel. Reexamining these elements that have been attributed to Joan's imagination in light of Todorov's study of the fantastic reveals that they do invoke hesitation in the reader about their reality status. Furthermore, this hesitation facilitates a feminist reading of the novel's fantastic. Hite points out that the supernatural events in Atwood's novel "invariably take the form of appearances of a female body" (136). She observes that while the text itself does not naturalize the appearances of either Frances Foster's astral body or the Fat Lady, male characters within the text do: "Arthur's gaze here acts as agent of the naturalizing impetus within the narrative, denying visibility to the spectacular by assigning it a psychic and indeed a pathological origin. Not coincidentally, naturalization of this sort is always a male move in *Lady Oracle*, while the tendency to see something instead of nothing is female" (141). Against Arthur's naturalizing impulse, both the Fat Lady and Frances Foster's astral body "bob disconcertingly above the 'real' actions, distracting attention despite the masculinist insistence that there is 'really' *nothing to be seen*" (141). Placing Hite's observation within the context of theories of the fantastic allows the reader to see how the hesitation experienced by Joan and by the reader invites revision of Todorov's theory. Exploring his concept of hesitation in the fantastic tale at its intersection with these feminist observations about *Lady Oracle,* we see that hesitation becomes gender-coded and as such constitutes not solely an ontological problem involving the reality status of strange events but a socio-historical problem involving masculinist interpretations of women's reality and the social construction of femininity.[7]

Before examining the supernatural instances associated with Frances Foster, it is first necessary briefly to contextualize those ghostly appearances in the troubled relationship between Joan and her mother. Massé writes that "the Gothic legacy of domination is forcibly handed on by maternal figures who demand that young girls learn to be 'natural' women" (254). The category of the "natural" woman includes what Rosowski points out are merely "fictional constructs" (89) such as beauty myths and the ideal of thinness. Joan's mother first indoctrinates Joan to traditional definitions of femininity by fixating on Joan's appearance and body image. An ungainly, overweight child whom her mother wants to conform to beauty standards of the day, Joan defies her by glorifying in and flaunting her corpulence, until her Aunt Louisa (Lou) Delacourt, who is also overweight and dies prematurely of a heart attack, stipulates that Joan must lose weight in order to claim the money Lou wants to leave her. Joan desires the money so that she can gain independence from her parents and agrees to diet. Although she becomes thin, the figure of the fat lady reappears at significant intervals in the novel, a figure that, according to Hite, "exceed[s] the patriarchal gesture whereby the real is defined and contained" (141). While the fat lady is an important figure in the novel, ultimately it is possible to naturalize her presence[8]; thus I concentrate instead on the other strange female body, the astral body of Joan's mother.

Other references to appearance and to the mother's attempts to indoctrinate Joan to conventional femininity that anticipate the later sightings of Frances's astral body include frequent references to cosmetics and to the three-sided make-up mirror that becomes an important image in the novel, one that has bearing on the reader's interpretation of both the astral body and of Joan's automatic writing experiments. When Joan dreams about watching her mother put on her make-up in her three-sided mirror, Frances Foster, model of conventional femininity, is portrayed as "a monster" with three heads and three necks (67) rather than as a woman. Just as *The Sea, The Sea* reverses the trope of monstrousness often associated in the female gothic with the questing and rebellious woman by linking it instead to the domineering male, so too *Lady Oracle* undermines convention by employing monstrousness as a metaphor for the domestic angel rather than for the rebellious female character. If mirrors function to reflect woman's image or surface as the patriarchal culture would like to see that image, then the surface image itself becomes a metaphor for the monstrosity of masculinist constructions of femininity.[9] Joan's own attraction to Chuck Brewer (the Royal Porcupine), the lover she takes during her marriage to Arthur, is couched in the same terms: precisely because he seems to embody the gothic hero, Joan is never sure if she is attracted to the man or to his cape (239), and when the Royal Porcupine transforms himself to just plain Chuck Brewer by shaving off his exotic beard and mustache and abandoning his career as an avant-garde artist, causing Joan to lose interest in him because he has shed the qualities of the gothic hero, Joan thinks of herself as "a monster, [...] irredeemably shallow" (271). In this instance, Joan implicitly links herself to the monstrous mother in the looking glass by deeming herself monstrous for being so concerned with appearances and, in this case, with the classic gothic definition of the rescuing male, another surface construction that denies the deeper reality and complexity of men's and women's subjectivities.

Many mirror scenes in the novel suggest the possibility of getting behind the false surface that only appears to reflect a reality. For example, when Joan's mother applies her make-up, Joan notes that sitting at the mirror makes her mother unhappy, "as if she saw behind or within the mirror some fleeting image she was unable to capture or duplicate" (66). Perhaps the mother looking behind or within the mirror suggests not the quest for greater artificial perfection, but the inner longing to do away with images, to free the trapped, natural body. Indeed, we learn later in the novel that she is deeply dissatisfied with her wholly conventional marriage, and her feelings of being trapped by social expectation manifest themselves in minor acts of violence: perusing the old family photo albums, Joan discovers that Frances has used a razor blade to excise the faces of both her husband and the man she apparently was involved with before her marriage, leaving only images of Frances herself "laughing gaily at the camera, clutching the arms of her headless men" (179). These images reverse sexist assumptions that a woman's head is the least important part of her body and demean woman's intellectual capacity, and Joan discovers them immediately upon musing that her mother is correct to have assumed that she is unappreciated despite the fact that "she'd done the right thing, she had devoted her life to us, she had made her family her career as she had been told to do" (178). These observations occur only after Frances has died, the first point in Joan's history when she has expressed sympathy with her mother rather than with her father and begins to realize that her father himself has been partially responsible for Frances's unhappiness.

It is also at this point that Joan even speculates that her father may have killed her mother, pushing Frances down the stairs, rather than Frances falling when she is intoxicated, having turned to alcohol in her unhappiness. Many critics view these suspicions, which are never confirmed (or disconfirmed), as evidence of Joan being unhealthily trapped in gothic plot conventions according to which husbands are suspected—often wrongly—to be murderers. However, one can instead read this shift in Joan's sympathies from her father to her mother as one of the many moments in the novel when the "unreal" plot structures do comment realistically on the actual conditions of women's lives in the mid-twentieth century: as Massé points out, "[t]he boundaries between Gothic and real clearly are not as fixed as we once thought" (19). Frances seems to suffer precisely from what Betty Friedan identifies in *The Feminine Mystique* as the "problem that has no name." If Joan's father has not literally killed her, nonetheless the patriarchal culture that he represents has played a role in Frances's death. Joan's mother might be read finally as functioning more positively than many commentaries on the novel suggest. While Joan's eventual rejection of "monstrous" conventionality emerges only very slowly throughout the course of the novel, unexplained supernatural events disrupt Joan's ties to conventional plot structures, eventually leading her to overturn them. One device Atwood employs in this transformation is the fantastic device of the mother's astral body appearing to Joan to suggest the dangers of conforming to socially defined femininity. This astral body can be interpreted as actually warning Joan of the pitfalls of conventional femininity rather than continuing simply to indoctrinate her to those conventions, the manner in which the astral body is often read.[10]

Joan first encounters the concept of the astral body when her Aunt Lou takes her to a revival meeting where the living attempt to commune with the dead. In her first experience at the revival meetings, the medium, Leda Sprott, tells Joan she has a message for her and describes an unhappy woman of Frances's age, clad in Frances's typical conservative apparel, "a navy-blue suit with a white collar and a pair of white gloves" (110). Leda accepts the presence of this fantastical figure without hesitation, though she mistakenly assumes that she is seeing the spirit of a dead person, until Joan informs her that Frances is not dead. Leda is unfazed; she simply states "placidly" that the apparition must instead have been Frances Foster's astral body (111). Joan, unlike Leda, is incredulous; she dismisses as "crazy" (112) the whole notion of the astral body, which, given the absurdity of Leda's general explanation of an astral body (111), is likely to be the reader's response as well. But as much as readers might like simply to dismiss this astral body, the text makes it impossible to do so. While one can account for Leda Sprott's lack of hesitation because she is a believer in the occult, one cannot account for the details she includes when she describes the astral body to Joan since Leda has never met Frances. These details and the fact that Joan herself never sees the astral body in this instance make it impossible for the reader to naturalize the appearance as simply Joan's or Leda's imagination (cf. Hite 136–141). Ultimately, when this "sighting" is contextualized with later appearances of the astral body and Joan's developing responses to those supernatural contacts with her mother, readers see that the hesitation invoked in this instance serves an important function by shaping how Joan and the novel's readers construe the "reality" of the conventional femininity embodied in Frances's apparition. While Joan at first struggles against believing in this apparition, ultimately it has a positive effect, and the contacts with the "other side" that Joan at first deems crazy ultimately lead her, in effect, to the other side of the mirror.

It is revealing to look at the contexts in which the mother's apparition haunts Joan later in the novel. The same astral projection reappears to Joan at telling points in Joan's development, almost as if to suggest that Frances is unhappy that her daughter is choosing a conventional path like the one she herself "had been told" to take (178). For example, the astral body reappears shortly after Joan has left home and fled to London. At this point Joan has taken her aunt's name, Delacourt, and celebrates the emergence of her "second self" (137), a stage in which she hopes fervently to avoid having her mother locate her. But in this stage, Joan develops relationships with two men that in many ways replicate the gender conventions that characterize her parents' marriage, first with Paul, the eccentric Polish count, and then with Arthur, a social activist in the Canadian nationalist movement, the man she will marry and who "rescues" her from Paul. Significantly, it is just when she has found Arthur and at the moment when she has decided to undertake a sewing project (in spite of the fact that she has never sewn) that her mother comes back, the astral body still clothed in the conventional navy-blue suit and white gloves (173).

At this point Joan, now herself witness to the apparition, seems to accept the supernatural. She is nominally frightened, but she is less incredulous that the astral body exists at all than she is disturbed that her mother seems to have found her in spite of Joan's efforts to hide. Since Joan presumes the apparition to be quite real, she takes measures against its returning: she explains, for example, how she rearranges the furniture in the apartment as one such measure, because Leda Sprott had claimed earlier that this strategy wards off "unfriendly spirits" (174). One might say that a device characteristic of the fantastic novel, a ghost of sorts who haunts the living, comes to be presented in the narrative mode of the magic realist novel, with its mundane presentation of the supernatural.

Even though the character does not hesitate, the reader still will wonder if this apparition is "real" within the world of the fiction. Since the apparition so clearly invokes gendered codes of behavior themselves (here the horror is not any trepidation about the presence of a ghostly body but the horror of the constraining effects on women of socially sanctioned femininity), the ultimate effect of the reader's hesitation is to call into question the reality status of conventionally-defined femininity itself, revealing, as Hite points out, the fantasies inherent therein. These constructs are ideologies, not truths, but they create, as we have seen, a bleak reality for Frances Foster. Indeed, the description of this supernatural body is both thoroughly enmeshed in references to domesticity—Joan's sewing and her explanation to her roommates about why she has rearranged the furniture, which they attribute to "housewifely instincts" (174)—and juxtaposed with Joan's discoveries about her mother's unhappiness only a few pages later (178–179). The way the appearance of the astral body is contextualized, then, calls attention to the constructed nature of definitions of femininity and facilitates an understanding of Frances's unhappiness with her circumscribed existence. Reading about the way Joan reinterprets her mother when she has returned to Canada after learning that Frances has died, the reader sees the astral body in a new light: not as any real threat to Joan, and not simply as a "comic gothic" device,[11] but as a force that sympathizes with Joan's plight and Joan's struggles with female subjectivity that represent the very real threat inherent in a culture that defines women narrowly—in short, as a force that offers an implicit warning.

The astral body appears again soon, when, in spite of Joan's discoveries about her mother's unhappiness in marriage, Joan marries Arthur. Indeed the astral body of Joan's mother is present at the wedding, almost as if sending a message to Joan about the dangers/unhappiness associated with marriage. A short time later, unhappy in her marriage to Arthur, Joan writes that she dreams frequently about the monstrous image of her mother, and the dream reveals the similarities between Joan's and her mother's marriage: Joan is locked in small, enclosed places, classic gothic enclosures, described in terms that recall the image of the mother's house as a "plastic-shrouded tomb from which there was no exit" (179–80). For in spite of Arthur's purported radicalism, he expects from Joan conventionally feminine activities such as cooking and housekeeping (209). When Arthur is depressed, Joan feels "inadequate" because she can't satisfy his expectation that her love will "preserve a man from this kind of thing" (212). Arthur's very name suggests that he is the "author" of Joan's self at this point, something of which her self-consciously styled, clichéd language shows she is aware, but she has not yet fully found a way to author herself. Although she has a secret identity as Louisa K. Delacourt, author of Costume Gothics, in this capacity she authors only wholly conventional pulp novels inspired by the influence of the Polish Count, with his nineteenth-century views of women. By participating in the novel's second fantastic device—so-called "automatic writing"—Joan becomes a different kind of author. Automatic writing, the mother's astral body, and Joan's incorporating the fantastic in her Costume Gothics in a manner that interrogates the underlying assumptions of those novels all merge as a means by which, in Hite's terms, feminine excess (that remainder which can be neither accounted for nor circumscribed by traditional notions of gender), persists to trouble masculinist constructions of femininity.

Joan's "Automatic Writing" and the Fantastic

Joan's childhood observations of her mother applying cosmetics in the three-sided mirror in Frances's bedroom begin as a wholly naturalized moment of the fantastic—Joan dreams about her mother appearing monstrous in the mirror—but modulate to a moment of the fantastic that is not naturalized when the adult Joan appears literally to enter into a world beyond the mirror's surface, like Alice through the looking-glass. Leda Sprott, who introduced Joan for the first time to her mother's astral body, has at the same time encouraged her to try experiments in automatic writing. The process involves sitting in front of a mirror, pen in hand, with a lighted candle, and mesmerizing oneself by watching the flame's reflection. One is then "moved" to write. When Joan first tries it, she accidentally sets her hair on fire and produces only "a single long red line that twisted and turned back on itself, like a worm or a snarl of wool" (114), which she cannot recall producing. Joan never interprets this first episode of automatic writing to mean anything; like the first appearance of the mother's astral body, it is deflated by her comic tone, and in fact she gives up the idea of the experiment for quite some time. The line that she produces, however, might well remind the reader of the narrative structure of *Lady Oracle* itself: Atwood's novel loops back on itself, meanders, and in general avoids the linear plot associated with the realist novel that many feminist critics (e.g. DuPlessis, Hite, Greene, Sally Robinson) theorize is an oppressive narrative form for representing women, a form that women writers' experimental fictions combat, even as these narratives embrace some elements of realism. Thus Joan's first experiment with automatic writing serves as an important figure for writing that gestures toward a feminist sensibility insofar as it constitutes a form of writing that opposes the literary conventions to which Joan's Costume Gothics conform with a vengeance.

Later, Sprott encourages Joan to try automatic writing again and reminds her of her great powers, telling her, "Don't say what you don't mean [...]. You do enough of that already" (206). While Massé interprets automatic writing as a loss of agency for Joan, just as Aunt Lou doesn't like automatic writing because it feels like "being taken over" (113), the experiment can be viewed otherwise, as a chance for Joan to abandon convention, to stop saying what she doesn't mean. For the truth is that Joan is to some extent "taken over" in writing her gothics: that is, she is taken over by genre conventions that prevent her from expressing anything that is not a product of the social forces she lives among, even if she is aware of those forces and conscious of the conservatism of her own novels.[12] Indeed, when Joan writes her gothics, she does so "with [her] eyes closed" in a quick, automatic way (131 and 219); they are automatic writing of a different sort.[13] Joan is, in Sprott's terms, "a receiver" rather than "a sender" (112)—a receiver of entrenched social norms that she simply repeats and sends back to the audience in her writing, untransformed. But in receiving signals during the occult automatic writing process, Joan is enabled as a sender, too, one who can transform and transmit messages other than those simply inculcated in her by the culture. The experiment, then, becomes a way for Joan to find a different voice. Leda Sprott reminds Joan of her own creative power and urges the experiment that will produce Joan's first writing outside the Costume Gothic mode. It is also significant that Joan, writing a pulp novel from a point in time near the end of *Lady Oracle*, after she has produced other types of writing, comments that she struggles to write her usual gothic fiction, no longer producing it automatically; the process is much slower with her eyes open (131), when she in effect struggles against the conventions.

Dissatisfied after her marriage to Arthur with an existence that amounts to "playing house" (216), Joan experiments again with automatic writing. When Joan tries writing this way this time, she notes that she recently bought a three-sided mirror, like her mother's (219), which will remind the reader of the monstrousness associated with conventional femininity and Frances Foster's feelings of being trapped in the mirror. Joan's second experiment with automatic writing coincides with a strategy that Todorov theorizes is a central structural feature of the fantastic: literalizing figurative discourse (76–82). Hegerfeldt, more so than Todorov, analyzes the ideological function of this feature in her study of magic realism, arguing that the technique suggests the truth function of such metaphors and, by extension, causes the reader to question distinctions between social truths and constructs (56–58). According to Hegerfeldt, magic realist texts maintain a tension between the literal and metaphoric readings when the figurative becomes literalized, thereby creating "hesitation about how it is to be understood" (59).[14] In *Lady Oracle*, the metaphoric becomes literal when Joan, during her automatic writing, seems literally to travel into the mirror, to its other side. This "other side" of the mirror exists simply as a metaphor earlier in the novel when Joan observes her mother looking longingly at something behind or in the mirror that seems to offer an alternative to the surface that that the mirror reflects, something beyond the shallow images of stereotypical femininity that Frances adopts when she "put[s] on her face" (66). When Joan later travels into the mirror's depths, she discovers precisely this alternative. Her literal journey into the mirror that her mother seemed to gaze beyond can then be interpreted still in a figurative context, as a means of moving beyond the surfaces and conventions of femininity that the society wants her simply to reflect. In this capacity, Joan's automatic writing leads to the interrogation and transformation of such constructs.

When she becomes entranced by the reflection of the candle in the mirror, Joan feels as though she is traveling through a mysterious passageway, in a search of something awaiting her, some "truth" (221). She undertakes this exercise for a period of many months, until one night she becomes trapped: "I went into the mirror one evening and I couldn't get out again" (223). The novel offers this explanation at face value — Joan never attributes her experiences to imagination induced by her trance-like state, and she actually produces quite a lot of writing in this state, though readers might be inclined to naturalize the situation and assume that the experience of going into the mirror is simply Joan's hallucination. But indeed the novel does produce hesitation in the tension between this seemingly rational explanation and Joan's insistence that the event is "extranatural" (223), especially given that Sprott has been the one to encourage automatic writing and that Sprott's sighting of the mother's astral body cannot be naturalized. And from this tension arises as well the tension between the literal and the metaphoric reading of the event, so that whether Joan literally enters the mirror or not, the figurative reading suggests itself and invites the reader to view the experience as one which participates in the earlier metaphor of the mother looking "beyond" the mirror's surface, seeking a "deeper" understanding of feminine subjectivity.

The writing that Joan produces during these journeys into the mirror reinforces this sense. Joan in fact undertakes automatic writing as a way to find inspiration for one of her gothic characters, Penelope, a female damsel in distress, but she becomes so intrigued by the fact that she produces a bit of writing, and by the possible meanings of this writing, that she goes back to the mirror experiment and "set[s] Penelope aside" (221), a phrase which itself suggests that she is traveling beyond the constraints of her formulaic, socially sanctioned Costume Gothic novels. At first, she writes only one word, "bow," which puzzles Joan and leads her to look up its meanings in the thesaurus. Many of the meanings suggest submission—bending to another's will and respecting authority—definitions that reinforce patriarchal conventions when contextualized in the descriptions of marriage and gender relations that characterize the surrounding narrative. One meaning, however, offers another possibility: the crossbow, a reference nearly buried among all the other meanings that suggest deference (see *Lady Oracle* 220), is a powerful weapon that shoots the arrow referenced in the poem Joan later produces, suggestive of an active principal rather than a passive one. Greene points out that "Joan incorporates the word 'bow' [as in the bow of a ship] into her poem as 'prow' […], thereby transforming submission to control, obedience to 'authority'" (181), insofar as the bow of a ship implies navigating, steering, charting one's course.

Many critics read the embedded text of Joan's "Lady Oracle" in a negative fashion, as being indicative of Joan's identification with Tennyson's "The Lady of Shalott," the "Victorian ideal of feminine self-renunciation" (Rao 135).[15] On some level, the female character in the poetry Joan produces in her entranced state does resemble the title character of Tennyson's poem. Like *Lady Oracle*, "The Lady of Shalott" employs the image of a mirror to comment upon the relationship between life and art. The Lady of Shalott dies when she leaves her tower and her mirror to enter the real world, attracted to the image of Sir Lancelot, her rescuing knight.[16] Yet Joan transforms Tennyson's speaker's fate: she does not die but instead fakes her death and finally emerges stronger for this experience: "I pretended to die so I could live, so I could have another life" (315). Ironically, the press interprets her death as illustrating the plight of the suicidal woman author and attempts to contain her in the conventional narrative for women: Joan notes, "I'd been shoved into the ranks of those other unhappy ladies, scores of them apparently, who'd been killed by a surfeit of words. There I was, on the bottom of the death barge where I'd once longed to be, my name on the prow, winding my way down the river" (313). Her language here is clearly ironic; her tone implicitly challenges the very premises of Tennyson's poem. Rather than exchanging one imprisonment for another, Joan's "death," along with the novel's fantastic devices, allows her to extricate herself from the romance plot that leads to the Lady of Shalott's death. Koenen notes that Joan "neither dies nor goes mad; rather, she stages her own death to start a new life dedicated to investigate the meaning of female subjectivity" (243).[17]

While Atwood's critics have commented extensively on Joan's connection to Tennyson's retiring Victorian Lady, the possibility that Sylvia Plath's speaker in "Lady Lazarus" is also a source for Joan Foster has gone relatively unremarked upon.[18] The red-haired exhibitionist Lady Lazarus, who comments that she has nine lives, considers herself to be an artwork created by others; with each transition that she makes in her various deaths and resurrections, feeling herself simply a performer who conforms to others' expectations of her, she notes that her various selves simply repeat earlier, culturally constructed selves. By the poem's end, however, the speaker's tone shifts when she issues a warning to the patriarchal forces that have attempted to create and identify her. In the poem's closing lines, the speaker becomes a creator rather than the created: in her final resurrection, Lady Lazarus defies the objectification of which she has been a victim early in the poem and becomes an agent who breaks out of restricting definitions of femininity, with all the threat that this move implies to the men who surround her. The speaker of Plath's poem bears a startling resemblance to Joan Foster in Atwood's novel, who is also a redhead and who is linked, like Plath's speaker, with a circus exhibitionist, the Fat Lady. Joan continually creates new selves, all of which seem until the novel's end to be different versions of the female self sanctioned by a conservative, patriarchal society. But in her final act of resurrection from the dead, Joan, like Lady Lazarus, breaks free from many of the constraints that have defined her sense of self throughout the novel, acting aggressively toward men (she renders a male reporter unconscious in an act of self-defense) rather than passively constructing herself according to patriarchal definitions of femininity.

In *Lady Oracle* one can read Joan's poem through the lens of the fantastic when, in the final moments of the novel, allusions made in Joan's automatic writing to "The Lady of Shalott" coincide with the final appearances of the astral body of Joan's mother. In the apparition's penultimate appearance, Joan explicitly revises the notion that she herself mirrors Tennyson's speaker. Joan hears a noise and is at first frightened but relaxes when she sees it is "only [her] mother," in her typical costume (329). Now she identifies her mother rather than herself as the "lady in the boat, the death barge" (330), allowing the reader to see the "fatal lady" as a metaphor for that part of Joan who has followed in her mother's footsteps. Joan's poem gestures, then, not toward Joan's own suicide but toward the act of killing off the self constrained by social convention. The "last song" that her speaker sings as she floats down the river is not literally her last song (226); rather, Joan has sung her last song that conforms to social expectations, her last song in her mother's voice, but she does not, like the Lady of Shalott, turn away from her art altogether: she continues to produce writing that explores precisely the complicated relationship between art and life, between fiction and reality, namely, her last Costume Gothic. For Joan, the complicated relationship between art and life becomes not a choice between one kind of death and another, but a means to interrogate through her art the very conventions of other art forms that relegate women to the Lady of Shalott's untenable position, an interrogation that takes place in significant measure in the novel's representation of the fantastic.

"GOTHIC GONE WRONG": THE FANTASTIC AND THE ENDING(S) OF THE NOVEL(S)

Joan's reason for faking her death stems from various circumstances in her life that make her feel the need to escape complicated plots in which she has become embroiled: she is mixed up in a plan to dynamite a bridge as an act of protest, a plot conceived by Arthur and his friends; she is confronted by a reporter, Fraser Buchanan, who has learned the secrets of Joan's past and threatens to expose the author of "Lady Oracle" as the author of the Costume Gothics that Joan has written under a pen name, as well as to expose Joan's affair with Chuck Brewer to her husband, Arthur; and some unknown person seems to be stalking Joan, leaving dead animals on her doorstep. To disentangle herself from these complications, she stages her drowning and flees to Italy. *Lady Oracle* is structured in such a way that the narrative seems to be generated from this point in time, with Joan recounting her past. The novel both opens and closes in Italy, and periodically this framing device interrupts the narrative that leads up to Joan's time in Italy. While there, she continues to work on her manuscript for the Costume Gothic titled *Stalked by Love*, and segments of this embedded novel, along with segments of other of Joan's writings, also disrupt the linear flow of her life story. As a result, the form of *Lady Oracle* is highly non-linear, so that the novel itself, like Joan's mysterious scrawl generated during her first experiment with automatic writing, twists and turns back on itself. As such, the novel is an example of the "self-begetting" feminist fictions Gayle Greene examines whose very self-consciousness becomes an "interrogation of narrative conventions" (17), specifically of narrative conventions that have negative implications for female agency.[19] One of these conventions is, of course, closure: in the opening pages, Joan promises "no loose ends" (7), but as her narrative continues, it exhibits, like Charles Arrowby's in *The Sea, the Sea* "a deliberate and extended refusal to end" (Dipple 276). Joan abandons the "neat" plots of the typical Costume Gothic with its strong moment of closure. When her narrative finally does come to a stop, rather than to a conclusion per se, she ends with the line "I don't think I'll ever be a very tidy person" (345); Joan, like Murdoch's character Charles, finally accepts the contingency and messiness of every day reality. Her narrative finally leaves many loose ends, not least of which is the failure to naturalize its own supernatural devices.

The hesitation invoked in the reader about the reality of these events, which, as we have seen, ultimately challenges social constructions of femininity, eventually makes its way into the pulp gothic novel that Joan is trying to complete in Italy, disrupting the moment of closure in a literary genre that would ordinarily contain no loose ends. Indeed, the penultimate appearance of the mother's astral body immediately precedes Joan's writing about rejecting the marriage plot. Joan now finds the plots she constructs, which conform to normative definitions of women's social roles, to be "not convincing" (334), whereas earlier she had always found "other people's versions of reality very influential" (160).

In her novel, Joan has created two women characters, Charlotte and Felicia, who seem on one level to represent typically dualistic representations of women in fiction, the angel and the rebel, respectively. Joan finds herself increasingly impatient with her "good" woman character, Charlotte, "with her intact virtue and her tidy ways" (319) and increasingly taken with her "bad" woman character, Felicia, who, like Joan herself, is decidedly untidy and who needs, according to her fictional husband Redmond, to be "contained" (319). But a careful examination of the descriptions of these two characters reveals that Joan shares characteristics with both and that she ultimately deconstructs the binary opposition between them; finally neither conforms to the stereotype of angel or demon, and finally neither one is "contained," so to speak, by the conventional plot of the gothic novel. Though Felicia is supposed to die, the fate of wives in formula fiction, Joan is having trouble getting rid of her (316). According to the formula, it is "against the rules" for Joan to create "sympathy for Felicia" (319), who is a cheating wife of "scandalous reputation" (129), yet it also becomes increasingly difficult for either Joan or the reader to sympathize with Charlotte, who initially appears to be an innocent victim in Joan's manuscript (see, for example, 128–131), but whose "virtue" is undermined by Joan's descriptions of a conniving character plotting to steal Felicia's husband in part for the wealth she will inherit from Redmond (316–317).

The two characters almost merge into one while Joan struggles to write this Costume Gothic. At one point, she concludes that Charlotte will have to enter the maze, a setting in the fiction within the fiction that becomes in *Lady Oracle* itself a metaphor for conventional marriage: the maze contains "the central plot" (241), and as such, represents everything that has entrapped Joan's mother, everything that Frances's astral body warns Joan against. Joan writes that "It was noon when Charlotte entered the maze" and composes a couple of pages in which Charlotte encounters a demonic Felicia there, only to be rescued by Redmond (332–333). Joan then observes, however, that what she writes "no longer felt right" (333), and a few pages later, in the next installment of *Stalked by Love*, Joan again writes "It was noon when she entered the maze," only for the reader to discover that "she" now refers to Felicia rather than to Charlotte (341). In this installment, Felicia encounters in the maze four women who all claim to be Lady Redmond and who resemble Joan herself, Aunt Lou, and the Fat Lady, as well as the astral body of Joan's mother. The various former Mrs. Redmonds, who proliferate in this fantastic appearance (Joan's manuscript had earlier indicated that Redmond had had only two wives prior to Felicia) warn Felicia that she, like they, is trapped in the maze. Charlotte seems to have disappeared from the story at this point, but as the woman who was to have replaced Felicia as Redmond's wife, she would have faced a similar fate. In Joan's imagination, Charlotte has earlier pondered going into the maze and wondered about its relationship to the impending marriage to Redmond that she desires, concluding that she needs to enter the maze to allow him to rescue her, so that she can become the fourth Mrs. Redmond. Joan herself warns her own character against going into the maze in this instance, but just as she has not heeded the warnings of her mother's astral body, implicitly invoked as she continues to write *Stalked by Love*, so too Charlotte fails to heed Joan's warnings (332).[20]

As Charlotte morphs into Felicia and the ghostly former Lady Redmonds proliferate, the gothic villain/hero Redmond makes a final appearance in the manuscript, where he too "began his transformations" (342), taking on in succession the appearance of the various men in Joan's life, from her father to Paul to Arthur and finally to a figure of death (343), whom the Felicia/Charlotte character resists in the final lines of Joan's manuscript. She refuses the "rescue" and promise of love that he offers and states "I know who you are" (343) in recognition of the dangers for women inherent in the conventional marriage plot. As Greene points out, "rather than exonerating the hero so that the heroine can join with him, Joan's version exposes his menace as real, part of the 'central plot' of patriarchy in which girl grows into woman to be replaced by 'the next one'" (187). The manuscript simply stops at this point, and Joan vows not to write any more Costume Gothics (345), having finally "overturned" the "orthodox plot" of the romance genre (Benson 111).

Stalked by Love becomes, then, a "gothic gone wrong"—a term the reader will read ironically, a term Joan has applied earlier to the manuscript for her "Lady Oracle," which "was upside-down somehow. [...T]here was no happy ending, no true love" (232). Both instances of the fantastic from Joan's own experience invade the world of the Costume Gothic and subvert its conventions: the astral body-like apparitions of the Lady Redmonds warn Felicia/Charlotte of the dangers of these very conventions just as Joan's mother's apparition has earlier warned Joan, and *Stalked by Love* comes to resemble Joan's "Lady Oracle" in its lack of resolution. Indeed, the early portions of *Stalked by Love* contain what the second-time reader of Atwood's novel will recognize as a reference to "Lady Oracle," which Joan has already written before going to Italy but which doesn't appear in Atwood's *Lady Oracle* for another hundred or so pages: Joan writes that "Redmond bowed to his wife, an ironic bow" (129), a line that echoes the word "bow" that Joan produces in her automatic writing and that becomes incorporated in "Lady Oracle." While Redmond's bow is ironic insofar as it does not imply any overturning of the idea that a woman should bow to her husband in marriage, Joan's use of this key word from "Lady Oracle" in her Costume Gothic has the effect of making Redmond's irony double back on itself since the term acquires connotations of power for women in its "Lady Oracle" context; and indeed, by the time Joan stops composing *Stalked by Love,* she has transformed her women characters so that they no longer "bow" in submission to the classic gothic conventions.

It should be noted that Joan's narrative throughout *Lady Oracle*, not just in her embedded gothic novel, reveals that she certainly does not uncritically adopt the conventions on which she comments. Her resistance always underlies her narrative, even when she explicitly claims that her life has "follow[ed] the line of least resistance" (7) by accepting rather than challenging the versions of femininity produced by the media and internalized by various figures in Joan's life: her mother and father; her first lover Paul, clandestine author of "nurse novels" who sparks Joan's interesting in writing Costume Gothics that perpetuate stereotypes about women and who trivializes Joan in various ways; Arthur, who claims to be a radical with enlightened political views but whose views on marriage and gender roles are entirely conservative; and finally, the Royal Porcupine (Chuck Brewer), who seems to fulfill the role of the classic gothic male. Many critics accept at face-value Joan's own statements about her limitations. Yet Joan's very self-consciousness about conventions suggests instead that she adopts them subversively, embracing a strategy of mimicry as defined by Luce Irigaray: "if women are such good mimics, it is because they are not simply reabsorbed in this function" (76). This self-awareness, in conjunction with the fantastic elements that disrupt the stories Joan constructs about herself, suggests that she is in a position to negotiate the images and plot structures that surround her rather than be passively constructed by them.

Eleanora Rao points out that Joan, retrospectively telling her story from Italy, exhibits "detachment in her ironic rethinking of her past, since a discrepancy is created between the 'self' who is telling the story and the various 'selves' represented in the narrative" (134–135). Joan speaks, according to

Rao, in a "double-voice," one "a public voice that is cheerfully accepting and selflessly accommodating," another "that is critical, enquiring, discontented, and desiring" (136).[21] Much evidence exists that in her retrospective narrative, this second, critical voice undermines the claims made in Joan's public voice, so that narrative self-consciousness and subversion of gothic and romance conventions mark not just *Stalked by Love* but also the novel *Lady Oracle* that Joan narrates retrospectively, evidence that counters many critics' claims about Joan's failure to distinguish formula fictions from the events of her life.[22] More aware from the outset than Murdoch's Charles Arrowby about the ways in which images and social constructs shape her desires, her narrative self-consciousness and the elements of her narration that render the novel postmodern are themselves a kind of "excess," to borrow Hite's term, which cannot be contained by the conventions of the realist novel, just as her own novel, *Stalked by Love*, finally cannot be contained by the gothic form it purports to fulfill.

Michelle Massé, drawing on Patrick Day's work on the gothic, identifies Joan as adopting, eventually, a strategy of subversion vis-à-vis gothic conventions that recalls Irigaray's description of mimicry: "Subversion, then, with its letter-perfect miming of what ideology demands, has a secret knowingness. It takes the tools of oppression and renders them impotent. As Day observes about the Gothic, 'The passivity and acceptance we see in the heroines is not a surrender to their situation, but a style of resistance and self-assertion' (20)" (Massé 250).[23] Instances of Joan's subversive mimicry abound in the novel. As a character in her tale, Joan frequently adopts a stereotypically feminine role to manipulate others for her own ends. As a narrator of her tale, she employs stylized discourse at almost every turn to illustrate that she remains aware of and outside the conventions that she subversively employs. In one instance, when she allows herself to be "rescued" from Paul by Arthur, she says, "I myself was bliss-filled and limpid-eyed: the right man had come along, complete with a cause I could devote myself to. My life had significance" (171). Joan's self-conscious use of Costume Gothics discourse calls attention to her self-ironization, exhibiting her awareness of the ideology behind her language and ultimately pointing to her resistance to gothic conventions, even before she describes her attempts to complete *Stalked by Love*.

Conclusion

Rather than having "mundane [...] explanations" common in the gothic novel (Hite 134), the supernatural appearance of the former Lady Redmonds, as well as Redmond's own transformations, remain unnaturalized in the final installment of *Stalked by Love*, just as the astral body and Joan's journeys into the mirror during automatic writing experiments are given no natural explanation within Atwood's novel. The fantastic moments serve a similar function to and on some level facilitate the emergence of Joan's critical voice. And just as *Stalked by Love* comes to an abrupt stop with seemingly supernatural events that challenge patriarchal constructions of reality and subvert the marriage plot, so too *Lady Oracle* ends on an abrupt note and, significantly, does not return Joan to the marriage plot. It remains entirely ambiguous what will take place in Joan's relationship with Arthur (though Joan suspects he will leave her), just as the identity of the man who has been stalking her is never discovered.[24]

Both McKinstry (63) and Barzilai ("Say that I had a Lovely Face" 249) conclude, however, that when Joan visits in the hospital the reporter that she has hit on the head with a bottle, she is entering a new romance plot by engaging in the narrative of the nurse novel, the very kind of novel her first lover Paul authored, and hence she in essence repeats the conventions of romance rather than subverting them. Yet a careful reading of the *Lady Oracle*'s final paragraphs reveals that if Joan does have romantic intentions regarding the reporter, she is attracted to him precisely because he knows something about her, not the self merely reflected in the mirror, the selfless self that Joan projects to the other men in her life. He knows a woman who in self-defense (albeit mistaken) "takes the offensive" (Fee 73) rather than hide, pretend, or rely on a male rescuer (see *Lady Oracle* 343).[25] In addition, one needs to take into account that when Joan encounters Paul again not long before her flight to Italy, her discourse about Paul's offer to "rescue" her from Arthur lays bare the absurdities of the conventions of the nurse novel by employing over-blown, self-conscious language that might be drawn from just such a novel. It is at precisely this point that Joan proclaims, "I was not the same as my phantom," (283), the damsel-in-distress character that Paul and other men have constructed for her. This "phantom" is nowhere to be found in the language Joan uses to describe the reporter, at a point in time when she has established that she wants to become another kind of ghost: "The trick was to disappear without a trace, leaving behind me the shadow of a corpse, a shadow everyone would mistake for solid reality" (7). Finally, the narrative that emerges from Joan's encounter with the reporter is not a nurse novel, but the text of the novel *Lady Oracle* itself, which both subverts the linear narrative strategy of the nurse novel and employs devices of the fantastic, sometimes in the narrative mode of the magic realist novel, in order to lay bare the very same conventions that Joan's critical voice calls attention to and undermines.

Both *Lady Oracle* and *The Sea, The Sea*, then, employ the fantastic to facilitate the narrator's self-consciousness about social constructions of femininity and to overturn a narrative genre—the classic gothic novel—that often reinforces socially sanctioned gender roles. While *The Sea, The Sea* portrays a male narrator's transformation from an author whose narrative practices are patriarchal and domineering to one whose storytelling conventions implicitly coincide with feminist narrative techniques, Atwood's novel employs a first-person female narrator to explore questions about women's narrative voice and authority. Though Joan seemingly tells her own life story in an autobiographical novel, however, Atwood raises the possibility in the last chapter that what readers have encountered is not Joan's own version per se, but her life story as penned by the male reporter: she muses that the story will be a strange one, "once he's written it" (344). This line causes Stein, for example, to speculate that "the entire novel may be his version of her story" and to point out, as a result, that "the novel raises the question of the woman author's control of her text, or indeed of any woman's authority over her own story. Has the journalist gained control of Joan's narrative, or has she retained control, shaping the story to suit her own purposes?" (*Margaret Atwood Revisited* 62). In a similar vein, Howells notes that the title of Joan's prose poem, "Lady Oracle," is not her own choice but is selected for her by the male publisher; furthermore, she points out, "[t]he most significant thing about an Oracle is that it is a voice which comes out of a woman's body and is associated with hidden dangerous knowledge, but that it is not her own voice" (*Margaret Atwood* 56).

From the text of *Lady Oracle*, it is impossible to determine if the reporter has reshaped Joan's narrative in any way, or if he has simply transcribed what she has told him, exactly in the way that she has told it. It is not even certain that he has in fact written the story—while it is suggested that he will do so, he has not already done so at the time that the narrative ends, and the possibility remains that while he might produce some version of Joan's tale, the version we have just read has been hers. (Greene, for example, reads the novel thus, with no mention of the male reporter's writing the novel.) Often, in novels in which one character narrates a story to another character who writes that story, or in novels in which a character finds and edits a manuscript about someone else, the framing narrative includes devices that call attention to the way the story has come to be produced. *Lady Oracle* contains no such commentary from a fictional editor or author, no framing device other than Joan's retrospection on her life from the present moment of the novel in the Italian setting. Yet even if the reader concludes that *Lady Oracle* is authored within the fiction by the reporter in spite of the fact that there exist no markers of such an embedded author, one can still interpret the narrative in a feminist light, and furthermore, the novel's treatment of the fantastic provides a key means for doing so. That is, his transcription of her story does nothing to naturalize the fantastic. If, as Hite argues, naturalizing the fantastic is a "male move" (141), then this reporter/fictional author does not engage in such a move and thereby implicitly sanctions not only the novel's and Joan's feminist narrative form but also Joan's acceptance of seemingly supernatural occurrences.[26] His difference from the other male characters who want to contain Joan in masculinist interpretations is thus captured in his implicit attitude toward the fantastical elements of her tale. If, as we have seen, naturalizing moments of the fantastic with the world of *Lady Oracle*, resolving them into the uncanny or considering them a hoax, is a move that reinforces a patriarchal world view, then the reporter implicitly challenges patriarchy in his failure to naturalize Joan's accounts of her mother's astral body and her automatic writing sessions.

The novels examined in Part II likewise raise questions about the female narrative voice and women's narrative authority. Just as many critics read *Lady Oracle* as a novel that ultimately compromises its own purported feminism and question Joan's reliability, so, too, many critics read *Housekeeping* and *The Stone Diaries* in a similar manner, stressing the ways in which these novels and their first-person female narrators preserve rather than challenge patriarchal definitions of femininity, and questioning the perspective of the narrators. These novels' uses of the fantastic, however, in conjunction with their self-conscious narration, facilitate a feminist re-reading of the narrative voice.

Part II

Ghostly Narrators and Narrative Voice

3

Narration from Beyond the Grave in Marilynne Robinson's Housekeeping

> The dead demand that we interrogate the alternative possibilities that seem to have withered and disappeared. [...T]he remainder: that haunts us, the ghost of potential, of alternative.
> —Arthur Redding, *"'Haints': American Ghosts, Ethnic Memory, and Contemporary Fiction" [180]*

> Robinson's double-gesture in the final pages—the negation of certainty and affirmation of possibility—compels characters and readers alike to unending constructions and deconstructions of what might be.
> —Elizabeth Meese, *Crossing the Double Cross: the Practice of Feminist Criticism [67]*

Introduction

When Joan Foster removes the clothes she has "drowned" in from a plastic garbage bag, she notes that "they smelled of my death, of Lake Ontario [...]. Jeans and a navy-blue T-shirt, my funerary costume of my former self" (19). This is a comic version of Marilynne Robinson's characters Ruth Stone and Sylvie Fisher, who purportedly drown but return to haunt the living, "leaving behind [them] a strong smell of lake water" (*Housekeeping* 218). Just as Joan's death is reported by newspapers, so too Ruth's and Sylvie's deaths are captured by the press: "Lake claims two," a headline in the local paper reads (213). While readers of Atwood's novel can be sure that reports of Joan's death are greatly exaggerated, readers of Robinson's novel cannot determine with any certainty that Ruth and Sylvie live, in spite of the fact that Ruth's narration continues past the moment of her reported death. The trope of ghostliness that Ruth frequently employs to describe herself before she claims to have died becomes, perhaps, more literal by the novel's end. Faced with the threat of the local sheriff removing Ruth from Sylvie's care, the two women attempt (unsuccessfully) to burn down their house and flee the town, to take up a life of transience together. As Sylvie ignites the pantry curtains with a burning broom, Ruth comments "there was an end to housekeeping" (209). Ruth and Sylvie leave the scene, never to be housed again, with the town assuming they have drowned in the lake while crossing a railroad bridge. "Since we are dead," Ruth writes, "the house would be [Lucille's] now" (217–18). How does one read this statement of Ruth's, or her nonchalant confirmation of the newspaper headline in her statement that "the lake claimed us" (214)?

Kristin King identifies two narratives in *Housekeeping*: the narrative of fact, through which Ruth straightforwardly sets out her own and her family history, and the narrative of desire, characterized by "extravagant metaphors and subjunctive moods [that] invite the reader to merge with the author, reconstruct altered versions of the past, and envision fantastic futures" (567). King links these two narratives with Lacanian feminist accounts of the workings of the symbolic and the imaginary orders. I would suggest that the hybrid aspect of the narrative along these lines also recalls, without replicating precisely, the hybrid nature of the magic realist narrative that blends its own "narrative of fact" with elements of the fantastic. The narrative of fact extends beyond the family history that Ruth sets forth to encompass as well historical conditions of women's lives as represented in a magazine such as *Good Housekeeping*, Depression-era economics, and the social conditions of and attitudes toward the homeless.[1] But this narrative of fact quickly merges into a narrative perspective that might be termed "fantastic" in two senses: Ruth's first-person narrative voice assumes the "superhuman privileges" (Lanser 19) of an omniscient narrator, offering to the reader information about her family past to which she could not realistically have access; and Ruth describes several events that might be deemed supernatural. In addition to her description of what is perhaps her own death, these events include an encounter with children who are possibly spirits, and descriptions of her actions following the moment of death written in terms that are clearly hypothetical, in which possibilities for what Ruth does after her death, real or metaphoric, replace one another in rapid succession, leaving the reader wondering what really does take place at the novel's end, and on what ontological plane.

Like most of the novels considered in this book, *Housekeeping* cannot be readily fitted into categories such as the fantastic or magic realism as they have been commonly defined. In some ways, it shares characteristics of Todorov's pure fantastic insofar as the novel's critics are divided in their interpretations of the ghostly elements: some readers naturalize them, while others posit that Robinson creates a supernatural world, and still others, without using Todorov's theory or terminology, read the ending as undecidable, as in effect encompassing hesitation between a natural and supernatural interpretation.[2] Robinson leaves it unclear if Ruth and Sylvie have in fact perished when a train comes while they are still on the bridge and return as literal ghosts in the novel's last few pages, or if they are only metaphorically dead to the rest of the world because their choices make them outcasts. Yet unlike the classic fantastic tale, there is no character hesitation represented, and no terror or trepidation surrounding the possible appearance of ghosts. It is impossible to tell from Ruth's narration if she believes in ghosts, if she becomes one herself, or if her talk of ghosts is simply figurative. In this regard, the novel employs a strategy common to both the fantastic and magic realism: it blurs the literal and the metaphoric, a chief effect of which is to give rise to hesitation in the reader, bringing to the forefront concerns about the real. As Nancy Walker puts it, "possible realities collide as *Housekeeping* concludes, resisting closure" (42). These possible realities concern social constructions of gender roles, and this resistance to closure lies in the novel's status as a fantastic text, in the very hesitation evoked in the reader about the ontological status of the narrator, which in turn raises questions about women's social roles.[3]

A critical controversy surrounding *Housekeeping*'s status as a feminist work stems from a divide among readers who approach the novel from a pragmatic, American-based feminism and those who, influenced by continental theoretical approaches, focus on the novel's representation of language itself. The best reading of *Housekeeping*, however, melds these critical discourses, exploring the ways in which the novel both develops alternative discursive practices and participates in the social realm. In spite of all the claims in *Housekeeping* that the main characters are "absent," the novel's various feminist narrative strategies and its use of the fantastic moment to call forth hesitation in the reader have the effect of rendering ordinary women's lives more "present" by restoring voice and visibility to the characters' lives, a strategy that opposes both normative closure and dominant ideologies of gender. By considering the novel and the body of criticism it has elicited against the background of the fantastic, readers can better understand and appreciate *Housekeeping*'s peculiar power. Whether the ghosts be literal or metaphoric, they do haunt the conventional world, to remind those left behind—the character Lucille and the reader—of the cultural conditions that have rendered these women silent and invisible, and in fact to break that silence through Ruth's narrative gesture.

THE NEGATIVE READING OF THE ENDING

Death by drowning is a common fate in *Housekeeping*: for example, when Ruth describes her grandfather, readers learn that he possessed the typical American dream of conquering the western frontier. Feeling confined in his Middle Western house, Grandfather Foster sets off in search of the wide open spaces of the American west. But Robinson shows the grandfather's efforts to be futile and undermines his masculine quest. After he works his way up the ranks in the railroad industry, his train plunges off a bridge into deep, icy water, never to be recovered. At the same time that women eschew the traditional male dreams that lead the grandfather to his death—"the troublesome possibility of success, recognition, advancement" (13)—they are often confined still by cultural constructs of femininity, which lead Ruth and Lucille's mother Helen, for example, to the same place: the bottom of the lake. After a conventional marriage, Helen "set[s] up housekeeping" (14), and later she gets a job "selling cosmetics in a drugstore" (22). Apparently dissatisfied both with motherhood and with her limited career, she drives herself over a cliff into the lake in Fingerbone. Her drowning, while it mirrors her father's, is fundamentally different in that he accidentally drowns while pursing adventure to escape confinement, while she commits suicide because she feels confined by womanhood and motherhood.

In contrast, Ruth's sister, Lucille, initially drawn like Ruth (though never to the same degree as Ruth) to the mysterious other-world that their Aunt Sylvie represents, eventually comes to embrace housekeeping with a vengeance, becoming the staunch representative of traditional femininity. As an adolescent, Lucille desires all the conventional trappings: she buys makeup, nail polish, sets her hair in pin curlers (119), wants to buy setting gel for Ruth (120), reads books on dinner table etiquette (132), asks for regular meals served on china (102), and takes a Home Economics course at school (136). Lucille adopts all these measures against Sylvie's non-conventional housekeeping: Sylvie prefers to sit in the dark, eats crackers that she keeps in her pockets, finds her clothes on the streets, doesn't serve regular meals, and lets the house revert to a state of nature. Eventually Lucille leaves the decaying house to live with the home economics teacher, completely dissociating herself from Sylvie.

Both Helen's and Lucille's endings are the endings met by so many women in nineteenth and early twentieth-century fictions, as both D.A. Miller and Rachel Blau DuPlessis point out in their studies of closure: like Lucille, they give up their transgression and are reinscribed in the social order; or, like Helen, they go mad, or they die. The question then becomes one of whether the fate that Ruth and Sylvie meet replicates this pattern or provides an alternative to it. According to Christine Caver, who belongs to the group of critics that does not read the novel as a successful feminist text, *Housekeeping*'s ending in essence repeats the endings of early twentieth-century works such as Charlotte Perkins Gilman's *The Yellow Wallpaper* and Kate Chopin's *The Awakening*: "the alternatives for women who long to escape from an abusive or repressive system are situated somewhere between madness and death," with Ruth's and Sylvie's purported drownings replicating Edna Pontillier's drowning at the end of *The Awakening* (113–4).[4] Those who are critical of the novel's version of feminism question the practical oppositional potential of the world that Ruth and Sylvie enter, focusing on the novel's movement toward death, its intermingling the language of rebirth with the language of the dissolution of Ruth's self.

The novel provides much evidence for the negative reading. Even before they are presumed dead, Ruth increasingly cuts herself off from the physical and social worlds. When the sheriff who wants to remove her from Sylvie's care speaks to her, she doesn't speak back. She likewise refuses to talk to the women who come from the church with food, noting that for several months she has spoken "only to Sylvie" (183). Focusing on Ruth's mention of Babylon near the novel's end, coupled with Ruth's difficulties communicating in "normal" language, Caver suggests that "she and Sylvie are entering a realm of confused languages, where they will no longer be able to communicate with the living communities whose perimeters they skim" (131–132). In some critics' views, then, Robinson's novel threatens to leave its women exactly where the oppressive society wants them: either "housed," like Lucille, or should they refuse to be housed, then silenced, dispossessed, disintegrated, ineffectual, and very possibly drowned. Admitting that it is tempting to read *Housekeeping* from a feminist perspective, many readers have commented on the novel's lack of a truly social vision and ultimately feel that the novel compromises its potential radicalism. For example, Sian Mile claims that Ruth's and Sylvie's "self-centered" exploration of their identities "is an insidious diversion from the problems of the social and political" (134).[5]

RECUPERATING THE ENDING (I): SEMIOTIC NARRATIVE STRATEGIES

A second group of critics, however, celebrates the novel's resistance to masculine plot structures for women and finds in the novel an alternative feminine world and an alternative feminine language that does indeed function in an oppositional manner. Ruth, with her transient Aunt Sylvie's help, pursues a transformative definition of the feminine: just as Sylvie lets the house in which they live return to a state of nature by refusing to "keep house," by allowing the elements of nature, wind, water, and animal life to enter into that space, so too Ruth rejects domesticity and in various ways merges with the natural world. Ruth undertakes several journeys outside her house that become key steps in her merging with Sylvie's character and finding in Sylvie the mother figure she yearns for. Robinson offers the reader the gradual merging of Ruth into Sylvie's world as an alternative to the traditional Oedipal quest for a father, and she portrays Ruth's entrance into Sylvie's world, described through the imagery of rebirth, as an alternative to the masculine quest novel in American literature.[6] For example, there is a long section of the narrative devoted to Ruth's journey away from the home to the shores of the lake with Sylvie, where Sylvie briefly abandons Ruth and then returns to her. As the two recline in a boat on the water, Ruth resting between Sylvie's legs, Robinson's language evokes the act of Sylvie giving birth to Ruth, suggesting a pre-oedipal bond between the two and apparently fulfilling Ruth's earlier wish that "the world will be made whole" (152) in the merging of this daughter-mother dyad. This anti-oedipal narrative both involves a rejection of masculinist plots and of conventional cultural institutions associated with what Lacan identifies as the symbolic. And because the narrative of this rejection participates in the fantastic by suggesting the possibility that Ruth's narrative is generated from beyond the grave, it becomes tempting to read the novel in light of Rosemary Jackson's theory of the fantastic and its intersection with Lacan's imaginary: "it has been possible to claim for the fantastic a subversive function in attempting to depict a *reversal* of the subject's cultural formation. [... T]he imaginary area which is intimated in fantastic literature suggests all that is other, all that is absent from the symbolic, outside rational discourse" (*Fantasy* 177).

This group of critics focuses upon *Housekeeping*'s representation of language itself, reading that representation as a positive resistance to patriarchal symbolic language. One can, for example, explore the novels' unusual, dense, poetic language not as an element that cuts Sylvie and Ruth off from communication with the world (Caver), but one that instead disrupts norms and undermines the structure of so-called masculine language, or the symbolic order itself—the language Lucille speaks but which Ruth, by the novel's end, can no longer hear. *Housekeeping* perhaps illustrates the claim Susanne Becker makes for "gothic forms of feminine fiction of the 1980s," arguing that Atwood's mid–1970s neo-gothic *Lady Oracle* "anticipat[es] a 'wilderness' that itself escapes the constructions of enclosures of houses" (196).[7] Becker views Atwood's Joan Foster as entering what Elaine Showalter terms the "wild zone" of women's discourse when she engages in automatic writing and senses her mother's presence during these experiments with language (167); similarly, Ruth's and Sylvie's act of torching the house, rejecting the indoor life of housekeeping for the outdoor life of transience, represents "an attempt to explore [...] a specifically female cultural 'wild zone,' a female space where mother and daughter struggle to have their voice heard and their subjectivity fulfilled" (Lin 209–210).[8] Ruth's rebirth into the "wild zone" of Sylvie's world is marked nearly complete when Ruth and Sylvie see Lucille on the street on their way back to the house, and Lucille, now dressed like her friends, refuses to acknowledge them. Later Lucille tries to take care of Ruth, to get her to change her wet clothes, and urges Ruth to leave Sylvie, but Ruth, so distant now from all conventionality, "could not hear a word she said" (175), can no longer even register Lucille's conventional language. This highlighting of language and Ruth's distance from conventional talk is emphasized earlier as well, when first she imagines she dies and cannot make out the words that pass between Sylvie and Lucille (118) and then just afterward cannot seem to participate normally in a conversation with Lucille (122).

Housekeeping's final passage is worth examining in detail for the ways in which it advances this semiotic reading. Ruth writes here about all the things she and Sylvie do not do when their ghostly selves watch Lucille, who, they learn, is now living in Boston:

> We are nowhere in Boston. However Lucille may look, she will never find us there, or any trace or sign. We pause nowhere in Boston [...] and the perimeters of our wandering are nowhere. [...] No one watching [Lucille] smear her initials in the steam on her water glass with her first finger, or slip cellophane packets of oyster crackers into her handbag for the sea gulls, could know how her thoughts are thronged by our absence, or know how she does not watch, does not listen, does not wait, does not hope, and always for Sylvie and me [218–219].

Several critics have theorized that Ruth and Sylvie form a new, feminine self, a pre-oedipal bond with one another that places them outside the culture that they find stifling and narrowly oppressive, in an oppositional relationship to it. Jean Wyatt, for example, drawing on Kristeva's theories of the semiotic, explains that Ruth's and Sylvie's "absence of being is beyond a language whose function is to represent what *does* exist. By forcing language to accommodate something that cannot be articulated in its terms—the invisible, the nonexistent—Robinson creates a new discourse" (*Reconstructing Desire* 98). Wyatt goes on to argue that all the descriptions of what Ruth and Sylvie do not do at the end of the novel have the effect of making the reader visualize them doing precisely those things that they disclaim, so that Ruth's new discourse "force[s] language to positivize negation, to realize absence" and thereby "generates an impossible poetry whose metaphors make emptiness palpable, concrete" (100).[9] Thus rather than simply being a sign of Ruth's inability to effect the world, her relegation to silence and her dissociation from conventional language instead precipitate the development of another kind of communication. The new discourse Robinson creates in describing her characters' absence forces the reader (and perhaps other characters whom their ghosts encounter) to reckon with this palpable absence, to confront the social circumstances that relegate these characters to mere ghostliness.[10] In *Housekeeping*, the transgressive characters Ruth and Sylvie do perhaps drown, yet in many ways their ghostly status at the novel's end continues their transgression rather than bringing it to an end, rather than wholly writing them out of the world that has no place for them.

Readings that focus on Robinson's representation of language itself, illustrating how the novel enlists semiotic strategies for subversive ends, recuperate the novel's feminism from the arguments of those critics who question *Housekeeping*'s engagement with the social real. Yet it is also possible to recuperate the novel's feminism by analyzing how its language enlists not only semiotic but also symbolic expression to assert Ruth's presence and the authority of her narrative voice, a means of approaching the concept of voice in this novel that perhaps more effectively than others addresses the concerns of those critics who are troubled by *Housekeeping*'s representation of women.

Recuperating the Ending (II): Symbolic Narrative and Narrative Authority

As Kristin King has shown, *Housekeeping* does not in fact reject the symbolic in favor of the semiotic: rather, "the novel's feminist charge resides equally in the tension it *sustains* between symbolic and semiotic realms" (565). While King acknowledges that all of the material on the dissolution of Ruth's self points toward Ruth's merging with a pre-oedipal mother, she also maintains that Ruth "has mastered rather than abandoned a symbolic order" (565). According to King, Ruth's rebirth scene in the rowboat with Sylvie constitutes a "rebirth to the power of her voice" (574), insofar as Ruth becomes, following this scene, a self-conscious storyteller, retelling Biblical accounts of creation, and "demand[ing] a voice" in these accounts just as she does in American literary traditions that have excluded women's voices (575). Thus unlike those critics who disparage the novel's attention to the semiotic and see its feminism as impractical, and unlike those who value its alternative feminist language at the expense of its symbolic moments, King focuses upon the novel's hybridization of these tendencies as the source of its peculiar narrative and feminist power.

Similarly, feminist narrative theorists such as DuPlessis and Sally Robinson explore the ways in which women employ what Showalter describes as double-voiced discourse, the necessity of speaking/ writing in two voices at once, both within and outside of the dominant discourse of the patriarchal culture. The "wild zone" of a feminine language that exists completely outside the dominant and that coincides in some ways with feminist psychoanalytic approaches to Robinson's novel is, according to Showalter, a utopian possibility or fantasy (263). In reality, women's discourse is always inscribed within the dominant. But as Sally Robinson explains, women do not need simply to adopt the subject positions "*offered* by hegemonic discursive systems"; rather, they can construct other positions, "wrenched from within those very systems" (18). The self-conscious use of language and narrative constitutes a key means by which women writers, including women characters who narrate and perhaps pen their own tales, negotiate the demands of subverting the dominant discourse even while employing it. Thus Ruth, a self-consciousness narrator, enlists language in a playful, self-reflexive manner rather than remain silent (King 571).[11] The novel's fantastic dimension and its exploration of ghostliness facilitates Ruth's storytelling powers, her ability to manipulate language and storytelling conventions, granting her an authorial voice as narrator of her own tale even as she adopts strategies of silence as a character within that tale. At one point in the novel, a teacher tells Ruth, "You're going to have to learn to speak for yourself [...]," to which Lucille responds, "she has her own ways"

(135). While Lucille is not referring to Ruth's authorial stance, generated from a point in time posterior to the events themselves and perhaps even from a different ontological plane, the reader can see in this remark a commentary on the narrative of *Housekeeping* itself: Ruth has indeed learned to speak and to think for herself in her own way, rather than simply remaining silent and ineffectual. Likewise, the reader can see a metaphor for Ruth herself as a narrator in Ruth's comment that one always feels the presence of the "accumulated past, which vanishes and does not vanish, which perishes and remains" (172): while she emphasizes her ghostliness and her bodily dissolution, her voice remains.[13]

Ruth's first-person narration contains numerous unusual features that can be illuminated through feminist theories of women's narrative voice. The unusual features of the voice also link it with the novel's use of the fantastic, since, in effect, the voice pushes beyond the boundaries of conventional first-person narrative in a manner that might be construed as "fantastical" but that nonetheless grounds the voice in the "real" through its critique of existing social structures and its engagement with alternatives to patriarchal narrative. For example, Joanne Frye, who valorizes the first-person voice in women's fiction, argues that while the narrating I "resist[s] and redefine[s] the premises of representation," it also allows a woman character to represent herself in ways that imply authorship and authority (55), rather than eschewing representation itself, as do many experimental narratives: the narrating female I has "the capacity to engage the normative and simultaneously to elude and critique it, to evoke realities at the same time that it interrogates our ways of defining them" (55).[14] Ruth's very self-consciousness about language throughout the narrative functions in precisely this way: she always calls attention to the ways that social realities are defined and offers a perspective that challenges conventional interpretations, without calling into question the status of all representation.

At other times, Ruth's first-person narration seems to shift to an almost omniscient perspective. Susan Sniader Lanser, in *Fictions of Authority: Women Writers and Narrative Voice*, argues like Frye that feminist narratives do represent the female self even while challenging conventional representation, but she complicates some of Frye's claims about the personal voice. Placing structuralist narratology within a feminist perspective, Lanser draws on the work of Gerard Genette to define the personal voice as belonging to those first-person narrators who are the protagonists of the stories they narrate and who tell those stories in a self-conscious fashion (18–19)—seemingly Ruth's position within the narrative of *Housekeeping*. Lanser points out, however, that while the personal voice "remains a structurally 'superior' voice mediating the voices of the other characters, it does not carry the superhuman privileges that attach to authorial voice"; and furthermore, the personal voice might simply be dismissed by the culture if it doesn't conform to existing cultural constructions of femininity. Thus the "authority of personal voice is contingent in ways that the authority of authorial voice is not" (Lanser 19).

While Frye views the omniscient narrator who speaks in a "public voice" as necessarily dependant upon "the oppression of dominant ideologies" (51), Lanser explores the positive possibilities for a female narrator who employs the public, authorial voice: "Since authorial narrators exist outside narrative time (indeed, 'outside' fiction) and are not 'humanized' by events, they conventionally carry an authority superior to that conferred on characters, even on narrating characters" (15–16). The authorial voice, not to be confused with the historical author's voice, grants powers of authorship to the narrator. Ruth's unusual first-person narration possesses precisely this quality and at times blends almost imperceptibly into an omniscient narrative voice since Ruth does in essence "exist outside narrative time" (Lanser 15)[14] with the power to comment on the narrative act itself. Since this has been a position typically denied to women, women writers' adopting an authorial narrative voice allows them to assume, in Lanser's terms, the authority "to establish alternative 'worlds' and the 'maxims' by which they will operate" (22). But because *Housekeeping* embeds this authorial stance within a story told largely through a first-person narrative voice, Robinson's narrative strategy also grants Ruth the advantages of personal voice, namely the authority "to construct and publicly represent female subjectivity and redefine the 'feminine'" (Lanser 22). The unusual narrative stance enlists simultaneously two different types of feminist narrative authority, the very combination tempering the potential drawbacks of each type—namely, reinforcing hegemony, in the case of authorial narration, and being dismissed as merely autobiographical, in the case of personal narration.

In *Housekeeping*, Ruth becomes "the self-assured voice speaking from somewhere beyond the bridge" (King 566). This fantastical space allows for narrative experimentation that decidedly—and paradoxically—reinforces the palpable presence of Ruth's voice, even in her purported absence. While King sees Ruth's voice as evolving from tentatively recounting only what she could know "to resounding omniscience and authorial confidence" by the novel's end (569),[15] readers in fact see evidence of Ruth's authorial stance right from the beginning, even before she has begun to reflect self-consciously on the nature of language itself. At times, Ruth's writings about the family past are qualified by such statements as "she must have felt" or "imagine that," or "say that," informing readers that Ruth is constructing the thoughts of others. In themselves, of course, these qualifiers underline Ruth's imaginative powers and her storytelling abilities.[16] But at other times, Ruth speaks as though she has direct access to others' minds with no such qualifying markers present, and early passages of the novel thus read as if they were third-person, internally focalized narration rather than first-person narration.

For example, as Ruth describes her grandfather's confining Midwestern house on the novel's opening page, her description captures Edmund Foster's point of view, in spite of the fact that Ruth has never seen the house and never met her grandfather, who died before she was born, a fact she reveals to the reader in the same paragraph in which she relates information as though from his perspective to convey his motives for heading west: "from within [the house], the perfect horizontality of the world in that place foreshortened the view so severely that the horizon seemed to circumscribe the sod house and nothing more" (3). Describing her grandfather's death a few pages later, she again assumes the stance of an omniscient narrator. Right after she notes that the train accident "was not, strictly speaking, spectacular, because no one saw it happen" (5–6), a phrase that in itself illustrates a good deal of self-consciousness about word choice and precision in language, Ruth proceeds to provide a strong visual image in describing the accident that no one witnessed: "the engine nosed over toward the lake and then the rest of the train slid after it into the water like a weasel sliding off a rock" (6). Ruth's weasel image might not particularly strike the reader as unusual were it not for the disclaimers about no one seeing the accident that both immediately precede it *and* immediately follow it: Ruth takes care to point out that two people who did survive the wreck also were not, strictly speaking, witnesses, since they were at the end of the train looking backward at the time of the plunge into the water. Given how much attention she calls to the wreck's not being "spectacular," then, her visual imagery seems to generate from an omniscient narrative perspective that comments from beyond the world of the fiction.[17] This unusual aspect of Ruth's authorial stance is perhaps made possible by her very ghostliness, which in effect dissolves the constraints of conventional first-person narration by dissolving strict bounds between character and omniscient narrator, giving her license to enter the consciousness of others, and hence facilitating her socially symbolic act of telling her story. (These kinds of narrative violations, as we will see, are even more pronounced in *The Stone Diaries*).

Moreover, Ruth as narrator fully recognizes that there are different versions of the same story, a fact that both highlights further her narrative self-consciousness and has implications for the novel's social vision. For example, when thinking of her mother, Ruth acknowledges that she and Lucille have different accounts of Helen's existence: Lucille would describe a socially acceptable mother, "orderly, vigorous, and sensible," while Ruth would describe a mother who "presided over a life so strictly simple and circumscribed that it could not have made any significant demands on her attention" (109). Or, when recounting the events of a night she and Lucille spend by the lake, Ruth comments, "Lucille would tell this story differently" (116) in order to explain events in a more commonsense way, while Ruth herself highlights the fantastic dimensions of their night away from home, speaking of ghosts and being "haunted" by Sylvie, stressing her own merging with the consciousness of the night. These passages foreshadow the moment when Ruth, left by Sylvie at a fallen house inhabited by ghostly children whose presence she senses, makes up stories about the children who represent not only Ruth herself, but all society's invisible people, like the hoboes, tramps, and transients who populate the novel. In these stories, Ruth significantly casts herself as a rescuer (158). Though she feels on some level that she has failed because she thinks she has merely imagined the children in the ruined house (159), she will later revisit the urge to rescue the unseen, the social outcasts, through the story that becomes *Housekeeping*. Just as she tells a different version of family stories than would Lucille, so too, Ruth tells a counter story to the town's dominant stories (or non-stories) about its "invisible" ranks.

As Ruth notes of the town's sheriff, he "preside[s] over [...] stories" (177) about violence and loss. In his world view, the idea that Sylvie should raise Ruth is a related story, a socially unacceptable story, because of Sylvie's status as a transient. Therefore the sheriff and others of the town, "believing that [Ruth] should be rescued, and that rescue was possible" (178), want to preside over her story by making it a socially sanctioned one. Ruth, then, in the townspeople's version of her story, would be rescued from oblivion, for the story of transience is not even one that can be told. That is, the town's residents would consider the town's many transients as having been erased from their own existence at the point that they become wanderers: "like the dead, we would consider their histories complete, and we wondered only what had brought them to transiency, to drifting, since their lives as drifters were like pacings and broodings and skirmishes among ghosts who cannot pay their way across the Styx. However long a postscript to however short a life, it was still no part of the story" (179). But rather than allow herself to be rescued according to the sheriff's and the townspeople's story, Ruth presides over her own story by putting into words the narrative whose very existence is denied, by telling the story of her transience from "beyond the grave," whether she be literally or merely socially dead. Ruth thus reverses the concept of "rescue" and does succeed in telling her own version of a rescue story. In so doing, she creates a narrative that substantiates the existence of society's other ghosts, a narrative for women who do not see themselves as domestic angels, without casting them as rebellious monsters.

Paradoxically, the importance of constructing alternate narratives and of preserving words for this purpose is further emphasized when Ruth and Sylvie at one point attempt to burn words. They ignite and try to get rid of all the newspapers and magazines Sylvie has accumulated, incriminating evidence that clutters the house, in the effort to convince the sheriff that they can be good housekeepers and that Ruth should remain with Sylvie. The passage that describes the burning of words contains many interesting contradictions: on the one hand, the act of burning is meant as an act of conformity, a gesture that will convince the town of Sylvie's normalcy. Yet the act of burning also convinces Ruth that "words, too, must be salvaged" (200). The preservation in language, then, of the story of transience and alternative definitions of femininity that *Housekeeping* becomes, constitutes an act of defiance to the norms. The passage also suggests that the story Ruth tells will be different, non-conventional, for the very things she and Sylvie burn represent the conventional world: a library book, issues of *Good Housekeeping*, and images of the American dream, including a baseball team and a Chevrolet (200). That these images are described as being "transfigured" by flame suggests the novel's alternative version of the American dream, invokes Ruth's alternative narrative to the town's dominant narrative, and foreshadows Ruth's and Sylvie's transformation into alternative selves when they become ghosts, whether literally or figuratively.[18]

Even before the two women meet an uncertain fate crossing the railroad bridge, Ruth imagines that she would become a ghost, "lost to ordinary society" (183) by cutting herself off from the world that the sheriff represents. But in another reversal of the conventional story, according to which Ruth would be restored to substance by leaving Sylvie's world and being housed "safely within doors" (183), Ruth imagines later that to become substantial, to be transformed into a mortal child, would be to become "lost to her kind" (204), and she registers this loss more profoundly than she registers her loss to ordinary society. As Galehouse points out, "it is only when Sylvie and Ruth drift outside of convention that they realize—that is, *become real to*—themselves" (123). Through the trope of ghostliness and invisibility, then, which can be transferred through the act of Ruth's narration from those who traditionally have no history, no stories, to those whose stories are more commonly told, Robinson suggests that the ghostly Ruth is in some ways more "present" than those who assimilate to ordinary society. Moreover, as Macpherson notes, Robinson suggests that "as ghost or transient, Ruthie [...] becomes an unsettling force for the women of Fingerbone" (198) who would like to house or contain her, insofar as Ruth returns to Fingerbone to haunt those dedicated to conventional living, disturbing their routines by opening doors, tracking in leaves, and rearranging domestic objects (*Housekeeping* 218). Ruth's and Sylvie's returns constitute an essential part of the novel's critique of conventional society and suggest their power to influence and transform it, not simply to escape from it, since, as Smyth points out, mere escape would leave conservative social forces unchanged (282).[19] Rather, in their returns, in the scent of lake water they leave behind, Ruth and Sylvie remind the living "of the alternative possibilities that seem to have withered and disappeared" (Redding 180).[20]

CONCLUSION

The novel's most prolonged act of speculation on Ruth's part, an extended passage that depicts an imagined future for Lucille, is interesting not only for what it tells us about Sylvie's and Ruth's presence-in-absence, but also for what it tells us about Lucille. We learn little else about Lucille after the point at which she leaves to reside with the home economics teacher, but at the end of the novel, years later and after Ruth and Sylvie are assumed dead, the two wanderers imagine where Lucille might be. When they occasionally pass the old house on the train, they see that someone is living there, and Ruth writes, "I imagine it is Lucille, fiercely neat, stalemating the forces of ruin. I imagine doilies, high and stiff, and a bright pantry curtain, there to rebuke us with newness and smell of starch whenever we might wander in the door" (216). Sylvie speculates that Lucille has likely married, and Ruth concurs (217). As Ruth noted earlier, "Lucille was determined to make something of herself" (132). For Lucille, this means adopting the very role assigned to her by patriarchal culture.

Yet for all Lucille's own resistance to Sylvie and her ways, there is an odd doubling of Lucille and Sylvie in *Housekeeping*'s closing passage, in which Ruth imagines Lucille not in the house, but in a restaurant in Boston. Here, Lucille adopts Sylvie's characteristic gesture of slipping crackers into her pocket (219), and Robinson deconstructs the binary opposition between Ruth / Sylvie on the one hand, and Lucille on the other. Lucille's attempt to write her initials, as if asserting her identity thus, in a medium so fleeting as steam on a water glass suggests a certain kinship between her and her lost family members whose ontological status has become so questionable. The passage implies perhaps two things at once.

First, in keeping with Ruth's discourse about her own status as a "ghost" and her reversal of that trope to refer to people with conventional ways, the imagery that Robinson employs suggests that although Lucille consciously embraces substantiality, her particular choice to adopt the domestic identity chosen for her by conventional society makes her as invisible as Ruth and Sylvie with their choice to become outsiders. Robinson also writes that Lucille's glass "has left two-thirds of a ring on the table, and she works at completing the circle with her thumbnail" (218). That the circle is "two-thirds" complete suggests that Lucille herself is the missing one-third in the Lucille-Ruth-Sylvie triad, Ruth and Sylvie being strongly associated with water imagery throughout the novel. Lucille, then, is described as an absence while Ruth and Sylvie are presences. In portraying Lucille the housewife as being as insubstantial as Ruth and Sylvie, Robinson transfers the status of ghost to the conventional angel in the house, an interesting twist on the common nineteenth-century monster/angel dichotomy, described, for example, by Gilbert and Gubar. In this trope, that which has been considered women's "real" existence by the patriarchal culture is revealed as unreal, a cultural construct belied by women's actual experience in the world.

Second, it is as if Robinson posits that subconsciously Lucille cannot really dissociate herself from Sylvie and Ruth's world, that some force links her, too, with the unconventional existence they lead. The paradoxical line "her thoughts are thronged by our absence" suggests that Lucille *does* register the loss of these two family members. As Koenen points out, Robinson's use of the word "always" in the last sentence of the novel "contradicts the gaps, the denial of loss and female community in Lucille's thought and exposes her longing against her repressions, an affirmation of female bonding against conscious negation" (292–3).[21] Although Champagne (325) has interpreted the line about Lucille's glass leaving a partial ring on the table that Lucille tries to complete to mean that Lucille seeks a conventional kind of closure, one should note that the imagery is circular rather than linear; perhaps this gesture instead suggests Lucille's unconscious attempt to enter the cyclic time associated with women in the novel, expressing some secret desire for an oppositional stance to the patriarchal story in which she has willingly inscribed herself. In the end, *Housekeeping*'s haunting conclusion coincides with Arthur Redding's observation about "haints": "Finally, ghosts return because it is we who want something of them; in this regard, it is not so much the dead that haunt the living, but the living that obsessively haunt the dead" (180).

In this light, it is interesting that Ruth would like to see the people who occupy the old house in which she, Lucille, and Sylvie once resided in order to "expel poor Lucille" (217) from her imagination, but just as Lucille remains haunted by Ruth and Sylvie, so, too, Ruth remains haunted by Lucille, compelled in her wanderings to obsessively imagine the sister left behind. Throughout the novel, Ruth's first-person voice frequently violates the conventions of that voice by entering realms it cannot know. Ruth wonders if she might return to the house in Fingerbone and find Lucille living in the house, noting the possibility that Lucille would, logically enough, own the house and still reside there, and is perhaps even raising a family there. But after imagining such a scene for a few minutes, emphasizing her reconstruction through her repeated use of the word "perhaps," explaining that these things have happened "in [her] mind" (217), she states, "If Lucille is there, Sylvie and I have stood outside her window a thousand times" (218). In this sentence, the voice shifts from the subjunctive to the indicative mood in such a way that it both calls attention to the constructed nature of Ruth's projection and asserts it as a fact, thereby interrogating the ways in which we construct realities but also lending an authoritative air to Ruth's hypothetical narration that causes the reader to hesitate, in reading this passage, about what is fact, what is merely possibility. This is not simply a case of unreliable narration from an untrustworthy narrator. Rather, it is a case in which an unusual, fantastical narrative stance is employed not to call into question the judgment of the narrator herself but to probe social conventions that render women invisible, given that Ruth is here contrasting Lucille's conventional path with her own and Sylvie's unconventional one. The hesitation is bound up with the fantastic insofar as readers remain unsure of

Ruth's ontological status at this point, but it is firmly grounded in considerations of the real and points toward the conflict between reality and fantasy inherent in social constructions of femininity.

The elliptical and haunting final pages in which Ruth does not merely imagine Lucille but moves almost by sleight of hand from one possibility for Lucille to another, slipping into her consciousness seamlessly, like a ghost passing through a wall, leave the reader not only with the strong images of Lucille engaging in all the acts that Ruth imagines her not engaging in (thereby, according to Wyatt, rendering the absent characters "palpable" and present), but also with the powerful presence of Ruth's authorial, quasi-omniscient voice. Whether Ruth is dead or alive, the narrative voice itself becomes fantastical. Her impossible, ghostly access that violates the boundaries of what is allowable in first-person narration is especially highlighted in Ruth's final narration, a gesture by which "the ghost of potential, of alternative" (Redding 180) cannot be simply remaindered but must be registered as a voice protesting those cultural forces that, like Fingerbone's Sheriff, preside over women's stories, ultimately displacing them with a feminist counter-story.

4

The "Invisible" Woman: Narrative Strategies in Carol Shields's The Stone Diaries[1]

> To play with mimesis is thus, for a woman, to try to recover the place of exploitation by discourse, without allowing herself to be simply reduced to it. It means to resubmit herself—inasmuch as she is on the side of the "perceptible," of "matter"—to "ideas," in particular ideas about herself, that are elaborated in/by masculine logic, but so as to make "visible," by an effect of playful repetition, what was supposed to remain invisible: the cover-up of a possible operation of the feminine in language. It also means "to unveil" the fact that, if women are such good mimics, it is because they are not simply reabsorbed in this function. They also remain elsewhere.
> —*Luce Irigaray, This Sex Which Is Not One [76]*

> Giving voice to the voiceless and making visible the invisible are two prime maneuvers in feminist poetics.
> —*Rachel Blau DuPlessis,*
> *Writing Beyond the Ending [41]*

INTRODUCTION

Carol Shields's novel *The Stone Diaries* presents the reader with a challenging narrative puzzle: the extraordinary violations of storytelling conventions include not only rapid shifts between first- and third-person narration but also a first-person narrator who both recounts details of her birth to which she could not realistically have access and appears to speak even after the moment of her death. When it seems that Daisy Goodwill Flett has in fact died, a first-person voice makes statements such as "I'm still here, inside the (powdery, splintery) bones, ankles, the sockets of my eyes, shoulders, hip, teeth, I'm still here, oh, oh" (352). Reviewer Marjorie Fee concludes that Daisy assumes the narrating role when she is in her eighties, during the portion of the novel that describes her illness and decline (174). While the date of Daisy's death is left as a blank in the novel (343, 347), and while Shields herself commented in an interview that Daisy's "construct is still in place before she dies, so she's just imagining what is happening to her after her death" (Thomas 58), the position of the narrator in time and space seems less clear cut than these comments would suggest: embedded in a section of the narrative in which her family and friends respond to her death and reminisce about her life, Daisy's comment about still being here suggests that this latter portion of her story is rendered through a ghostly narrator.[2]

In this respect, *The Stone Diaries* resembles *Housekeeping*. Both novels employ the trope of invisibility to describe their central female characters, clearly linking invisibility to gender; both raise the possibility that the narrative is generated from a point in time following the narrator's death; and both violate the conventions of first-person narrative by giving the narrators access to others' thoughts and to events that they could not have witnessed or have reconstructed from others' accounts in as much detail as they do, so that these events and other characters' interiority are rendered as if from an omniscient perspective. In *Housekeeping*, the suggestion that Ruth narrates after her death is much stronger than the suggestion in *The Stone Diaries* that Daisy tells her story from beyond the grave; nor does *The Stone Diaries* contain, as *Housekeeping* does, other references to ghosts or to the supernatural that suggest the novel belongs to the mode of the fantastic. Shields's novel is, in fact, the most tangentially fantastic novel included in this book. And yet the suggestion about the ghostliness of the narrative perspective invites the reader to reinterpret the whole of the narrative in light of the ending. From the first page, the narration itself can be construed as fantastical, its violations of normative conventions being far more exaggerated than the violations in *Housekeeping*. Generated from a seemingly impossible narrative perspective, the novel prompts the reader to wonder who is telling this story. One might say that the novel invokes the reader's hesitation not only with regard to Daisy's ontological status by the story's end, but also with regard to the source of the narrative from the very beginning. Indeed, as David Williams points out in a recent article on Shields, "in one form or another, the specter of multiplicity still haunts criticism of *The Stone Diaries* a decade after its publication"; this "spectre" involves questions about the narrative voice, questions about to whom it belongs and whether there is one or more than one voice rendering Daisy's life (10).[3] Although Williams himself does not employ theories of the fantastic or feminist narrative theory in his discussion of the narrative voice, nonetheless, his use of the language of the supernatural in the opening line of his essay is both intriguing and apt.

Many of the novel's critics have concluded that Daisy is simply not a sophisticated, self-conscious enough narrator to have generated the whole of *The Stone Diaries,* positing instead that multiple voices weave the story of her life. However, reading the novel both through theories of the fantastic and feminist theories of narrative, including theories of women's autobiography, provides a different answer to the question of who tells this story. I would like to consider *The Stone Diaries* as a fictional autobiography, narrated throughout by Daisy herself, who adopts multiple voices in the act of employing various feminist narrative strategies to restore voice and visibility to her apparently voiceless, invisible character. Although Daisy initially appears to be thwarted by social constructions of femininity, she might instead be viewed as a highly self-conscious narrator of her life story who distances herself from the character "caught in a version of her life, pinned there" (147). In Irigaray's terms, she ultimately "remains elsewhere" in the narrative, outside of the conventional definitions that she seems at times to adopt, just as she, perhaps, remains elsewhere than resting quietly in her grave after the moment of her death.

The plot of *The Stone Diaries* is difficult to summarize because so little of it focuses directly on the main character, whose narration contains countless digressions into the lives and minds of other characters. Daisy's story begins with her own birth and her mother's death during the process of childbirth, and then progresses through her childhood. Before being reunited with her father, Cuyler Goodwill, at age eleven, Daisy is raised by a neighbor, Clarentine Flett, and the neighbor's son Barker, whom Daisy later marries, following her disastrous first marriage. The sections of the novel that recount her childhood and two marriages also provide a great deal of information about Daisy's friends, about the Flett family, and about Cuyler Goodwill. The novel then turns to Daisy's experiences as a mother, her subsequent work as a gardening columnist, the death of her husband Barker, a period of depression in Daisy's life, her later travels with her niece to pursue family history, her move to a retirement community, her old-age illness, and finally her death. Each section of the novel, each major segment of Daisy's life, modulates in its narrative perspective, at times seeming to generate from Daisy's first-person, autobiographical voice, and at other times seeming to generate from the other characters' viewpoint and/or from a third-person, omniscient narrator.

For readers to make their way through the narrative maze of *The Stone Diaries*, the work of Simone Vauthier on point of view and the curious shifts between first- and third-person narration in *The Stone Diaries* provides a helpful starting place, though I would like to substantially revise Vauthier's conclusions about the narrative perspective. According to her analysis, readers take the novel first as autobiography, accepting the lapses into third-person narration in the "Childhood" chapter as a "strategy" that allows the narrator "to render the sick child's disorientation" (182); yet the categories soon blur, leaving readers confused as to whether they are reading a fictional autobiography or fictional biography. Ultimately, Vauthier identifies two third-person voices: one an outside biographer, an internally focalized, extradiegetic narrator who recounts events of Daisy's life; and another that Vauthier terms the voice of "the critic" (184), a hidden author who comments self-reflexively on the narrative limitations of both biography and autobiography. Both these voices are separate entities from Daisy's first-person, homodiegetic narrative voice. All three generate the text of *The Stone Diaries*. Rejecting the idea that the split voices all belong to Daisy, Vauthier concludes that the novel's complicated narrative structure "seems too much of a burden for a character like Daisy" (184). Vauthier even goes so far as to suggest that the "I" who appears throughout the narrative might not always be Daisy's "I"—this voice perhaps belongs instead to the "outside biographer" (185). Vauthier, then, does not grant Daisy herself much of the novel's narration, which, she writes, "destabilizes the authority of the narrating voices" (177). Winifred M. Mellor takes a similar view, writing that "the plurality of diaries in the title *The Stone Diaries* suggests that there is not only one story and not only one teller" (98), and concluding that the novel undermines "Daisy's authority to tell her own story" (103).[4]

I would like, however, to argue that Daisy is in fact the only narrator of *The Stone Diaries*, that Daisy splits her own narrative voice into first and third person in ways that coincide with feminist theories of narrative, and that the speaking tone and the kinds of knowledge evidenced in the different narrative voices might be understood not ironically as a "gap between the autobiographical narrator's lesser and the biographical narrator's greater knowledge" (Vauthier 184), but as an effect of Daisy's relationship to her own story and to language itself, her self-consciousness about her social position as a woman.[5] As a character in a story about a conventional woman's life, Daisy seems limited because the social circumstances of her day severely circumscribe her role, but as a narrator who speaks from some ambiguous point in time and space, she is capable of transcending these limitations to articulate a great deal about her life, evidenced in the narrative complexities of her fictional autobiography. When she seems to exist on a different ontological plane than does the character Daisy, the narrator Daisy is able to grasp and to convey to the reader the ways in which dominant ideology has defined her, and ultimately to exceed those bounds.

Shields herself, when asked in an interview about the split between the first- and third-person voices, commented that "it was my intention that everything in *The Stone Diaries* should be filtered through the consciousness of Daisy Goodwill. [...] Sometimes—at least once in every chapter—Daisy has a moment of clarity, and it is in those sections that I used first person. But mostly, she is a baffled, seeking, third-person character, ever wandering through the construct that she calls her life story" (Hollenberg 347). Shields, then, claims to produce a certain kind of fictional autobiography, one in keeping with Sidonie Smith's comments about the typical nineteenth-century woman's autobiography. Describing those women producing autobiographical prose prior to the twentieth century, Smith writes that "the ideology of gender makes of woman's life script a nonstory, a silent space, a gap in patriarchal culture" (*Poetics* 50), and further, that "the woman autobiographer must "negotiate...

[the] sets of stories" that are all "written about her rather than by her" (*Poetics* 51).[6] Even though Shields, unlike some of her critics, does grant Daisy the central consciousness of the novel, she sees her own character as nonetheless limited, circumscribed by her story. Yet the novel provides much evidence for reading it against the grain, for construing Daisy's voices, both first- and third-person, more positively than does Shields herself, just as there is much evidence for reading it against the grain of many of Shields's critics, for not taking at face value Daisy's repeated claims about the limitations of her own narrative voice. In considering this evidence through theories of women's autobiography and through feminist narrative theories, readers of the novel can discern several types of first- and third-person voices employed by Daisy: her subversive semiotic voice undermines the seemingly conventional third-person voice, as do her self-conscious, first-person voice, her authorial first-person voice, and her "extrarepresentational" (Lanser) third-person voice. These different types of narrating voices do not emerge one by one in any particular order in the novel; rather they are scattered throughout the narrative from beginning to end. Ultimately, the narrative combines all these different voices as Daisy resists patriarchal language and narrative practice.

THE NINETEENTH-CENTURY WOMAN AUTOBIOGRAPHER/THE THIRD-PERSON REPRESENTATIONAL VOICE

The characteristics of pre-twentieth century female autobiography seem initially to describe the dynamic at work in Shields's novel. From the start, *The Stone Diaries* comments explicitly upon language and its relationship to gender in a way that suggests the limitations of the female voice as compared to the strength of the male voice. Daisy herself, along with other women in the novel, is denied access to symbolic language at many points in the narrative. When she writes to her future husband Barker, for example, "she elects the language of childhood, deliberately naive" (149), writing in sentences that are "breathy," "uneven," and "incomplete"; and while Daisy has collected her husband's letters, "her letters to him have not survived" (145). Similarly, Daisy's step-mother Maria's language lacks social register: "she jabbers and jabbers, and no one understands one word she says—except for her husband who claims he can usually get the 'gist'" (129). Daisy's mother Mercy possesses a "helplessness with words and with the difficult forms the real world imposes" (60), being described throughout the portions of the narrative that concern her primarily in terms of her immense body. The physically slight Cuyler, in contrast, is described largely in terms of his voice, which, when he is reunited with Daisy, "continued all night long" (90); "he felt, rightly, that he owed her [...]

the whole of his story" (91). Daisy's father-in-law, Magnus Flett, who in his old age memorizes whole books, is described as "a pump primed with words" (101).

Daisy's relationship to language, then, appears to be a troubled one, her autobiography to resemble those typical of the nineteenth-century women writers that Sidonie Smith describes. It is from this impression that some critics are reluctant to attribute to Daisy much, if any, narrative authority. On the surface, it appears that Daisy is a representative of traditional femininity, a woman who adopts patriarchal culture's definition of her role and becomes "invisible," a selfless and un-self-conscious wife, mother, and housekeeper. She refers constantly to her own emptiness, "hollowness" (330) and "absence" (281); and she frequently undermines the very idea that she could produce an autobiography (75–6). A diarist whose writings include almost no details about her own experience of the world, she seemingly accepts the stripping of her subjectivity by masculine constructions of femininity, her life story appearing to be determined by a series of abstract positions or stages of life: birth, childhood, love, marriage. Summarizing Georg Misch's work on autobiography, Smith points out that

> For Misch, the "normative" definition of autobiography and the criteria used to evaluate the success of any particular autobiography lie in the relationship of the autobiographer to the arena of public life and discourse. Yet patriarchal notions of woman's inherent nature and consequent social role have denied or severely proscribed her access to the public space; and male distrust and consequent repression of female speech have either condemned her to public silence or profoundly contaminated her relationship to the pen as an instrument of power [*Poetics* 7].

As Daisy herself puts it, "the acts of her life form a sequence of definitions" (*Stone* 148). Many theorists who see narrative itself as gendered comment on this phenomenon. For example, as was noted in the Introduction (a point worth repeating here, since it is particularly apropos to Shields's novel), Sally Robinson writes, "narratives, in the broad sense in which I mean that term, address readers in gender-specific ways and very often seduce women readers into complicity with the erasure of female subjectivity, seduce women into becoming Woman" (18). Or, in Smith's terms, "participating in a certain conservative 'truthtelling,' the autobiographer might constitute a 'truth' consonant with the regimes of truth operating culturally and temporally by configuring experience according to established conventions and practices" ("Construing Truths" 155–6).

In many sections of the narrative that seem at first glance to be in keeping with theories of nineteenth century woman's autobiography, Daisy employs what Lanser identifies as the "representational voice," a narrator who reports the words and deeds of other characters without offering interpretive commentary (16). According to Lanser, this voice "make[s] a more limited claim to discursive authority" (17) than does the extrarepresentational authorial voice.

Daisy's third-person voice frequently engages in simple acts of representation, whether she is describing her own thoughts and actions or whether the narration is focalized through the thoughts of another character, as it often is. In this mode, Daisy appears to be caught inside her story. A prime example of this mode is found in the chapter titled "Motherhood," which contains virtually no self-conscious narrative commentary until the final pages. In the early parts, Daisy's daily routine and her relationships with her children are described in the third-person voice, with one section being told from each child's narrative point of view. Daisy is referred to throughout as "Mrs. Flett" and indeed is defined in the chapter through her relations to others: "deeply, fervently, sincerely desiring to be a good wife and mother, Mrs. Flett reads every issue of *Good Housekeeping*" (185). In the vast majority of this chapter, Daisy's third-person voice simply describes the life and thoughts of Daisy Goodwill Flett, the un-self-conscious social construct that I will call the *narrated* self. Though the novel begins with an autobiographical I—"My mother's name was Mercy Stone Goodwill" (1)—it quickly changes to the third-person representational voice, and Daisy is presented to us as a "she." According to Joanne Frye, "if a female pronoun recurs throughout a text, it repeatedly reminds us of cultural expectations for what it means to be female; it reminds us, inevitably, of the femininity text" (65), or cultural expectations accepted as truths about the role of women. Daisy's slippage into the third-person representational voice, then, seems to be in compliance with assumptions of both the femininity text and the nineteenth-century woman's autobiographical voice, concepts that are closely related to one another.

It would seem, then, that like Daisy's relationship to language itself, Daisy's relationship to narrative is troubled, passive, as she allows herself to be consumed/ constructed by others' stories for her, especially society's story for women of her time: as she observes, "She is powerless, anchorless, soft-tissued—a woman. Perhaps that is the whole of it, that she is a woman. Yes, of course" (150). But as Sally Robinson goes on to note after describing how narrative can circumscribe women, narrative can also become a tool whereby women confront their erasure, creating self-representations rather than accepting their place as sign or representation in masculinist narratives. Women writers exist both inside and outside hegemonic discourse:

> to be "inside" hegemonic representation of gender means to be framed within/by *the* sexual difference—that is, Woman's difference from Man. To be "outside" does not mean to occupy a space that is somehow "objective," free from ideology; rather, it means to occupy, self-consciously and critically, a position of marginality that enables women's self-representation [19].

This latter dynamic is what takes place in *The Stone Diaries* when Shields manipulates the narrative voice. In keeping with Robinson's comments about women confronting their erasure in narrative and self-consciously occupying a position on the margins, Shields writes of Daisy, "she lives outside her story as well as inside" (123). Here Daisy emerges as a *narrating* self, a self that is evidenced in several different kinds of narrative voices that she employs, alternatives to the self-effacing voice typical of the nineteenth-century woman autobiographer.

THE TWENTIETH-CENTURY WOMAN AUTOBIOGRAPHER

Even Daisy's self-effacing statements referenced above reveal her self-consciousness about her gendered representation and her relationship to the narrative that patriarchal culture has constructed about her life. To appreciate the narrative complexities of *The Stone Diaries*, readers must move beyond Daisy's repeated claims about her own absence in her fictional autobiography. She is, after all, a (fictional) twentieth-century autobiographer. Whereas the pre-twentieth-century female autobiographer might, in Smith's terms, tell a "truth" consonant with established cultural truths, as Daisy seems to do at many points in *The Stone Diaries*, a more sophisticated autobiographer might engage in what Smith calls "contestatory 'truthtelling' since that which seems to be 'truthful' to regimes of truth many in fact be false; and that which appears to be 'untruthful' may in fact be another kind of 'truthtelling'" ("Construing Truths" 156). In Shields's novel, Daisy's various other voices emerge to contest the "truth" told by the voice that seems merely to reinforce cultural stereotypes about women. We can see at least two ways in which Daisy challenges her own self-proclaimed voicelessness: first, in the ways in which the novel's narrative forms and modes of discourse might be defined as subversively semiotic; and second, in the narrative voice's self-consciousness about narrative's shaping role and the moments in the novel that emphasize Daisy's own narrative power (rather than the narratives that overpower her). Like Robinson's *Housekeeping*, Shields's *The Stone Diaries* melds what might be termed alternative, semiotic ways of speaking for women with what Lanser terms acts of "overt authoriality" (*Fictions* 17), yielding a novel that explores the difference of women's relationship to language without sacrificing women's access to symbolic uses of that language.[7]

The Semiotic Voice

Smith, even as she acknowledges the problematic nature of French theories of women's language, refers to Kristeva's semiotic, noting that "the subject position from which woman speaks may be, like the voice of the mother, outside time, plural, fluid, bisexual, de-centered, nonlogocentric" (*Poetics* 58). Indeed, the narrative of *The Stone Diaries* does seem to emanate from a point outside time, since Daisy appears as a witness at her own birth and perhaps concludes her narrative from a point in time after her death. Certainly the fluidity of the narrative voice and the plurality of modes in which Daisy speaks might be accounted for by theories of women's language and the semiotic,[8] theories that, as we have seen, are often linked to narratives of the fantastic.

In addition, and in keeping with theories of the semiotic and theories of women's twentieth-century narrative, Daisy seeks a connection with her deceased mother. Overtly, Daisy tries to reconnect with her biological father and her father-in-law—traditional, Oedipal father quests that would seem to undermine her feminist sensibility. Nonetheless, Daisy's niece Victoria, who does not herself care about fathers, believes that Daisy is truly interested in finding her mother, and that her purported interest in her fathers "is only a kind of ruse or sly equation" (269). Shields herself undermines the father quests, for they prove fruitless. The fact that the novel is titled *The Stone Diaries* reminds us of Daisy's connection with her mother, whose pre-married name is Stone. When, for example, Daisy speaks of the moment of her death, she says, in keeping with theories about the connection between mother and child that characterizes the imaginary order, "Stone is how she finally sees herself [...]; she loves [the image], in fact, and feels herself merge with, and become, finally, the still body of her dead mother" (358–359). The family tree on Mercy's side extends back no farther than Mercy herself, whose father is indicated only with a question mark on the genealogical chart that begins the novel, so that "Stone" cannot be traced to any particular father and is associated, as a name and sense of identity, only with Mercy. The "stone" of the title of course also refers to the numerous references to literal stone that fill the novel, and especially to Cuyler's career as a stone cutter. Yet in Daisy's mind, the image of stone connects her finally to her mother.[8] Rather than follow the sequential oedipal plot, Daisy instead returns to a maternal attachment. As DuPlessis points out, some "female quest plots loop backward to mother-child attachments" as women writers "undertake a reassessment of the process of gendering by inventing narrative strategies [...] that neutralize, transcend, or minimalize any oversimplified oedipal drama" (37). The novel's ironic treatment of the father-quest thus illustrates another strategy identified by Smith as characteristic of the twentieth-century female autobiographer, tracing one's origins to the mother (*Poetics* 57).

Mimicry is another strategy by which Daisy undermines the conventional "she" or "femininity text," a strategy identified by Smith as one that feminist autobiographers adopt in exposing cultural "truths" ("Construing Truths" 158). According to Irigaray, on whom Smith draws, women can indirectly challenge masculinist constructions of femininity through mimicry; Irigaray views direct challenges as "demanding [that women] speak as a (masculine) 'subject'" (76). But mimicry avoids this perceived problem of not acknowledging sexual difference in language: "One must assume the feminine role deliberately.

Which means already to convert a form of subordination into an affirmation, and thus to begin to thwart it" (76). Even some portions of the narrative that initially seem to emanate from Daisy's conventional self might be viewed instead as moments when Daisy deliberately adopts a feminine role for the purpose of undermining that construction. For example, Shields at one point writes in a heavy-handed way about Daisy's "golden childhood" and her relationships with her adoptive family, and then her good fortune in being reunited with Cuyler, "a remarkable (everyone said so) self-made man [...]" (148). The passage concludes with the observation that Daisy "does insist on showing herself in a sunny light, hardly ever giving us a glimpse of those dark premonitions we all experience. And, oh dear, dear, she is cursed with the lonely woman's romantic imagination and thus can support only happy endings" (149). Moments in the passage suggest that Daisy's happy recollections, merely fictions, belong again to the category of the socially constructed narrative. But her very typical childhood experience and the comments about her father that derive from public opinion ("everyone said so") suggest her awareness of and resistance to the narrative imposed upon her by others. Moreover, the claims made in this passage are often heavily ironic: readers know from the narrative that has preceded and from what follows that much of what is said in this passage about Daisy's construction of herself and her past is simply not true; the material of the novel is in fact strikingly less "sunny" than we are led to believe here. In the claim about the romantic imagination and the happy ending, Daisy adopts the typical feminine role, but she does so in language that qualifies itself exactly in the manner Irigaray suggests. Indeed, readers can find one unromantic counterexample to this claim later in the novel when the first-person Daisy reflects upon her second husband's death and admits that she has spent "very little" time reminiscing about their twenty years together (230). *The Stone Diaries*' narrative voice calls into question the "reality" of Daisy's conventional narrative influenced by patriarchal society and creates for Daisy an alternate subjectivity, a voice that, through the strategy of mimicry, actually makes visible the otherwise invisible story of the experiential rather than idealist Daisy.

In this example and others, we see evidence that, in Irigaray's terms, Daisy "remains elsewhere" in the narrative, other than where she initially appears to be, caught inside her story or trapped in Frye's "femininity text." Several features of Daisy's discourse raise the possibility that there is more to Daisy than meets the eye; subversive moments in her narrative suggest that she has evolved a way of asserting herself as a speaking subject while seeming not to. Another good example of semiotic discourse manifests itself in the chapter "Work," where Daisy takes over her deceased husband's gardening column. Her "narrative" is indirect: the chapter consists solely of letters authored by others to Daisy, and not a single word of Daisy's own. Yet others regale her with praise for her linguistic ability: she is frequently commended for clever turns of phrase, and one admirer writes, for example, "You've got a real gift for making a story out of things" (222). When the job is taken away from her after eleven years, the letters written to Daisy all express concern about her silence: she has in effect lost her voice again—to a man who wanted her job and who was allowed to take it because of a policy on the newspaper granting writers choice of columns according to seniority. While many critics have viewed this chapter as evidence of Daisy's absence and lack of narrative prowess because she never speaks directly herself, readers do in fact get a very strong sense of Daisy at work. From the letters written to her, the reader actively reconstructs the letters and columns that Daisy must have written. And when she feels wronged when her job is taken away, we can hear in the editor's replies to her letters Daisy's hurt, her sense of loss and injustice. Even though we don't see her writing itself, the narrative compels us to imagine it and thus renders it present. One might argue that Daisy has evoked herself in the very act of not writing directly about herself, creating an absence so strong that it is felt as a presence and rendered so in unusual modes of discourse. As Daisy herself realizes early in her life, "the absent are always present" (90).[10]

Other characters observe of Daisy, "there's some wily subversion going on" (251) whereby Daisy manages to achieve this presence. The ending of the novel provides more concrete instances of this phenomenon. Gaps in Daisy's life story are filled in after her death, when readers see her children going through her possessions and discovering things about her that they never knew while their mother was alive, including her scholarship—the college notes she has bequeathed to her son Warren—and her trousseau from her first brief marriage, each item embroidered with a signature daisy (350). From beyond the grave, Daisy as narrator is witness to others' discoveries about her, and from this position as an observer, she is able to "sneak" into the narrative information that has seemingly been omitted. Thus when Warren, speaking earlier about Daisy's scholarship, concludes that someone "yanked out her tongue" (252), the narration reveals his misreading of his mother and to some extent replaces this lost language by working into the story some of the facts about Daisy's writing and her intellectual self.

The reader's first impression in reading *The Stone Diaries* might well be an impression shared by the children: Daisy is a woman with so little sense of herself that she purports to write her own diary while telling us almost exclusively about other people. But after the reader finishes the novel, he or she might suspect that Daisy, more wily than it initially appears, has in a subtle way written about herself under the guise of writing about other people. One way of accounting for the seemingly disproportionate amount of Daisy's autobiography devoted to stories other than—but connected to—Daisy's own is through Susan Stanford Friedman's claim about the construction of the female autobiographical self. Drawing on Nancy Chodorow's psychoanalytic theories of female development, and paraphrasing Mary Mason's early work on women's autobiography, Friedman observes that "women's sense of self exists within a context of a deep awareness of others" (43).[11] Or, in considering the degree to which Daisy seemingly disregards her own story, the reader might also recall a comment made by one of Daisy's children: "evasion can be a form of aggression" (346). This insight proves true, for Daisy's semiotic narrative strategies have the effect of making the reader search for her—not Daisy the socially constructed wife and mother, but some other Daisy. Daisy's daughter Joan in fact recognizes that there are two Daisys, a public and a private one (172); for the reader, Daisy's secret existence is subtly evoked through the ways in which the narrative makes her absence a felt presence.

However, these alternative (non)-narrative strategies, many of which seem to rely upon a technique that has been termed "writing-without-having-written" (Laennec 35), are paradoxically encompassed within a fictional autobiographical text that at times possesses an extraordinary degree of self-consciousness about storytelling and discourse.[12] At one point, for example, reflecting on the limitations of the narrative, the narrator tells us that the account is "written on air," in "invisible ink" (149). Yet this statement, while it accurately accounts for some aspects of Daisy's covert narrative, is also highly ironic, for at other moments Daisy speaks in a commanding, authorial voice. We are constantly reminded of her own reliance on narrative self-consciousness to render herself, her story, visible. For example, Daisy's connection with her deceased mother's body represents not merely a moment of physical connection with the mother, for as Daisy has written earlier, on an another occasion when she feels linked to her mother, she is struck by "the notion that Mrs. Flett has given birth to her mother, and not the other way around" (191). This passage thus reminds us of the creative linguistic power that Daisy has developed as an authorial presence in the narrative of her life. That is, rather than thinking of herself as a physical/biological creation of her mother, Daisy thinks of herself as the author of her mother's life, a stance evident already in the first chapter of the novel when Daisy, recounting her mother's life story, speaks from the unusual position of an omniscient, first-person narrator.

While Irigaray might view direct challenges to patriarchal constructions as putting woman in the position of speaking like a man, other feminist theorists adopt a different perspective on voice and women's writing. Lanser, for example, drawing precisely on Irigaray's discourse on mimicry, argues that "'female voice' is not an 'essence' but a variable subject position whose 'I' is grammatically feminine. The particular characteristics of any 'female voice,' then, are a function of the context in which that voice operates" (*Fictions* 12). For Lanser, an authorial female voice can "be a powerful tool for dislodging an existing authority" (*Fictions* 278), as can a female narrator's personal voice; both strategies are employed in *The Stone Diaries* along with the semiotic strategies already discussed.

The Narrating Female "I" and the "Femininity Text"

In sorting out the various types of voices Daisy employs when she seems to be very self-consciously and overtly (rather than covertly) challenging woman's place in patriarchal culture, it is useful to turn again to theories of woman's narrative voice advanced by Frye and Lanser. Earlier, in accounting for ways in which Daisy's narrative seems simply to acquiesce to cultural constructions of femininity, I drew upon Frye's observations about the representation of woman as "she" in narrative and Lanser's comments about the third-person, representational voice, with its limited claims to authority. Yet each theorist also explores ways in which women's voices gain narrative authority. In order to see how *The Stone Diaries* accomplishes this end, we need to return to an analysis of the novel's shifts between first- and third-person narration, exploring their relationship to Daisy's position as a self-conscious author of her own story and her resistance to the stories written about her.

Frye, for example, writes about how a woman character's "I" functions subversively to undermine the socially constructed "she": "The 'she' can easily lull us into complacent and conventional expectations; the 'I' keeps us conscious of possibility and change" (65). One way to account for some of Daisy's modulations between first- and third-person narration, then, would be to consider the "she" or third-person Daisy as the culturally constructed Daisy, while thinking of the "I" as Daisy's personal voice, the voice of a self that rejects the construct. In *The Stone Diaries,* we see numerous examples of Daisy's rapid modulation between first and third person especially toward the end of the novel. In her old age Daisy at times refuses to identify herself with the woman whose existence has been defined by patriarchal culture. "I'm not myself" (324), she says. At one point she is unsure if "Grandma Flett" has actually voiced these words: "She's not sure. She's lost track of what's real and what isn't, and so, at this age, have I" (329). Though "I" and "Grandma Flett" are literally the same person, Daisy posits them as two, her narrating self distancing and refusing to claim her narrated self. The versions of herself that she would reject have been peeled away by the novel's end when Daisy's act of splitting herself in two deconstructs conventional notions of womanhood, or what Frye calls the "femininity text." Similarly, on the last page of *The Stone Diaries*, Shields gives us two closing statements. We encounter Warren's benediction at Daisy's funeral: "Daisy Goodwill Flett, wife, mother, citizen of our century: May she rest in peace." Yet "Daisy Goodwill's final (unspoken) words" are "I am not at peace" (361).[13] Here again is a kind of subversive fracturing of Daisy into two: the conventional Mrs. Flett, distanced by the use of the third person, may be put to rest; but Daisy Goodwill, whose ghostly presence haunts the story of her life, will not sleep quietly in her grave. Warren and others who attend the funeral are like the naive narrator of *Wuther-*

ing Heights, Lockwood, who wonders to himself "how anyone could ever imagine unquiet slumbers for the sleepers in that quiet earth" (320). But unlike Brontë's Catherine who declares Heathcliff to be more herself than she is and is buried so that their bodies will commingle in death, Daisy is secretly not much bothered by either of her husbands' deaths, and she has composed her own tombstone inscription to include the fact that she chooses to be buried alone (347).

Frye, who valorizes the first-person voice in women's fiction, argues that while the narrating "I" "resist[s] and redefine[s] the premises of representation," it also allows a woman character to represent herself in ways that imply authorship and authority (55), rather than eschewing representation itself, as do many experimental narratives: the narrating female "I" has "the capacity to engage the normative and simultaneously to elude and critique it, to evoke realities at the same time that it interrogates our ways of defining them" (55). Like other women narrators whom Frye describes, Daisy might be said to "find in her life experiences those capacities that the culture text has denied and use them to develop an alternative narrative explanation," in effect "re-emplot-[ting]" her life story to make it her own rather than the culture's (Frye 59). Indeed, Daisy notes at one point:

> men, it seemed to me in those days, were uniquely honored by the stories that erupted into their lives, whereas women were more likely to be smothered by theirs. Why? Why should this be? Why should men be allowed to strut under the privilege of their life adventures, [...] while women went all gray and silent beneath the weight of theirs? [....] Well, this particular irony haunts the existence of Daisy Goodwill Hoad [...] who's still living in the hurt of her first story, a mother dead of childbirth, and then a ghastly second chapter, a husband killed on his honeymoon. Their honeymoon, I suppose I should say. Wherever she goes, her story marches ahead of her. Announces her. Declares and cancels her true self [121].

In this passage where the narrative voice shifts four times between "I" and "she," the first-person narrative voice begins by pointing out the cultural discrepancy between the value attached to men's and women's stories. In this register, the first-person Daisy is aware of the way in which this discrepancy has affected her, slipping back into the third-person voice when she says "this particular irony haunts the existence of Daisy Goodwill Hoad." Significantly, Daisy at this point bears the name of her first husband. The narrator refers to "his" honeymoon, but then the first-person voice quickly corrects this language by pointing out that it is "their" honeymoon. Readers know from the narrative that it was in actuality more "his" honeymoon than "theirs," but here the first-person voice offers precisely the kind of critique Frye discusses in which the narrating female "I" calls into question the ways we define realities, or stories for women. The passage ends with another representation of Daisy in the third person: her story, or her culture's story for her, "declares and cancels her true self," but the very presence of the narrating "I" in the passage challenges the culturally constructed story and makes clear that Daisy is not simply encapsulated by it—her "true self" might be said to emerge in the "I" who explicitly critiques the way women's stories, including Daisy's, are represented in the culture.

THE THIRD-PERSON EXTRAREPRESENTATIONAL VOICE

Yet in the slippery narrative world of *The Stone Diaries*, the question of voice and narrative authority becomes more complex still, for many of Daisy's authoritative statements about women's relationship to narratives of femininity issue from a third-person rather than a first-person voice. As we saw in the discussion of *Housekeeping*'s narrative perspective, Lanser complicates some of Frye's claims about the authority of personal voice. Lanser explores the advantages for a female narrator of employing the omniscient, authorial voice, a voice that narrates from beyond the time-frame of the fiction. In discussing authorial narrators, Lanser further distinguishes between narrators who employ the third-person representational voice to report actions and dialogue within the fiction and narrators "who undertake 'extrarepresentational' acts: reflections, judgments, generalizations about the world 'beyond' the fiction, direct addresses to the narratee, comments on the narrative process, allusions to other writers and texts" (16–17.) Lanser concludes that narrators who engage in such extrarepresentational acts possess the quality of "overt authoriality" insofar as they "expand the sphere of fictional authority to 'nonfictional' referents and allow the writer to engage, from 'within' the fiction, in a culture's literary, social, and intellectual debates" (17). In Shields's novel, the "debate" pertains precisely to the issue of gender and men's and women's roles in the society. When Daisy engages in extrarepresentational narrative acts, she challenges head-on masculinist narratives and thereby gains a kind of narrative authority different than that of both the semiotic voice and the first-person voice. As Lanser points out, "fiction in the personal voice is formally indistinguishable from autobiography" so that "the use of personal voice also risks reinforcing the convenient ideology of women's writing as 'self-expression,' the product of 'intuition' rather than of art"; hence women novelists might employ the third-person voice to avoid these limitations, to avoid having their work "be taken for autobiography" (19–20). Such a voice "claims broad powers of knowledge and judgment, while a personal narrator claims only the validity of one person's right to interpret her experience" (Lanser 19). Viewed in this light, it is as if Daisy, author of her autobiography, is a self-conscious and savvy enough narrator to adopt a third-person voice precisely to overcome the limitations of the personal mode, at the same time that she exploits the potential of first-person narration to grant her own voice the narrative authority associated with that mode.

In *The Stone Diaries*, then, Daisy's *narrating* self is evidenced not only in the autodiegetic, personal voice, but also in a version of the third-person voice. That is, Daisy's third-person voice often assumes a different register than the representational voice discussed above (the voice in which Daisy as narrator speaks in ways that coincide with what Frye calls the "femininity text"), slipping into what Lanser terms the "extrarepresentational" acts of an authorial narrator. The voice thus becomes a strange hybrid of homodiegetic and heterodiegetic narration, a character/narrator who adopts a perspective that distances her from the character construct and allows her to engage in critical commentary on the substance of her own life rather than simply to report it. (This is the voice that Vauthier identifies as the "critic" [184] but that I argue is another manifestation of Daisy's own voice.) In other words, while Daisy frequently represents herself in third person as she would be represented in the biography of a conventional woman, at times she steps outside that representation, calling attention in another third-person voice to its status as a fiction and undermining it as a completely truthful portrait of her existence: "Daisy Goodwill's perspective is off" (148). Thus Daisy's critical, authorial third-person voice, as well as her personal voice, frequently challenges the conventional third-person voice that Daisy often adopts.

A good example of this self-consciously narrative, authorial voice is found toward the end of the "Motherhood" chapter, when the third-person Daisy notes, "she carries the cool and curious power of occasionally being able to see the world vividly. [...] The narrative maze opens and permits her to pass through. She may be crowded out of her own life—she knows this for a fact and has always known it—but she possesses, as a compensatory gift, the startling ability to draft alternate versions" (190). While many readers of the novel might say that this musing simply calls into question the truthfulness of Daisy's life story, such a passage might be interpreted instead as evidence of Daisy's awareness of cultural constructions of femininity, evidence of how she is able to "live outside" the story constructed for her by constructing "alternate versions," including not just alternative ways of telling-while-not-telling her life story, but also alternate ways of self-consciously wresting narrative control of her story, of assuming overt authoriality. Indeed, according to Lisa Johnson's commentary on this passage, "author of her own life, Daisy [...] recognizes her ability to counter the official stories that would erase her" (213).[14]

By having Daisy shift from personal to authorial voice, by granting her a voice that seems to come from outside the fiction, Shields confers on her an authority greater than that of Daisy the narrating character. At the same time, Daisy's "I" frequently blurs the boundaries between personal and authorial narration. Because of the violations of traditional narrative modes, often Daisy's first-person voice, as well as her third-person voice, might be seen as authorial rather than personal. That is, Daisy almost immediately assumes the "superhuman privileges" (Lanser) of the authorial voice even before the reader encounters the first reference to Daisy as a "she" rather than an "I." Information about other characters' private thoughts is focalized through Daisy's first-person perspective, so that she narrates events to which she couldn't realistically have access as a character, as would an omniscient narrator. By having Daisy engage in extrarepresentational acts in either mode, first- or third-person, Shields grants her the power to participate, in Lanser's terms, in the social and intellectual debates of her time, thereby placing her narrative strategies squarely within the symbolic realm as she calls attention to cultural constructions of femininity and explores through the complicated narrative strategies questions about women's identity in patriarchal culture.

Finally, it should be noted that another manifestation of Daisy's third-person voice is figural, as opposed to authorial, narration. Lanser, drawing on the work of Franz Stanzel, distinguishes between these two modes: "while authorial narrative permits what I am calling narrative self-reference, in the 'figural' mode, all narration is focalized through the perspective of characters, and thus no reference to the narrator or narrative situation is feasible" (16).[15] In *The Stone Diaries*, as has been noted, large sections of the narrative are focalized in third-person through the perspective of characters other than Daisy herself. On the one hand, as I argued earlier, the sections might be viewed as a subversive, semiotic strategy for invoking Daisy's voice while seeming not to. On the other hand, even these passages might be read as evidence of Daisy's authorial stance. In *The Stone Diaries*, which one reviewer calls "deliciously unclassifiable" (Stephens 3), Daisy's narration becomes an odd amalgamation of the personal, authorial, and figural modes. In some ways the novel collapses this distinction between the third-person modes, authorial and figural narration, since within the context of *The Stone Diaries*' whole narration, the figural passages call attention to and raise questions about the narrative voice, in a backhanded way thus highlighting the narrative situation itself even if the figural mode per se does not allow for narrative self-consciousness. By extension, the passages highlight in a backhanded way the variety of Daisy's narrative voices and her feminist narrative authority.

Conclusion

Critics who have attributed the novel's narration to several narrators have generally concluded that the complexities of the narrative voice challenge the notion of the unified self and have interpreted the novel within the framework of one version of postmodernism, stressing its decentering of the subject and its calling into question the reliability of the narrative.[16] There is no doubt that *The Stone Diaries* complicates notions of the self. But theories of women's autobiography that urge a middle ground between the humanist and the postmodern subject, in conjunction with feminist theories of narrative, provide a way for readers to understand *The Stone Diaries* as a fictional autobiography narrated only by its central character, a means to explore the relationship between the novel's depiction of the female self and the multi-faceted narrative voice that weaves Daisy's story without concluding that, for example, disparate voices "in the mosaic narrative reinforce Daisy as a nexus lacking 'presence'" (Slethaug 68). Rather, as numerous theorists of women's autobiography caution, readers need to conceive the female self in a way that neither simply essentializes women nor "retreat[s] into a pure textuality that consigns woman—in a new mode to be sure—to an unrecoverable absence" (Brodzki and Schenck 14).[17]

This position on female subjectivity coincides with the position of feminist narrative theorists who argue that contemporary women's fiction occupies a middle ground between postmodern experimentation and realism. As we saw in the Introduction, this approach to feminist narrative practice itself coincides with D'Haen's view of ex-centric postmodernism and magic realism: magic realist authors employ the techniques of mainstream postmodernist authors in a subversive way, to provide a corrective to the way in which reality is perceived not only in the traditional realist text, but also in "central" postmodern challenges to realism that construct all reality as a mere fiction ("Magic Realism and Postmodernism" 195). Though *The Stone Diaries* little resembles the typical magic realist text, it nonetheless shares in this project and does contain a suggestion of the fantastic whose function is precisely to call into question the nature of the real vis-à-vis social constructions of femininity without, in Brodski and Schenck's terms, merely replicating the effects of dominant discourse by "consign[ing] woman [...] to an unrecoverable absence" (14).[18] As in the case of *Housekeeping*, the suggestion that the narrative is generated from some fantastical space outside the world of the fiction has the effect of restoring presence and visibility to feminine forces that the culture positions as absent and invisible.

In addition, Shields's novel occupies a middle ground insofar as it melds alternative, semiotic ways of speaking with self-consciously authorial acts. On the one hand, Daisy "remains elsewhere" (Irigaray) as a subversive, covert narrator on the margins of her story who has "wily" or "sly," roundabout ways of writing herself into her story while seeming not to; on the other hand, her authorial voice is everywhere central to the generation of the novel, and she also "remains elsewhere"—outside the conventional narrative—in the sense that her narrative voice quite self-consciously calls attention to the limits of the mimesis in which she often times seems to be simply caught, and calls attention to its own presence through its manipulations of conventional narrative perspectives. *The Stone Diaries*' violations of narrative conventions and the multi-faceted voice of its central character can be accounted for by a range of feminist perspectives that illuminate ways in which women writers resist dominant modes of representation. The hesitation invoked in the reader about the source of the novel's narration—including not only the fantastical suggestion that Daisy narrates the moment of her own death and continues her story from beyond the grave but also the peculiarities of the narrative voice throughout the whole of the novel—calls into question the very premises about these dominant modes, their "realism" or the "reality" status of patriarchal representation of femininity. Looking beyond the Daisy who seems wholly defined by others, the absent center of her own life story, readers can see through to the Daisy who is quite conscious of the way in which her society positions her and whose various narrative strategies fracture that representation.

Part III
The Historical Novel and the Fantastic

5

'The Eyes in the Trees': *Transculturation and Magic Realism in Barbara Kingsolver's* The Poisonwood Bible

> To live is to be marked. To live is to change, to acquire the words of a story.
> —Barbara Kingsolver, *The Poisonwood Bible [385]*

> The implicit cultural exchange this hybrid form [magic realism] represents contributes to the process of transculturation.
> —Wendy Faris, *Ordinary Enchantments: Magical Realism and the Remystification of Narrative [155]*

INTRODUCTION

Barbara Kingsolver's *The Poisonwood Bible*, which explores the Price family's missionary work in the Congo/Zaire prior to and after independence, is a novel about transculturation, or the ways in which a colonized nation shapes the mindset of the colonizer and the ways in which that colonizer represents colonialism. Kingsolver's treatment of her characters' relationship to language, to representation, is a key means by which she demonstrates the transculturation process, showing how the women characters in particular, through a multifaceted understanding of language, influence and are influenced by the Africans they encounter. Central to this process, and related to the novel's treatment of language itself, is the novel's fantastic element: the final section is narrated from beyond the grave by the youngest Price daughter, Ruth May. Killed by a poisonous snake in the middle of the narrative, Ruth May apparently transforms into a snake or spirit herself by the novel's end. Though *The Poisonwood Bible* has been considered as a postcolonial novel (Demory), a disability novel

(S. Fox), an historical novel (Kunz; York), and a neo-domestic novel (Jacobson), it has not yet been explored as a novel of the fantastic. Examining Kingsolver's work through this particular lens further illuminates its postcolonial project and allows critics to account for the novel's mysterious narration in the final chapter, an element often left unaddressed in the criticism.

This fantastical element of the novel resembles to some extent the narration from beyond the grave by Shields's Daisy Goodwill and Robinson's Ruth Stone, except that in the case of Ruth May, there is no doubt whatsoever that the character has indeed died. The presentation of this fantastic moment involves no character hesitation: indeed, although no characters interact directly with the deceased Ruth May, many of them implicitly acknowledge her continued existence and implicitly link her spiritual presence to African beliefs about the relationship between the living and the dead. Because it is presented matter-of-factly, and because the novel is so thoroughly enmeshed in colonial and postcolonial politics, the fantastic moment in *The Poisonwood Bible* can be illuminated through theories of magic realism. The magic realist novel's events, according to Wendy Faris, are "partially detached from the dominant realistic form of narrative authority, yet they are still grounded in social and historical reality" (*Ordinary Enchantments* 87). In *The Poisonwood Bible*, Ruth May's embodiment of African spiritual beliefs in her reincarnation as a snake or spirit is couched within an otherwise realistic, historical novel and is accepted as part of the truth of the novel's world. Through its exploration of transculturation in most of the Price women, and especially through its use of magic realism as an agent of transculturation, *The Poisonwood Bible* challenges dominant modes of discourse and the colonial construction of the colonized in mid-twentieth-century Congo.[1]

Though Kingsolver is not a postcolonial writer per se, her novel might be considered a fictional travel piece about colonialism and the process of decolonization, and thus it invites analysis along these lines. In 1959, Baptist preacher Nathan Price moves his wife, Orleanna, and their four daughters, Leah, Adah, Rachel, and Ruth May, from Bethlehem, Georgia to the Belgian Congo to undertake missionary work. *The Poisonwood Bible* details the family's arrival in Africa and reception by the Africans, their efforts to establish themselves in the community, and the community's resistance to Nathan's efforts to bring American and Christian ways to the region. The women, less intent on changing the African people to their ways, become much better integrated into the community than Nathan does, and they make significant and lasting connections with various of the Congolese characters in the novel. Chaos, however, erupts in several episodes, including the family's fleeing from carnivorous driver ants that invade the village, the Congo's achieving independence from Belgium in mid-1960, Rachel's becoming involved with an American diamond smuggler who has ties with the CIA plot to assassinate the country's new leadership, and Leah's breaking traditional African gender roles by participating in a village hunt. Tragedy is visited on the family when, probably in response to Leah's actions, a green mamba snake is left in the chicken house and bites Ruth May, killing her. Shortly after Ruth May's death in 1961, Orleanna takes Adah back to the United States. Rachel and Leah both remain in Africa, as does Nathan, who simply disappears into the bush and is not heard from again, though the family does eventually learn of his death. The surviving daughters narrate their sections of the remainder of the novel from the early 1960s to the mid–1980s, while Orleanna muses retrospectively on the family's African experience from Sanderling Island, Georgia, in an unidentified year, commenting extensively on the lasting effects of that experience.

The telling of the family's story through the voices of Orleanna, Adah, Leah, Rachel, and Ruth May works in conjunction with the novel's fantastic element to destabilize the assumptions of traditional realist representation that underlie colonial and patriarchal narratives of domination. In previous chapters, the work of feminist narrative theorists on personal and authorial narration provided a means to examine the complex interplay of the fantastic, feminism, and narrative voice. Kingsolver's novel is unusual in that it approaches a third possibility for storytelling, the communal narrative voice that Lanser identifies in several twentieth-century novels written by women, a voice that "necessarily threaten[s] novelistic conventions of representational coherence and structural unity" (263). The oppositional potential of such a narrative strategy coincides with Faris's observation that "magical realism creates a new decolonized space for narrative, one not already occupied by the assumptions and techniques of European realism." In the magic realist text, with its unusual narrative stance of presenting what Faris terms "irreducible elements" in a mundane fashion as though such elements were ordinary, the effect is to "destabilize habitual structures of order and authority" (*Ordinary Enchantments* 135). Kingsolver's novel combines an unusual narrative technique throughout the novel — sequential communal narration — with the mode of magic realism to destabilize the centralized authority accorded to the figure of Nathan Price (the only member of the Price family who does not narrate a portion of the tale). In the novel's final chapter, Ruth May's own narration is even more unusual in its perspective than the communal perspective of the rest of the novel. Together with her transformed state, her narration further challenges the assumptions of realism and Western modes of thought generally, explicitly revising through her discourse and through her unconventional narrative perspective the monologic perspective of the white male colonizer.

TRANSCULTURATION AND REPRESENTATION

Often when one considers the relationship between a colonized nation and its colonizers, one considers cultural influence to be a one-way street, yet this formula oversimplifies complex interactions. Mary Louise Pratt, in her work on travel narratives, writes that

> while the imperial metropolis tends to understand itself as determining the periphery (in the emanating glow of the civilizing mission or the cash flow of development, for example), it habitually blinds itself to the ways in which the periphery determines the metropolis—beginning, perhaps, with the latter's obsessive need to present and re-present its peripheries and its others continually to itself. Travel writing [...] is heavily organized in the service of that imperative [6].

Pratt advocates instead what she calls a "'contact' perspective," which "emphasizes how subjects are constituted in and by their relations to each other. It treats the relations among colonizers and colonized, or travelers and "travelees," not in terms of separateness or apartheid, but in terms of copresence, interaction, interlocking understandings and practices, often within radically asymmetrical relations of power" (7). Similarly, postcolonial critic Francoise Lionnet argues for a means of understanding colonial relations in terms other than what she sees as the reductive approaches of "assimilation" and "acculturation" for "describing patterns of influence that are never unidirectional" (10–11).[2] Paraphrasing the Cuban poet Nancy Morejon, Lionnet writes that transculturation "describe[s] a process of cultural intercourse and exchange, a circulation of practices which creates a constant interweaving of symbolic forms and empirical activities among the different interacting cultures," an exchange which is "mutual and reciprocal" (11). These theories speak to the ways in which being a presence in Africa transforms many of the American women characters in *The Poisonwood Bible*. This fictional travel narrative is organized precisely to explore the influence of the periphery on the metropolis, at least for the Price family women. The family patriarch, Nathan Price, in his attempts to represent African others to himself, uses Western modes of discourse unselfconsciously, assuming a "unidirectional" (Lionnet) relationship between the center that he represents and the margin. Other characters, however, adopt the "contact" perspective that Pratt describes; they hold a more self-conscious view of how others are represented in language and of how African cultural and linguistic practices shape their world views, their understanding of self and other.

Moreover, if we consider Kingsolver's novel as a magic realist one, we can explore the ways in which the magic realist element challenges dominant modes of representation, especially the ways in which the colonizer, in this case Nathan Price, represents the colonized African people. Indeed, Faris writes extensively about how magic realism and postcolonialism coincide, suggesting that magic realism not only "reflect[s] the cultural moment of postcolonialism" but also that it "achieve[s] substantial work within it" insofar as it "radically modifies and replenishes the dominant mode of realism in the West, challenging its basis of representation from within. That destabilization of a dominant form means that it has served as a particularly effective decolonizing agent" (*Ordinary Enchantments* 1). In *The Poisonwood Bible,* as in other magic realist novels, the fantastic element functions in two related ways: it challenges the authority of authoritarian versions of that history, the history as told from the conqueror's perspective; and because the fantastic is presented in the novel not as strange or surprising to the characters or the narrator, it locates the reader's surprise or disbelief in the biased representation of historical events themselves, so that readers see the real as being in some sense fantastical (cf. Faris 14; Hegerfeldt 59). The *Poisonwood Bible*'s magic realist element is part of its treatment of transculturation as Kingsolver challenges dominant representations of the Congo and its people through the ways in which the Price women are transformed by their experience in Africa.

But before turning to a discussion of Ruth May, in whose literal transformation readers most clearly see magic realism working as an agent of transculturation, we must first examine how the important (if non-magical and less dramatic) transformations of Ruth May's mother and sisters are illuminated by these theories. Transculturation breaks down in the novel along gender lines since the women undergo the process to a far greater degree than does Nathan, who represents not only imperialism in the African setting but also patriarchy within the family. Orleanna comes to recognize that "Africa shifts under [her] hands" (10), while Nathan becomes increasingly convinced of his ability to remake Africa in his own image. The novel thus illustrates the argument made by Sidonie Smith about the differences between men's and women's travel writing. Smith, drawing on Pratt's *Imperial Eyes*, surveys numerous kinds of male travelers in the first chapter of *Moving Lives* (1–11); Nathan Price most resembles the missionary traveler, dedicated to "'uplifting' the dirty work of colonization (and perpetuating it) through the ideology of the 'civilizing' mission. Such narratives reflected the cultural work of recreating the country, the social organization, and the peoples of 'uncivilized' lands in the image of Europe and Euro-America" (*Moving Lives* 6). Interestingly, in Kingsolver's novel, the male traveler is given no narrative voice, one of the ways in which Kingsolver undermines the authority of the traditionally masculine travel narrative.

Unlike a male traveler, however, who imposes himself upon foreign lands to remake them in his image, Smith notes that a woman traveler, "in becoming another kind of subject, in grounding herself in an other's identity, [...] imagines herself un-becoming Western. Shedding conventional identities and behaviors, [...] she becomes other to her ordinary, unheroic, 'feminized' self" (*Moving Lives* 32), a process that accurately describes, for example, Orleanna's growing disillusionment with her very conventional marriage to Nathan Price and her willingness to act for herself and for her family in ways that defy his wishes. Throughout the novel, Kingsolver makes clear the link between the colonized Congo and women who are oppressed by patriarchal culture, and the resulting greater ability of women than men to recognize and embrace the process of transculturation. For example, Orleanna refers to the "poor Congo, barefoot bride of men who took her jewels and promised the kingdom" (201), and Adah calls the Congo "a woman in shadows, dark-hearted, moving to a drum beat" (495), comments in keeping with critic Patrick Hogan's observation that "indigenous cultures were seen as feminine and effeminate and the metropolitan culture as masculine" (17–18). Nathan's domineering, patriarchal style in his household mirrors his domineering attitude in his missionary work, his single-minded efforts to impose his point of view on others and determination to bend his will to no one's. In contrast to his wife and daughters, Nathan remains unchanged by his experiences, and in his attempts to convert the Congolese to Christianity, he certainly refuses to recognize any reciprocal effects of the African people on his character or belief system. Leah describes him, for example, as a father "whose strong hands always seized whatever came along and molded it to his will" (368), while Orleanna observes that "Nathan felt it had been a mistake to bend his will, in any way, to Africa" (97). Themselves in effect colonized by Nathan—a dynamic made explicit in Orleanna's comment that her family was "swallowed by Nathan's mission, body and soul. Occupied as if by a foreign power" (198) and by her reference to herself as "the conqueror's wife [,…] a conquest herself" (9)—Orelanna and her daughters find themselves naturally allied with those they meet in the Congo.[3]

Pratt, in her work on transculturation, is particularly interested in modes of representation, in how "signifying practices" of travel writing produce meaning in colonized cultures, and in turn how they are produced by those cultures. Just as the magic realist treatment of Ruth May's death (discussed in more detail below) challenges Western ideas about reality and destabilizes the assumptions of the realist novel, Kingsolver's novel also challenges Western representations of Africa by exploring the characters' different relationships to language itself and the impact of those relationships on the process of transculturation.

Indeed, Nathan's resistance to the transculturation process stems in part from his relationship to language, his inability to see multiple meanings or to adapt to the African language in which signifiers carry many, often contradictory, signifieds. Orleanna observes that "the same word slanted up or down the scale can have many different meanings" (94). This comment is in keeping with the writings of Janheinz Jahn, on whose work Kingsolver drew in composing *The Poisonwood Bible*: Jahn points out that in the Yoruba language, for example, a language in which words have many meanings, one "who utters a word must first designate it by his utterance. It is he who gives it its immediate meaning, while giving a new interpretation to every word he speaks […]" (152). Given that the Prices experience a new approach to language itself, Leah compares the whole family to Adam learning language in the Garden of Eden (101). (The comparison is not entirely apt, as we will see, given differences in the conception of "the word" between Christianity and traditional African religions.) Nathan, however, dismisses the Congo as the Tower of Babel (168) and repeatedly refuses to acknowledge the ways in which language works there. For example, as Adah notes, her father mispronounces a key word in his weekly sermons when he proclaims *"Tata Jesus is Bängala!"* The term *"bangala,"* Adah points out, "means something precious and dear" (276). But in Nathan's pronunciation, the term refers instead to the poisonwood tree, a plant that causes a rash and whose smoke, if it is burned, can even cause death.

Nathan's own stubbornness repeatedly interferes with his ability to convey the Christian message that he wishes to convey. More insidiously, his dogmatic adherence to narrow interpretations of Biblical language renders him unable to understand or accept any religious perspective that does not exactly match his own. For example, in an argument with a fellow missionary about translation and interpretation of the Bible, when Brother Fowles acknowledges his perplexity at a verse, Nathan Price replies, "Sir, I offer you my condolences. Personally I've never been troubled by any such difficulties with interpreting God's word" (251). As Adah declares, "Our Father has a bone to pick with this world, and oh, he picks it like a sore. Picks it with the Word. His punishment is the Word, and his deficiencies are failures of words" (213), or the failure to understand the complexity of words,[4] a fact that reflects his attitude of dominion, his conviction that, contrary to theories of transculturation, it is the role of the colonizer to change the colonized in a non-reciprocal relationship. His use of language, then, including his implicit storytelling practices, reinforces Western practices of representation. From the information readers glean of Nathan through the novel's various narrators, we can deduce that the story he does not narrate would exemplify traditional realist conventions; his attitude toward language is characterized by what Faris terms "the univocal narrative authority that characterizes much realist fiction" (*Ordinary Enchantments* 142). Or as Koza points out, "Nathan's identification with the Word [...] emphasizes his phallocentric viewpoint" (286).

In contrast, African religion presents a very different concept of "the word," one that coincides with the fact that in African language, single words carry many different signifieds, depending on context and slight variations in pronunciation. Jahn explains that the African concept *Nommo*, roughly translated as "the word," differs from the Christian principle of the Word become flesh:

> Nommo does not stand above and beyond the earthly world. *Logos* becomes flesh only in Christ, but nommo becomes "flesh" everywhere. According to the apostle [John], *Logos* has made all things, once for all, to become as they are, and since then, all generated things remain as they are, and undergo no further transformation. Nommo, on the other hand, goes on unceasingly creating and procreating, creating even gods [132].

Through the concept of nommo, language itself becomes associated with metamorphosis: "nommo, the word, creates images upon images, and transforms them and the poet with them. For he himself never approaches things unchanging; since he too is in his nature a force among forces, he changes with them and from them" (Jahn 138). In short, "nommo, the word itself is [...] fluidity" (139). As Dona Richards likewise points out, "*Nommo* manifests itself in our ability to transform the English language, to give it new life." Africans use words "out of ordinary context and place them in new ones. *Nommo* defies the logic of European semantics" (282). Nathan's very fixed concept of language, completely at odds with African philosophy and religion, together with his dogmatic and narrow interpretations of Christian doctrine, renders him unable to conceive of or participate in transculturation. Most simply, his inflexibility manifests itself in his insistence on baptizing African children in the river in spite of the fact that the Africans are terrified of the rite because crocodiles pose a real threat, and in his obstinate attempts to use gardening methods that erode the African soil and to sow American plants that cannot be pollinated in the African setting, with the result that the family's entire garden dies, leaving the Prices with no source of food.

In contrast, the attitudes toward language held by several of the Price women coincide with African beliefs about nommo and enable the process of transculturation, which is itself implicitly embedded in African religion and philosophy. Of the Price women, Leah is perhaps the most straightforwardly involved in the transculturation process. She arrives in Africa very much enamored of her father and his missionary project, but she soon grows disillusioned with Nathan. Unlike her father, Leah recognizes the complexities of language, commenting that "everything you thought you knew means something different in Africa" and giving a detailed account of the word *nzolo*'s different meanings (505). Becoming deeply involved in African culture and politics, she in fact marries the African teacher/activist Anatole who has been associated with her family since her childhood, and she decides by the novel's end to live and raise their children in Africa. Leah refers to herself as "the un-missionary, [...] beginning each day on [her] knees, asking to be converted" (525). Koza notes that Kingsolver's representation of Leah and Anatole in effect reverses "the colonial view that the colonized have nothing to teach the colonizers" (287). Leah receives from Anatole a new name, Béene, symbolic of her personal transformation, in which he acts as "catalyst" (Goldblatt 46).[5] Kingsolver's treatment of the bi-racial Leah-Anatole relationship offers a corrective to earlier colonial love stories. In Pratt's account of such eighteenth-century narratives, Pratt writes that "As an ideology, romantic love, like capitalist commerce, understands itself as reciprocal" (97). Yet in bi-racial colonial tales of love,

> While the lovers challenge colonial hierarchies, in the end they acquiesce to them. Reciprocity is irrelevant.
> Such is the lesson to be learned from the colonial love stories, in whose dénouements the "cultural harmony through romance" always breaks down. Whether love turns out to be requited or not, whether the colonized lover is female or male, outcomes seem to be roughly the same: the lovers are separated,

the European is reabsorbed by Europe, and the non–European dies an early death [Pratt 97].[6]

Leah's story, in contrast, explicitly revises conventions typical of colonial versions of romance between the Euro-American and the African and as such participates in the transformative power of nommo and in the recasting of Western modes of representation.[7]

The novel's most interesting revisions to Western narratives and Western discourse generally, however, and its most intriguing depiction of the process of transculturation, reside in its treatment of spirituality and the fantastic, located mainly in the stories of Adah and Ruth May. In contrast to their father's single-minded approach to language and interpretation, Adah has a self-conscious and complex relationship to language, and though Ruth May is too young as a character in the novel (age seven when she dies) to possess this self-consciousness, nonetheless, she is doubled with Adah and, as a narrator from beyond the grave, she employs language that explicitly revises her father's language. Both characters challenge dominant ideas about the unidirectional influence of the colonizer on the colonized through their discursive practices, and both embody the concept of metamorphosis associated with nommo, Ruth May in a specifically fantastic context.

Adah's transformation is, like Ruth May's, both spiritual and physical, though non-magical. Nonetheless, it is in part through Adah that elements of the novel that will seem fantastical to the Western reader are introduced and explained. Born with a disorder in which one hemisphere of her brain failed to develop normally (hemiplegia), Adah is partially paralyzed on one side and does not speak but is very adept at processing language, reading widely and avidly, and amusing herself with various language games. Her ability to see words' multiple meanings and to read backward provides her with a far broader understanding of others than her father possesses and with the flexibility to adjust her world view. She comments at one point, for example, that she reads a book not only from beginning to end, but also in reverse, noting that this re-examination of a text enables her to discover new meanings that a "singular plowing through" (58)—the conventional reader's method—doesn't allow. Unlike her father, whose views are singular and monologic, and who consequently sees cultural change as unidirectional, Adah realizes that Africa "talk[s] back" (298). After some time in Africa, she observes that all of her family members other than Nathan have changed from the experience, proceeding to provide backward versions of their names to suggest that their experience has influenced their identities in fundamental ways (276). In addition, she frequently creates palindromes that complicate words' usual connotations and in effect defamiliarize terms in order to challenge Christian imperialism. For example, in re-writing for herself the words to "Amazing Grace," Adah composes the line "*A, he rose...ye eyesore, ha!*" which, as DeMarr points out, connects "resurrection [...] and ugliness," and constitutes "Adah's mute comment on her father's attempts to convert the villagers" (137).

Adah herself finds much greater acceptance in the Congo, none of the isolation she experienced in the United States as a result of her physical afflictions (72). She sees herself transformed through African spiritual beliefs and the Congolese concept of the self, which differs from the American concept. Thus when she returns to Atlanta where medical treatments correct her "crooked" walk, she laments the change and seems to prefer her African self, holding on to the idea that she "will always be Ada [sic] inside, a crooked little person trying to tell the truth" (496). Her notion of truth is still linked to Dickinson's poem "Tell All the Truth But Tell it Slant," and Adah's "slanted" truths differ markedly from the single-minded concept of truth that Nathan has tried to impose on the Congolese. Interestingly, she misspells her own name in this and other instances (Ada), turning it into a perfect palindrome, a reminder of her ability to look at things forward and backward, from multiple perspectives. Yet despite what she considers the drawbacks of her changed physical state, which results in her deciding to speak, her metamorphosis in America allows her to pursue a medical career studying AIDS and Ebola at Emory University; her experience in Africa has drawn her out of herself, has enabled her transformation, and has led her to dedicate herself to improving health conditions in Africa.

Though she ultimately becomes a scientist, it is Adah who describes African spirituality to the reader, while Ruth May literally embodies these beliefs. At one point Adah, reflecting upon all the things that she and her family do not know (in contrast to Nathan who claims to know all), notes that "Here in the Congo I am pleased to announce there is no special difference between living people, dead people, children not yet born and gods—these are all *muntu*" (209). Jahn writes that "*Muntu* [...] is usually translated as 'man.' But the concept of 'Muntu' embraces living and dead, ancestors and deified ancestors: gods" (18). In the novel, Adah frequently ruminates about the concepts of *muntu* and *nommo*, anticipating Ruth May's demise, her transformation, and her participation in the African philosophy of language. Like Adah, Ruth May becomes fascinated with African beliefs about *muntu*, but while Adah interprets and muses about these beliefs from an adult intellectual's standpoint, the youthful Ruth May accepts the beliefs without necessarily thinking about their implications and comes literally to embody them by the end of the novel when she is transformed through death to a snake/spirit, *muntu*, whose presence watches over her family and speaks to her mother, her sisters, and to the reader in the novel's closing chapter. Ruth May, it should be noted, does not develop as a character in the novel as do her sisters and mother; rather, her very literal transformation is symbolic of the transculturation process. In her final narration, she speaks in an adult voice, very different from the voice of the young Ruth May whose narration we have heard throughout the sections of the novel preceding her death. It is here at the moment of closure that she speaks in ways that challenge and revise Nathan's monologic approach to the interaction between colonizer and colonized, ways deeply imbued in the African culture and in the process of transculturation: the magic realist event in the novel challenges the colonial project and colonists' means of representation.

RUTH MAY'S METAMORPHOSIS: REVISING COLONIAL DISCOURSE

Nearly every chapter narrated by Ruth May prefigures her fantastical reappearance at the novel's end, the moment when she speaks following her demise. According to Faris,

> while it is true that all magical realism embodies a mode of discourse that suggests the integration of a world of the spirits into ordinary reality, this interchange is especially important in postcolonial societies, which suffer from the imposition of a dominant culture on a subordinated one in a the realm of ordinary reality, so that an enactment of contact with a different realm serves as an efficacious form of counterdiscourse. And it is a counterdiscourse that transforms not only the discourse of the colonized but that of the colonizer as well [*Ordinary Enchantments* 154–55].

Ruth May's transformation into an African spirit/snake is a form of "counter-discourse" to her father's univocal Christian discourse that is linked quite explicitly to the novel's commentary on language itself. That is, the passages that foreshadow the magic event of Ruth May's transformation further connect Ruth May to Adah, with the latter's complex understanding of words' multiplicity. The doubling of Ruth May and Adah underlines Ruth May's own complex relationship to language, in spite of the fact that Ruth May's relationship to language is much less well-developed than Adah's. Nonetheless, we learn from Leah that Ruth May, at age five, can easily communicate with the Congolese people while the rest of the family struggles with the language barrier (106). Perhaps because she is the youngest and least enmeshed in American cultural traditions, Ruth May forms bonds easily with the various African characters, particularly her friend Nelson, who teaches her a great deal about African world views.

Ruth May and Adah are doubled through various means, especially African beliefs about *muntu*.[8] Adah, forbidden by her father to witness African religious ceremonies, seeks out at night funerals for the deceased African children and feels their spiritual presence, which often takes the form of an owl (296). Connected to the African beliefs surrounding death, Adah also has presentiments of Ruth May's death; even before her sister's actual demise, she makes comments about Ruth May's muntu, existing in her sister's body during Ruth May's short life, but also existing before her birth and after her death (346). Likewise Ruth May, influenced by her interactions with Nelson, is fascinated with the owls/spirits, and with the concept of *muntu*. In fact, Ruth May speaks frequently of her death and of coming back as a snake in the trees that can observe everything around her (124; 273; 304). Indeed, when she is bitten by the snake and does die, Leah observes that all the family members cast their eyes to the trees rather than looking at Ruth May herself (363). And later Orleanna muses about Ruth May's judgment of her as a mother who took her daughter to Africa where she would die from a poisonous snake bite, referring to her daughter as "the eyes in the trees" and wondering if Ruth May belongs to her or to Africa, even as she notes the extreme difficulty of differentiating between the "two rivers," the Delaware that she observes in Georgia, and the Congo that played such an important role in her life in Africa (385).[9]

In its foreshadowing of Ruth May's death and final narration, the novel calls attention to Ruth May's voice. The idea of "the word" is frequently associated with Ruth May at the time of and following her death, and this association invokes the African ideas of muntu and nommo. When she is bitten by the green mamba snake and the family looks into the trees, Leah observes that "[j]ust for the moment it was as if she'd disappeared, and her voice was thrown into the trees" (363). Later, back in Georgia, Adah says, "we must wait to hear word from [Ruth May]" (414), and at one point Leah remarks that she feels Ruth May is still with her as long as she can hear "her voice in my ear" (438), comments that reveal the sisters' adoption of African beliefs about the interaction between the living and the dead, or muntu. The comments also highlight the importance of the word or nommo and gesture toward the Africanized discourse that characterizes Ruth May's final narration.

At one point in the novel, Ruth May compares herself to Jesus because she can see into her mother's thoughts (216). Later, after Ruth May's recovery from malaria, Adah speaks somewhat sardonically of her sister as having "risen" (277), and Leah speaks of her "transfigured shadow" (371). But in the end of the novel, Ruth May's "resurrection" has transformed from a Christian one to an African one, in which her muntu seems to have metamorphosed into a snake. At the same time, Ruth May's language explicitly revises her father's Christian discourse and participates in the transformative spirit of nommo. Nathan, obsessed with the fear that African children will die before being baptized, conducts a series of baptisms immediately following his youngest daughter's death; as he walks around the circle of African children, he "implor[es] the living progeny of Kilanga to walk forward into the light" (375). In Ruth May's final narration, after her voice has disappeared from the novel for well over two hundred pages, Ruth May echoes and revises her father's language. She offers her mother forgiveness and begs her mother to forgive herself, and perhaps implicitly, to forgive Nathan: "Slide the weight from your shoulders and move forward. You are afraid you might forget, but you never will. You will forgive and remember. [...] Move on. Walk forward into the light" (543).[10]

In this passage, the language takes on characteristics of African poetry. Both Jahn and Richards note that nommo, the word, constitutes a force that makes things happen: Richards terms it an "activating principle" (282), and Jahn explains that "the word alone alters the world" (133), has the power to affect change. As a result, "since the word produces, commands, and conjures, [African] poetry speaks in imperatives. Its basic form is the command. [...] The event is created in the vision. The vision is always an imperative addressed to time; the future is commanded how it is to be." Lines of African poetry do not constitute merely "a description of a future occurrence, but an invocation of it" (Jahn 136). Thus the power of nommo in Ruth May's final narration, replete with imperatives, both actualizes the forgiveness that she urges her mother to adopt and actualizes a broader world view than that held by Nathan. Its notion of truth, of light, is distinct from Nathan's attempts to impose a Western concept of truth on a non–Western nation. The same words, spoken in a new context, take on the characteristics of words in the African language that mean many things at once, the phenomenon commented on earlier in the narrative by Orleanna, Leah, and Adah. In her discourse, the transformed Ruth May exemplifies the earlier ruminations of her mother and sisters on the nature of language itself, its multiple, many-layered meanings. In this capacity, the healing and forgiveness that Kingsolver addresses at her novel's end extend beyond the rifts in the Price family itself to the larger cultural and historical circumstances in which those rifts have developed. Several magic realist novels that Faris identifies, including *The Palace of the Peacock, Beloved,* and *The White Hotel,* for example, "involve—in their different ways—the partial magic healing of socially damaged relationships through communication with beings from beyond the grave" that leads to "a settling of scores from the past" (*Ordinary Enchantments* 84). *The Poisonwood Bible* might well be added to this list.

NARRATIVE VOICE AND MULTIPLE POINTS OF VIEW

The previous sections have been written as though the novel's final chapter is narrated by the transformed Ruth May, and indeed, this is partly true. But the story of the narrative voice is more complex. The passage that echoes but revises her father's earlier exhortations for the Kilanga people to "walk forward into the light" (375) of Christian beliefs emanates from a voice identified only as "*muntu* Africa, *muntu* one child and a million all lost on the same day" (537). The section titled "The Eyes in the Trees" is the only section of the novel not identified in a subheading as emanating from the perspective of a particular character because Ruth May per se has ceased to exist though her *muntu* lives on. (It is also, as DeMarr notes, the only section of the narrative that does not bear a biblical title, another of the ways in which *The Poisonwood Bible* revises Nathan's imperial Christian mission [122; 141].[11]) The disembodied narrative voice decenters narrative authority, in a manner that Faris suggests is typical of magic realist narration; the voice itself "is elusive, virtually unlocatable, what we might term unanchored" (*Ordinary Enchantments* 135).

In the case of *The Poisonwood Bible,* Kinsolver's final narrative voice exaggerates the unlocatable, unanchored focalization typical of the magic realist text; it also exaggerates what Hegerfeldt identifies as the ex-centric focalization typically used in magic realism insofar as the narrative voice is extremely de-centralized and non–Western in spite of the fact that Ruth May is an American: it belongs simultaneously to a child, to a dead person, to a spirit who is and is not the dead child, to a community of spirits, and to the continent of Africa itself. Once again, the magic realist qualities of the voice can be illuminated not only through the work of theorists of magic realism, but also through a feminist narrative theory of narrative voice. The chapter begins in a first-person singular narrative mode, addressing Orleanna in the second person as the voice's mother. But the narration shifts quickly to a first-person plural mode; Ruth May speaks as a "we," part of a community of the dead, who, according to African beliefs, exist in communication and in a continuous relationship with the living. This particular manifestation of the communal voice in the novel provides a brief example of what Lanser identifies as simultaneous communal voice, couched within a narrative that is otherwise an example—or close to it—of sequential communal voice.

Lanser explains that in sequential communal narration, "each voice speaks in turn so that the 'we' is produced from a series of collaborating 'I's.'" (256). She distinguishes this communal "we" from narrative generated in a series of first-person voices that provide competing versions of events or that offer very different perspectives on the same story (262), narratives in which perspectivism and unreliability of point of view are highlighted. Instead, communal narratives "offer multiple stories, each one contributing to a fuller portrait of a specific community" (262–3), even as the multiple stories emphasize the individuality of the narrating "I." In *The Poisonwood Bible*, the narrators do have great differences and individual perspectives that are highlighted in their distinctive storytelling voices, but reliability of the different voices is not an issue. Readers appreciate the differences among the women members of the Price family but do not necessarily question the veracity of their accounts, which generally complement rather than compete with one another. That is, as Ognibene points out, "the narrative point of view creates a field of reciprocal subjects" (21). At times, the narratives even blend seamlessly into one another. For example, in the book titled "The Judges," one sister's narration picks up on the heels of another as together they recount the night the family and village fled from the ants that devour everything in their path, contributing to the communal flavor of the narration. The different voices do not constitute an ethnic community per se, as do many of Lanser's illustrative texts, but they nonetheless comprise a white woman's community in the colonial and postcolonial setting.[12] And although Rachel in many ways replicates her father's colonialism to a greater extent than do the other sisters—each one, in some way, shares traits with her father—still the sisters and Orleanna form a community of women united in their opposition to the domineering, patriarchal attitudes of Nathan, and each one undergoes a transformation that places her in contradistinction both to her former self and to the untransformed Nathan.[13]

Both forms of communal voice—sequential, which characterizes the novel as a whole, and simultaneous, which characterizes a brief portion of the final chapter—challenge the conventions of the realist novel, its "individualist narrative authority" (Lanser 256). This authority is closely connected to what Faris identifies as "the univocal narrative authority that characterizes much realist fiction" (*Ordinary Enchantments* 142), the very narrative voice that would surely characterize Nathan Price's own account of his family's ventures in Africa, were he granted a narrating voice in the novel. The communal voice thus offers another kind of feminist narrative authority to displace masculinist authority; it works in conjunction with magic realist storytelling practices that challenge conventional narrative authority. Thus when the final chapter of the novel employs simultaneous communal narration, when Ruth May seems to have been absorbed into an African "we," part of a collective of spirits or muntu (537), the unusual narrative perspective emphasizes, together with Ruth May's fantastical physical transformation, the process of transculturation itself, thereby offering a further critique of Nathan Price's imperial world view.

At the same time that she participates in both types of communal voice, Ruth May (who in this final section of the novel is both Ruth May and more than Ruth May, just as Toni Morrison's Beloved seems to be both Sethe's daughter and more, an entire community of forgotten African voices) also narrates in a personal voice and in an omniscient, authorial voice. She thus employs all three of the types of narrative that Lanser identifies as having the potential to interrogate masculinist narration.[14] This voice speaks of Ruth May in the third person (538) as well as emanating from Ruth May's first-person perspective; she at one point identifies Orleanna in the third-person, too, as "the great-grandmother," rather than addressing her as "you" (541) like she does elsewhere in the chapter. The voice is able to observe the movements of her family members as they search for her grave and is able to enter the consciousness of both the people and the animals that she observes, and it is capable of extra-representational acts, briefly commenting on the complicity of everyone in determining the course of history. Stating that it is no worse to be dead than alive, just different, the voice observes that "the view is larger" (538). As in the case of statements made by *Housekeeping*'s Ruth Stone and *The Stone Diaries*' Daisy Goodwill, these authorial statements both illustrate "a woman's bold appropriation of the philosopher-historian's role" traditionally reserved for male narrators (Lanser 90) and expand Ruth May's consciousness beyond the contingent authority of the personal voice, especially the first-person voice of a young child. Finally, that the narrative voice of the final chapter takes on many different narrative perspectives at once, appearing variously as a personal, communal, and authorial voice, illustrates the necessity of multiple perspectives to understand complex people, cultures, and political situations. As such, it poses an alternative to Nathan's singularity of voice, just as Ruth May's Africanized concept of the word, *nommo*, challenges Nathan's monological interpretations of the Christian word.

CONCLUSION

Lanser proposes that when a communal narrative "creat[es] its characters not simply as voices but as storytellers, the novel legitimates every woman's diegetic and mimetic authority" (265). *The Poisonwood Bible*'s self-consciousness about language and storytelling certainly invites readers to see its women narrators as storytellers; indeed, the epigraph used for this chapter, words spoken by Orleanna Price, highlight this element of the novel, emphasizing the connection between change and "acquir[ing] the words of story" (385).[15] Adah, with her self-consciousness about language and representation, and Ruth May, speaking finally through the voice of African cultural beliefs, answer questions raised by Pratt's work on modes of representation in travel writing: "with respect to representation, how does one speak of transculturation from the colonies to the metropolis?" (6). Kingsolver's magic realist fictional travel writing demonstrates the changed discourse and world views that result in the contact zone from the reciprocal interactions between the Americans and the Congolese. These changes often manifest themselves in the uses of language and narrative: the stories told by many of the Price women acknowledge the many layers and ambiguities of language itself. The novel as a whole adopts a narrative voice that decentralizes narrative authority, and the particularly complex shifts in narrative voice in the final chapter dovetail with the fantastic transformation of Ruth May from an American child to African *muntu*: these shifts among first-person singular, first-person plural, and third-person narrative voices themselves suggest the broadened view and the altered perceptions of the self and the colonies held by members of the Price family who went to the Belgian Congo to change it and its people, but some of whom instead emerged from the experience with a completely new perspective and new ways of articulating that perspective.

6
Telling Beloved's Story

> The community of survivors established by the text allow themselves to be haunted in order that a continuity between past and present be established. The potentially dreadful haunting of the unburied dead may thus be translated into the weighty but more benign haunting that we call historical consciousness.
> —Kathleen Brogan, *Cultural Hauntings* [92]

> Beloved defies interpretation. Beloved is.
> —A. Timothy Spalding, *Reforming the Past: History, The Fantastic, and the Postmodern Slave Narrative* [69]

INTRODUCTION

In contrast to Robinson's and Shields' ghostly narrators who haunt only very tentatively the conventional world they react against, and in contrast to Kingsolver's Ruth May who briefly narrates after she has died but does not interact with her surviving family members, Morrison's character Beloved makes her presence and her anger known. In *The Stone Diaries* and *Housekeeping*, other characters are affected by the ghostly narrators in subdued, almost unconscious ways: Daisy's children have moments of insight into their mother's nature, realizing that she is more complex than they had previously allowed insofar as she exceeds the bounds of patriarchal constructions of femininity, and Lucille seems to want something more, something less conventional than the life she has chosen, expressing in the novel's closing images a likeness to Ruth and to Sylvie. But for the most part, the effects of the ghostly narrators lie in the reader's experience of these novels—the manner in which the reader hesitates about the narrative voice, its point of origin, its relationship to the masculine world that constructs femininity in particular ways, its resistance to these modes of construction. The same is true of *The Poisonwood Bible:* characters are obliquely aware of Ruth May's spiritual presence, but it is chiefly the reader who is affected by the fantastic. Within Morrison's story world, in contrast, Beloved profoundly affects the other characters, especially

Sethe, Denver, and Paul D. While Beloved has, at the end of the novel, much the same status as Robinson's and Shields' characters—discounted, disremembered, invisible—"she cannot be lost because no one is looking for her" (274)—nonetheless, her presence catalyzes the other characters' telling formerly untold personal stories, as well as the narration of the horrific Middle Passage, a chapter in African American history not adequately addressed in official histories. A chief function of the novel's fantastical element, then, lies in the recovery of voices and experiences discounted or unrepresented in traditional historical narratives, particularly though not exclusively the experience of enslaved mothers.

Morrison's narrative technique, which blends realistic narrative conventions with narrative experiment, takes a dual approach to recovering silenced voices. On the one hand, it promulgates the social value of narrative or storytelling itself. On the other, it subverts conventional narrative forms. Margaret Homans, arguing that the practices of black feminist writers who insist on the importance of the narrative gesture to restore/restory their untold and/or misrepresented histories can be reconciled with the views of white feminist narrative theorists who equate narrative form with social structures that oppress women, puts it this way: "celebrating narrative, [Morrison] nonetheless do[es] not practise narrative in any straightforward way" ("Feminist Fictions" 10). That is, *Beloved*'s formal characteristics reveal a suspicion of closure and of linear narratives that prove inadequate to capture the characters' complex psychology and their non-linear relationship to history and the passage of time. *Beloved*'s fantastic dimension is inextricably bound up in its self-consciousness about language, which manifests itself both in the way that the novel highlights the act of narration and in the way that it calls attention to patriarchal uses of language that oppress African American women—and men.[1] The postmodern feminist fantastic lays bare ideological constructions behind storytelling practices. With its attention to a woman slave's story and the mother-daughter relationship under slavery, together with its innovations in the language used to tell this story and its experimental narrative structure, Morrison's novel employs feminist narrative strategies enabled by the fantastic, but uses them in a specifically racialized context.

In adopting what Homans calls a "middle ground" (9) between opposing assessments of narrative's relationship to social practices, Morrison adopts an approach that very much resembles the approach of experimental feminist writers explored by theorists of feminist narrative such as Greene, Hite, Frye, and Sally Robinson.[2] As we have seen, these theorists locate recent women's storytelling practices between realism and postmodern experimentation.[3] In this multi-layered, complicated novel, Morrison in fact employs a middle ground or "both/and" approach in a variety of ways: she hybridizes seemingly incompatible genres; she makes truth claims for the representation of blacks' histories even while exposing the problems of prior representations, thereby employing conventions of realism and conventions of postmodernism; she presents the supernatural as real but also creates in Beloved a character who exists on the border between the marvelous and the uncanny (in other words, she combines strategies of magic realism and strategies of the fantastic as Todorov defines it); and she evokes a "maternal symbolic" (Wyatt) or "cultural semiotic" (Moglen 216), thereby merging symbolic and semiotic discourses, in much the same manner that Carol Shields and Marilynne Robinson explore alternative feminist discourse in their novels. Because this last approach has been well-developed elsewhere,[4] this chapter focuses on the ways that Morrison interweaves seemingly opposed approaches to narrative, to genre conventions, and to the fantastic itself, which constitutes an integral part of how Morrison treats narrative and genre. The reader's experience of hesitation and the reader's interpretation of the stories catalyzed by the fantastic figure Beloved comprise a crucial element of how the irreal intersects with the real to challenge patriarchal storytelling practices.

HESITATION: CHARACTERS, NARRATOR, READER

Linking *Beloved*'s middle position on the possibility of representation specifically with its status as a novel of the fantastic, narrative theorist Shlomith Rimmon-Kenan analyzes the role of ambiguity in the novel, which is "crucial both for the novel's problematization of the possibility of gaining access to reality and for its tentative retrieval of representation" (116). One form of this ambiguity, according to Rimmon-Kenan, is Todorov's pure fantastic (119). In fact, several critics identify *Beloved* as belonging to this mode, though the vast majority accepts the presence of the supernatural in the novel, rather than concluding that hesitation about Beloved's identity persists throughout the narrative.[5] Because Morrison employs a third-person narrator in both *Beloved* and *Paradise*, her narrative technique differs from that of the first-person narratives explored earlier in this book, requiring careful attention to the point of view adopted by the third-person narrator. Focalization within the narrative profoundly affects the reader's experience of the novel's fantastic dimension.[6]

The novel opens with an omniscient narrator's unfazed account of the baby ghost haunting 124, driving away the two boys Buglar and Howard, so that *Beloved*'s initial narrative strategy resembles that of the magic realist text with its straightforward presentation of the strange or impossible, rather than the strategy of the fantastic tale that invites hesitation about the uncanny or marvelous nature of mysterious events.[7] And when readers are shortly introduced to the opinions of various characters about the ghost, we see that although they respond to it differently, ranging from terror on the part of the boys to acceptance on the part of Sethe, Denver, and Baby Suggs, all agree without hesitation that the house is haunted by a ghost. Even Paul D, an outsider arriving at the house after an eighteen-year absence from the region, expresses no hesitation whatsoever about the idea of a ghost (9–10)—he simply mistakenly assumes that the ghost is that of Baby Suggs. As we have seen, Todorov postulates that the lack of hesitation in the presentation of the seemingly impossible, when such an event is present within a world that is not a marvelous world, signals the end of the classic fantastic tale and ushers in the era of the generalized fantastic tale, which other theorists in turn identify with the strategies of mainstream postmodernism. Yet Morrison employs codes of magic realism for ends that counter claims made about the generalized fantastic and its relationship to historical reality. Hesitation persists in the experience of the reader who does not believe in ghosts, and is ultimately tied inextricably to questions about the representation of history.

Of course, such a reader is not the only reader of Morrison's novel. Indeed, Travis notes that Morrison "has claimed she writes with a black audience in mind" (182), and Lanser analyzes Morrison's oeuvre in terms of the author's shift from a narrative perspective or authorial voice that allows space for a white reader to enter the text to the perspective adopted in *Beloved* that "increasingly refuse[s] to accommodate a white audience" (138). Yet Travis, drawing on the work of Peter Rabinowitz to distinguish among implied, actual, and authorial readers (197, n. 8), observes that white readers who likely do not share Morrison's African American-based sense of reality do constitute part of the actual audience. Both she and Lanser, then, analyze the effects of the narration on the white reading audience (Travis 184–186 and 194–195; Lanser 120–138), with Lanser acknowledging that the magical aspects of Morrison's later novels constitute an important part of her project to expose the "inadequacy of Western epistemology" (134). In a similar vein, Harris notes that "Morrison [...] draws us into active intellectual participation in the novel by challenging [western] beliefs about ghosts" by treating Beloved's presence in the household as "a probable occurrence" (144–145). Exploring the dynamic that takes place among white (or, for that matter, non-white) readers who may not believe in ghosts through the lens of theories of the fantastic and magic realism and in terms of hesitation provides an important means by which to understand the operation of the novel's narrative perspective on that reader.

Such a reader will, as Hegerfeldt points out in her work on magic realism, experience hesitation insofar as the magic realist text by definition employs codes of the realist mode, including a realistic setting, that are belied by the presence of the supernatural: "the uncertainty over which set of conventions to apply in reading draws attention to these conventions as cultural constructs" (55). Within *Beloved*, the dynamic that Hegerfeldt describes works in the following manner. The novel does indeed employ realist codes in its opening descriptions, including codes of the historical novel such as details that identify Cincinnati's geographic limits and the status of Ohio's statehood in 1873

(3), details about typical Ohio winter weather (4), and descriptions of the historical effects of slavery on the enslaved, such as the pain caused to Baby Suggs when her children are sold and separated from her (5). The introduction of a ghost assumed by narrator and characters to constitute an unproblematic part of this empirical reality does indeed begin to invoke in the reader questions about which generic conventions to apply to this novel.[8] In playing with reader expectations and generic conventions, Morrison enacts feminist and Africanist revisions to various genres. The introduction of the ghost also raises questions about the nature of reality itself and the role of cultural construct in that determination. As Morrison writes later in *Beloved*, "definitions belonged to the definers—not the defined" (190), a statement that has bearing on the novel's treatment of history itself and the very nature of historical discourse, especially where the history of a people actively oppressed by another people is written from the oppressors' perspective.[9] Todorov's concept of hesitation as a structural device of the fantastic tale, whether it occurs in the reader's responses to the magic realist mode employed in the novel's opening or in the reader's responses to the character of Beloved who appears a short time later, can thus be usefully recuperated in a socio-historical context. As Denise Heinz points out,

> Morrison's ultimate purpose in using the supernatural in art is not to prove its existence—her novels intentionally represent it ambiguously—but to create this ongoing dialectic between the seen and the unseen, the known and the unknown, the signified and the Signified—the supernatural as a trope on reality. The effect of this is a redefinition for some and reaffirmation for others of a consensus reality that dilutes the debilitating effects of double-consciousness, racism, and oppression [160].

Hesitation encoded in the reader's experience of encountering both realist and non-realist codes in the novel's opening is furthered by the narrative technique itself, which causes the reader to experience a great deal of hesitation about the action of the novel, its time frame and plot details, and about the characters and their relationships to one another, raising question after question and providing no conventional exposition by which the reader might become firmly oriented to the story. Within the first thirty pages of the novel, for example, Morrison incorporates no fewer than twenty-five shifts in time and fifteen shifts in point of view, so that within single time frames the perspective changes, and within passages focalized through one character's perspective, the time frame frequently modulates. As a result, until the reader moves beyond these thirty pages, no one narrative segment (an event set in one time frame and told from one consistent point of view) lasts for more than two or three pages. The effect is profoundly disorienting. As a part of the disorientation produced by the rapid modulations in time and focalization, Morrison incorporates brief, unexplained mentions of past events that are not clarified for quite some time. For example, we read about a baby's throat having been cut very early on (5) but learn no details of this central event behind the entire narrative of *Beloved* until the end of the long first section of the novel (148–165).

Morrison explains in her essay "Unspeakable Things, Unspoken" that she intended to disorient the reader so that he or she is "[s]natched just as the slaves were from one place to another [...] without preparation, and without defense"; she creates "compelling confusion" in the reader, "without comfort or succor from the 'author,' with only imagination, intelligence, and necessity available for the journey" (32–33). The effect of both the jarring narrative technique and the presentation of 124's haunting as an accepted reality is both to broaden the reader's understanding of slavery and to lay bare conventions of realism as ideological constructs rather than truths. Later in the novel, the presence of the character Beloved furthers this end, when the novel shifts from the omniscient narrator's unfazed presentation of the baby ghost in the magic realist mode to the narration focalized through various characters about Beloved's status in the novel's fantastic mode. Like the magic realist element of the novel's opening, the postmodern fantastic mode used in *Beloved* paradoxically enables the recovery of reality, since more than simply figuring history in the fantastic character Beloved, Morrison uses the device to lay bare the narrow ways in which history has been constructed in the first place.

The characters' perspectives on Beloved, when she appears at 124, do in fact create a great deal of hesitation about her status, contrary to Cutter's claims about the narrative.[10] While it is true that much of the story is focalized internally through Sethe and Denver, a significant portion of the narrative is filtered through Paul D, who never accepts that Beloved and the baby ghost are one and the same: he questions Beloved's status throughout in spite of accepting readily the idea that 124 is haunted by the baby ghost, speculating about who Beloved is and where she came from. Until the end of the novel when he asks Denver if she indeed thinks Beloved was her sister (266), he is inclined to assume that she is fully human, not a spirit at all; a conversation that he has with Stamp Paid late in the novel, after Paul's departure and return, suggests that Beloved might have been a girl locked up by a white man who recently died (235). Nor do Sethe and Denver share the same view of Beloved. Denver is much quicker than Sethe to suspect that Beloved might be an incarnate version of the baby ghost, Denver's murdered sister, while Sethe maintains doubt for quite a long time, accounting for Beloved's strange behavior and infant-like characteristics through a natural explanation very close to the one that Paul D. and Stamp Paid discuss (119). Sethe's opinions about Beloved work against the reader's simply accepting Denver's point of view, especially since readers might easily account for Denver's haste in identifying Beloved as her sister through the fact that she is so desperately lonely, especially after Paul D has driven away her one companion, the baby ghost, and taken much of Sethe's attention for himself.

While Sethe and Denver do for a time share the perspective that Beloved is the embodied form of the murdered baby girl, very shortly after Sethe's conclusions come to match those of Denver (175–6), the narration modulates into the sections narrated in the first person from Sethe's, then Denver's, then Beloved's point of view, before merging into a mélange of these voices in a brief prose-poem (200–217). This section of the narrative is important in maintaining doubt about Beloved's status because Beloved's own narration does not confirm Denver's and Sethe's claims that Beloved is sister or daughter: as Cornwell aptly points out, "Beloved's narrative [...] appears to have little if any reference to the terrible fate of the 'crawling already?' baby girl," seeming to give details instead of Beloved's experience of being captured in Africa by slave traders and transported to America (206). The Middle Passage sections of the novel suggest that while Beloved might represent in part the murdered, unnamed baby girl, she represents as well a Middle Passage survivor, perhaps even Sethe's own mother.[11] While Sethe and Denver cannot, of course, conceive of her in this way, the narration clearly cues the reader to do so, juxtaposing accounts of Beloved's past that do not coincide with one another so that we cannot simply adopt Sethe's and Denver's points of view. And Denver herself eventually suggests that Beloved represents not simply the embodied murdered child but also, as Denver puts it, "more" (266), a manifestation of the "sixty million and more" referenced in the novel's epigraph.

Finally, the novel's coda returns us to the perspective of an authorial narrator; the internal focalization or figural narration that has comprised the bulk of the novel disappears altogether in the enigmatic final two pages (274–5). The effect of this narration is to recast doubt on any certainty the reader might have reached because the authorial narrator offers no definitive interpretation.[12] The novel's shift away from characters' perspectives and the interpretive difficulty of the novel's externally focalized coda restores a high degree of ambiguity to the question of Beloved's identity.[13] The externally focalized narrative voice speaks in seemingly contradictory ways at the end of novel, insisting that "It was not a story to pass on" (274, 275), though the bulk of the narrative has been devoted to precisely this enterprise. On the one hand, the other characters, having remembered Beloved, need to forget her in order to move on, so that forgetting is contingent on remembering. Still, the narrator's tone expresses regret that a culture seems to have forgotten its Beloveds. On the other hand, Beloved paradoxically continues to serve in her very mysterious and "unknowable" state as a reminder to a culture which would narrowly define her and forget her: her non-name, Beloved, constitutes the last word of the novel. James Phelan provides a compelling reading of the "stubbornness" of the novel's ending, arguing that the impossibility of interpreting Beloved necessarily reveals to the reader "the limitations of interpretation's desire for mastery" (240) and challenges the reader's claims to be able to "master" or fully understand the novel rationally, thereby placing the reader in contradistinction to those who claim mastery—especially to Schoolteacher, who claims mastery over Sethe and her story.[14] Though Phelan does not draw on theories of the fantastic, his observations in effect provide evidence for identifying the novel as belonging to the mode Todorov defines as the pure fantastic and moreover, coincide with observations made about the function of the fantastic by subsequent theorists who consider its socio-ideological effects.

The narrative point of view merits emphasis because it has important bearing on the reader's experience of hesitation. Morrison's novel in some ways defies the opposition critics make between magic realism and the fantastic insofar as the novel employs both modes but for similar ends: in both the opening magic realist mode, and in the novel's subsequent shift to a predominantly fantastic mode when the baby ghost disappears and Beloved materializes, readers grapple with ways in which to understand the conflicting codes of realism and the fantastic. In turn, this hesitation demands that readers notice and interpret genre conventions in a self-conscious way, interrogating the manner in which familiar conventions of realism portray historical knowledge, often revealed to be mere representations or fantasies; and, concomitantly, to recognize the socio-historical dimension of the fantastic tale, to see the complicated ways in which the irreal invokes the historical real. In the space where history and the fantastic intersect, Morrison's novel illuminates Fredric Jameson's comments on generic "sedimentation": "[generic] form is immanently and intrinsically an ideology in its own right. When such forms are re-appropriated and refashioned in quite different social and cultural contexts, this message persists and must be functionally reckoned into the new form" (140–41). In *Beloved*, the generic layering of historical and fantastic conventions causes the reader to reexamine the assumptions of each of these genres and to arrive at a new understanding of how each functions in the context of postmodernity.

Revising the Historical Novel and the Slave Narrative

Morrison began writing *Beloved* when she read a news story about a woman name Margaret Garner who attempted to kill her children rather than see them returned to slavery. In the novel, the only written account of Sethe's act exists in a newspaper clipping that Stamp Paid carries with him and eventually shows to Paul D. Yet this piece of the historical record proves inadequate and distorting since it represents the event only from the white point of view. Paul D, who can't read the article, also doesn't doesn't recognize the photograph of Sethe (154–155). The photo misrepresents Sethe just as the printed story fails to account for the complexities behind the event and fails to take into account Sethe's perspective. Even Sethe's own community will not tell her story: when Sethe is driven away to prison following her murderous act, the narrator notes that the community refuses to sing for her. After she pulls out of sight, they merely hum: "And then no words. Humming. No words at all" (152). Sethe herself, for eighteen years following the baby's death, considers her act "unspeakable" and begins each day with the serious work of "beating back the past" (73). She views any possibilities for the future as dependant on her ability to keep that past hidden from Denver: "the future was a matter of keeping the past at bay" (42). Denver treasures Sethe's "told story" (29), Sethe's account of her escape, which stands in implicit contrast to the "untold story" of the killing, but it is only when that untold story comes to light that Denver can, in fact, move into the future. The most horrific of slavery's consequences, then, remain untold in the novel's 1855 setting; not until 1873 when the young woman who calls herself Beloved appears, when this fantastic character forces the others to confront the past, does this unnarrated event, which is paradoxically unnarratable and yet somehow told nonetheless, become restored to the historical record from which it has been erased. Brogan, who distinguishes "cultural haunting" from other types of ghost stories, argues that this genre constitutes an exploration "not only of the individual psyche but also of a people's historical consciousness. Through the agency of ghosts, group histories that have in some way been threatened, erased, or fragmented are recuperated" (5–6).

The presence of the fantastic within the documentary historical framework of the novel causes the reader to modify his/her assumptions about the historical novel. Traditionally, history is presented as a story-like record that systematically accounts for past events in chronological fashion with clear cause-effect connections. As we saw in Chapter One in conjunction with Iris Murdoch's *The Sea, the Sea*, Hayden White, theorizing historiographic discourse, describes the relationship between traditional historical narrative and realist fiction, positing that history's narrative form lends it "scientific" legitimacy in a culture that values Enlightenment ways of interpreting experience. As White points out, however, the chronicle or annals, non-narrative records of the historical past, preserve its "reality" more accurately than do narrativized accounts of historical events (24–5). Morrison's own narrative technique and the fantastic itself, which defies clear explanation and remains unresolved, counter the teleological form of traditional written history. The disruptive, discontinuous narrative strategy of *Beloved* calls into question the smooth, seamless flow of traditional historical narrative and, as we shall see, of the traditional slave narrative.

Morrison's narrative also foregrounds point of view, a strategy, historian Robert Rosenstone points out, "that does not change facts but, rather, the ground for constituting facts and the meanings one can draw from them" (12). Similarly, according to Waxman, Morrison's novel emphasizes in particular the gendered, maternal perspective as it contrasts with "the views of white male historians and storytellers" (57), exploring "absent resonances in white patriarchal interpretations of slavery's history" (58). Because Morrison provides first Schoolteacher's account of finding Sethe in Ohio when he has attempted to reclaim his property, and then Sethe's own account of the novel's central event when she attempts years later to explain her actions to Paul D, these two accounts juxtaposed in two nearly contiguous sections of the novel (pages 148–153 and 159–164) invite the reader to compare the vastly different perspectives, the one cold and clinical, the other filled with emotion. As Maggie Sale argues in her discussion of African American oral traditions in *Beloved*, "in contrast to master versions of history, which erroneously present themselves as independent of their makers and so of any particular perspective, the history created in *Beloved* both emphasizes the importance of perspective and requires the articulation of many perspectives" (43).[15] Thus Morrison employs internal focalization to challenge a traditional Western concept of history.

In one significant section, however, the narration is focalized through a white slave holder. In *Beloved*, the character of Schoolteacher represents a white, patriarchal approach to narrating historical events; as Mae Henderson points out, "his methodology [...] suggests the role of the cultural historian (or ethnologist)"; moreover, like the historian who never becomes aware of the ideology of form, "Morrison's historical investigator remains hopelessly unconscious" of the limits of his own methodology (69–70).[16] Thus when schoolteacher and the other white men come to take Sethe back to Kentucky, the scene they encounter at 124—the scene that constitutes the documentary historical event of Margaret Garner's act on which Morrison loosely based her novel—is described in cold, clinical terms. When they go to the shed to get the "pickaninnies," they see that "two were lying open-eyed in sawdust; a third pumped blood down the dress of the main one—the woman schoolteacher bragged about, the one he said made fine ink, damn good soup, pressed his collars the way he liked besides having at least ten breeding years left. But now she'd gone wild, due to the mishandling of the nephew who'd overbeat her and made her cut and run" (149). Here the white characters impose a definitive cause-effect interpretation on Sethe's actions, one the reader knows to be incorrect since Sethe had planned "to cut and run" long before the beating took place, a fact made clear from the most detailed account of the escape attempt provided in the entire novel, appearing in Part III (see pages 222–229). The Nephew likewise thinks she commits murder "on account of a beating" (150); the sheriff thinks of the event as "testimony to the results of a little so-called freedom imposed on people who needed every care and guidance in the world to keep them from the cannibal life they preferred" (151).

The account of Sethe's actions focalized through the white characters recalls not only traditional historiography but also scientific discourse; Henderson points out that schoolteacher functions "as a data-collector, cataloguer, classifier and taxonomist concerned with matters of materiality and empiricism [...]" (70), evident in the scene in which he measures Sethe's head and instructs Nephew to list her animal characteristics on one side of the paper, her human characteristics on the other. In both his cause-effect, linear historiography and his pseudo-scientific discourse, Schoolteacher constructs knowledge according to two Western modes of knowledge that, Hegerfeldt maintains, magic realism deconstructs, "criticizing their claim to provide an objective and complete picture of the world." Magic realists texts often employ in counterpoint a paradigm of "narrative knowledge, drawing on the oral traditions of myth, legend, and fairy tale, as well as personal accounts and memories" (158), a mode of knowledge "devalued in the West with the rise of science" (64). In *Beloved*, Sethe's discourse, as well as the novel's own narrative structure, evocations of the oral tradition, and representation of the African ancestor tradition, provide this kind of narrative knowledge as an alternative to conventional historigraphic narrative and pseudo-scientific knowledge claimed by Schoolteacher.

Countering these seemingly rational explanations, Sethe's own account of her actions that follows shortly on the heels of Schoolteacher's and the other whites' musings contrasts sharply with the linear, logical version told from the whites' perspectives. Ultimately the sections of the narrative focalized through Sethe herself undermine the authority of schoolteacher's narrative:

> Sethe knew that the circle she was making around the room, him, the subject, would remain one. That she could never close in, pin it down for anybody who had to ask. If they didn't get it right off—she could never explain. Because the truth was simple, not a long-drawn-out record of flowered shifts, tree cages, selfishness, ankle ropes and wells. Simple: she was squatting in the garden and when she saw them coming and recognized schoolteacher's hat, she heard wings. Little hummingbirds stuck their needle beaks right through her headcloth into her hair and beat their wings. And if she thought anything, it was No. No. Nono. Nonono. Simple.

Morrison repeats the word "simple" here ironically, since the killing is triggered by emotions that are not nearly as simple as a reaction to a beating. Sethe's "explanation" counters the exclusionary and oppressive narratives of the dominant ideology in the circularity (rather than linearity) with which she addresses the subject. In fact, Mbiti points out that in African religion and philosophy, the circle constitutes an important symbol of continuity, signifying the unending quality of the universe and emphasizing that "continuity on a large scale is more important than change in small details" (*Introduction to African Religion* 37 and 40). Sethe sees her action as ensuring continuity— "my plan was to take us all to the other side where my own ma'am is" (203)— to reunite three generations of the family, restoring familial continuity and the continuity between the living and the dead disrupted by the institution of slavery. Hence descriptions of the way she both circles the room and circles her subject as she talks with Paul D invoke an African belief system. The circle image associated with the slaveholders—that of the circle of iron around the

African's necks that encircles and encloses—contrasts sharply with the positive circle symbol of African cosmology. In addition, the "explanation" Sethe offers—hummingbird wings—further counters the whites' cold explanation: as Teresa Washington points out in reading of *Beloved* based in Yoruba myth, Sethe's actions recall those of spiritually powerful women, associated with creation and motherhood (171). These women, with whom Washington identifies Sethe, are furthermore "associated with birds that act as spiritual media. The Spirit Bird, Eye Òrò, is capable of aesthetic creativity, astral *cum* physical destruction, and sublime protection. [...] When this spiritually-charged Bird emerges and goes on outings, its power and potential are awesome" (176–177). Thus the "hummingbird wings" referenced in Sethe's account of her action invoke motherhood and a protective act. The image also participates in the novel's fantastic dimension; echoing elements of African spirituality, it counters Schoolteacher's discourse and reductive assessment of Sethe's actions in *Beloved*'s crucial scene.

Morrison calls attention throughout *Beloved* to the white slave holders' closed and oppressive narratives that exclude the humanity of the black characters. In addition to Schoolteacher's distorted account of the killing itself, of key importance is the scene in which Schoolteacher asks his nephew to divide Sethe's characteristics into two columns labeled "human" and "animal" (193). This scene of classification scars Sethe's psyche much more severely than the beating scars her back; she later tells Beloved that it is one of the reasons she sent her to the other side: "And no one, nobody on this earth, would list her daughter's characteristics on the animal side of the paper. No. Oh no" (251). In addition, Sethe's discussion of the meaning of the word "characteristics" with Mrs. Garner immediately after the scene prompts Sethe's later discussion with Halle about Schoolteacher, leading her to the eventual realization that her family will be broken apart and to the initial thoughts of escape, though it takes Paul F's being sold before the threat of separation inspires a plan (see *Beloved* 193–198).

Analyzing the accounts of the novel's central events—Sethe's escape and the subsequent murder of Beloved—focalized through Sethe reveals both that the content of the narration differs markedly from the content of the version focalized through Schoolteacher and that Sethe's "circular" form counters his linear narrative. Ultimately, issues of motherhood and family connections drive much of Sethe's version, as well as much of the novel itself. Mae Henderson views Sethe as feminist historian whose own historiography provides a counterdiscourse to Schoolteacher's: through Sethe's tellings, "Morrison uses the metaphor of maternity to establish an alternative to the metaphor of paternity common in white/male historical discourse" (75). Henderson goes on to demonstrate how the metaphor of "delivery"—figured in the repeated tellings of Denver's birth and of the birth imagery employed when Sethe first sees Beloved—"becomes a means of 'deliverance' from the dominant conception of history as a white/paternal metaphor" (76).[17] Narration focalized through Sethe, her acts of memory, include stories about her own lost mother and the mother figure Nan, who nursed Sethe, as well as about Schoolteacher's Nephew stealing Sethe's own milk, an act which in Sethe's mind overshadows the subsequent beating as a violation of her personhood. During the escape itself, the novel not only renders "childbirth as high adventure" in a gesture that Wyatt sees as a feminist revision to the quest narrative (475) but focuses on Sethe's need to get her milk to her still nursing "crawling already? baby." Nursing becomes a trope that dominates the novel, too, in the later interactions among Sethe, Denver, and Beloved. This maternal history, along with accounts of the Middle Passage generally, comprises an absence in official histories, as reflected in Schoolteacher's utter lack of consideration of her role as a mother in the account of Beloved's death filtered through his limited perspective. In a comparison of *Beloved* and Susan Glaspell's "A Jury of Her Peers," Koolish aptly notes that Schoolteacher, the sheriff, and the other white men who come to reclaim Sethe "are unable to read the text of a woman's life, are unable to make sense of the gendered evidence before them" (431). The authority of the white male view is thus undermined by the feminist view that dominates the novel.[18]

In addition, the form of the novel's alternative history to the white, patriarchal narrative challenges the teleological assumptions of Schoolteacher's version. Sethe's own account of her actions, her reasons for running and her reasons for cutting her baby's throat, as told to both Paul D and to Beloved, are presented in piecemeal fashion, scattered throughout the narrative. The reader must work to put these pieces together, and even when readers connect one bit of information with another, the complexities behind Sethe's actions are so vast, and readers' responses to her killing the baby so torn between understanding and the inability to understand, that the novel's central event cannot be firmly understood, never "pinned down" in certain terms. Morrison's work thus not only restores a forgotten narrative that has been omitted from the official narratives of history, but she challenges the form of the official narrative. According to Spearey, *Beloved* "map[s] out an alternative historiographic methodology which forestalls teleological imperatives" (175).

In this black feminist novel, Morrison thus employs narrative strategies that coincide with feminist narrative strategies described, for example, by Homans and Henderson, but these same strategies also invoke an African world view and concept of historical time. The oral tradition of African peoples underlies the narrative, with its high degree of repetition and hence circular rather than linear structure. Busia, for example, in her work on the form of contemporary black women's novels, points out that black women writers "can subvert the inherited form of the novel" (16) by adapting African modes of storytelling and myth.[19] As Mbiti notes, "the linear concept of time in western thought [...] is practically foreign to African thinking" (*African Religions and Philosophy* 17).[20] Because traditional African people have no concept of future time, as Mbiti explains, beyond events in the immediate future that are certain to take place, there can be no sense of teleology in the African world view, no sense of history working toward some particular end, no sense of progress and no grand schemes that often characterize Western models of history (*African Religions and Philosophy* 22), including the foundational myths of America itself, myths upon which the institution of slavery itself was in part based.[21] Thus the novel invokes African cosmology in part to critique dominant models of Western thinking that have been used specifically to justify slavery and generally to oppress and marginalize others.

Moreover, *Beloved*'s fantastic dimension participates in this project. In employing a *revenant* or spirit of the recently dead from the African ancestor tradition, Morrison employs a ghost who originates from an African American belief system. The hesitation experienced on the reader's part about this ghost's reality—both in the in the opening pages of the novel that have features in common with magic realism and in the subsequent story of the young woman calling herself Beloved that shares characteristics of the fantastic tale—thrusts the Western reader into what might well be an unfamiliar cultural context. Describing *Beloved* as a novel that employs conventions of the fantastic Western tale as defined by Todorov and others, critic Helene Christol also observes that "behind the surface text hides another text, signifying resistance, rediscovering what Morrison called a 'black cosmology'" (165) through which "she questioned and transcended Western conceptions of time and reality" (168); Morrison's own "vision of reality struck at the very heart of Western civilization, questioning a post–Enlightenment reason that objectified the other and unnamed millions of black people" (Christol 168). In Morrison's own words, she wanted the reader to confront "a reality unlike that received reality of the west" ("Memory" 88).

In addition, Morrison points out that what many Western readers might commonly term "fantastic" or "irreal" constitutes a very real part of the African-American tradition: what she calls "enchantment" is not "a thing you do on Sunday morning in church, it's not a tiny, entertaining aspect of one's life—it's what *informs* your sensibility" (Davis 144). Given that "enchantment" constitutes a significant part of the reality of the people about whom Morrison writes, she feels "it seemed impossible for *me* to write about black people and eliminate that simply because it was 'unbelievable'" (144). Morrison's character Stamp Paid makes a similar point: somewhat skeptical of Ella's claims that Beloved is a spirit, Stamp at first resists this interpretation. But when Ella reminds him that "'people who die bad don't stay in the ground,'" Stamp "couldn't deny it. Jesus Christ Himself didn't" (188). Morrison thereby makes an explicit comparison between Christian myth and African beliefs, inviting Western readers to see the latter as no more strange or unbelievable than the former.

Beloved's ghostly status not only invokes an alternate cultural reality, but it also underlines the inherent fantasy in Western "official histories." Morrison herself describes the relationship between the fantastic devices and historical-political concerns in her work: "the fully realized presence of the haunting is both a major incumbent of the narrative and sleight of hand. One if its purposes is to keep the reader preoccupied with the nature of the incredible spirit world while being supplied a controlled diet of the incredible political world" ("Unspeakable Things" 32). She has commented elsewhere to narrative theorist Rimmon-Kenan that "the 'Fantastic' status of the title character may be a displacement of what seems to her much more central and much more unbelievable, [...] namely 'the slavery stuff'" (120). In effect, slavery imposes social death on its subjects, rendering them non-persons or ghosts of sorts (Keizer 109); Beloved's possibly being a ghost, then, literalizes this metaphoric death, blurring the bounds between the fantastic and the historical real.[22] Morrison's comments also suggest that atrocities committed in the name of slavery rival anything she could invent in fiction and suggest that such acts of violence committed in the name of Western rationalism and progress are—or ought to be—more unbelievable and unacceptable than another culture's spiritual belief system, the African ancestor tradition.

Morrison's treatment of "the slavery stuff" also revises generic conventions of the classic slave narrative. Like traditional historiography, and influenced by the conditions under which such narratives were produced—namely, to convince white readers of the need for abolition by "pander[ing] to the abolitionist polemics of victimization" (Hamilton 433)—these texts, too, are fraught with problems in the way they represent the slaves' experience. Typically they employ a linear, teleological plot structure as they map the journey from slavery to freedom and display a strong sense of closure upon the protagonists' achieving that freedom. Typically they emphasize the action of the escape story rather than the complex psychology of the slaves who are seeking freedom. Morrison's novel departs from the classic slave narrative pattern both in its recursive, non-linear narrative structure and in its focus on characters' interiority through its use of internally focalized narrative. It privileges the thoughts and perceptions that dominate the narrative over details of the action—indeed, the full story of the escape, given the plot's complex arrangement of story events, does not emerge until very late in *Beloved*, toward the end of the second section. By combining the documentary historical event of Margaret Garner's escape and subsequent act of killing her child with elements of the gothic tale and its psychological dimension, Morrison is able to write a history of the slave's experience that extends beyond the account given in slave narratives that embrace the conventions of literary realism.[23]

Just as Homans notes that Morrison's novel adopts a dual approach to narrative, just as Morrison's novel exhibits the both/and approach to realism and postmodernism characteristic of feminist narrative praxis in the contemporary age, so Spalding notes that Morrison

> posit[s] an alternative historiography that can claim the best of both worlds: the claims of truth and coherence evidenced in traditional history and the ambiguity and expansiveness of non-mimetic forms like the gothic. *Beloved* achieves narrative authority over the past by both asserting slavery's elusiveness and gothic dimensions as a historical reality and conceptualizing the past as a knowable component of the present [74].

Moreover, as Hamilton points out, the novel's gothic dimension not only questions the form and nature of traditional representations of slaves' histories, but it also does so within a specifically gendered context by challenging the domestic ideology of the nineteenth century, according to which "the fallen women of the sentimental novels paid for their seductions with pain and often with death," an ideology that manifests itself in the classic slave narrative's relative silence about matters of sexual violence and the rape of enslaved women by white men (435), or in a presentation of sexual violence that emphasizes victimization and also plays to the reader's voyeuristic tendencies. Morrison, in contrast, depicts violence and victimization in such a way that she counters "the limited, partisan, and voyeuristic perspective of the traditional slave narrative, transforming a discourse of victimization into a narrative of the capacity of individuals and communities to support and heal those subjected to brutality" (Hamilton 438). Morrison's revision of the narrative of victimization extends from the slave narrative genre to the gothic as well: Morrison employs the conventions of the gothic both to challenge literary realism and also to revise traditional gothic conventions themselves.

REVISING THE GOTHIC NOVEL

As we saw in the chapters on Margaret Atwood's *Lady Oracle* and Iris Murdoch's *The Sea, the Sea*, recent women writers interrogate the typical role for women in the classic gothic tale—leading lady of a love story often victimized and persecuted, whose leading man quests for power and independence. In their gothic novels, contemporary women writers also challenge the monstrousness associated with independent, rebellious women in conventional gothic novels. Atwood transfers monstrousness to women who follow societal conventions regarding femininity, while Murdoch transfers the trope of monstrousness to a male character who victimizes the traditional gothic heroine. Morrison not only subverts gothic conventions in a racialized context to call attention to the fantastic, gothic horror inherent in slavery itself but also subverts those conventions in a gendered context to advance her feminist treatment of the experience of the enslaved mother in particular and to challenge white social constructions of black masculinity.[24]

Like *Housekeeping*, *Beloved* begins with the concept of house and home and all the complex cultural significance such a notion carries. Denver and Sethe, both of whom have a narrow sense of the outside world and who have essentially imprisoned themselves in 124, are not victims of domestic enclosure by male culture at large but more specifically of white patriarchal culture. The house is, in effect, haunted by the specter of racism; because Sethe has murdered her daughter Beloved there, the house is a gothic prison in which the characters are trapped, separated from the larger community. The novel charts the way the house at Bluestone Road is exorcised of its ghost—real or imagined—so that it can once again become a home to its inhabitants, but significantly, *Beloved* revises the role of the traditional gothic "rescue" of women characters Sethe and Denver by revising the role of Paul D as traditional gothic hero—and does so within an Africanized context by drawing on an African conception of masculinity.[25] The novel thus does introduce gender as well as race as an important category in its revisions to gothic conventions, even if it does not locate the original cause for the house's haunting in a "gendered conflict."[26]

The gothic dimensions of the novel are highlighted immediately in the opening descriptions of the baby ghost's mischief. When Paul D first comes to 124 Bluestone Road, not having had any contact with Sethe or her family during the eighteen years that have intervened since the escape in 1855 and Paul's return to the area in 1873, one of his first actions is to rid the house of the baby ghost (18–19), assuming the role of male protector of the women who live there. He believes he is doing them—especially Sethe—a favor, but Denver regards his actions otherwise: "Paul D messed them up for good. With a table and a loud male voice he had rid 124 of its claim to local fame" (37). Denver in fact twice emphasizes Paul D's maleness when she ruminates on how she prefers the ghost's company to Paul's. Paul himself, much later in the novel, muses that when he drove off the baby ghost, he assumed that Sethe "could not do it" herself; that as a woman living alone with husband and sons gone, she has been "helpless" and has had to live in "apologetic resignation" (164). He thereby conceives of himself as male rescuer. Paul's actions are further located within conventions of masculinity by the fact that he himself ruminates twice in the early parts of the narrative on Mr. Garner's granting the status of manhood to his slaves (10 and 22). As Sitter points out, however, Mr. Garner's own treatment of his slaves vis-à-vis their manhood is problematic in various ways, including the way in which Garner's definition leads Paul to adopt a white American patriarchal version of masculinity (Sitter 24), a version contrasted with the African masculinity embraced by the character Sixo and endorsed by the novel itself, as well as finally by Paul (Sitter 26–27).

Thus before Paul undergoes a change late in the novel, he not only initially "rescues" Sethe from the baby ghost (or thinks he has, not knowing the full story behind the child's death or the impact that the story has on Sethe's psyche), but he also tries to remove the young woman calling herself Beloved from the house as means of asserting his own power and dominance. When Beloved seduces him and gradually moves him out of the house, he is naturally disturbed by his lack of power, his lack of self-definition, but his means of trying to reassert his dominance in the household and reclaim Sethe's affections from Beloved partake of conventional masculinity as portrayed in the classic gothic tale, among other genres of the novel: when he feels that his manhood has been stripped by Beloved's actions, he tells Sethe that he wants to impregnate her: "suddenly it was a solution: a way to hold on to her, document his manhood and break out of the girl's spell—all in one" (128). Sethe resists this suggestion, dismissing it as absurd, and a short time later, when Paul learns the story of the murdered baby and Sethe's role in it, he is shocked to discover that Sethe is not an "obedient" woman. She in fact becomes a figure of terror for Paul: her actions—and even more so her reasons for her actions—frighten him, and he confers on her a version of the label "monster" associated with rebellious women in the classic gothic tale (164), implying in addition that she is animalistic when he tells her that she has two feet rather than four (165).

Following Paul's departure, a "rescue" of Sethe and Denver from the hold that Beloved has over the house and the family does take place, but in a manner that provides a feminist alternative to the rescuing male figure of the traditional gothic. At first, Denver fantasizes that her father, Halle, will return to protect her and her mother (207); Harris points out that her stories resemble "fairy tales, with the passive princess waiting to be rescued" (142). When it becomes clear to Denver, however, that she must take some action to save her mother, it is the ghost of her grandmother, Baby Suggs, who speaks to Denver and urges her to leave the yard (244). Morrison thus again employs the African ancestor tradition to subvert the conventions of the European fairy tale and gothic novel, as well as invoking the matrilineal line as an alternative to the rescuing male hero. The role of women in the rescue continues when Denver, following Baby Suggs' words of encouragement from beyond the grave, takes initiative in appealing to Lady Jones and the other women of the community to provide sustenance for Sethe; in turn, the women's gossip amongst themselves about what is taking place at 124 Bluestone Road and about the presence of Beloved prompts them to intervene by enacting an exorcism of sorts, so that a community of thirty women, along with Denver, ultimately ends Beloved's destructive hold over Sethe and ends the haunting of the house.

By the time Paul D returns, then, there is no role for him as the rescuing male figure, and in his final interactions with Sethe, he feels no need to dominate: he wants to rub her feet rather than to count them (272); and "[h]e wants to put his story next to hers" (273), suggesting equality, rather than to inscribe Sethe in his own story for her, as he did earlier—indeed, as Schoolteacher attempted to do in his white, patriarchal discourse about Sethe. Admiring Sethe for leaving his manhood intact, he has redefined for himself what manhood means and, by extension, has redefined femininity as well, no longer expecting Sethe to conform to a passive feminine ideal. The initial presence of the baby ghost and the novel's opening gothic conventions prompt Paul's initial behavior. The more complicated presence of the young woman Beloved in the novel's fantastic mode serves as a catalyst not only for Paul to unlock his rusted shut tobacco tin—the novel's metaphor for his inability to process the complex emotions associated with his period of enslavement, his time on the chain gang and the sexual abuse he endured, his many years on the run, and the psychological aftermath of these and other trials—but also as a catalyst for him to adopt a masculine identity that does not hinge upon white, patriarchal definitions of manhood. Morrison's revisions of both the classic slave narrative and the gothic tale, then, challenge the domestic ideology of the nineteenth century.

Conclusion

Other novels that employ the fantastic to disrupt the domestic ideology inherent in the gothic tale end by disrupting the heterosexual romance plot— *The Sea, The Sea, Lady Oracle, Housekeeping*. Rewriting the gothic within a specifically racialized context, however, Morrison employs the fantastic to challenge conventions of domesticity and femininity in ways that are not identical to the challenges posed in the novels written by white women. Taken from their original homes in Africa, Morrison's characters see "home" as crucial to their self-definition. They cannot, like Robinson's women, burn down the house and take up a life of transience, since these women's lives have been circumscribed by the transience and homelessness associated with the institution of slavery, both in the displacement that occurred during the slave trade and in the manner in which slaves were sold from one plantation to another, with family units being destroyed by these acts of displacement. *Beloved* devotes a great deal of attention to both of these forms of displacement, and the house at Bluestone Road, in spite of being haunted, is an important symbol of freedom and a locus of self-definition for the characters. At one moment in the novel, for example, Sethe thinks to herself that she can't possibly, at Paul D's urging, simply leave her house because it is haunted, "as though a house was a little thing" (22).[27] Indeed, as Dubey points out, "[...] the ending of *Beloved* achieves the goals typical of the realist novel—the heterosexual union of Sethe and Paul D., the consolidation of the familial unit of father, mother, and daughter, and the reintegration of Sethe with the social world—all three of which were put at risk by Beloved's appearance" (197). Even the paradoxical coda, which in many ways opens the novel up again beyond the moment of closure achieved in the reunion of Sethe and Paul D and the expulsion of Beloved, reminds the reader of Beloved's existence and laments the fact that a culture has forgotten its Beloveds in part to remind the reader of the importance of the nuclear family: she is, after all, insofar as she represents Sethe's murdered daughter, a sister who should rightfully join Denver in the new family constituted in the novel's penultimate chapter. She is a reminder of the strength of Sethe's motherlove.

While Paul D and many critics of the novel argue that Sethe's love is "too thick" (*Beloved* 164), that Sethe needs to achieve individuation from Beloved to achieve full selfhood, O'Reilly argues that Sethe in fact "secures subjectivity through her mothering" (132), and moreover, that her commitment to motherhood constitutes an act of political resistance. That is,

> the nineteenth-century cult of moral motherhood said that women were born with a maternal instinct, which rendered motherhood natural to them. The racial specialization of gender ideology in the nineteenth century precluded black women from this so-called natural law by defining them as breeders and not-mothers. In *Beloved*, Sethe claims the rights and responsibilities accorded to white women under the cult of moral motherhood.
> [...]
> In the sociohistorical context of slavery, a black woman who defines her selfhood through and in her mothering is resisting the ideological construction of the slave mother as breeder [O'Reilly 135–136].

Thus O'Reilly points out that those readers who criticize Sethe's motherlove and assume she cannot achieve selfhood fail to understand "Morrison's maternal stance"—fail to understand that it is "through motherlove [that] one obtains self-love" (138). To read Sethe's racialized experience of motherhood through the lens of dominant, white views of motherhood, a reading which would assert that Sethe is too motherly and hence reinforces cultural constructions of femininity, is to read Sethe in such a way as to erase political differences between social attitudes toward white mothers and black mothers. And such an erasure constitutes a grave disservice to feminist readings of Morrison's work. As Koenen points out, "the reconstitution of the nuclear family at the end of the novel [...] is not an affirmation of cultural hegemony, but its subversion" (123).

Beloved subverts cultural hegemony through its use of the fantastic. For Sethe, the belief that her daughter has come back in the character of Beloved leads to her new-found ability to articulate the story of her motherlove and thereby to combat what O'Reilly calls the construction of the slave as "not-mother." Her actions in the 1855 setting of the novel have in themselves positioned her in contradistinction to the white culture's positioning of her, but never has she told the tale of why she did what she did. Her telling the story in the 1873 setting, adopting the role of feminist historiographer (Henderson) restores that untold story of motherhood under the institution of slavery. The figure of Beloved enables that telling for Sethe and demands by her very nature a story told in a manner that revises received forms and assumptions of the historical novel. The hybrid nature of the novel, its codes of realism and the fantastic, its revisions to the conventional historical novel, invite the reader to reevaluate assumptions about the representation of history itself. Morrison takes up this question again in her next novel, *Paradise*, in which the characters are much more self-conscious historians than the characters in *Beloved*. *Paradise* examines and subverts cultural hegemony through its use of the fantastic as well, this time exploring not only the cultural hegemony of white society but also hegemonic constructions of gender, race, and nationhood within the black community of post–Civil War America.

7

The Gospel According to Consolata: Alternative Christianities and Toni Morrison's Paradise

> If cultures define themselves not at their calm centers, but at their peripheral conflicts of inclusion and exclusion, then Gnosticism, whatever we mean by it, is more than an antiquarian curiosity. It stands as a continuing testament to difference in the face of our cultural tendencies toward closed homogeneity.
> —Richard Smith, *"The Modern Relevance of Gnosticism,"* afterword to The Nag Hammadi Library in English *[549]*

> These heretical women—how audacious they are! They have no modesty; they are bold enough to teach, to engage in argument, to enact exorcisms, to undertake cures, and, it may be, even to baptize!
> —Tertullian, DE PRAESCR. *41, quoted in* Elaine Pagels, The Gnostic Gospels *[60]*

> The Sons of Zebedee, being bolder than the rest, went to Jesus privately and suggested that they, in particular, should be his right-hand men when he came into his Kingdom. But Jesus shook his head with that look of profound sorrow he often had when they spoke to him of their expectations. "No," he insisted, "we must have a different view of the world to come. It must not be a world where one ruler replaces another, but a world where rulers and ruled are no more."
> —Rosemary Radford Ruether, *Feminism and God Talk [5]*

INTRODUCTION

"The Church has four Gospels, but the heretics have many," writes Origen of Alexandria, a third-century theologian.[1] In Toni Morrison's novel *Par-*

adise, the orthodox community of Ruby recognizes four gospels, while the women who inhabit the Convent, considered heretics by many townspeople, engage in spiritual practices that implicitly recognize gospels excluded from the New Testament canon. *Paradise* critiques exclusionary communities on several levels, one of which is by juxtaposing orthodox Christianity with alternative religious traditions. It is in the depictions of these alternative traditions that the novel's fantastic element primarily rests: a supernatural figure appears at the Convent; the character Consolata Sosa undergoes a transformation and receives magical powers; and at the end of *Paradise*, the "heretical" Convent women are brutally slaughtered, but their bodies mysteriously disappear. The women subsequently reappear, both in this world, and in an apparent afterlife realm. While many elements of these fantastical moments can be illuminated by African religious beliefs, they also invoke elements of early Christian traditions. The novel obliquely employs—and critiques—Gnostic theology as part of its project of countering exclusionary communities, an element of *Paradise* that has gone largely unexamined. The novel's epigraph, whose source is not identified by Morrison, is drawn from "Thunder, Perfect Mind," a cryptic Gnostic text discovered at Nag Hammadi that has significant bearing on the novel's feminist challenge to patriarchal traditions.[2] In addition, the later chapters in the novel that focus on Consolata and the various women who seek refuge with her at the Convent resonate with many of the cryptic sayings in the *Gospel of Thomas*, among other Gnostic texts. While many aspects of Gnostic practice and belief are consonant with Morrison's vision, she recasts other aspects—especially Gnosticism's anticosmological stance—in light of African religion and feminist Christianity to suit her own purposes and her own conception of an earthly, inclusive paradise, as captured in the novel's final pages.[3]

The fantastic elements of *Paradise* have received far less critical attention than the fantastic elements of *Beloved* and have generally been confined to complaints about the novel's ending. While *Paradise* employs the fantastic in a more limited way than does Morrison's earlier novel, it nonetheless does so in equally important ways that function similarly to the manner in which the fantastic functions in *Beloved*. Hence it, too, can be fruitfully examined as a novel of the fantastic. Briefly, the fantastic restores alternative versions of history, disrupts racist, patriarchal narrative practices, and privileges a feminist world view through feminist narrative practices. Rather than dealing primarily with slavery and white racial oppression as does *Beloved*, *Paradise* critiques racism practiced by a group of dark-skinned blacks against both whites and blacks with light skin. The novel's fantastic dimension—presented largely through supernatural elements associated with spiritualities other than mainstream Christianity, including Gnosticism, feminist Christianity, and African religion—undermines all forms of hierarchy, be they based on race, class, gender, or religious beliefs. It is not so important whether Morrison herself subscribes to any particular spiritual tradition, although as shown in the chapter on *Beloved*, she has stated that what might be called "magic" inherent in African religion is part of the reality with which she grew up, a form of knowledge that has been discredited in the West (Davis 144).[4] What is important is the manner in which these spiritualities function in the novel to remind the reader of alternative kinds of knowledge and alternative histories, and to subvert the patriarchalism of the dominant versions of Christianity espoused by various characters in *Paradise*. They thus serve an important demythologizing function.[5]

Megan Sweeney, who offers an excellent reading of the novel's alternative Christianity, catalogues numerous objections to the fantastic quality of *Paradise*'s concluding pages, pointing out that "with astonishing frequency, critics and readers alike dismiss this conclusion as 'implausible' and 'contrived'" (56). For example, she cites Adam Mars-Jones' review in *The Observer*: "'If Morrison had resisted the temptation to bring in possession, ghosts and amateur miracles, *Paradise* might have attained the status of masterpiece' (Mars-Jones 2001)." Sweeney notes that while many

> readers view Paradise's fantasy-driven conclusion as "hokey" (Kakutani 1998), other readers charge that the conclusion operates as a palliative, an aestheticized attempt to compensate for the slaughter of women that takes place at the level of the social real. Proponents of this viewpoint argue that Morrison falls back on the relief that the foundational myth of crucifixion and resurrection provides, rather than positing much-needed, real-world possibilities for women's survival and resistance [57].[6]

Like many of the novel's reviewers whom Sweeney cites, critic Elisabeth Jay is likewise unhappy with the novel's fantastic ending: comparing it to Kingsolver's *The Poisonwood Bible*, she writes that it is unfortunate that these novels, among others, "have to resort to an otherworldly voice as a gesture toward a positive final message" (38).

Sweeney, however, dismisses such objections on the grounds that they overlook how "*Paradise* rescripts the foundational myth of Christianity" (57).[7] Taking into account the novel's engagement with Gnosticism as part of this rescripting, something Sweeney does not do, suggests a strong connection between the novel's fantastic devices and the very real history of the early Christian era, especially the process by which various gospels were marginalized when others were canonized, and the resulting historical fact that women's roles in spiritual leadership were vastly diminished during the emergence of orthodox Christianity. *Paradise*'s publication (1998) roughly coincides with scholarly and popular interest in the early Christian period and examination of lost scriptures that present alternative Christianities to orthodox Christianity. The third novel in Morrison's trilogy follows Elaine Pagels' influential work *The Gnostic Gospels* (1979) by nearly two decades; indeed, given that Morrison and Pagels are friends and colleagues at Princeton who spend time together each week,[8] it is not unreasonable to surmise that Pagels' early work on Gnosticism is a source for Morrison in her oblique employment of Gnostic beliefs in *Paradise*. Morrison's novel precedes by just a few years a long list of publications on a host of "lost Christianities," to borrow Bart Ehrman's title.[9] By historicizing and contextualizing Morrison's work amidst scholarly debate on the diversity of early Christianities, we can examine her use of the fantastic to critique the manner in which the concept of paradise always marginalizes or others certain groups, insofar as Gnostic Christianity was marginalized and denounced as heretical by the church that its practices threatened. In addition, fantastic devices in Morrison's novel invoke a tradition of African-American women as spiritual leaders and counter patriarchal practices of the early African-American church that sought to exclude female spiritual leadership. Far from being asocial or simply otherworldly, then, Morrison employs the fantastic to remind the reader of the socio-historical experience of women in various Christian churches, both in late antiquity and modernity. Like the other novels in this book, *Paradise*'s fantastic devices disrupt masculinist narratives—specifically the masculinist narrative of the town of Ruby, which mirrors the narrative of various Christian orthodoxies in its partriarchalism—with feminist narrative strategies.

* * *

In her epigraph to the novel, Morrison employs the final lines of the poem "Thunder, Perfect Mind":

> For many are the pleasant forms which exist in
> numerous sins
> and incontinences,
> and disgraceful passions
> and fleeting pleasures,
> which (men) embrace until they become
> sober
> and go up to their resting place.
> And they will find me there,
> and they will live,
> and they will not die again.[10]

The poem as a whole captures several key tenets of Gnostic thought, though it should be noted that "Gnostic" is a broad term used to categorize under one rubric a wide variety of texts and traditions from the early Christian era, not all of which are Christian—Gnosticism by no means comprises a unified religion. As Kurt Rudolph observes, it is better considered "an historical category" than a religion per se (57). Briefly, Gnosticism teaches that humankind originates from a perfect home called the pleroma but finds itself on an imperfect earth, where humans have forgotten their original, true natures. Salvation comes from gaining insight into the true nature of the self and its capacity for the divine; those who possess this insight, or gnosis, will return, through a difficult journey, to the lost home or paradise.[11] In Christian Gnostic texts, Jesus teaches humanity about its lost nature and offers salvation by restoring insight about humankind's capacity for divinity. The salvific aspects of Gnostic theology differ from those of orthodox Christianity insofar as Jesus does not die on the cross to save humankind from sin; salvation comes rather from his teachings themselves, from the wisdom and knowledge of the self and of God gained therein by those who understand his message. Gnostics differentiated themselves from other Christians, claiming a true understanding of the divine that contrasted with what they viewed as others' blind faith in proto-Orthodox traditions; they rejected the idea that one can achieve salvation merely by professing belief and participating in rites such as baptism sanctioned and administered by the Church.

The "Thunder, Perfect Mind," though not an explicitly Christian text, captures aspects of this rough outline of Gnostic theology. Biblical scholar Bentley Layton describes the entire poem as "a riddlesome monologue spoken by the immanent savior," in this case a female figure, who educates the audience about how she has descended to earth for the purpose of recalling humans to their true nature, to enlighten them (*Gnostic Scriptures* 77). According to Layton, the poem's framework, including the first few lines and the last several lines that Morrison chose for her epigraph, describes the soul becoming trapped "in a disastrous cycle of reincarnations" before being returned to the Gnostic true home, thereby reaching salvation ("Riddle" 41).

Several features of "The Thunder, Perfect Mind" have bearing on Morrison's project in *Paradise*, and this chapter is divided into four parts that expand upon those features. The first section explores how Morrison treats the nature of storytelling in the town of Ruby, drawing parallels between the town's history and the history of the process by which the four New Testament Gospels were canonized, consigning other texts, including Gnostic scriptures such as "the Thunder," to the margins. The second section explores the novel's feminist alternative to the town's patriarchal Christianity, through an examination of Consolta's transformation from Catholic convert to a female divine power (like the speaker of "the Thunder") and spiritual leader of the Convent women whose practices resonate in intriguing ways with Gnosticism. Some of the fantastic elements of the novel are related to Consolata's achieving "insight." The third section focuses on the nature of the paradise that Morrison envisions for the women of the Convent and for Ruby itself, exploring the ways in which this vision explicitly revises the idea of transcendence inherent in both orthodox Christianity and in Gnosticism. Morrison in essence "signifies upon" (to borrow Henry Louis Gates's term) the final line of the epigraph, "And they will live/ and they will not die again," so that the fantastical afterlife realm she creates has strong ties to the earthly real. The novel combines elements of Christian belief with elements of African religious belief. The fourth, concluding section explores the ways in which Morrison's use of the final line in the epigraph, in conjunction with other elements of the novel's closing chapters, suggests that the town of Ruby breaks free from a harmful pattern of repetition without a difference, embracing change and accepting multiplicity in its response to the fantastic disappearance of the Convent women's bodies.

NARRATIVE, CANON FORMATION, AND MARGINALIZATION

Recent research into Gnosticism in the wake of discoveries at Nag Hammadi and elsewhere reveals that early Christian traditions were far more diverse than scholars had previously thought. The very fact of this diversity has bearing on Morrison's *Paradise*, whose project is to counter the intolerance of the Ruby citizens and their narrowly defined Christianity. As Bart Ehrman explains in his work *Lost Christianities*,

> scholars have concluded that there are *numerous* religious perspectives represented in the various Gnostic documents surviving from antiquity and that these perspectives are not always consistent with one another. Probably different documents come from different communities with different worldviews, mythological systems, beliefs, and practices [...]. Rather than one thing, then, the Nag Hammadi library contains numerous things, various perspectives presented in any array of texts including a whole host of lost Christianities. It is impossible to synthesize the views, presuppositions, religious perspectives of these into one monolithic system [115].

In contrast to orthodox Christianity, as Kurt Rudolph points out, "there was no gnostic 'church' or normative theology, no gnostic rule of faith nor any dogma of exclusive importance [...]. There also was no gnostic canon of scripture" (51). That different perspectives—even different versions of texts—existed alongside one another, and that "Gnostic communities evidently did not lay any claims to exclusiveness against one another" testifies to Gnosticism's "tolerant position" (Rudolph 51), an aspect of this world view prominent in late antiquity that would surely hold appeal for Morrison. Yet through the fourth and fifth centuries, the varieties of Christianities, Judaisms, and other traditions that flourished in the early Christian period were marginalized through the process of canonization of the current four New Testament gospels and the religious perspectives embodied therein that became orthodox Christianity. The details by which this process took place, and the details of the resulting beliefs and practices that came to constitute the orthodox Church, are beyond the scope of this chapter.[12] Among the resulting effects of this process, however, were the severe diminishment of women's leadership roles within the Christian faith, the establishment of clear lines of authority and a strict hierarchy in the administration of Christian rites, and the ongoing oppression of other religious groups that did not embrace the one true Christian God, effects that are all captured in Morrison's depiction in *Paradise* of the Ruby Christian patriarchs and countered in her depiction of the spiritual practices that take place in the Convent.

Significantly, the Convent is located on the outskirts of the Ruby community, and the town itself, which vehemently rejects diversity and resists any challenges to what it considers orthodox Christianity, is laid out along Central Avenue, suggestive of its centralized vision that excludes anything on the margins, with side streets to the west named for the four canonical New Testament Gospels.[13] When a new street is needed, the townspeople name it St. Peter, in keeping with Peter's role as the lead apostle and head of what became the Orthodox Church. And when still more streets are needed, the community builds continuations of the older ones to the east of Central Avenue and simply names the newer side streets "Cross John," "Cross Luke," "Cross Matthew," and "Cross Mark" (*Paradise* 114), both reinforcing the centrality of these four gospels and emphasizing the importance of the cross to orthodox Christian theology, a point of contention in Gnostic theology.[14] The very process by which the New Testament that we know today and has come to be accepted as *the* gospel through the exclusion of other Christianities is mirrored in *Paradise* by the manner in which the story of the foundings of Haven and Ruby has become the town's own gospel, a story which forcibly excludes other stories, other versions of spirituality, and even various of the founding families themselves who do not abide by the strict practices established by the town. Thus Gnosticism provides an apt backdrop to Morrison's novel, whose project is precisely to expose and counter "cultural tendencies toward closed homogeneity" (Smith 549), to offer a vision of paradise that is heterogeneous—accepting of a wide variety of religious traditions and historical backgrounds, inclusive of peoples of all different races and social classes, and non-discriminatory on the basis of gender.

The town of Ruby is a replica of an earlier all-black town, Haven, founded in the late nineteenth century as part of the Exoduster movement. The term "Exodusters" itself suggests the Biblical exodus and the religious foundations of the movement—African Americans moving west to establish their own communities considered themselves God's chosen people, on a mission to settle a new promised land, much like the founding fathers of America itself. Generally, slaves and former slaves in the nineteenth century "interpreted the Bible in a unique fashion, making it immediate, a living part of their sense of historical and mythic experiences. The battles and victories of the Old Testament could be reenacted in their time" (Taylor-Guthrie 128). The African Americans' sense of themselves as being morally superior to the Europeans is exaggerated in Morrison's portrayal of Haven's founding fathers: when the founders of Haven are cast away from an all-black community because the Haven group

7—The Gospel According to Consolata

is darker skinned than the group from which they seek assistance, those in the Haven group, and later in Ruby, decide to celebrate their coal-blackness and to isolate themselves not only from whites but also from lighter-skinned blacks. The original exclusion of the group of founding families comes to be known as the "disallowing." When in the 1950s townspeople sense that the white world is encroaching too much on the town of Haven, and when they experience a second version of the disallowing in prejudice against African Americans who fought in World War II, they move the town to a more remote location and rename it Ruby.

Over and over again, Morrison's readers hear the story of the founding(s) of Haven and Ruby, usually from the perspective of the two most powerful Ruby men, Deacon and Steward Morgan. Morrison writes that in hearing tales of the community's history, "They listened to, imagined, and remembered every single thing" (16); "between them, they remember everything that ever happened—things they witnessed and things they have not" (13). Collapsing memory and imagination, Morrison comments upon the power of stories to shape one's conception of reality: the twins have their world view cemented in particular and narrow ways through repeated tellings of the story of Haven's founding, a story termed the "controlling one" (13), heard "time after time" (15). Early on in the novel, we read that the Morgan brothers, through "stories told and retold," understand "how narrow [was] the path of righteousness" (14).

This sense of righteousness, as well as the tendency of the town elders to turn unreliable memory into fact, is captured well in the vehement arguments that take place between the older and younger generations who interpret the inscription on the Oven, a huge brick structure that serves as a community gathering place and a monument to their achievements. Constructed in Haven, it was moved brick by brick to Ruby, but in the process, the first word in the inscription was obscured. Nonetheless, the older generation insists that the inscription reads "Beware the Furrow of his Brow," a statement that implies a warning to those who enacted the Disallowing(s). In spite of the fact that the only surviving witness to the original inscription was a small child at the time whose memory the novel paints as unreliable, this interpretation of the Oven's motto has become gospel truth. This process is a commentary on the larger story of Haven/Ruby that in turn mirrors the way that the canonical gospels came to be the controlling Christian stories. In one key example of an act of erasure of a discrepant version, we see that in Petrine Christianity, Peter is considered the first witness to Christ's resurrection in spite of the fact that many alternative gospels and two of the canonical New Testament gospels themselves name Mary Magdalene as the first witness (a point explored in more detail later in this chapter.)

Similar to the way a patriarchal, Petrine Christianity came to dominate the Christian story, Deacon and Steward's ancestors, Big Papa and Big Daddy, figure centrally in the story the two brothers tell and retell, and as these names suggest, their history is a strongly patriarchal one. In order to preserve pure bloodlines in the town and to preserve what comes to be known as the "8- rock" skin tone, the town patriarchs control relationships in the town, casting out those who marry outside the community and "taint" that community with lighter-skinned blood, a practice whose chief side-effect is the oppression of the townswomen. In one rumination, for example, we hear of the Morgan brothers trying to control the "shape" of their nephew K. D.'s offspring, since their family line constitutes the true family line, given than Deacon and Steward have followed in the footsteps of Big Daddy and Big Papa by creating Ruby in the image of Haven (113). This passage anticipates what the character Patricia Best later discovers in her attempt at a town genealogy: her father has been ostracized because he did not follow the terms of the 8-rock blood rule tacitly embraced but never explicitly acknowledged in the town (195). She also recalls that another Rubyite, Menus, has been forced to turn his back on the woman he intended to marry because she has lighter skin and hair color than the 8-rocks. Observing the strange and comical conflation of the Exodus story and the story of Jesus's birth portrayed in the town's annual Christmas pageant, Pat observes that the number of holy families on the stage, meant to reflect the number of families who founded Haven/Ruby, has diminished from nine to seven since two families have been outcast from their privileged position because they violated the blood rule. Pat concludes her narrative, in which she traces tangled blood lines and realizes the amount of inbreeding that has probably taken place in the town, by reflecting upon the "deal" that the town has struck with God: as long as the founding families maintain the purity of the 8-rock blood and as long as that blood remains in the claustrophobic community of Ruby, then no one in the community will die. Pat realizes, then, that the men concern themselves with the women's sexual behavior (217). As Pat's daughter Billie Delia puts it when a disagreement arises in the town about the marriage between K. D. Morgan and Arnette Fleetwood, "the stallions were fighting about who controlled the mares and their foals" (150).[15]

Morrison makes clear that the town's oppression of women, evidenced everywhere in the novel, is linked to the normative Christian practices of the townspeople, stemming ultimately from a literal interpretation of New Testament scriptures about the role of women. For example, Karen King points out that passages from the Bible traditionally used "to silence women's voices [...] are supplemented by appeal to the patriarchal household codes (Ephesians 5:22–24; Colossians 3:18; 1 Peter 3:1–6)" ("Afterword: Voices of the Spirit" 336). Biblical passages that urge women's servility are extended in *Paradise* to include descriptions of housekeeping codes as well: for example, Morrison writes that Deacon, driving along Central Avenue, is pleased to see the industry and orderliness practiced by the women in the houses (111). The Convent women, in contrast, fail to meet these housekeeping codes; their messiness and

7—The Gospel According to Consolata 155

disorder is stressed throughout the novel's prologue when the townsmen enter the Convent just prior to the slaughter. Their justification for attacking the Convent includes a list of accusations against the women that recall not only accusations against women in Puritan times during the Salem witch trials, but also accusations leveled against the Gnostics by proto-orthodox Christians about homosexuality and licentious behavior and "no telling what else" (*Paradise* 275–276; cf. Ehrmans 190), all rooted essentially in the townsmen's perception of the women's godlessness. Thus when the men "take aim. For Ruby" at the Convent women, they do so with "God at their side" (18).

Morrison's descriptions of the attack on the Convent illustrate a strategy that Anne Hegerfeldt associates with magic realism, whereby "a rhetoric of banality is used [...] to characterize events of war or cruelty" as being themselves unbelievable, more unreal than fantastic events, even when neither character or narrator calls attention to this fact. Hegerfeldt writes, "[i]nappropriate to the subject matter, a rhetoric of banality highlights the absurd, nonsensical, fantastic nature of reality" (209). Examples of such rhetoric abound in *Paradise*'s prologue, from the statement about the men having "God at their side" (18) to the "chill" that they feel from the "female malice" that accompanies the "yeast-and-butter smell of rising dough" (4). The initial description of their entrance into the Convent states matter-of-factly that "they are nine, over twice the number of the women they are obliged to stampede or kill and they have the paraphernalia for either requirement: rope, a palm leaf cross, handcuffs, Mace and sunglasses, along with clean, handsome guns" (3). The incongruity of this description—the ironic uses of the words "obliged" and "requirement," the inclusion of a palm leaf cross and sunglasses in the list of "requirements" for the mission, the glaring mathematical error that the astute reader will notice at once, since there are five women and nine is not "over twice" five—calls attention to the fact that this act of brutality is more fantastic than the threatening supernatural powers the men are reacting against.[16] The slaughter itself becomes, or at least ought to be, more "unreal" than the mysterious disappearance of the murdered women's bodies. This narrative stance, typical of the magic realist text that by definition "install[s] the realist mode" (209) puts in tension the horrific occurrence and the realist text's assumptions about humanist values, laying bare the failure to adhere to ethical values at the same time that it insists on their necessity (Hegerfeldt 208–209).

In addition, the feminist narrative strategies employed in *Paradise* further lay bare the assumptions of realism that support patriarchy in favor of a narrative form that supports alternative points of view. The very arrangement of narrative information within the novel itself "breaks the sequence" (DuPlessis) of the linear, teleological narrative of the town patriarchs, a narrative that the reader can recognize as embracing such a form despite the fact that it is not presented in a linear, teleological fashion. Rosemary Jackson observes of fantastic feminist writing, "linear narrative (realism, illusionism, transparent representation) is broken or dissolved" (186, n. 10). Morrison's novel as a whole counters the linear narrative practices of the town patriarchs and defies the monological world view that they embrace. Not only does *Paradise*, like most of Morrison's fiction, fracture chronology by shifting rapidly from the novel's present time frame (roughly 1968–1976) to the complicated history of Haven/Ruby's founding, a narrative which is itself fractured and emerges only piecemeal through several different tellings, but the novel also interweaves the stories of the townspeople in the present and past with the stories of the women who seek refuge at the Convent. Connie has been living at the convent the longest, since she was nine years old, but her history is deferred through much of the novel, being presented as the last of the five narratives about the women. And though most of the novel's chapters are named for the five women, often the information about the title character is buried within the chapter and told in elliptical fashion, interspersed with narratives about the townspeople. Finally, the real story of the disallowing—its basis in race, in lighter-skinned blacks ostracizing darker-skinned blacks and the resulting reverse discrimination in Ruby against those who don't have the 8-rock skin tone—is withheld until late in the narrative, the disallowing being originally couched in terms of class: those who constitute the Haven group don't have enough resources to be welcomed in the Exoduster town they first approach.[17]

As DuPlessis observes, drawing on Virginia Woolf's *A Room of One's Own*, a key means by which feminist writers disrupt patriarchal narratives is by breaking the sequence, thus creating a "rupture in habits of narrative order" (34). For Woolf and DuPlessis, this narrative order includes the usual ending for women in the nineteenth-century novel—marriage—or, should a woman character transgress social norms and refuse marriage, then death. Yet as DuPlessis points out, "breaking the sequence can mean delegitimating the specific narrative and cultural orders of nineteenth-century fiction—the emphasis on successful or failed romance, the subordination of quest to love, the death of the questing female, the insertion into family life" (34–35). In *Paradise*, this conception of breaking the sequence through the non-linear narrative form employed is played out thematically as well as formally in the narratives of the Convent women, all of which portray failed heterosexual relationships in the women's pasts and many of which critique violence and patriarchal domination that characterize these relationships. For example, Mavis's husband abuses her, K. D. uses Gigi for sexual purposes, Pallas has been raped, and Deacon exhibits unspoken fears of Connie's strong sexuality that eventually lead him to abandon her. All these narratives eventually, however, subordinate failed romance to the women's quest for knowledge of self and spiritual wholeness, with Connie as their guide. Embedded as they are amidst the stories of marriage in Ruby, which on the surface seem to conform to reigning ideology about male-female relationships within marriage and the willing and happy subordination of the women characters to the men (and as such are consonant

7—The Gospel According to Consolata

with the way that scriptures have been interpreted in patriarchal terms), the narratives about the Convent women also reveal the underside of the love plot in the Ruby community. Indeed, the townsmen who carry out the attack on the Convent justify their actions not only through their belief that the Convent women assume that they "don't need God," but also through their belief that the women think they "don't need men" (276).

Moreover, the narrative breaks the sequence by challenging the traditional novel's ending of death for transgressive women who do not subscribe to the traditional marriage plot: the fantastic nature of *Paradise*'s conclusion allows Morrison to "write beyond the ending" in more ways than one. The afterlife realm that she depicts counters not only the women's brutal murder by men, but it counters also the reinsertion of the women into family life, as DuPlessis suggests is typical of traditional narrative, since it shows the murdered women interacting with their families only briefly. The novel ends instead with the women pursuing their quest and taking solace in each other's company as they work to enact social change. As Koenen observes in her work on women's fantastic narratives, such stories overturn the conventional marriage plot in favor of "plots of power" (52–57).

In spite of the fact that information about the women characters is sometimes buried within a chapter, nonetheless that all the novel's chapters are named for women (both Convent women and townswomen) underlines what Judylyn Ryan identifies as "a *democracy of narrative participation* that enables a more expansive presentation of characters who would otherwise be considered 'marginal,' endows them with their full human complexity, and allows them to occupy the narrative foreground" (*Spirituality as Ideology* 18). The various women's stories that emerge through the novel's use of free indirect discourse, coupled with the formation of a female spiritual community in the "Consolata" chapter informed by African spiritual practices, emphasize the interconnectedness that Ryan sees as characteristic of recent African American women writers' narratives. The community that emerges in the Convent recalls DuPlessis's observation that late twentieth-century women's writing employs a "collective protagonist" in fictions that "replace individual heroes or sealed couples with groups, which have a sense of purpose and identity, and whose growth occurs in mutual collaboration" (179).[18] Thus, in spite of the recurrence of the patriarchal narrative of Ruby/Haven's past focalized through either Deacon or Steward (for example, see pages 13–17, 95–99, and 108–110), in fact the majority of the novel is focalized through the perspectives of the women characters marginalized by the patriarchal narrative. As Lanser observes of *Beloved* with its similar use of the authorial voice and free indirect discourse, such a narrative strategy "can be a powerful tool for dislodging an existing authority" (278). Similarly, the novel employs the fantastic to restore voice and visibility to feminist Christian texts marginalized by dominant interpretations of the gospels.

Given the complexity of *Paradise*'s narrative form itself, Morrison's choice of the epigraph from "The Thunder, Perfect Mind," which first signals to the reader the novel's engagement with Gnosticism as an alternative to orthodox Christianity, is apropos. For the form of this mysterious piece of writing, which Layton terms the "most bizarre of all works from the Nag Hammadi corpus" ("Riddle" 38; *Paradise* might be said to be the most bizarre and difficult novel in Morrison's corpus), mirrors both Morrison's narrative technique and her meditation on the nature of paradise as a realm where many different traditions coexist, where exclusionary practices don't determine who can enter paradise. According to Layton, "The Thunder, Perfect Mind" (or "Thunder, Perfect Intellect" in his translation) combines three distinct literary forms — the Isis/Wisdom proclamation, the philosophical sermon, and the riddle — forms that are not normally employed in conjunction with one another (44).[19] The text's pastiche nature and defiance of normative literary classifications would naturally appeal to Morrison, who, within the postmodern narrative of *Paradise*, combines many literary modes, including the historical novel, myth, the fantastic, and various sermons, rendering her work difficult to classify according to conventional genre categories. In addition, as Layton points out, the third of the modes incorporated in the *Thunder* — the riddle — constitutes an "occasion for rethinking the sense of what seems obviously impossible, a time for a shift in perspective, a search for a deeper meaning." He goes on to explain how a riddle demands to be reread even after it is solved, and he compares "the hermeneutic of riddles" with Gnostic practices of rereading scriptures. This practice of reinterpretation within Gnosticism has the effect of "lead[ing] the reader into a new relationship with" texts ("Riddle" 44), in stark contrast to the practices of the town elders whose history has become "a closed book, not a text to be rewritten — or, for that matter, reinterpreted — with each generation" (Davidson 361). Morrison's project in *Paradise* — in which even the plot is notoriously difficult to piece together, in which characters are so numerous and their relationships to one another so difficult to untangle that many readers become frustrated, and in which allusions abound and symbols intersect in complicated patterns — is precisely to encourage the type of active reading and reinterpretation that Layton describes.

Indeed, the method of exegesis of older texts practiced by Gnostic Christians, which Rudolph terms "a 'protest exegesis' in so far as it runs counter to the external text and the traditional interpretation" (54), also counters the method of exegesis practiced by African Americans who reinterpreted their own enslavement in light of the Israelites' experience in the Old Testament, which, as critics writing about Morrison's critique of jeremiad rhetoric illustrate, repeats rather than transforms the way the Puritans interpreted the original Biblical texts. For example, Romero points out, "although originally framed in opposition to mainstream American principles of exclusion, violence, and oppression of the non-exceptionalist 'Other,' the black national community's sense of 'peoplehood' is symbolically predicated on similar principles. The Exodusters' all-black towns historically repeat these symbolic exclusions and oppressions" (422).[20] In contrast, Morrison both implicitly invokes Gnostic exegesis of Biblical texts as a "protest exegesis" to normative Christian interpretations of the Bible and performs her own act of exegesis on Gnostic texts to transform them for her own inclusive purposes. That is, Morrison in effect blends Gnosticism and Afro-American spirituality, both already syncretistic religions that incorporate many traditions, an element of *Paradise* that readers see in her treatment of two key spiritual women characters, Consolata Sosa and Lone DuPres, who are the chief means by which we encounter the fantastic in this novel.

TWINSHIP WITH JESUS: CONSOLATA AS SPIRITUAL LEADER

Countering practices that subjugate women and are justified by particular interpretations of the Bible held by Steward Morgan and his followers, the women at the Convent engage in alternative spiritual practices, many of which seem to be based on ideas expressed in the Gnostic gospels about insight into self as a way to achieve knowledge of God, about the role of women in spiritual leadership, and about the ability to achieve spiritual salvation outside of organized religion. Some scholars champion what they see as Gnosticism's feminist alternative to patriarchal practices associated with the emerging Orthodox Church. Elaine Pagels' work, for example, stresses greater opportunities for women in Gnostic thought and practice, opportunities which the Orthodox Church discouraged for socio-political reasons (*Gnostic Gospels* 60–69). Karen King argues that *The Gospel of Mary* "presents the most straightforward and convincing argument in any early Christian writing for the legitimacy of women's leadership" (3).[21] And Rosemary Radford Ruether, in her book on feminist theology, acknowledges that in some forms of Gnosticism, "woman, far from being scapegoated for sin, was given a privileged relation to the divine Sophia who mediated redemptive revelation. In the person of Mary Magdalene and other early female disciples of Christ, women's apostolic authority was defended in Gnostic Gospels, in contrast to Petrine Christianity" (34–35). *Paradise* explores precisely the Ruby townsmen's desire to scapegoat the Convent women for misfortunes taking place in Ruby: in the initial description of their attack on the Convent, the men agree that all the strange things happening in their community are somehow linked with the Convent and "those women" (11), women later referred to as "black bodacious Eves unredeemed by Mary" (18). Gnosticism's role for women, then, would have appeal in the time frame of the novel, its present moment coinciding with the women's movement. Indeed, one of the women in the town, Anna Flood, even refers to God as "her" at one point (159), in keeping with the alternative feminist spirituality practiced at the Convent, as well as with the female divine power who speaks "the Thunder, Perfect Mind."

In the late chapters of the novel, Consolata offers spiritual guidance to the four troubled women who have found sanctuary in the Convent, and these chapters—"Consolata," "Lone," and "Save-Marie"—reinforce the novel's engagement with Gnosticism that is first raised by the epigraph itself, in addition to introducing elements of African religion and Afro-Christianity, all of which provide alternatives to orthodox Christianity. These chapters also contain most of the novel's fantastic devices, which, through their engagement with the Gnostic world view and an Afro-centric world view, remind the reader of alternative realities and reveal the constructedness of the dominant Christian narrative. The story of how Consolata becomes a female divine figure is a complicated one, but elements of the Gnostic conception of the relationship between Jesus and humankind illuminate Consolata's transformation from Catholic convert to a spiritual leader whose practices depart significantly from Catholicism. Of central importance here is Connie's affair with Deacon Morgan and the treatment of Deacon as a Christ figure, an element of the "Consolata" chapter infrequently analyzed by the novels' critics. The affair, which begins shortly after the founding of Ruby, roughly twenty years prior to the end of the novel, is described in a highly elliptical way, rendering this part of the "Consolata" chapter one of the most puzzling sections of the novel.

Deacon is an unlikely Christ figure to be sure: for the bulk of the novel, he exhibits the same racist, patriarchal values as his brother Steward, but during the section of the "Consolata" chapter that treats the affair, he is differentiated from Steward—a difference later accentuated in the novel's close—and is in fact given attributes that recall the Gnostic Jesus. Consolata refers to Deacon throughout the description of the affair as her "living man," echoing the Gnostic term "the living Jesus," a connection made most explicit when Connie believes she sees Deacon pulling up in his truck (she is in fact mistaken—it is Steward) and thinks of the person at the wheel as both "my Jesus" and "the living man" (235).[22] A description of God becoming incarnate in Christ and a reference to him as the "living God" is followed by the statement that Connie's many years of devotion "cracked like a pullet's egg when she met the living man" (225). In many ways, Connie's departure from the Catholicism with which she was raised recalls the differences between an orthodox, normative Christian view of Christ "as God's manifestation on earth [who] wholly transcends human modes of thought and experience" with the Gnostic view of "seeing Jesus as if he were simply 'one of us'" (Pagels, *Beyond Belief,* 146–147). At the same time that she begins to see Deacon in the town and that he begins to seek her out at the Convent, the Convent school is in the process of being shut down by the state, another sign of the passing of the Catholicism practiced by Mary Magna as Connie's primary spiritual influence and the growth of some other spirituality within her. The Convent, already having shifted from an embezzler's mansion filled with erotica to the nuns' school for orphaned girls, will now shift again, becoming a place where a new brand of spiritualism is practiced, captured in the descriptions of Consolata's interactions with the four troubled women who make their home there. Unlike Mary Magna and the other nuns, who want to obliterate the practices of the native American girls by converting them to Catholicism and redeeming them through knowledge of the only true God (227), Consolata's home for women will offer the chance for redemption in more inclusive, less imperial ways.

Connie's ensuing relationship with Deacon is described in terms that blend sensuality with religious imagery.[23] Her love for Deacon, expressed in an intensely sexual affair, is described as having an "edible quality" (228) and takes on characteristics of the Eucharist when during one of their encounters Connie bites Deacon's lip and licks the blood, thinking of herself as "a woman bent on eating him like a meal" (239). At this point, Deacon, seemingly threatened by Connie's strong sexuality, ends their relationship.[24] Mourning her loss, Connie wants to tell Mary Magna "he and I are the same" (241). This line echoes Gnostic teachings fairly explicitly and bears a striking resemblance to lines from the *Gospel of Thomas*, when Thomas himself becomes like the living Jesus, stating that Jesus revealed to him, "He who will drink from my mouth will become like me. I myself shall become he, and the things that are hidden will be revealed to him" (*Gospel of Thomas* 108, Robinson 137). Consolata has literally drunk from her living Jesus's mouth, has become that person insofar as she, too, gains mysterious spiritual powers—"he and I are the same"—and has had formerly hidden things revealed to her. As Elaine Pagels points out, Thomas's "name means 'twin.' By encountering the 'living Jesus,' as Thomas suggests, one may come to recognize oneself and Jesus as, so to speak, identical twins" (*Beyond Belief* 57; see also Pagels' *Gnostic Gospels* 18–19; 131). Because Deacon is an identical twin, the idea of twinship is incorporated in the novel, though the "twinship" referenced in Connie's "sameness" with Deacon as a Jesus figure is not a form of destructive repetition but the innate spiritual capacity in all humans used ultimately for their salvation from ignorance.

The fantastic powers that Connie receives from her interaction with Deacon include the ability to revive Soane and Deacon Morgan's son Scout after a fatal car crash and to prolong Mary Magna's life long past the point that she should have died. Raised Catholic by Mary Magna, Connie believes her powers to be alien and sinful, but Lone, a woman from Ruby who practices folk medicine and spiritual healing, urges Connie to accept and use them. While Lone calls Connie's ability to raise the dead "stepping in" (247), Connie, who has been struck blind when she identifies herself and Deacon as "the same" (241), renames her powers and calls them "'seeing in.' Thus the gift was 'in sight,'" a gift that increases steadily as Connie's eye sight deteriorates (247).

Elaine Pagels notes that "as the gnostics use the term [gnosis], we could translate it as 'insight,' for *gnosis* involves an intuitive process of knowing oneself [...]. Yet to know oneself, at the deepest level, is simultaneously to know God; this is the secret of *gnosis*" (*Gnostic Gospels* xix; see also 124). Christian Gnostics achieve gnosis through understanding the teachings of the living Jesus.

Plagued with guilt and reluctant to act in ways that violate Mary Magna's teachings, Connie does not fully appreciate her twinship with Jesus at the moment that she is "spoken to" (241). This process takes many years; her ultimate transformation does not occur until January, 1976, in a puzzling passage in the novel that further draws on the idea of twinship and also lends support to a Gnostic reading of Consolata's spiritual awakening/rebirth. At that time, a mysterious stranger, a seemingly supernatural figure, appears to Connie and seems to think that she should know him, though she claims not to. His cryptic responses to Consolata's queries about his identity recall Jesus's responses to disciples' queries about his identity in *The Book of Thomas*.[25] At first, his features are masked by shadow and by his cowboy hat and reflective-type sunglasses, but later, as he moves very close to her and removes his hat and glasses, she sees that he has long "tea-colored hair" and eyes "as round and green as new apples" (252). Connie herself is described as wearing aviator-style sunglasses (43) and as having green (emerald) eyes and tea-colored hair (223). Descriptions of the man's hair (252) echo descriptions of Connie's hair when the reader first meets her in the "Mavis" chapter (38–9). It is almost as if this mysterious man is Connie herself—like she says of Deacon, she and he are the same—and also a spiritual guide, another manifestation of the living Jesus.[26] This fantastic figure who appears to Connie recalls the Gnostic belief that for one to achieve gnosis, "the intervention of a celestial mediator is required. He descends from above to call the Gnostic, to rouse him from earthly sleep and drunkenness to take him back to his divine homeland" (Filoramo 40).

For many years, Consolata has led an existence characterized by lots of sleeping and drinking. She is, of course, also blind. In Gnostic scriptures (see especially *The Gospel of Truth* and *The Gospel of Thomas*), those who do not recognize their own potential are referred to as being sleepy, blind, and drunk—in essence "unconscious" of their true natures (Pagels *Gnostic Gospels* 126). Says Thomas at one point, for example, "Jesus said, I took my place in the midst of the world, and I appeared to them in flesh. I found all of them intoxicated. [...] When they shake off their wine, then they will repent" (*Gospel of Thomas* 28, Robinson 130). Likewise, the epigraph from "Thunder, Perfect Mind" speaks of becoming "sober." Thus immediately after the mysterious stranger appears, the seeming representation of Connie's inner self and spirituality, Connie "shakes off her wine"—literally the wine stored in the Convent's basement—wakes up, becomes sober, and works purposefully to prepare a meal for the Convent women. She transforms from Connie to Consolata and,

7—The Gospel According to Consolata 163

having also undergone a mysterious physical transformation that makes her almost unrecognizable to her companions, she addresses them as a spiritual leader: "'I call myself Consolata Sosa. [...] And I will teach you what you are hungry for" (262).[27] Connie seems finally to have gained full insight, to be willing to develop the "something [that] God made free to anyone who wanted to develop it" (*Paradise* 247), to fulfill her capacity to become Jesus's twin, and to take on the role of spiritual counselor for others.

For Gnostic Christians, achieving insight or gnosis meant understanding the divine potential within the self, recognizing how humankind has fallen away from its original state and been tempted by worldly pleasures. For Morrison, the process of insight involves understanding not that the world itself is a fallen place but understanding the social circumstances that have led people away from their ideal natures and alienated them from themselves. Connie helps others achieve insight into their circumstances so that they may come to terms with the various traumas they have faced, which, as the women's histories make clear, stem from racism, classism, and sexism. Unlike the townspeople, the women represent racial and class diversity. The novel's opening line identifies one of them as white, but Morrison makes it impossible to identify which one, in effect discounting race as an essentialist marker of identity and confounding racial stereotypes. Mavis, who flees an abusive husband and misunderstanding by the press in the wake of a tragic accident in which her twin infants suffocate in a hot car, is the first to arrive at the Convent. Gigi, whose father is on death row and who has been recently traumatized in race riots in Los Angeles where she witnessed a young black boy killed, arrives next. They are joined some years later by Seneca, a young woman abandoned in childhood by her mother and used recently as a sex slave by an older woman; when she arrives at the Convent, she has been engaging in acts of self-mutilation, having internalized the abusive treatment she has received. Finally, Pallas, a young, wealthy girl whose class status stands in contrast to that of the other women, arrives at the Convent pregnant, either by a rapist in a recent attack on her by a dark lake that is the source of her immediate trauma, or by her boyfriend Carlos, whom Pallas's own mother has stolen away from her.

Consolata's experience and her teachings for the women in the Convent resemble many of the cryptic sayings of Jesus reported in the *Gospel of Thomas*. Paraphrasing this gospel, Pagels points out that "when the disciples asked Jesus to show them where he was so that they might reach that place as well, he refused, directing them instead to themselves, to discover the resources hidden within" (*Gnostic Gospels* 131). Pagels describes Jesus as one who, "instead of coming to save us from sin, [...] comes as a guide who opens access to spiritual understanding" (*Gnostic Gospels* xx), much like Consolata does for the women toward the end of *Paradise*. In one key example, Seneca leads Pallas to Connie when Pallas has just arrived at the Convent after being sexually assaulted, and on the way to see Connie finds herself comforted by the thought. In the atmosphere of the Convent's "blessed malelessness," Pallas feels "[a]s though she might meet herself here—an unbridled, authentic self" (177). This passage suggests the relationship between Connie's healing powers and the Gnostic theology of insight, of knowing one's true self, set in the social context of a female-centered community that does not exclude men but that does provide a safe space for refugees from sexual violence.[28]

Later, Consolata draws a template of each woman on the floor on which each one lies down. Just as Consolata struggled to overcome inertia in her own transformation, so too the women "wriggled in acute distress" on these templates "but were reluctant to move outside the mold they had chosen" (263). Their struggles reflect the distress that Jesus tells Thomas seekers will encounter in the process of self-discovery leading to enlightenment (*Gospel of Thomas* 2, Robinson 126). At Pallas's urging, the women transform these mere outlines into works of art. Their drawings help them express their pain to one another and to begin to heal from it, each one revisiting her traumatic past and communicating about it through her art, creating original and individualized representations of the self that help the women achieve self-knowledge or insight. The women also participate in a process called "loud dreaming" (264) in which they seem to step into one another's memories and gain insight into their companions as well as to themselves, offering one another support in the process so that they can let go of past wounds. The spiritual fellowship that takes place among the women—who earlier in the novel have engaged in many petty battles with each other—resembles the Gnostic idea that what characterizes a "true church" is not adherence to particular tenets or the relationship to authority figures in the church hierarchy, but the fellowship of the members (Pagels, *Gnostic Gospels* 106–107).

The spiritual nature of Connie's teachings thus differs significantly not only from the orthodox Christianity practiced in the town, but also from the imperial efforts of the nuns to make the Indian girls forget their histories. During the ceremonies, "with Consolata in charge, like a new and revised Reverend Mother, [...] they altered" (265), becoming, in contrast to the citizens of Ruby, no longer mired in the past but able to grow and heal from their joint remembrances of past traumas. At the Convent, the nuns instruct "stilled Arapaho girls" in the art of forgetting their cultural heritage (4); in contrast, Consolata's teachings involve the active participation of the women in the learning process and are based on memory rather than forgetting, in keeping with the Gnostic idea that the human race needs to be summoned to the memory of its true nature. The women's ultimate release comes during the women's dance in the rain just prior to their slaughter, a ceremony that recalls Pagels' descriptions of the Gnostic practice of a second baptism (*apulotrosis*) that takes place when one achieves *gnosis*, a ceremony that takes many different forms. The Greek term translates as "redemption" or "release" (Pagels, *Beyond Belief* 140), which in essence characterizes the experience of the women at this moment, each of whom experiences a release from the particular trauma that has led her to seek refuge in the Convent (283).

It is important to note that Consolata, in her role as spiritual leader, is a "facilitator" rather than one in power over others, as Michael argues in her examination of community and coalition building in *Paradise* (654). In a similar vein, Sweeney writes that while Connie "takes charge of the redemption rituals, the other women fully participate in, and negotiate, the collective process of healing" (58). Connie's role is in keeping with the Gnostic conception that one does not need to look to authority for salvation and in the emphasis on the possibility of equality with Jesus. According to Pagels' reading of *The Gospel of Thomas*, once one recognizes this equality with Jesus, one no longer has need for an authority figure for spiritual guidance (*Gnostic Gospels* 131); in fact, in Gnostic thinking, one is "no longer a Christian but a Christ" (*Gospel of Philip* 67, Robinson 150; see also Pagels, *Gnostic Gospels* 134). This model stands in stark contrast to the town fathers' conception of God and the authority of the church. Indeed, according to Pagels, one reason that Gnosticism was perceived as threatening and denounced as heretical in early Christian times rested in its lack of organization: "the structure of authority can never be fixed into an institutional framework: it must remain spontaneous, charismatic, and open" (*Gnostic Gospels* 25). In this respect, the unorganized spirituality practiced at the Convent challenges the organized religion of the town and counters the negative effects of Ruby's authoritarianism.

Morrison's Earthly Paradise: Revising Gnostic Transcendence

Even as Morrison draws on Gnostic teachings and suggests the analogy that Gnosticism is to orthodox Christianity as the Convent women's spirituality is to the town's patriarchal Christianity, she also revises a central tenet of Gnostic thought: its emphasis on transcendence of the earthly and the concomitant dualism of spirit and matter. Her revision is captured in two related aspects of the Convent women's spirituality. First, Consolata's teachings explicitly critique a Gnostic world view that castigates the material realm and creates a binary opposition between spiritual and material reality; and second, the Convent women's "resurrection" after their deaths counters the Gnostic view of an afterlife as a realm wholly transcendent and other than the earthly realm. In both of these elements, Morrison draws on religious ideas that are more African than Western, and that also resonate with elements of feminist Christianity. She synthesizes aspects of different religious traditions in an implicit gesture toward a world view broader than that held by the Christian patriarchs of Ruby and by the Catholic Mary Magna, than that held by those historical figures who shaped the New Testament, and than that held by even Gnostics themselves, who sometimes labeled orthodox Christians "heretics" and whom some scholars consider elitist in their insistence on their own specialized understanding of Christian theology.[29] By revising Gnostic theology even as she draws upon it, Morrison, in essence, repeats with a difference or signifies upon older texts, thus countering her characters' tendencies to enact repetition without a difference. Overcoming the impulse toward repetition is inherent in the subject matter of all of Morrison's novels in the trilogy of *Beloved, Jazz,* and *Paradise*. In *Paradise,* Morrison creates a fantastic, spiritual vision that resists repeating patterns of dominance and oppression and embraces instead elements of feminist Christianity that "imply a rejection of every elevation of one social group against others as image and agent of God, every use of God to justify social domination and subjugation" (Ruether 23).

Consolata gives a cryptic speech to the women at the time of the ceremony that departs significantly from Gnostic beliefs about the body. After recounting how she first denied her body to devote herself to God and then denied her spirituality to devote herself to the affair with Deacon, Consolata concludes by synthesizing these two approaches to her life, insisting that "bones" and "spirit" are not mutually exclusive: "Hear me, listen, never break them in two. Never put one over the other. Eve is Mary's mother. Mary is the daughter of Eve" (263). As Tally points out, "Consolata finally adopts a fusion of the spirit and the flesh in her search for wholeness, integrity" (17). In contrast, the townspeople maintain a rigid binarism, labeling the Convent women whores or "black bodacious Eves unredeemed by Mary" (18).

But Gnosticism itself doesn't necessarily counter the townspeople's binarism, and feminist theological scholars, even as they are attracted to the leadership roles for women in Gnosticism and the idea of a divine female power, take issue with its privileging the spirit over the body, breaking them in two.[30] What Consolata advocates is less like Gnosticism than like African religion. In the African world view, Dona Richards points out, spirit and matter, as well as other terms perceived as opposites in the West, instead constitute "*complementary pairs*" that are "interdependent and necessary to each other in a unified system" (252), quite different from the dualistic, world-denying aspects of Gnosticism. African religion also provides means to legitimate the work of female spiritual leaders. There is an emphasis on the earth being itself divine, a "mother earth" or goddess to be highly respected (Mbiti *Introduction* 36). In general, though African religion certainly contains sexist elements, Omoyajowo states that "we can safely conclude that African traditional religion is, generally speaking, less sexist in its masculine image of God than other religions. This may be the factor that makes it possible for men and women to perform sacerdotal functions" (74). Moreover, African religion, like Gnosticism, portrays the deity as both male and female. As Ryan points out, "the interconnectedness of the male and female aspects of Deity in African cosmology may well account for Black women's undaunted conviction of their own entitlement to and capacity for spiritual leadership" (*Spirituality as Ideology* 44). Finally, Mbiti suggests that myths that scapegoat woman for humankind's fall "are proportionally few" ("Flowers" 62), an important counterpoint to the scapegoating of women within the Ruby community.

A careful examination of the spiritual traditions set forth in the "Consolata" chapter of *Paradise* allows readers to see elements of both Gnosticism and African religion, as well as both feminist and African-American revisions of Christianity (Afro-Christianity), interwoven and commenting on one another in the novel's complex spiritual vision. Just as Gnosticism provides an alternative to the hierarchy of the organized Church and its strict adherence to particular doctrines, so too Ryan notes that "within [the African] cosmology, the expression of spirituality is not restricted to religious praxis, which perhaps explains why theology, as an institution or discourse, is neither dominant nor centralized." Also like Gnosticism, Afro-Christianity is concerned with ways of knowing: "It determines what knowledge is valuable, for what purposes, what responsibilities this knowledge confers, and what functions these have within and outside the community" ("Spirituality and/as Ideology" 269). Connie's practices, as has been noted, echo the Gnostic emphasis on self-knowledge, but more so than invoking Gnostic beliefs in particular, her practices resonate with those that Ryan identifies within black women's narratives. Like Consolata and her transformation to a divine figure, in these works, "characters display aspects of divinity, especially the capacity for righteous/creative agency and access to other ways of knowing. In these works, spirituality constitutes the foundation on which the artist constructs her vision of empowerment, and from which the characters derive knowledge of self and strength" (*Spirituality as Ideology* 26).[31] These spiritual ways of knowing, however, in contrast to the Gnostic emphasis on transcendence of this earth, "promote healing, survival, growth" in the earthly realm and as a response to specific, historical circumstances such as slavery (Ryan, *Spirituality as Ideology* 53).

Morrison's use of spiritual traditions in her depiction of the fantastic in *Paradise*, then, recalls not only the history of the early Christian epoch, the process of canonization of the New Testament, and the exclusion of women from an active role within the church, but it also recalls the historical experience of African American women exercising spiritual leadership within the parameters of the Black church in the nineteenth century. While, as Ryan points out, enslaved women did not experience resistance to their spiritual leadership, "the move away from the plantation and the development of theologies brought an orthodoxy—borrowed from Euro-American theologies—that opposed Black woman's spiritual leadership" (*Spirituality as Ideology* 43). With the exception of Reverend Misner, the Ruby community practices normative Christianity, not African-American Christianity, another manifestation of the town patriarchs' repeating rather than transforming the acts of their white oppressors. In contrast, Consolata and Lone DuPres exhibit what

Peter Paris observes of slaves: "creative genius" in adapting Christianity, "in making the Euro-American cultural forms and practices serve as vehicles for the transmission of African cultural elements."[32]

Like Consolata, the character Lone DuPres is associated with the fantastic and plays an important role in the novel's synthesis of Gnosticism and African American Christianity. Lone tells Connie at one point, "You need what we all need: earth, air, water. Don't separate God from his elements. He created it all. You stuck on dividing Him from His works. Don't unbalance His world" (244). This comment embraces the same African world view inherent in Consolata's urging the women at the Convent to overturn the binary opposition between spirit and matter. As Helen Othow points out, "Lone's last name, DuPres, suggest that she may be from Haiti, Brazil, or Louisiana, areas of the African Diaspora where the *vodun* religion (now called voodoo) most notably have been preserved" (370) so that the novel links Lone with African religion. Her use of magic in folk healing and her ability to foresee the slaughter at the Convent likewise evoke African beliefs in mystical powers available to some people (Mbiti *Introduction* 41–2). Within the community of Ruby, Lone—seemingly a member of one of the Christian churches—is nonetheless looked upon with suspicion. Her own blend of Christian theology and African spirituality recalls the Spiritual Church of New Orleans, the city from which Lone might originate, whose female "leaders are reputably able to heal illness and manipulate events by performing magico-religious rituals" (Estes 164) and who generally sought acceptance in the community "by proclaiming their Christianity and denying any connection to Voodoo" (Estes 159). The suspicion of Voodoo or the *vodun* version of aspects of African religion rests not only in the white community of New Orleans, as Estes points out, but also in the black male community that "perpetuate[s] an ideology of gender that denies women's spirituality" (164) since, "in the history of African American religion, preaching has been restricted almost exclusively to men on the basis of a literal interpretation of New Testament teachings about the role of women" (174). This, certainly, is the interpretation adopted by the Ruby patriarchs.

In addition to recalling African American women marginalized in the black church, Lone also recalls Mary Magdalene and invokes *The Gospel of Mary* insofar as she, like Mary, is a discredited female witness. Both she and Mary are alone on the scene of a miraculous occurrence, and their act of eye witnessing is discredited because they are women: just as Mary Magdalene is the first to see the risen Christ, so Lone is the first to witness the disappearance of the Convent women's bodies, and according to her version of the story, the women were indeed shot by the men, but then their bodies disappeared. In the wake of the Convent women's slaughter, multiple versions of what happened circulate in the town to account for the disappearance of the bodies, neither of which includes murder: one version holds that "the women took other shapes and disappeared into thin air" when the townsmen go simply to ask the women to leave town, and another holds that the women were attacked by some of the men but escaped in Mavis's Cadillac unharmed (296–7). The two versions of the "official story" (296) of what happened to the women are "rapidly becoming gospel" (297), just as official versions of Biblical stories became, through a politicized process, the four canonical New Testament gospels. Morrison in fact privileges Lone's version, another of the ways in which Morrison's treatment of religious ideology restores/restories the narratives suppressed by the dominant discourse. Her treatment of both Consolata and Lone, then, invokes the historical processes of exclusion of women from spiritual leadership in the early Christian era and more recently, in nineteenth-century America, and also revises elements of Gnostic world view by incorporating the interconnectedness of matter and spirit essential to the African world view.

A second, related revision that Morrison makes to Gnosticism's anti-cosmological stance rests in her treatment of what happens to the women after they are shot by the Morgan brothers and their cohorts, one of the key means by which the novel incorporates the fantastic. Gnosticism emphasizes humanity's return to a true home or paradise. Morrison links the idea of going home with Connie and Deacon's affair in a way that explicitly echoes Gnostic theology: Connie says, after she bites Deacon's lip and drinks from his mouth in the passage that recalls sayings in *Thomas*, "Dear Lord, I didn't want to eat him. I just wanted to go home" (240). But Morrison revises the Gnostic conception of a transcendent home. Morrisons's earthly vision of paradise/home is made explicit when Reverend Misner converses with Pat Best about the nature of home, distinguishing between heaven and "a real earthly home" (213). This home that Misner describes seems to be captured also in Connie's visions of the mythical character Piedade, associated with Connie's original Brazilian home.

A beautiful, lyrical passage anticipates the novel's ending with references to "emerald water," Piedade's hypnotic singing, and travelers on ships entranced by her song (284–5). Finally, in the novel's closing passage that is set in a fantastic realm, Morrison writes of the "solace" of finding an idyllic world of communion with others, "the unambivalent bliss of going home to be at home—the ease of coming back to love begun" (318).

The closing lines of the novel's epigraph promise that those who are saved from the earth's darkness will "go up to their resting place [...]/ and they will not die again"; yet Morrison's language in the novel counters the idea of *ascending* to paradise; the realm that her characters enter after death is decidedly more cosmic than transcendent. At the site where the women's bodies disappear, for example, Anna Flood sees a "door needing to be opened" and wonders "what would happen if you entered? What would be on the other side? What *on earth* would it be? What *on earth*?" (305, my italics). The women's actions and environment as described on this "other side" in the novel's coda also suggest that the realm they enter through the door is "other earthly"

(Krumholz 30) or "an alternative earthly realm" (Sweeney 47) rather than a transcendent realm envisioned by both orthodox Christians and Gnostics.

In the last several pages of the novel, each of the four women who has come to the convent for refuge interacts in a decidedly realist way with the family she has left; it is as if the women had not died at all but had returned to their prior lives to speak with those they left behind, in two cases (Mavis's and Gigi's) reconciling with family and reaching closure on the traumas that prompted them to leave home in the first place. If it had not been suggested that the four women were shot and killed, a reader might assume that these encounters were simply a realist ending to the novel. But as we have seen, the novel's moment of closure does not in fact reinscribe women in family life. The encounters with family members give way on the novel's last page to another realm, where Consolata is described in the position of Jesus in the pieta—identifiable as Connie through references to "tea-brown hair" and "emerald eyes" (318)—resting in the arms of the woman Piedade. This description, too, though mythical and less realistic than the descriptions of the four other Convent women, is decidedly earthly: the ocean-side environment in which Consolata and Piedade exist is littered with "sea trash," the very kind of jetsam and flotsam one would find washed up on a typical beach. Ships arrive on the shore with "disconsolate" passengers who "will rest before shouldering the endless work they were created to do *down here* in Paradise" (318, my italics). The notion of paradise captured here, then, describes a landscape far from ideal and an action of ongoing work to better the human condition, rather than a state of eternal rest. This paradise-on-earth can never be static or replicate the unchanging nature of the false paradise of Haven and later Ruby.[33] The "life everlasting" that the women achieve is quite different from the Ruby patriarchs' contract with God that is based on the subjugation of women: Morrison's treatment of what happens to the Convent women after their deaths is based on a feminist theology. The women reach into the wider world, greeting shiploads of the disconsolate who arrive on the shores of their mysterious realm; their expansiveness at the end contrasts with the rigidly defined, claustrophobic, monological Ruby community that wants to dispel any element of difference and to drive out all travelers who come to the town.

This home in which the women find themselves also carries elements of Africa and the characters' original roots. While the older Ruby citizens reject, as part of their insularity, any suggestion that Africa has anything to do with their heritage and disparage the younger generation's and Reverend Misner's interest in Africa (Pat Best, for example, tells Misner she is "really not interested" [210]), Lone's practices can be linked to African religion, and several other elements of the novel simultaneously invoke alternative Christianities and African religion. For example, when Connie first sees Deacon Morgan, he is associated not only with the Gnostic living Jesus, but also with African traditions that Connie remembers from her days in Brazil. Connie feels an immediate kinship with the eight-rock group—"Consolata knew she knew them"—and hears while she observes them in the act of establishing Ruby "a faint but insistent Sha sha sha," a rhythm associates with black people from her early years in Brazil before Mary Magna took her from her native land to the Convent (226). Moreover, the healing ceremonies that the women undergo in the Convent bear resemblance not only to Gnostic practices as discussed above, but also to African spiritual practices. Of the women's templates on the Convent floor, for example, Justine Tally writes that

> through inscription of the body on an external surface traumatic memory is reworked and vocalized. Pallas insists they complete their drawings with paint and chalk, an interesting African addition to the idea of renewal, in what Judylyn Ryan calls an "*efun*esque transformation of double consciousness. (*Efun* is ritually prepared chalk which is used for cleansing in Yoruba religion. It is said to have the power to transform the negative energy within an entity into a positive potential" [Tally 43].[34]

The rituals in which the Convent women participate to heal their traumas resemble Richards' descriptions of African ritual through which "trauma is avoided [...]. In ritual, the African combines life with artistic expression" (254). The ceremonies not only partake of the artistic element of African ritual, but they also recall the communal nature of testifying and listening to others testify as a way of combating the individualism imposed by slavery: the women "become one" in the loud dreaming sessions insofar as they seem to share one another's painful pasts, to all "step into the dreamer's tale" (*Paradise* 251; cf. Richards 268).

In addition, Consolata, who appears to Soane after being shot (301), and the other Convent women who appear to their families, resemble African conceptions of spirits of the recently dead or "the living dead" who "are believed to live close to their homes where they lived when they were human beings" and who "show interest in their surviving families" (Mbiti *Introduction* 77). The African concept of the ongoing relationship between the living and the dead differs from both Gnostic transcendence and the general "Christian formulation" that "heaven" consists in "eternal life *without* continued relationship to earthly existence" (Richards 285). This continued relationship to earthly existence, manifested less in the dead women's brief contact with their families than in their ongoing, collective efforts for social change in the fantastic realm that Morrison depicts, is crucial to Morrison's vision in *Paradise*.

Finally, Tally writes that "Piedade, the woman 'black as firewood' [*Paradise* 318], figures here as mother to all races, and calls to the ideological narrative which reinforces the idea of Mother Africa and the black race as progenitors of mankind" (Tally 92), while Bouson identifies her as a "morphed" version of Mary Magna, from white Catholic nun to "Black Madonna" (215). Bouson makes a very convincing case for the connections between Consolata's spiritual practices and the practices of Candomblé, an Afro-Brazilian religion that Morrison encountered on a trip to Brazil. Like Tally, he links Consolata with ancestor figures in African religion.[35] But as Romero points out, with reference to Bouson's work, "attempts to limit Morrison's more expansive view of religion to one particular religious belief system would detract from the novel's representation of a multiplicity of enabling beliefs and ways of organizing community" (428–429 n. 4). What is remarkable about *Paradise* is that it blends so many religious traditions, just as it depicts, in the make-shift community of the Convent, a community that transcends racial and class distinctions. The novel's fantastic devices—Connie's transformation to spiritual leader, Connie's and Lone's magical powers, and especially the reappearance of the murdered Convent women in the other-earthly realm where they work for social change—facilitate this democratic vision of paradise and overturn the principles of exclusion on which Ruby's patriarchal Christianity rests.

Conclusion

The conclusion of *Paradise* enacts in fiction what feminist Christian scholar Ruether portrays in an imagined play about Mary Magdalene: Mary ruminates that the disciples have fundamentally misunderstood Jesus's message, bemoaning that they will continue a cycle of domination and oppression by "'rebuk[ing] the Jews and conquer[ing] the Gentiles, lording it over them as the Romans now lord over us,'" rather than recognizing that "'a new God is being born in our hearts to teach us to level the heavens and exalt the earth and create a new world without masters and slaves, rulers and subjects. No, not even men come first with women behind in meek servility'" (11). Ruether emphasizes that "The Word of God does not validate the existing social and religious hierarchy but speaks on behalf of the marginalized and despised groups of society. [...] This reversal of social order doesn't just turn hierarchy upside down, it aims at a new reality in which hierarchy and dominance are overcome as principles of social relations" (136). In *Paradise*, the Ruby patriarchs' interpretation of their history and of Biblical scripture reinscribes the very hierarchy that they aim to surpass. To return to Morrison's epigraph, we should recall the portion of "The Thunder" that deals with a harmful cycle of reincarnation from which the saved are finally released. These lines might be applied to the destructive patterns of repetition in the novel, such as the repetition of Big Daddy (Zechariah) in his son Big Papa (Rector), the repetition of the town of Haven in the town of Ruby, the repetition of Puritan jeremiad rhetoric in the Exoduster movement, and the twinning of Deacon and Steward Morgan. The various cycles of repetition in the novel need to be broken; characters need to be released into the process of change itself. In an ironic twist on the epigraph's closing line—"they will not die again"—Morrison shows the unhealthy stasis and repetition that characterize Ruby to be bound up with the pact with God that no one will die in the town as long as the townspeople stay within the confines of Ruby and follow the blood rule. But instead, salvation is delivered precisely when Save-Marie, one of Sweetie Fleetwod's sick children, finally dies. Her illness, it is strongly implied, comes from the incestuous relationships that the blood rule necessitates. Her death, along with the mysterious circumstances surrounding the Convent women's disappearance, introduces the necessary process of change that frees the town from its stultifying stasis. The townspeople's ignorance, their lack of gnosis or insight, has lain in their unquestioning belief in the univocal and exclusionary story of their past; as much as they decry the disallowing, they have repeated it in various forms, something Deacon and Misner explicitly recognize (302 and 306).

Morrison, in contrast, employs the fantastic and feminist narrative strategies to privilege a world view that involves questioning, re-visioning, engaging in complex acts of interpretation, and accepting multiple meanings and open-endedness rather than settling on a fixed, gospel truth. She employs fantastic devices that recall Gnostic beliefs and practices, but in so doing, she performs what Rudolph calls a "protest exegesis," revising those beliefs by filtering them through African religion and cosmology to counter the Gnostic belief that "salvation will come not by trying to make [the world] better but by escaping it altogether" (Ehrman 114). As we have seen, her vision of salvation and the attainment of paradise involves overcoming human ignorance and achieving enlightenment in an earthly, social, and democratic way. In so doing, she counters the town patriarchs' acts of exegesis that enact repetition, not transformation.

But the end of the novel suggests that the town, too, will transform. Implicitly invoking *The Gospel of Mary* through Lone's witnessing of the women's bodies' disappearance, Morrison provides the perspective of an excentric figure that serves as a corrective to the "centralized" truth embodied in the town patriarchs' versions, and as such, like other post-modern magic realist fictions, *Paradise* enlists the fantastic, "to create an alternative world *correcting* so-called existing reality, and thus to right the wrongs this "reality" depends upon" (D'Haen 195). In spite of the fact that at first the town's versions of the women's disappearance seem to be "rapidly becoming gospel" (297), ultimately the very disagreement in the town about what has happened to the Convent women itself counters the single-minded, "controlling" story of Ruby's past: Reverends Cary and Pulliam "had [not] decided on the meaning of the ending and, therefore, had not been able to formulate a credible, sermonizable account of it" (297).[36] In the shattering of the closed narrative form that has characterized Ruby's story of its own past, in the ultimate failure of attempts to find a final, "sermonizable" account of what has happened to the Convent women, the town, too, seems to have broken out of its destructive cycle of repetition without a difference. The hesitation experienced by the characters with regard to this fantastic moment invites a broadened understanding of the characters' own conceptions of reality, a recognition of the constructed nature of their teleological account of the Haven/Ruby history, illustrated primarily through Deacon Morgan's change of heart at the end of the novel. At the same time, the novel's depiction of the women's disappearance also invites the reader to hesitate. In the town's accounts, Morrison provides both natural and supernatural explanations of the women's mysterious disappearance, though Morrison seems ultimately to ask readers to accept the supernatural as part of the novel's reality. But in so doing, she invites Western readers who may be Christian believers to reject a reading of the women's attaining life everlasting that is consonant with patriarchal versions of Christian doctrine.

In a not dissimilar vein, Karen King writes of the *The Gospel of Mary*:

> According to the master story of Christian origins, Jesus passed down the true teaching to his male disciples during his lifetime.[...] According to the *Gospel of Mary*, however, [...m]en like Peter and Andrew misunderstood the Savior's teaching and sowed discord within the community. According to the master story, the full doctrine of Christianity was fixed by Jesus and passed on in the doctrines of the Church. The *Gospel of Mary* instead suggests that the story of the gospel is unfinished. Christian doctrine and practice are not fixed dogmas that one can only accept or reject; rather, Christians are required to step into the story and work together to shape the meaning of the gospel of their own time. Because human passions and love of the world incline people to error, discerning the truth requires effort, and it insists that communities of faith take responsibility for how they appropriate tradition in a world too often ruled by powers of injustice and domination [189–190].

This is the lesson of Toni Morrison's *Paradise*, in which the teachings of the woman spiritual leader Consolata, the fantastic dimensions of the novel, and Morrison's feminist narrative techniques disrupt the town of Ruby's fixed gospel/master story and ultimately disrupt the harmful cycle of mastery and oppression of others. Morrison's engagement with Gnosticism, with ways of knowing, provides an appropriate conclusion to this book insofar as the fantastic in general concerns itself with ways of knowing (Malekin 41). The feminist fantastic in particular, as it is manifested in all of the novels in this book and as it shapes the narrative strategies adopted by these writers, is aptly captured in Morrison's vision of the endless work to shoulder "down here in Paradise" (318). Her novel highlights the necessity for the reader to step into the narrative in active ways, resisting received interpretations of the past, reshaping the patriarchal story, and re-envisioning the truth for the twenty-first century.

Chapter Notes

Preface

1. For more discussion of this difference between classical structuralist narratology and feminist narratology, see also Lanser's "Toward a Feminist Narratology," as well as her subsequent exchange, published in *Style*, with Nilli Diengott.

Introduction

1. Koenen's work *Visions of Doom, Plots of Power: The Fantastic in Anglo-American Women's Literature* comes closest to my own insofar as she, too, is interested in "the fantastic elements in 'mainstream' women's literature" that, she notes, are "persistently overlooked" (2). Her book, unlike many others on feminist uses of the fantastic, does situate the works she examines within both the theoretical discourse on the fantastic and feminist theory, though she does not extensively employ feminist narrative theory. While her interest in certain works and authors overlaps with mine to some extent, she also considers feminist utopian/dystopian fictions, vampire novels, and cyborg fictions, all of which fall outside the bounds of my book insofar as such works approach fantasy rather than the fantastic. Like Koenen, Armitt explores Anglo-American works in *Contemporary Women's Fiction and the Fantastic* (2000), yet she does not contextualize these works amidst theories of the fantastic or feminist narrative theory, in spite of having produced an earlier work titled *Theorising the Fantastic* (1996). While she claims in her later work to use the term "fantastic" in keeping with Todorov's theory (13), she does not seem to develop a consistent approach and examines works that are not always fantastic in Todorov's terms. Her work also uses a Freudian approach that is not especially useful for my purposes. Clark examines a handful of South American short stories to make a more explicit connection between feminist narrative theory and theories of the fantastic. Likewise, Duncan examines the narrative strategies of some Argentine short stories that employ the fantastic, noting the use of the first-person point of view for calling attention to the speakers' perception of events, wherein, as Todorov points out, the fantastic lies (Duncan 235). Her brief observations about perception and who speaks in these tales have bearing on the discussion of narrative authority and women's voices in several chapters of my book. Finally, Bachhilega focuses upon narrative strategies in postmodern feminist rewritings of fairy tales, exploring the ways that "woman" and "story" intersect (4). While her emphasis on the relationship to gender of storytelling practices such as narrative voice, focalization and the framing of a tale is consistent with my approach, she makes these observations in the context of a fantasy genre rather than in the mode of the fantastic; hence the body of works she examines is quite different from that examined in this book.

2. Clark's reference is to Mary Ann Doane, Patricia Mellencamp, and Linda Williams, eds. "Introduction." *Re-Vision: Essays in Feminist Film Criticism*. Los Angeles: University Publications of America, 1984. 1–17.

3. While Jackson's work is valuable and influential in its examination of the subversive function of the fantastic, her formulations about the twentieth-century fantastic are disappointing insofar as her vocabulary emphasizes lack, absence, or "hollowing out the real" without exploring the positive social functions of the fantastic. There is a dissatisfying vagueness in her terminology—for example, in the phrases "nameless things" and "thingless names" that she employs repeatedly and that other critics also seem to adopt (e.g. Horstkotte and Koenen.) In this respect, her ideas almost coincide with the concept of the generalized fantastic, explored in detail below. Nor does she engage as extensively with feminist theory or women's literature as one might expect from the general focus of her work on subversions of socially constructed realities.

Finally, her heavy reliance on Freudian and Lacanian theory makes problematic the relationship of her work to feminist readings of fantastic texts. Indeed, she finds Todorov's refusal to engage Freud a chief shortcoming of his work, writing that "it is in the unconscious that social structures and 'norms' are reproduced and sustained within us" (6). Koenen offers important revisions to Jackson's and other theorists' tendency to use Freud's uncanny as a reference point, arguing that the uncanny functions quite differently in women's literature than in men's (55). While I appreciate Jackson's ideological applications of psychoanalytic theory and Koenen's insistence on revising psychoanalytic interpretations of the fantastic, and while some of this theory is incorporated in my analyses of the novels in this book, other sociohistorical critical methods ultimately prove a more fruitful way to examine the ideological function of the fantastic in most of these novels. Elsewhere, in the introduction to the collection of women's ghost stories *What Did Miss Darrington See?* Jackson provides a more extensive discourse about feminism and the fantastic than she does in *Fantasy: The Literature of Subversion*. However, she identifies women's ghost stories that challenge patriarchal constructions of reality as being produced "*outside* the frame of reason," as being "anti-reason, unreasonable, unrealistic" (xvii), as "attempting [...] to articulate senses and experiences which are frequently [...] beyond social definitions altogether" (xviii). Such statements seem to bear out the concerns expressed by Clark, who indeed cites Jackson's introduction in her discussion (Clark 241). Moreover, the feminist fictions that I examine contain unrealistic elements but are certainly not wholly unrealistic—the fantastic in effect heightens the socially realistic aspects of these novels.

4. See also Cornwell's overview of the theory in *The Literary Fantastic: from Gothic to Postmodernism* 1–41 and Koenen's chapter "Theories of the Fantastic" (37–71).

5. Koenen makes useful observations about self-reflexivity in feminist fictions of the fantastic, writing that "in fantastic literature by women, the self-reflexivity that Rabkin sees as one of the constitutive factors of the fantastic texts is one of the most prominent and pervasive features, reflecting women's consciousness of and rebellion against their historical silencing" (59). [Koenen's reference is to Rabkin's *The Fantastic in Literature* 165–177.] But she also writes that in self-referential fictions, "The fantastic elements do not refer to an extra-textual reality, but only to themselves and the absence, the gap it signals" (58), a finding with which I disagree. I illustrate how the novels' self-consciousness about textuality often invokes a very specific, extra-textual and sociohistorical reality.

6. Todorov uses the term "genre," but many other theorists revise Todorov's terminology, likewise finding that the fantastic is less an identifiable genre than a mode (Jackson, Chanady, Horstkotte, Murphy and Barr, Koenen, Cornwell) or an element (Brooke-Rose). As Koenen points out, "the fantastic in the (post)modern text is no longer contained in separate genres like science fiction, but mixes freely with realism" (1).

7. Others have noted that Pynchon's *The Crying of Lot 49* also fits the "pure" fantastic mode, despite Todorov's insistence that works of its time period are not properly fantastic at all, an element of Todorov's work considered in detail later in this introduction.

8. On the distinction between fantasy and the fantastic, see, for example, Chanady 2–3; Hegerfeldt 50 and 53–54; Horstkotte 34–38; Koenen 42; Watson 164–5. Horstkotte observes that Jackson, among others, fails to discriminate between the two terms, using them in effect interchangeably in *Fantasy: the Literature of Subversion* (Horstkotte 35). Koenen is guilty on this front: claiming not to be interested in the genre of fantasy (42), she goes on to use the terms fantasy and fantastic more or less interchangeably. Kathryn Hume uses the term "fantasy" broadly as well, to describe any work that "departs from consensus reality" (21). The work of Cranny-Francis on women's genre fiction provides a good example of the differences between feminist fantasy and feminist uses of the fantastic, insofar as she treats literary works that may seem to the reader "far removed from the representation of the 'real' to which s/he is accustomed" (78), whereas the works I am concerned with are set squarely within the "real" world. Cranny-Francis treats, in her chapter on fantasy, secondary world fantasies, reworked fairy tales, and, to a lesser extent, horror and gothic fictions. Nonetheless, Cranny-Francis's comments on the function of women's fantasy are relevant to the function of the fantastic in the novels included in my book: "Women, the experiential subjects rather than the idealist construct, are not only invisible; they are entirely imperceptible. Feminist fantasy explores the problems of being for women in a society which denies them not only visibility but also subjectivity. It scrutinizes the categories of the patriarchal real, revealing them to be arbitrary, shifting constructs" (77). This operation may be even more pronounced in feminist novels that incorporate moments of the fantastic within narratives that are set in the historical world, whose dominant mode includes a great deal of realistic detail related to the historical circumstances of women's lives.

9. Traill makes another kind of distinction that comes close to describing many of the

works I consider. She sets forth five modes of fiction that employ the supernatural. Her ambiguous mode resembles Todorov's concept of hesitation and describes accurately some of the novels I examine. Others perhaps fall into her fifth mode, the paranormal mode, in which supernatural events "are not physically impossible; they are extraordinary and mysterious, natural—physically possible [within, I would add, the world of the text]—but latent and awaiting explanation" (138–9; see also 17–18).

10. In fact, an early essay on literary magic realism that identifies *The Metamorphosis* as a work of magic realism was published in 1955, well before Todorov's study of the fantastic, but Todorov makes no reference to it, nor, as noted above, does he employ the term magic realist. See Angel Flores, "Magical Realism in Spanish American Fiction," *Hispania* 38.2 (1955): 187–192. Hegerfeldt explores later critical responses to Flores' essay in detail in her work, 24–27.

11. Cornwell, drawing on the work of Brooke-Rose, also makes the observation that when Brooke-Rose schematizes Todorov's categorizations of fiction from realism to the marvelous in a circular rather than linear diagram so that realism and the marvelous constitute contiguous slices of the pie diagram (see Brooke-Rose 84; Cornwell 38), the category of "marvelous realism" results (38). Brooke-Rose speculates that this "mixed genre" of the marvelous and the real, a genre deemed impossible in Todorov's theory, in effect comprises science fiction (84), while Cornwell, further elaborating the category of the marvelous, identifies one end of the spectrum as a subdivision that he terms "what if," which in essence includes "works set in what seems to pass for 'our' world, but with a single (or at least a small number of) element(s) of the manifestly impossible." This subcategory, he points out, is what Chanady identifies as magic realism, and "she indeed specifically wishes to include *Metamorphosis* in the magical realist category (Chanady, pp. 48–50)" (Cornwell 40). The works that I examine in this book, when they seem to invite the reader ultimately to accept the presence of the supernatural either with or without thematizing character hesitation, can be fitted into Cornwell's "what if" category, insofar as none of the works is marvelous, involving a secondary world with its own set of laws, all of them being set firmly within the real, historical world of the reader.

12. Hoffman's much more recent work, *From Modernism to Postmodernism: Concepts and Strategies of Postmodern American Fiction* (2005), contains a chapter on the fantastic that identifies five types of the fantastic, the fifth one being the one dominant in postmodernism: "the hermetically fantastic world that questions, and, as it were, engulfs the idea of the real and of order, not differentiating between reality and fiction" (233). Hoffman observes that postmodern American fiction also employs three other types of fantastic: first, "the fairy tale fantastic mode" (234); second, a fantastic splitting of the character between conscious and unconscious actions, akin to Todorov's fantastic insofar as the reader might hesitate between a marvelous and uncanny resolution of the character-split (237–39); and third, a fantastic that, "making visible the invisible in society and culture, [...] serves an additional perspective like the satiric or the grotesque and the absurd" (239). But Hoffman gives no examples of this third type, and his examples of all the other types of postmodern fantastic, like in his earlier work, are drawn from the canon of white male American authors. He finds that a fourth type of the fantastic, magic realism, is not postmodern, a view with which other critics would disagree. D'Haen, for example, uses Hoffman's 1982 article as a point of departure for his essay "Postmodernism: from Fantastic to Magic Realist" and views much of the recent postmodernism produced by multiethnic, women, and post-colonial writers as "continu[ing] to work in what can be termed an extension of Hoffman's fantastic," while "others work in the mode of magic realism, a mode which [...] should be construed as *supplement*, in the sense used by Homi Bhabha, to Hoffman's fantastic" (284; D'Haen's reference is to Bhabha's *Nation and Narration* [London: Routledge, 1995], p. 305). D'Haen also notes that "it is inevitable" that Hoffman concentrates on a "select group of white, male, U.S. authors" (283) given the 1982 publication date of his article; Hoffman's continued reliance on this select group in a book published in 2005 seems less understandable.

13. In spite of the fact that McHale's own considerations do not account for recent feminist uses of the fantastic, nonetheless McHale makes important observations about hesitation taking place in the reader's response to the displaced fantastic; his discussion of the problems inherent in Todorov's analysis of *The Metamorphosis* is succinct and insightful—see especially 74–77.

14. I do not mean to suggest that theories of the generalized fantastic or the works to which these theories pertain are necessarily ahistorical or apolitical, or that the critics and authors subscribe to a view that reality is simply textual, rather than being available to us only through texts. Hutcheon makes this point clear in both *A Poetics of Postmodernism* and *The Politics of Postmodernism*. Nonetheless, the terminology used in this strand of theory about the postmodern fantastic does seem to stress textual play in and of itself and seems quite diffe-

rent in tenor from magic realist theory and more recent theories of the fantastic that stress the mode's engagement with the historical real and consider a broader range of authors. See, for example, Koenen's work, in which she writes that "the prevalent definitions of the fantastic, in their references tacitly privileging white male literature, recognize the fantastic in the opposition between a communal, established reality, suggesting that the fantastic is marginal and in conflict with the center; without ever acknowledging the decisive importance of perspective, they thus imply that the fantastic is actually a discourse of marginal and powerless groups, of, among others, women" (54). See also Cornwell, Chapter Four (140–208), or consider his statement that the fantastic has developed "a strong social, political, and ethical thrust" in recent literature (211). In a similar vein, Malekin points out that the fantastic often "involve[s] an overhauling or replacement of accepted cultural matrices" (41) and that "works of the fantastic […] often attempt to get outside Western culture" (42). The shift from theories of the generalized fantastic to theories influenced by postcolonial, magic realist theory closely resembles the shift in discussions of what D'Haen calls "central" postmodernism to "ex-centric" postmodernism ("Magic Realism and Postmodernism"), including feminist theories of women writers' postmodern practice, discussed in more detail below.

15. Brooke-Rose describes the relation of the fantastic to the real through a structural analysis of fantastic and realistic narratives that reveals that the characteristics of realism appear frequently in fantastic works (apart from their supernatural elements), such as the referential and symbolic codes which recur in texts like Tolkein's *Lord of the Rings* trilogy (123; see also her analysis on pages 72–102 and 233–255). However, her work implies the parallelism of fantastic and realistic works, without exploring the ground where they intersect. Most important for the purposes of my discussion is the coincidence she notes between realistic and fantastic texts of a general "megatext" or "parallel story," defined as elements of a real, historical world (e.g. recognizable geographic places, historical names) that ensure in the realistic novel the effect of the real (86). While, as Brooke-Rose points out, in marvelous worlds like Tolkein's, this "megatext" is purely invented, the fantastic texts I examine privilege an actual, historical megatext much as a realist novel would and hence are fundamentally different kinds of works than those Brooke-Rose examines.

16. Compare Carpenter and Kolmar, for example, who find a "relatively unexplored" woman's tradition of writing ghost stories in both the nineteenth and twentieth centuries (2). In distinguishing between men's and women's ghost stories, they find that "women writers seem more likely to portray natural and supernatural experience along a continuum. Boundaries between the two are not absolute but fluid, so that the supernatural can be accepted, connected with, reclaimed, and can often possess a quality of familiarity" (12). Thus they do not look at the blend of the marvelous and the real as a phenomenon of incompatible modes or as a generalized fantastic. Similarly, Winsbro, in her work on ethnic women writers' use of the fantastic, borrows Gloria Anzaldua's concept of the "borderland" to account for the melding of two kinds of worlds in the fictions she examines: "All individuals have the option of positioning themselves on one side of a boundary or the other or of creating […] a zone of borderlands, a new zone situated at the boundary itself. From this new space, one can draw beliefs from both sides to construct an individual world view, reality, and identity that constitute one's center" (25). Finally, Brogan identifies an important but "unrecognized" genre of "cultural haunting" that comprises "an extraordinarily hybrid category of literature […]" (6) and that tends to be authored more frequently by women than by men (24); such stories are characterized "by their conjuring of ghosts to perform cultural work" (17). These works contain useful formulations but do not situate themselves within the current theoretical discourse on the fantastic or magic realism.

17. Durix, without mentioning the generalized fantastic, likewise objects to Todorov's "tendency to reduce reality to texts. Todorov's analysis may well apply to postmodernist Europe or North America where the novel has at times lost all pretension to social relevance" (21). Durix fails to distinguish between Todorov's assessment of the classic fantastic's tale relationship to the real world and the twentieth century manifestations/transformations of the genre and their relationship to reality, but nonetheless his point that postcolonial, magic realist fictions "represent a certain vision of reality which may not be essentially intertextual" (21) is well-taken, a position adopted by magic realist theorists generally that also applies to feminist fictions.

18. McHale makes this same point about what he calls the displaced fantastic, without ever employing the term magic realism. He also rightly points out that character hesitation is not a strict requirement of Todorov's definition of the fantastic (75).

19. This is a crucial part but not the whole of Hegerfeldt's working definition of magic realism, which unfolds over fifteen pages and contains numerous points about magic realist

fictions' blending the realistic and the fantastic, incorporating reader hesitation in spite of narrative matter-of-factness about fantastic events, employing various types of focalization to present the fantastic, literalizing metaphors, making the real seem fantastic, and challenging Western modes of knowledge production (50–65). I will return to many of these points in later chapters, though not all are strategies employed in the novels I examine.

20. In *The Poisonwood Bible*, as in *Housekeeping* and *The Stone Diaries*, other characters do not interact with the narrating character who may be generating the narrative from beyond the grave, but in the case of Kingsolver's novel, several other characters explicitly acknowledge the persistence after death of Ruth May and implicitly seem to acquiesce in the idea that she has become a snake, "the eyes in the trees."

21. Chanady also postulates that a work does not become fantastic or magic realist if a supernatural element is introduced in a dream, for example, and is thus not an integrated part of the reality of the work, and with that conclusion I would agree. (This case seems to me the same as a work being resolved into the uncanny, in Todorov's schema.) But her assertions about the degree of the supernatural event or presence determining a work's status as magic realist or fantastic seem more problematic to me insofar as even a small element can certainly effect the entirely of a work and doesn't necessarily render the work "unconvincing" or "poorly constructed" (61).

22. Cf. Armitt, who expresses frustration with the fact that theories of the fantastic often consist of taxonomies that do not fruitfully illuminate fantastic works but instead attempt mainly to classify them according to generic limits (*Theorizing* 3 and *Contemporary Women's Fiction* 13). Traill also observes that "many narratives, happily, blend features of more than one mode [of the supernatural's relationship to the real] and so resist attempts to slot them neatly into a category" (20; see also 135–6).

23. Faris also makes this observation. She fully recognizes that magic realist fiction may encompass hesitation and notes that "much of magical realism is thus encompassed by Tzvetan Todorov's well-known formulation of the fantastic," going on to complicate Todorov's argument by taking into account that that "some readers in some cultures will hesitate less than others" ("Scheherazade's Children" 171). Here she implicitly acknowledges that there is no such thing as what Kathryn Hume terms "consensus reality."

24. Hegerfeldt's work is very helpful, but she, too, maintains a distinction between the fantastic and magic realism that doesn't entirely hold, writing that "in magic realist texts, narrative unreliability is handled in a more self-reflexive way, directing attention away from the fantastic's questions about ontological possibility or impossibility, focusing instead on social meanings of concepts like truth and reality" (101). In a work that is clearly fantastic and not magic realist such as *The Sea, the Sea*, however, the narrator's unreliability and the novel's fantastic elements focus on social meanings, not solely on the ontological status of the seemingly impossible events. Hegerfeldt also finds that "in the literary fantastic, the reader must adopt the focalizer's world view" and that the chief effect of the fantastic is "apprehension" on the part of the reader, as on the part of the character (203). But the adoption of the focalizer's perspective is not necessarily the case, nor must apprehension be the sole effect of the fantastic text on the reader.

25. Homans' brief article cogently condenses the work of many feminist theorists whose ideas I have drawn upon in this book, including Hite, Greene, and DuPlessis; to her list should be added Sally Robinson's *Engendering the Subject*. Lanser's work *Fictions of Authority*, which deals less with concerns about narrative form than with concerns about narrative voice, is also quite valuable to my discussions of certain novels.

26. Compare Horstkotte's study *The Postmodern Fantastic in Contemporary British Fiction*, in which he describes British postmodern fiction as more "muted" than American postmodern fiction insofar as it uses postmodern devices to a lesser degree and thus "represents a stance between tradition and innovation." For Horstkotte, the difference is "quantitative, not qualitative" (56–57). While the first claim accurately describes women authors' postmodern fictions, I disagree that the difference is simply one of degree and argue in the pages that follow that their use of postmodern devices is in fact qualitatively different from American male metafictionists' brand of postmodernism. Horstkotte, unfortunately, does not consider any British women writers, beyond a brief mention of Angela Carter and Jeanette Winterson in which he notes that they "employ magic realism to problematise questions of gender and of patriarchy in society" (40).

27. Greene's citation is to Gerald Graff's *Literature against Itself: Literary Ideas in Modern Society* (Chicago: University of Chicago Press, 1979), p. 20.

28. D'Haen postulates that critical consensus now views magic realism as a subset of postmodernism. For a dissenting view, see Hegerfeldt 34, n. 56. Magic realism's relationship to postmodernism is troubled in ways similar to feminism's relationship to postmodernism. In

both cases, it is crucial to speak of postmodernisms, in the plural, rather than defining postmodernism monolithically, with reference only to those authors who belong to what D'Haen terms a "central" position. A variety of ex-centric postmodernisms challenge the premises of "central" postmodernism. Cf. D'Haen's "Postmodernism: From Fantastic to Magic Realist."

29. Koenen makes a similar point (38).

30. The feminist narrative theory I am drawing on here was published largely in the late 1980s and the 1990s. While some of the theory of the fantastic and of magic realism that I draw on was published later, still by the late 1980s and early 1990s a significant critical discussion about the fantastic and about magic realism had emerged but is not taken into account in the feminist readings of novels of the fantastic.

CHAPTER 1

1. Dipple, for example, frequently refers to the unresolved uncanny events that take place through the course of the novel but does not draw upon Todorov or other theorists of the fantastic (see 278–279; 296–297). Heusel, summarizing Dipple's work, uses the term "magic realism" in conjunction with Murdoch's oeuvre and comments that unrealistic elements "invade a realistic story to make a serious comment on reality" (132). While it is certainly the case that the unrealistic elements of *The Sea, the Sea* function in this manner, the novel fits definitions of the fantastic much more closely than definitions of magic realism, given the degree to which character hesitation is thematized.

2. Many critics view Murdoch simply as a realist writer. Leavis does comment that although she is often held up as a counterexample to modernism, "she at times comes close to the modernist or 'post-modernist' kind of interest in fiction [...]" (137), and Sullivan briefly describes the interplay of realism and experimentalism in Murdoch's fiction (57). For a more recent and extensive consideration of both the difficulty of placing Murdoch within the contemporary canon and of the relationship between realism and experimentalism in post-war fiction, see Nicol, chapter 1. Many critics have also commented on feminists' tendency not to consider Murdoch's novels. As early as 1974 Goshgarian (writing, of course, about Murdoch's early novels, not about *The Sea, the Sea*) comments that "few people, if any, have called attention to a strong feminist attitude that informs both [Murdoch's] intents as a novelist and relevancy as a moralist" (519). In a very recent volume of critical essays on Murdoch, Turner suggests that "there are original and insightful essays in this volume that place Murdoch within cultural materialism and feminist studies; regrettably, this is an exception in scholarship." (121). Similarly, Grimshaw laments the "dearth of criticism" on Murdoch's representation of sexuality, gender, and power. Though Grimshaw herself does not analyze *The Sea, the Sea*, the purpose of her work is precisely to examine "the overlooked theme of power in Murdoch's fiction, particularly the interplay of power, gender, and sexuality in her characters' personal and social relationships" (17). Deborah Johnson's work, devoted to exploring Murdoch's patriarchal male narrators from a feminist perspective, represents another exception to the rule in the criticism of Murdoch's fiction.

3. Compare Murdoch's comments in "Against Dryness," in which she posits that form falsifies by imposing wholeness on the individual and the world, resulting in fantasy. In contrast, "[r]eality is not a given whole. An understanding of this, a respect for the contingent, is essential to imagination as opposed to fantasy. Our sense of form, which is an aspect of our desire for consolation, can be a danger to our sense of reality" (30–31). Reality, according to Murdoch, is something that transcends the individual (26) and that is difficult to know. In "The Sublime and the Beautiful Revisited," she makes similar comments about the need for a novel's form to show "respect for reality with all its odd contingent ways" (271). In fact, the reader might identify Arrowby as the type of novelist Murdoch speaks against: he is one who ignores the contingent messy reality of everyday life and who creates characters that are not free, namely Hartley. In the "novel" that he produces, Hartley's "freedom" (in Murdoch's terminology, "free" is synonymous with "real"—a free character behaves like a real person in the real, contingent world) is severely restricted because Charles, who casts Hartley into a conventional social role, resembles modern authors who are guilty of "denying freedom to the fictional individual either by making him merely part of his creator's mind, or by treating him as a conventional social unit" ("The Sublime" 266). For a critique of Murdoch's attempt to redeem some art forms while agreeing with Plato's assessment of others, see Whibley, who writes that "It is unlikely, however, that her creative, yet misleading interpretation of Plato's aesthetic theory allows her to promote art as a vehicle for moral knowledge without doing violence to the original Platonic schema" (383).

4. See, for example, Stein's argument that recent women authors revise the Gothic form by "changing [...] victimhood and persecution into new sources of strength" (137). Likewise, Massé identifies two contemporary gothic novels, *Linden Hills* and *Lady Oracle*, that resist what she identifies as the masochistic strain in

earlier gothic fictions. According to Massé, many, but not all, contemporary women authors writing in the gothic mode create fictions in which women are freed from patriarchal authority and do establish identities of their own. See also the portion of Massé's argument that addresses the gothic's relation to social and historical reality and refutes claims that the gothic is merely "escape literature" (18–20).

5. In considering the structure of Murdoch's novel and her narrative strategies, one should compare the implications of her form to what Hayden White postulates. White argues that the value attached to narrativity in the representation of real events arises out of a desire to have real events display the coherence, integrity, fullness, and closure of an image of life that is and can only be imaginary. [...] Does the world really present itself to perception in the form of well-made stories, with central subjects, proper beginnings, middles, and ends, and a coherence that permits us to see the "the end" in every beginning? Or does it present itself more in the forms that the annals and chronicle suggest [...]? (24)

Earlier in the same essay, White points out that "the chronicle [...] often seems to wish to tell a story, aspires to narrativity, but typically fails to achieve it. More specifically, the chronicle usually is marked by a failure to achieve narrative closure. It does not so much conclude as simply terminate" (5). These ways of writing history correspond remarkably to Murdoch's project in *The Sea, the Sea*, where Charles's "History" section is narrativized history, marked by all the wishful thinking White identifies as inherent in this mode, while the "Prehistory" and "Postscript: Life Goes on" more closely resemble the chronicle.

6. Massé also writes that in the traditional Gothic, "Heroines of the Gothic [...] have the same expectations as those around them for what is normal. Their societal contract tenders their passivity and disavowal of public power in exchange for the love that will let them reign in the interpersonal and domestic sphere" (18).

7. Compare Murdoch's statement in "The Sublime and the Beautiful Revisited," where she comments on what she sees as the romantic, solipsistic character of recent fiction, in which authors seem to shy away from "history, real beings, and real change, whatever is contingent, messy, boundless, infinitely particular, and endlessly still to be explained," favoring instead "the timeless non-discursive whole which has its significance completely contained in itself" (260).

8. Stein's citation is to Joanna Russ, "What Can a Heroine Do? Or Why Women Can't Write," *Images of Women in Fiction: Feminist Perspectives*, ed. Susan Koppelman (Bowling Green, OH: Bowling Green State University Press, 1972), 9.

9. Not only Charles but all the characters who act possessively out of jealousy become demons to the other characters in some form. Charles links Rosina, jealous of his relationship to Lizzie, with the monster on at least two separate occasions. Ben, we learn from Hartley, is jealous of Charles and for years has suspected his wife of a secret affair with him; Hartley describes Ben's preoccupations with Charles as being "like demons in our lives" (229). Finally, Perry, too, who is jealous of Charles's affair with Rosina, comments that when one is wounded in love, "one becomes a sort of fiend oneself" (161). Compare also Murdoch's statement in an interview that people "play the role of demons for other people" (Rose 68).

10. For quite some time Charles excludes Lizzie, another former lover, from his association of women with the monstrous. Lizzie remains in his mind completely submissive, the ideal gothic heroine. She finds Charles's power and possessiveness attractive (189), and Charles in turn refers to her as being like an obedient dog (359). Yet when Charles finds out that she and his cousin James have known each other prior to his introducing them, he immediately assumes they have a sexual relationship and considers Lizzie "spoiled," associating her, too, with the terrifying singers (409).

11. The siren connotation is especially appropriate in *The Sea, the Sea* since the sirens lured men to their deaths by drawing them near to the dangerous coast, where they would be dashed against the rocks and drowned. Ben and Hartley's son, Titus, dies in precisely this manner, when he is unable to climb safely out after swimming and drowns from a blow on the head. But in this context, too, Murdoch undermines Charles's revulsion at female sexuality, for Titus is not the victim of siren-like singers but of Charles's own egotism. In his eagerness to appear strong and youthful to Titus, he neglects to warn the boy that climbing out of the sea can be treacherous. He realizes later, "My vanity destroyed him" (459), just as James laments that his vanity destroyed his companion Milarepa (447).

12. Charles describes Rosina, for example, as the "most stylish, the most gorgeously artificial" (73). He also sees portraits of the women from his past in various well-known artists' paintings in the London museum he visits (170). While he has not seen Hartley's portrait among the artworks displayed the museum, such is the case only because he has not yet painted it. Charles thinks of Hartley like a work of art he can create, which in his mind has the qualities of a truth rather than a fiction (428). The novel's attention to the exterior/interior opposition, its fascina-

tion with both surfaces (portraits, mirrors, windows that act as mirrors) and interiors (inner rooms and open mouths), also plays an important role in Murdoch's critique of patriarchal domination, especially of those versions of the gothic which refuse to grant women any identity other than shallow and supplicating victim of male aggression. Charles's fear of interiors is commensurate with his obsession with his own narrative form: in his attempt to write a perfect, coherent, seamless novel about himself and Hartley, he must ignore depth, the messy contingency of history and the events that surround him, and quite aggressively attempt to force them into the pattern he creates in his mind.

13. Kahane analyzes how Gothic mansions reflect the female body and discusses women characters' ambivalence toward the maternal body; in *The Sea, the Sea*, the association of the inner room with Hartley and her sexuality comments more explicitly on Charles's response to the female body than on Hartley's own, just as Murdoch reverses the trope of monstrosity to reflect upon the male character rather than the female.

14. While Charles believes that he is offering Hartley "freedom," his own discourse is full of dramatic ironies that suggest the collapse of boundaries between Charles and Ben. (See, for example, 357).

15. Cf. Irigaray, who writes that women who mimic masculine discourse "remain elsewhere," not trapped within that discourse (76). The relevant passage from *This Sex Which Is Not One* is discussed in more detail in Chapter Four.

16. See Johnson for a careful feminist consideration of the role of male narration in many of Murdoch's novels, both its advantages and its potential drawbacks (9–19).

17. Later, when Rosina breaks the mirror as part of her haunting, Charles is distraught and intends to keep the undamaged frame (55), but at the end, when he leaves Shruff End and takes up residence in James's London flat, he notes that he is able to overcome the urge to keep the mirror (479), suggesting his progress beyond conforming to cultural expectations reflected in the surface of the mirror.

18. James also has the power to will his own death, according to the doctor who signs his death certificate. Charles puzzles over James's unexpected death and even devises a theory that James has not died at all but has had his disappearance staged by British Intelligence (486). This instance provides another example of James's association with a fantastic event and the resulting hesitation invoked in Charles and in the reader, since no definitive account of what happened to James is ever provided. Punja also points out that the novel never explains the fact that James knows how to locate Charles during Charles's retreat to Shruff End: "His knowledge is on the edge of being uncanny although there is always a sense that it could be perfectly natural" (59). This, then, is another way that James is linked with the fantastic. See Punja 55–62 for an interesting overview of the gothic elements of *The Sea, the Sea*.

19. Critics have tended to view James either too negatively or too positively. Dipple considers him to be someone sinister and dangerous, as much to be condemned as Charles for his use of magic (293–96); she takes too literally his own self-assessment. Tucker, on the other hand, believes James to be a source of pure good, a saint, yet she fails to examine critically some of his problematic statements and attitudes ("Released from Bonds"). Gordon's reading of James is similar to Tucker's. Murdoch's novel suggests something between these two extreme views about the nature of James's magic. Capitani provides a balanced examination of James's relationship to goodness and magic.

20. See Tucker's comparison of the various characters in *The Sea, the Sea* to characters in Shakespeare's work; see also Sanders, 119–129. Sanders postulates that *The Sea, the Sea* is a precursor to postcolonial and feminist readings of *The Tempest* that dominated criticism of that play in the 1980s and 1990s (124).

CHAPTER 2

1. In "Great Expectations," the autobiographical foreword to VanSpanckeren and Castro's collection of essays on Margaret Atwood, Atwood mentions the work of both Simone du Beauvoir and Betty Friedan as being important influences on her writing (xvi).

2. Atwood stated in an interview that "Lady Oracle was more tragic to begin with—it was going to start with a fake suicide and end with a real one. As you know, it turned out differently" (Sandler 45).

3. Benson and Howells (*Margaret Atwood*), for example, discuss the relevance to *Lady Oracle* of Janice Radway's *Reading the Romance: Women, Patriarchy, and Popular Literature*, London: Verso, 1987. Davidson and Davidson also address the conservative social function of fantasy romance.

4. Koenen, however, dedicates only a few pages to discussing *Lady Oracle*. While she, like numerous of the novel's other critics, focuses on the gothic dimensions of the novel and Atwood's revisions to classic gothic conventions, she unfortunately does not treat elements of the fantastic, the appearances of the astral body of Joan's mother and Joan's automatic writing sessions. Critics have generally not rigorously analyzed *Lady Oracle* as a fantastic text:

as was noted in the Introduction, feminist narrative theorists who employ the novel as a central text in their studies of feminist narrative praxis do not draw on theories of the fantastic, and even theorists of the feminist fantastic like Koenen and Armitt seem to overlook the novel's truly fantastic dimensions.

5. Rao writes that as the novel "reworks older fictional forms—the Gothic, the sentimental novel, the picaresque and fairy tales—it becomes the locus where a plurality of styles and traditions are revisited. Such a medley probes notions of unity in generic classification to subvert conventional hierarchies" (133). Additionally, as numerous others point out, *Lady Oracle* may be considered a kunstlerroman. For an extensive analysis of Atwood's revisions to the picaresque novel, see Freibert. See Massé's excellent analysis of Joan's gothic writings and the ways in which *Lady Oracle* subverts gothic conventions; see also McMillan's analysis of Atwood's transformations to the genre.

6. Hite lists a number of works that treat *Lady Oracle* thus, including those by Sharon Wilson, Frank Davey, Sherrill Grace, Clara Thomas, and Catherine Ross (130, n.2). Barbara Hill Rigney's book might be added to the list. Hilde Staels' reading of Joan was published several years after Hite's study but falls into the same camp as those readings to which Hite objects. Other treatments of the novel locate Joan's troubles in the social realm rather than the personal. In addition to Hite, see Massé, Greene, and Bouson.

7. Although Hite perhaps overstates the case of this gender-coding (at Joan's wedding, a male character, Mr. Stewart, does witness without naturalizing the astral body of Joan's mother [205]), nonetheless, her point largely holds true and can be extended to the device of Joan's automatic writing. While Joan firmly believes herself to be in some "extranatural" state (220) when she composes her poem "Lady Oracle," all the male reviewers and interviewers dismiss her revelation about the manuscript's composition as a joke or as a marketing gimmick (see *Lady Oracle* 237–238 and 250).

8. Hite herself seems divided on the matter, arguing that she "intrude[s] herself into the action in ways that are less and less reconcilable with the premise that she is Joan's fantasy" (140), but suggesting that the scene in which the fat lady seems to appear on national television at a hockey game "can be also be read as the production of Joan's involuntary imagination, as full-scale hallucination" (141). I am inclined to agree with this latter assessment: Joan's description of the hockey game emphasizes her perspective, so that when a television commentator remarks upon the fat lady's presence, the novel reads "I heard the commentator say" (274) rather than "the commentator said." In addition, as Hite points out, Arthur never remarks upon the Fat Lady as he watches the game in which she, according to Joan, skates onto the ice. Shortly before this episode, Joan notes that her "daydreams about the Fat Lady returned" (251); in contrast, she never identifies the fantastic events of seeing her mother's astral body or becoming trapped in her mirror during an automatic writing session as daydreams. For an excellent analysis of the fat lady, gender expectations, and the female body, see, in addition to Hite, Boynton, 56–60.

9. Numerous critics have commented on the importance of the mirror in *Lady Oracle*. See Hite's analysis of the mirror in *Lady Oracle* (161–163), where Hite ultimately argues that the mirror reveals feminine multiplicity, which she identifies positively with monstrosity (161). Likewise, Givner insists that the triple mirror works against dualistic and reductive ways of defining femininity, and Godard makes a similar point about the function of the mirror (17). Becker proposes a reading of mirror similar to Hite's, writing that "aspects of Joan's subjectivity suggest the aspects of the 'monstrous-feminine'" of nineteenth-century fictions (159). Later, noting that Frances seems unhappy with her reflection, Becker postulates that the trope of monstrosity comes to be associated with the very "discrepancy" between actual woman and social constructions of Woman (165), and that Joan ultimately "'accepts' the 'monstrous'" when she stops trying to satisfy her mother (168). My reading, in contrast, suggests that monstrosity and the mirror are linked insofar as the mirror reflects only the surface and singularity. Although Frances and later Joan appear in a triple mirror, the reflection produced is really only three versions of the same. It is only when one "gets behind" the mirror that one voyages beyond the trope of monstrosity conventionally associated with the female in the gothic and approaches a more positive definition of femininity in all its plurality. It is true that Joan describes herself as a witch or monster near the end of the novel when the people of Italy interpret her as having "the evil eye" (325), but it is clear from Joan's language in her description of herself as "[a] female monster" that this particular fantastic interpretation of Joan is one she dismisses and deliberately ironizes (336). Bromberg's view of the mirror is closer to my own: she writes that "mirrors symbolize [...] the crippling emphasis that society places on the female image as a consumer item. Atwood shows that the mirror, long a literary symbol of female narcissism and childish self-absorption, more truly reflects a culture where women are objectified and packaged for the marriage market" (13); but she proposes a neg-

ative view of Joan's grappling with mirror images, concluding that Joan never escapes from the culturally sanctioned view of the mirror that her mother embraces (22). Greene, in her analysis of the mirror, draws on Irigaray's statements about the mirror being a device that signifies women reflecting man's image back to him, but Greene illustrates how Joan's journeys into the glass overturn this traditional function of the mirror (174–5 and 181).

10. See, for example, Massé's reading of the final appearance of the astral body in which Massé writes that "Joan is terrified by her brush with merger," viewing the mother as a force trying to make Joan conform, rather than warning her against conformity with convention (262).

11. Cf. Vincent. The pattern in the novel is to describe, through Joan's first-person narration, this seemingly supernatural occurrence in such comic terms that all apprehension is removed. In the first instance, Leda Sprott's explanation of the concept of the astral body is so absurd as to be laughable in spite of the fact that the reader cannot dismiss Frances's apparition as an hallucination on either Joan's or Leda's part; in the second instance, Joan's own language comically deflates the situation (see 173). In this respect, the fantastic/gothic elements of *Lady Oracle* differ substantially from those Murdoch employed in *The Sea, the Sea*, a novel that more nearly matches Todorov's model of the nineteenth-century pure fantastic insofar as the character always hesitates about the supernatural and the possibility of the supernatural always creates apprehension.

12. See also McKinstry, who argues that Joan divides herself into "self-as-creator and self-as-created" (63). Likewise Godard notes instances where Joan employs both the first- and third-person voice to distinguish between the self as subject and the self as object; see her analysis of the appearance of the Fat Lady at the hockey game (19). But Joan's self as creator of Costume Gothics that McKinstry comments upon is in a way simply another created self, a double of herself as the lover/wife of the various men in the novel. See, for example, Greene's reading: in many ways Joan's second self, author of Costume Gothics, is only "exchanging[ing] one confinement for another, for she has slotted herself into a stifling marriage and fixed herself there by means of the formulaic repetition, in her fiction, of the 'central plot' of patriarchy—'true love and happy endings'" (178). Joan's self as creator emerges more fully in the text of her poem, "Lady Oracle." One might compare Joan to Daisy Flett in *The Stone Diaries*, whose narrating self ("I") rejects the self narrated for her by conventional society ("she"). The implications of this splitting the self for a feminist analysis of narrative voice are considered in more detail in Part II of this book. See also Grace, who argues that *Lady Oracle* illustrates theories of female autobiography in its narrative conventions, including challenging "the notion of a teleological Self, authoritative, conscious, centered, developing inexorably towards its public goal, which, in turn, affects the causal, unidirectional, climatic plotting, familiar from male autobiography. The female autobiographical 'I' is more like a process than a product" (191). Theories of female autobiographical voice are discussed in more detail as well in Part II.

13. Howells makes a similar point about Joan's Costume Gothics as automatic writing (*Margaret Atwood* 56).

14. Hegerfeldt distinguishes between magic realism and the fantastic by arguing that "in magic realism the figurative dimension always remains visible, hovering, so to say, on the surface of the text, whereas in the fantastic it can be recuperated only through the process of interpretation" (59). This distinction does not seem entirely useful; again, the novels examined in this book often defy distinctions made between the techniques of magic realism and techniques of the fantastic.

15. In Hite's estimation, Joan's automatic writing produces only another kind of limited, conventional writing about women's roles (158–159). In addition, Rosowski views Joan as "the blank lady" referenced in her "Lady Oracle," still awaiting at the end of the novel some cultural construct to define her (97). Massé, too, has a negative view of automatic writing—Joan "figuratively constructs herself while in a trance state that denies her agency and voice" (253). Rao herself offers a more positive reading of Joan's poetry, and McKinstry emphasizes how Joan revises "The Lady of Shalott" (67). Greene's reading of "Lady Oracle" is a very positive one, emphasizing Joan's newfound powers (180–183). Other critics recuperate the feminist element of Joan's writing by noting the coincidence of Joan's automatic writing with theories of *écriture féminine*. See, for example, Davies (65–66); Tucker, who compares Joan's writing to Kristeva's *semiotique (Textual Escap(e)ades* 45); or Givner, who draws on the theories of Cixous and Irigaray to illuminate Joan's use of the word "bow" in "Lady Oracle." Becker, in contrast, sees the poem not as illustrating but as making a "parodic allusion to the French concept of *écriture féminine*" (167). But Bok, who dislikes the mysticism associated with the device of automatic writing (91), argues that in the coincidence of Joan's writing with French feminist theories of women's writing, Atwood "risks sustaining the ideologies of gender that she seeks to critique" (88) by relying on essentialist ideas and reinforcing stereotypes about

women, ultimately devaluing women's writing itself (91). Bok's points are well-taken, his general argument addressed in conjunction with Marilynne Robinson's *Housekeeping* and Carol Shields's *The Stone Diaries* in chapters that explore in greater depth the issue of women's narrative voice and semiotic versus symbolic language.

16. See Barzilai's essays for intriguing and detailed analyses of Atwood's use of Tennyson's poem and of various fairy tales. See also Wilson's *Margaret Atwood's Fairy-Tale Sexual Politics*, 120–135.

17. Judith Spector makes a very similar point: Joan in effect "stages a mock drowning to 'kill' Joan as the wife of Arthur, Joan as mistress to the Royal Porcupine/Chuck Brewer" (42), or those socially sanctioned versions of herself that she struggles against throughout the novel. Thus she writes beyond the ending not by generating narrative from beyond the grave like other narrators considered in this book but by refusing the moment of closure so often reserved for women characters who defy social norms: she refuses both the "happy" ending of the conventional marriage plot and the suicidal gesture.

18. Of the analyses of *Lady Oracle* that I've encountered, only Spector's "The Fatal Lady in Margaret Atwood's *Lady Oracle*" mentions Plath's poem. Analyzing "fatal ladies" represented in literature as well as women authors who take on that role by committing suicide, Spector mentions some parallels between Joan and Lady Lazarus, noting that the poem's "life/death dualism would have a more hopeful ring to it if we were not so acutely aware of the women poets like Plath who did not manage to rise from their ashes" (42). Though Tucker does not mention "Lady Lazarus," she does juxtapose her discussion of Plath's *The Bell Jar* with her discussion of *Lady Oracle* and draws comparisons between Plath and Atwood's narrator *(Textual Escap(e)ades* 35–36).

19. Compare also Hite's insightful comments on the non-linear form of the novel and its feminist sensibility (165.)

20. The parallels between Joan's life and her *Stalked by Love* manuscript are numerous and complicated; a full discussion of their implications is beyond the scope of this chapter. For additional analyses, see, for example, Greene, 184–188; Hite 150–153; Rosowski, 96; Massé, 261–64; McKinstry, 64–66.

21. See also Beran, who identifies three distinct voices in Joan's first-person discourse: "her natural voice, her gothic voice, and her poetic voice" (55).

22. A host of sources comment on Joan's lack of self-awareness: Parsons suggests that Joan "does not recognize, but we do, the half-likeness of [her gothics] to her own life" (105).

Staele suggests that Joan cannot really distinguish clichés from reality (87), that she adopts clichéd roles uncritically. Lecker views Joan as never being able to escape from her problems in real life or in fiction, which reflect one another (198). Barzilai takes a different tack, analyzing in detail Joan's self-consciousness about narrative constructs and identifying her "ironic distance" from these constructs, but concluding that this distance "does not provide adequate insurance or protection against the powerful grip of such narratives" ("Bluebeard Syndrome" 252).

23. Compare also Bouson's comments on Atwood's use of parody, in which he draws on Bakhtinian theory to illustrate how laughter operates in an oppositional fashion (*Brutal Choreographies* 77).

24. Fee points out that this aspect of *Lady Oracle*'s conclusion indicates that Joan really is being victimized and points to the need for people to "examine the system that creates victims" instead of "blam[ing] the victim" (61).

25. Compare Joan's prior statement, when she sees a scorpion in her room in Italy, that earlier she would have screamed and called Arthur to remove it, whereas now she simply dispenses with the scorpion herself (25). Atwood herself comments on the male reporter in an interview, suggesting that he differs from the other men in Joan's life, and that any relationship that develops between them "will be on some kind of honest basis" (Struthers 66).

26. For a different view that does not couch itself in terms of the fantastic, see Hite's own feminist recuperation of Joan's mentioning that she tells her story to the reporter, who will then write it down. Hite views Joan as having "wiggled out of the authority for her own story" (156), but unlike Howells or Stein, she interprets this move positively, as a means of resisting closure. She does not consider that the ending resists closure also by not definitively allowing the reader to conclude that the reporter writes Joan's story; rather she assumes that he indeed does so (156–57 and 165). See also Barzilai, who notes that the reporter has not yet written Joan's story and who writes that "This is one story that he (the reporter) will not have written because she (Atwood) already has" ("The Bluebeard Syndrome" 268). In other respects, Barzilai's feminist interpretation of this moment in the novel resembles Hite's.

CHAPTER 3

1. See Galehouse (118–119) for a consideration of the Depression-era setting and treatment of vagrancy and Smyth (281–282) for so-

ciological commentary on female homelessness in particular.

2. Perhaps some evidence for literal drowning occurs in an earlier passage in which Ruth imagines Sylvie returning from the drowned (84). Ruth also imagines the resurrection of ghosts, especially her mother (96), compares reeds in the lake to "drowned hair" (112) and is required to recite in school Emily Dickinson's "I Heard a Fly Buzz When I Died" (77), whose speaker narrates the moment of her death. Those critics who see the drowning as being perhaps literal but who don't consider this ambiguity explicitly in terms of theories of the fantastic include Caver (passim), Foster (96–7), Burke (723), Kirkby (106), Anghel (434), and Walker, who writes that "Ruth narrates *Housekeeping* as though from beyond the grave" (40). Koenen briefly considers *Housekeeping* as a novel of the fantastic (see 288–292) mostly insofar as the narrative is located "outside of time" (288), without, oddly, considering the statements at the end about Ruth and Sylvie being dead. Others focus as well on the passage in which Ruth visits a ruined house that contains children who might be real or might be ghosts (*Housekeeping* 153–160), interpreting this passage as a possible manifestation of the supernatural. See, for example, Anghel (432–33), Burke (719) and McDermott (263). Those critics who see the purported deaths as strictly metaphoric and hence do not consider the novel to have any supernatural dimension include Bohannon (77), Heller (95), Lin (222), Galehouse (235), Kaivola (672), Ryan (85), Rubenstein (225) and Geyh (118). Rosowski is "amused at speculations that Ruth and Sylvie died in their attempt to cross the bridge," concluding that "the question of their death is quite beside the point" (*Birthing a Nation* 187).

3. For a somewhat different analysis of the ways in which the novel blurs the boundaries between the real and the unreal, see Burke, who allows for the possibility that the novel is fantastic but stresses how *Housekeeping* reveals that the phenomenal world represents reality in ways that distort it: "Ruth desires to shatter the glass of the phenomenal world to expose a more substantial reality. [...] Like her aunt and her mother, Ruth sees the world as a surface that must hide some other and more permanent reality" (722–723). Placed in an ideological and gendered context, these comments about *Housekeeping* recall the ways in which the mirror in *Lady Oracle* reflects merely a specular surface that one must "shatter" or get behind to find some other reality or "truth" (*Lady Oracle* 221). As Geyh points out, "Lucille has mastered appearances—or they have mastered her, since she believes them to be reality" (111). Lale Davidson addresses the manner in which Robinson blurs boundaries between the real and the unreal from a deconstructive approach, focusing on the novel's metaphoric language and its treatment of desire and absence (24–33).

4. For an alternative view, see Galehouse, who argues that "Sylvie and Ruth are 'uncontainable' by traditional narrative standards" precisely because they are "major female characters for whom romantic love and/or death do not figure in the resolution of their conflict" (135–136), a view that of course hinges upon a nonliteral reading of the novel's ending and that downplays the idea of death inherent in the language that Robinson employs when she describes Ruth's and Sylvie's actions after they have crossed the bridge. O'Brien offers a similar interpretation, viewing Robinson's characters as defying the fate of nineteenth-century women characters that DuPlessis describes, precisely because they do not die (231).

5. The avoidance of the social marked in the female characters' association with nature is supported by a brief comparison of *Housekeeping*'s ending with the ending of Charlotte Brontë's *Jane Eyre*. First, Sylvie's and Ruth's act of burning down the house recalls Bertha Mason Rochester's act of torching Thornfield Hall, site of her imprisonment by a representative of patriarchal culture, her husband, Rochester. In addition to bearing some resemblance to Jane's repressed alter-ego Bertha, Ruth in many ways resembles Jane herself, who, resentful of being locked in the red room, imagines running away or starving herself (28). Ruth, in contrast to Jane (who overcomes this death wish and speaks out against injustice), ends her story with acts of self-starvation and running away when it is suggested that she should be indoors, all houses being for Ruth the equivalent of Jane's red room. But in spite of Jane Eyre's progress through the course of the novel, many critics, including Sandra Gilbert, have noted that she effectively withdraws from the social realm at the novel's end. As Gilbert points out, unlike the other houses where Jane has been which each represent some social institution (school, church, marriage), Ferndean "is notably stripped and asocial"; she further comments upon the "spiritual isolation" of Jane and Rochester and wonders if Brontë's feminism "compromise[s] itself in this withdrawal?" (500). Jane's retreat to Ferndean might be compared to the dominant movement of *Housekeeping*, where Ruth, like Jane, finally travels to a natural, wild world, away from the institutions that have been represented in the novel: school, home, law, and church.

6. *Housekeeping* has long been critically examined against the background of the American literary tradition, and numerous scholars have set forth arguments about the way that the

novel transforms the mythic frontier experience and the male quest story into a feminist story. See especially Heller, Lassner, Maureen Ryan, Anghel, and Ravitz. See also Macpherson, 197–200.

7. The novel bears something in common with the British gothic tradition as well as with the American quest novel. The two girls in *Housekeeping*, who like traditional gothic heroines initially "play out intricate, urgent dramas of entrapment and miraculous escape" (86), might be seen as the two types of women characters Gilbert and Gubar identify as characteristic of nineteenth-century women's fiction: the rebel and the angel. Lucille, the angel, stops attempting to escape and conforms, devoting herself to housekeeping, while Ruth escapes. However, as Koenen points out, there is none of the terror in the house that typifies gothic houses as places of female entrapment (272).

8. Koenen also refers to Showalter's essay "Feminist Criticism in the Wilderness" in her chapter on the domestic fantastic, of which her consideration of *Housekeeping* is part—see 271–272. Both she and Lin (209, n. 7) provide clear explanations of the diagram that Showalter employs to indicate that realm of women's expression that falls outside the dominant discourse; see "Feminist Criticism" 262. Lin points out, however, what Koenen does not: that Showalter considers this zone to be "only 'a playful abstraction'" (209; Showalter 263). Below I discuss other ways that women's discourse, including Ruth's, challenges the discourse of the dominant culture by self-consciously subverting it even when employing it, rather than trying to locate itself outside of the dominant altogether, an impossible task.

9. Wyatt also argues that the novel is actually a *bildungsroman* in reverse, and thus it undermines the linearity of the traditional novel of development, giving Ruth and Sylvie instead a new kind of "female" development that eschews linear logic and rational progress. *Housekeeping* begins with Ruth's self-defining statement: "My name is Ruth" (*Housekeeping* 3) but ends with the dissolution of her character (Wyatt 83). According to Wyatt, "this discursive reversal of the process of ego formation undoes both the conception of the self as a closed structure and the fixed position of the subject who is generating the present discourse, eroding the principal supports of the symbolic order" (84). For another semiotic reading of the novel, see Aldrich's essay, which focuses on Lucille's use of symbolic/metaphorical language and Ruth's use of semiotic/literal language. See also Foster's insightful application of Julia Kristeva's "Woman's Time" to *Housekeeping*, as well as Rubenstein's detailed reading of the novel's treatment of the mother/daughter bond, the "transformative" po-

tential of Ruth and Sylvie's relationship, even when the "psychic disorder and even destruction" of Ruth's character seems "initially regressive" (*Boundaries of the Self* 227).

10. Meese, like Wyatt, stresses the novel's rejection of male symbolic language and views the characters' choice to take up a life of transience as "an exercise of female autonomy, a necessary outcome of woman's refusal to participate in the socially imposed economy of gender roles" (62). Foster maintains that the novel's refusal of capitalistic practices makes it politically engaged (93–4); he also argues that Sylvie and Ruth's final "state of existence exceeds the closure of dominant stories or histories" (96) and that the future tense used in the end of the novel marks a "proleptic troping of a possible future condition" for women (98). Mallon, like Wyatt, views Ruth and Sylvie as "present in their absence" (104) and locates in their transience "a constant source of power and possibility" (97–98), as do Lassner and Nancy Walker. Gernes gives the ending a different spin, reading it from a religious standpoint to argue that Sylvie "empowers the protagonist to move toward a truer self: [...] Ruth, under Sylvie's tutelage, rejects the world of property, law, and logic in favor of flux, female community, and the mystical embedded in the natural world" (163), a position Gernes views as positive since it "empowers women to satisfy the hunger of their spirits" rather than their merely physical needs (164). Bohannan makes a similar point about the characters' spiritual self-awareness. Geyh is disturbed by *Housekeeping*'s ending but focuses on Sylvie's and Ruth's secret returns to the house, in which she sees "progress" for the characters, who "disrupt" normative cultural formations of female subjectivity (120).

11. Cf. Lassner, who also stresses the "self-parody" in Ruth's narration, arguing that "Ruth becomes a woman writer who is a reader of the past," recasting traditionally male stories into stories for women (50). As Lassner points out, "Unlike the biblical Ruth, who disappears from the story that bears her name but which she did not write, Ruth in *Housekeeping* engineers her own disappearance and writes her own story [...] in order not to regenerate patriarchal myth" (52). Walker makes a very similar point about Robinson's revisions to biblical stories and Ruth's power of authorship (37–38).

12. Cf. Silverman's account of the relationship between woman's body and woman's voice in *The Acoustic Mirror: the Female Voice in Psychoanalysis and Cinema*. For a very different reading of Ruth's voice, see Caver, who stresses Ruth's silence as a character within her narrative and views her as exhibiting difficulties with language typical of trauma victims.

13. For yet another view of Ruth's voice, see

Champagne, who maintains that Ruth refuses to "re/present," that her strategy is "anti-representational," since to represent is by definition to falsify and constrain that which is represented. Champagne, then, emphasizes that the novel's resistance to patriarchy is located in the fact that "Ruth is a speechless narrator" (326). Anghel also theorizes that Ruth resists patriarchy through silence (431). It seems to me, however, that the novel's narrative strategies can be best illuminated through feminist theories of narrative voice that offer alternatives to voicelessness or speechlessness. Ryan also draws on the theories of Joanne Frye to interpret Ruth's first-person narration as evidence of Ruth's "appropriation of her own voice [...that] resists narrative conventions and social restrictions" (83).

14. Interestingly, as noted above, Ruth's existing outside narrative time is the factor that renders the novel fantastic for Koenen (288). My application of Lanser's work is developed also in the next chapter on Carol Shields's *The Stone Diaries*, a novel which even more explicitly than *Housekeeping* invites analysis along these lines. It should be noted that the narrative voices employed in these two novels do not precisely match the categories that Lanser establishes for the varieties of first- and third-person narration (15–20) precisely because Robinson's and Shields's narrators blur the bounds among them. For example, Ruth's authorial acts are not strictly speaking heterodiegetic as defined by Lanser (who draws on the work of Gerard Genette—see *Fictions of Authority* 16), since Ruth is a homodiegetic, first-person narrator. But many of her narrative statements nonetheless partake of the qualities associated with heterodiegetic, authorial narration.

15. King refers briefly here to the work of Lanser on authority and the female narrative but does not expand upon the ways in which Lanser's theories illuminate *Housekeeping* and Ruth's narrative authority (578 n. 14).

16. Kaivola likewise notes such instances, emphasizing how Ruth blurs fact and fiction so that "what she invents is so intricately and seamlessly interwoven with what she knows as to be almost imperceptible" (687), though her point about Ruth's narration is quite different than mine. See 687–688, including note 12.

17. Walker likewise notes that Ruth "sometimes assumes the stance of the omniscient narrator in describing scenes she could not have witnessed" and that "Robinson employs several rhetorical devices to simultaneously underscore Ruth's power as storyteller and call attention to the fictive, contingent potential of all narrative" (40). In addition to King, Walker provides a useful analysis of the novel's feminist narrative strategies (see especially 40–42).

18. Compare Heller's interpretation of this passage: "Robinson's novel grants motion to the words that would otherwise keep women stationary, fixing them eternally as daughters, mothers, wives. Ruth's own narrative awareness emphasizes her revelation that the wreckage of the past is preserved only through a fragile weaving of language which is ultimately volatile, fragmentary, and dangerously combustible" (103).

19. Geyh makes a similar point in her discussion of the importance of the women's return (120–121). McDermott, drawing on the theories of S. Boym (*The Future of Nostalgia*, New York: Basic Books, 2001), offers a compelling reading of what she considers an act of nostalgia on Ruth's and Sylvie's part, arguing that such nostalgia is not simply a conservative longing for what they left behind, the "socially hegemonic," but rather a nostalgia "for what has not yet been presented," a way of "imagining what might have been; as such, it is a crucial aspect of feminism's yearning for what has not been, yet" (268). In a similar vein, Walker writes that Robinson employs the negative not just in the ending but throughout the novel thus: "to say that something is *not* is to suggest that it might have been; the shadow remains even while substance is denied" (42).

20. Redding's article, an excerpt from which is used as the epigraph to this chapter, comes from a special issue of the journal *Mosaic* devoted to representations of the supernatural in American fiction.

21. Geyh also notes the doubling of Lucille and Sylvie in this passage (118–119). Galehouse interprets Lucille's gesture as one that illustrates her "desire for resolution, if not reconciliation," with regard to the broken family circle represented in the novel (135), again suggesting the continued presence of Ruth and Sylvie in Lucille's imagination.

CHAPTER 4

1. The original version of this chapter appeared under the title "The 'Invisible' Woman: Narrative Strategies in *The Stone Diaries*" in the *Journal of Narrative Theory* 36.1 (Winter 2006): 90–120. (c) *JNT: Journal of Narrative Theory*, published at Eastern Michigan University. I am grateful to editors Craig Dionne and Joseph Csicsila for permission to include a revised version.

2. For another view of Daisy's narrating the moment of her own death, see Wasmeier's article on *The Stone Diaries*, in which the author explores the relationship between death and the act of life writing and concludes that "the desire to create security and reliability in a life marked by fragmentation and struggle for identity, and

pervaded by death from the very beginning, is the protagonist's incentive for creating the account of her life and death" (447). She views the novel as an example not just of fictional autobiography, but of "autothanatography" as well.

3. Williams is one of few critics who attribute the voice in all its variations to Daisy herself (see note 5 below). He accounts for the voice through neural biological theories of perception, drawing especially on the work of Paul John Eakin (*How Our Lives Become Stories: Making Selves*. Ithaca, NY: Cornell University Press, 1999), and concluding like Shields and like Fee that Daisy is still alive at the novel's end, when she simply imagines "a self […] extending beyond death" ("Making Stories" 27).

4. Other critics concur. For example, Clara Thomas writes that "the shifting voice of the narrator, [is] often Daisy's herself, but by no means always" (158), and while Billingham provides several ways to understand the third-person voice as coming from Daisy herself, she also notes that at times, "[w]here the text appears to be focalized through a consciousness other than Daisy's, the narrator could readily be mistaken for the omniscient narrator of realist convention" (284). Hansen-Pauly notes the presence of an omniscient narrator that she assumes to be some voice other than Daisy's (302, 306, 313); it is at various points in the story "when Daisy appears quite passive, unable to assess what is happening to her, that other narrators take over" (303). Wasmeier refers to "a chorus of narrators recounting [Daisy's] life (444), though she does also speculate that Daisy reconstructs her own life from a third-person perspective (446–447). Bak addresses "the highly tenuous and problematical status of Daisy Goodwill as a narrating self," emphasizing Daisy's "weak sense of self" (15). Many reviewers reach similar conclusions about the narrative voice. Fitzgerald focuses upon Daisy's "failure to find a language" and contrasts her with the novel's narrator (19); Sherman writes that "Daisy, unfortunately, never finds her own voice" (23); and Parini refers to "Ms. Shields's several diarists" (3). Among those reviewers who see Daisy as speaking for herself are Clayton, who notes a discrepancy between Daisy's outer and inner lives and who "senses she is at last beginning to live for herself, to write her own story" (19); McGill, who notes that "by writing her life in the third person she becomes her own observer, knowing that the outer person and the inner self often diverge" (34); and Fee, who distinguishes between the "domestic Daisy" and the "liberated Daisy," concluding that "only the reader hears the voice of the liberated Daisy" (174).

5. Readers should see the middle section of Vauthier's article (182–187) for a careful consideration of evidence suggesting that Daisy's voice and the third-person voice are not the same. However, it seems to me that instances in which the narration changes from first- to third-person in midsentence suggest that only Daisy is speaking: for example, "The long days of isolation, of silence, the torment of boredom—all these pressed down on me, on young Daisy Goodwill and emptied her out" (75). Williams shares the view that many sections of the novel narrated in third person about characters other than Daisy are "product[s] of Daisy's own imagination" ("Re-imagining a Stone Angel" 136). Later Williams queries, "was the absent autobiographer ever really so absent? Or was her virtual absence more likely a sign of her omnipresence as a third-person omniscient narrator?" (138). In his more recent article, Williams points out that in the opening of *The Stone Diaries*, Daisy "announc[es] from the outset her ubiquity in time and space, attributes that link her to an old-fashioned omniscient narrator" ("Making Stories, Making Selves," 16) and finds two ways to support the case that "the whole account in chapter seven of Daisy's 'Sorrow' belongs to Daisy herself" (23), this chapter being focalized through the perspective of many different people who have known Daisy. (See Williams' compelling explanation of these two factors, 23–25.) Likewise Osland, in an intriguing article about parallels between *The Stone Diaries* and *Jane Eyre*, suggests that Daisy might be the primary narrating consciousness (95 and 109, n. 20); although she does not fully explore the narrative strategies that give her this sense, Osland concludes that "if, as I have been arguing, Daisy herself […] is the product of Daisy's imagination making, then the 'glittering joke' that is buried with Daisy is Shields's own 'wily subversion' of a narrative tradition that makes it seem as if people like Daisy have had their heads cut off or their tongues 'yanked out' (252)" (105).

6. Roy also analyzes Shields's novel in light of theories of women's autobiography, arguing that Shields "turns autobiography into critical practice by engaging with feminist theories of life writing" (114). On the question of narrative voice, Roy's view approaches my own: "Whether Daisy's is the controlling consciousness of the narrative remains ambiguous, although the repeated references to her autobiographical project strongly suggest that she is imagining others' responses, as well as events in her life and others' lives, as she writes her autobiography with invisible ink" (121). Briganti likewise engages with the novel's relationship to autobiography, with especial attention to Shields's "reclaiming of the maternal body and the elaboration of its relation to language in

a genre that has traditionally banished the body from representation" (185). Finally, Hansen-Pauly addresses Shields's novel through theories of autobiography, though her view about the narrative voice differs substantially from mine, and her article deals mostly with the limitations of an autobiography's ability to capture truth.

7. In thinking about the ways in which the novel employs these two kinds of narrative strategies, I was aided a great deal by Kristin King's reading of Marilynne Robinson's novel *Housekeeping*, to which *The Stone Diaries* bears some interesting resemblances. Like *Housekeeping*'s narrator Ruth Stone, Daisy Goodwill Flett reclaims access to symbolic, authorial expression from a place outside the story written for her by the culture.

8. Readers interested in learning more about this aspect of the novel, especially its relation to the theories of Kristeva, should consult Briganti.

9. Cf. Howells, who makes a similar point (*Contemporary Canadian Women's Fiction* 87), as do Roy (131) and Briganti (195).

10. Shields's strategy for portraying Daisy resembles Marilynne Robinson's strategy in *Housekeeping* for portraying that novel's invisible characters, Ruth and Sylvie. Wyatt's work on *Housekeeping* has also shaped my reading of *The Stone Diaries*. One might say of Daisy that like the characters and readers haunted by Ruth and Sylvie at the end of *Housekeeping*, the readers of *The Stone Diaries* are "thronged by [Daisy's] absence" (*Housekeeping* 219).

11. Roy takes a somewhat different approach to this feature of Daisy's autobiography, noting that the large sections of the novel focalized through other characters "illustrat[e...] sacrifice of individuality" both to demonstrate that women's lives are often defined through their relationships to others and to demonstrate the limits of such a way of writing a woman's life story (124–125).

12. Sidonie Smith comments on how the twentieth-century woman autobiographer employs both semiotic strategies and also others which are not "outside time and history" (*Poetics* 58). Rather, she may claim "the legitimacy and authority of another subjectivity" (59).

13. Vauthier claims that Daisy's last words—"I am not at peace"—are "recorded by another voice," reinforcing her view that Daisy is "voiceless, like many women of her class and generation" (186). Yet if one interprets the split voices as emanating from Daisy herself, these contradictory statements provide a way for her to articulate her own feelings.

14. Johnson emphasizes throughout Daisy's authority in her narrative and seeks quite explicitly to counter the criticism of the novel that stresses Daisy's absence, arguing that readers must focus less on "what *isn't* there [...] attending instead to what *is*" (202). She views "the split or multiple narration [...] as a critique of sexist inequality" (218), though she does not necessarily argue that Daisy is the sole narrator: at one point, she mentions "the novel's many narrators" (220).

15. Lanser's reference is to Franz Stanzel's *Narrative Situations in the Novel*, trans. James Pusack (Bloomington: Indiana University Press, 1971). Lanser points out that critical discourse on narratology, which considers first-person and third-person narration to be opposed narrative modes, "conceals similarities between them" (20); Shields's novel provides another good example of a novel that that blurs the bounds between these modes. Lanser herself includes *Oronooko* (Aphra Behn) and *Scenes of Clerical Life* (George Eliot) in this category (20).

16. For example, Vauthier's main concern is not with feminism but with the novel's "ruptures" and its relationship to theories of chaotics and postmodernism. Slethaug similarly employs chaos theory to examine Shields's treatment of the self and of narrative (62). While Slethaug is interested in "Daisy's socially gendered position" (64) and the feminist issues that novel raises, he ultimately does not consider *The Stone Diaries* in light of feminist theory. Mellor does examine the novel from a feminist perspective and discusses the ways in which Daisy is a "textual creation" (103), but she never views Daisy as recuperating a sense of self outside of social constructs of femininity and instead emphasizes what she views as the novel's poststructural dismantling of the notion of self. For a refreshingly different view of the novel's relationship to postmodernism, readers should see Johnson's consideration of the troubled relationship between feminism and postmodernism, in which she argues that the novel offers a much more positive version of the female self than many prior critics allow, with "its trajectory toward hope and self-knowledge" (202). Shields, she writes, "approaches the postmodern novel [...] not as an apolitical renunciation of reality, but as an act of love" (222)—a stance typical of the authors included in this book whose use of narrative experiment in conjunction with the fantastic counters dominant constructions of the postmodern fantastic.

17. Similarly, Friedman observes that for women, the self is not a poststructural self but a self exhibiting "an awareness of the meaning of the cultural category WOMAN for the patterns of women's individual destiny. [...] Writing the self shatters the cultural hall of mirrors and breaks the silence imposed by male speech" (41). See also Neuman, who observes that "the answer for many recent critics is the adoption of

a theory of the subject that accepts neither the ontological nor post-structuralist positions but negotiates a space and a 'subject' between them by acknowledging the specific 'epistemologies' behind the speaking/writing 'I'" (3–4). Buss's article addresses the split nature of the self in several women's autobiographies; her argument about doubled discourse also works quite well in conjunction with the fictional autobiography *The Stone Diaries*.

18. Billingham draws on the theories of Hutcheon, employing the term "self-conscious realism" to describe Shields's work, and noting that "while her texts sometimes include postmodern elements, she also maintains a humanist focus upon the internal consciousness and daily lives of her characters" (276). Bak also observes that the novel blends postmodernism and traditional realism, calling the novel "a curiously hybrid or amphibian book" (13).

CHAPTER 5

1. Kingsolver has been criticized for her portrayal of African peoples in her novel. For example, Stephen Fox, who explores the shortcomings of Kingsolver's representations of disabled Africans, argues that "Kingsolver is able to humanize metaphors that elsewhere exploit people with disabilities, but she trades them for romantic (and romantic Marxian) metaphors about Africans. In the process she does a grave disservice to individuals with disability in developing countries by minimizing their actual plights" (412). Kunz, acknowledging that Kingsolver is correct in her representation of the historical facts surrounding U.S. involvement in Congo politics in the 1960s, nonetheless finds Kingsolver's interpretation of U.S. foreign policy and African politics "touchingly naïve" (296). Jacobson, considering Kingsolver's treatment of "cross-cultural discourse," concludes that the novel "is finally more concerned with its own discursive constructedness than with the history and the political, material reality of the Congo" (116) and finds that it fails to portray true cross-cultural discourse. I offer here a different reading of the novel's self-consciousness about language. Koza, who is also somewhat critical of Kingsolver's representation of Africa, does point out, however, that Kingsolver's "primary goal, then, is not to represent Africa, but to revise America's representation of itself" (288) in its involvement in Africa. My argument focuses on the ways in which the novel's American women revise themselves and their world-views through the process of transculturation. In spite of shortcomings in her representation of Africans, Kingsolver is nonetheless very interested in offering a corrective to reductive versions of the ways in which cultural influence works in a colonial and postcolonial setting.

2. Pratt notes that the term "'transculturation' was coined in the 1940s by Cuban sociologist Fernando Ortiz [...]. Uruguayan critic Angel Rama incorporated the term into literary studies in the 1970s. Ortiz proposed the term to replace the paired concepts of acculturation and deculturation that described the transference of culture in reductive fashion imagined from within the interests of the metropolis" (228 n. 4).

3. Drawing on the theories of Homi K. Bhabha, Koza notes that in the Price household, "the family structure replicates the power structure of colonialism" (285). See also Demory, who notes that "the day-to-day engagement with [the] necessities [of survival] requires the women to learn how to live with their environment, rather than imposing their wills upon it" (185).

4. Cf. Ognibene, who writes that Nathan "fails to see how the language of the region, rich in tonal ambiguities, describes far better than his English the complex antithesis that face people in his congregation" (28).

5. Leah's new name translates as "as true as the truth can be" (287). Unlike her father, and like her sister Adah, Leah recognizes that truth is relative and multiple.

6. Pratt's reference is to Peter Hulme, *Colonial Encounters*, Cambridge University Press, 1987, p. 249. On biracial romance in a colonial setting, see also Smith, p. 7; and Goldblatt, pp. 46–47.

7. Rachel, too, remains to live and work in Africa, but in a very different way than Leah: most like her father of the four Price daughters, she represents neocolonialism in Africa by becoming an astute businesswoman and running a resort hotel there. She is "'Changed the Least'" (494) of the sisters insofar as she is identified by Leah as "worldly" from the start (16) and holds racist views that persist throughout her adulthood (477). In spite of recognizing that she has become "someone different" (367), she nonetheless asserts that she won't let Africa "influence [her] mind" (516). Interestingly, Rachel, like Nathan, has a troubled relationship with language. While he is rigid in his interpretation of words (and the Word), Rachel's language is plagued by malapropisms. The infelicity of these two characters with language, juxtaposed with the other characters' ability to read multiple meanings and to find appropriate language for their stories, invites the reader to compare their approaches to Africa, in spite of the fact that Rachel's worldliness sets her apart from Nathan. But Rachel's neocolonialist capitalism is the flip side of her father's missionary imperialism. Indeed, Rachel might be identified with the typical male commercial traveler that

Sidonie Smith describes: "For these travelers, the land was 'underdeveloped' and its inhabitants backward, dirty, and lazy, in need of a secularized version of the civilizing mission. These travelers assembled in their narratives protoethnographic accounts that served mercantile interests" (6). In addition, Rachel's extreme materialism invites the reader to contrast her with her self-sacrificing sister, Leah, who lives in poverty; with her more spiritually oriented sister, Adah; and finally with her youngest sister, Ruth May, who by the novel's end literally embodies African spiritual beliefs, has herself become a spirit.

8. For example, when the family is fleeing an invasion of driver ants, both Adah and Ruth May need to be carried. Orleanna chooses to carry Ruth May, but Adah later observes, "In the end she could only carry one child alive out of Africa and I was that child" (413). In addition, Adah's survival instinct at the time of the ant invasion causes her to conclude, "that is what it means to be a beast in the kingdom" (306), and Ruth May is referred to repeatedly by her mother as "little beast" (385). Both Adah and Ruth May are threatened by native wild life: a lion stalks Adah at one point, and of course the snake is responsible for Ruth May's death. The motif of spying further connects Ruth May and Adah; both learn secrets about Eben Axleroot, Ruth May about his smuggling diamonds and Adah about his role in Congolese leader Patrice Lumumba's assassination. Adah comments explicitly about spying, observing that "night is the time for seeing without being seen" (295), while Ruth May, who breaks her arm when she falls from a tree while spying, speaks of spying also in the next life, looking down from the trees, unseen by human eyes as she gazes on the living (273).

9. That Leah and Adah have some presentiment of Ruth May's transformation speaks to their own process of transculturation, their own participation in African spirituality. That Orleanna engages in direct address to her dead daughter throughout her portions of the narrative provides further evidence of Africa's effects on her: "Africa rose up to seize me [...]. You've played some trick on the dividing of my cells so my body can never be free of the small parts of Africa it consumed. [...] It seems I only know myself, anymore, by your attendance in my soul" (87).

10. Orleanna's guilt over her role in Ruth May's death and the continuing presence of Ruth May in the novel after the time of her death also recall Morrison's *Beloved*, explored in the next chapter.

11. See DeMarr's insightful commentary on the relationship between the titles of Kingsolver's books within *The Poisonwood Bible* and their biblical/apocryphal counterparts (122–124 and 137–141). DeMarr posits that that the last section constitutes, "[in] some senses [...] the true 'Revelation' for this Poisonwood Bible" in that it "not only presents a new perspective (and a new narrative method) but it also mystically reveals a spiritual conclusion to all the events and meanings of the novel" (141).

12. A prime example Lanser identifies is Amy Tan's *The Joy Luck Club*. Kingsolver's novel approaches this kind of narrative structurally, since the sisters' and Orleanna's narratives are interwoven, with each one speaking multiple times and in no particular pattern. (Orleanna's narration always opens Books One through Five, but then the order of the daughters' narration within the different books is fairly random.) Ruth May's voice disappears at the time of her death, until it reappears in Book Seven. The sisters' stories are indeed multiple, especially after the point in the novel that the family splits up. The two sisters who remain narrate their own stories that are quite distinct from one another; Adah's story concerns her return to the United States with her mother and her ensuing medical career, and Orleanna's story centers on retrospective reflections about Africa and Nathan, with direct addresses to the deceased Ruth May. As such, it is generated from a different point in time than the daughters' narratives that relate events as they unfold. The story is perhaps more singular, however, than in novels like *The Joy Luck Club* or Louise Erdrich's *Love Medicine* (which, Lanser points out, is a communal narrative that is told sometimes from an authorial point of view, sometimes from a first-person point of view), insofar as the episodes are less disjointed and unfold largely chronologically, with the exception of Orleanna's sections. Still, Kingsolver's novel satisfies other criteria of this narrative voice.

13. Even Rachel recognizes that "you can't just sashay into the jungle aiming to change it all over to the Christian style, without expecting the jungle to change you right back" (515); she explicitly distances herself from her father and even rejects the constraints of traditional marriage that at one time defined Nathan's relationship to Orleanna and Rachel's hopes for her own future. Finally, in her penultimate chapter, Rachel describes the scene in which she, Adah, and Leah discuss Nathan's death, a scene in which the three sisters, disparate as they are, decidedly act in a communal fashion as they contemplate Nathan's end (487–488).

14. Lanser is careful to point out that the function of each type of narrative voice—personal, authorial, communal—depends on its context, and that all three have potential drawbacks as well as potential advantages for nar-

rating women's experience (278–279; see also 22).

15. Ognibene emphasizes especially Oreleanna's and Adah's status as storytellers (23–24 and 29).

CHAPTER 6

1. My reading focuses especially on the experience of the female characters and highlights how the narrative revises genre conventions in a specifically feminist manner. However, readers perhaps underestimate what a significant portion of the novel is devoted to Paul D's story and how much of the narration is focalized from his perspective. My treatment of him relates to the feminist framework of this project, but interested readers should also see Barnett's argument that Morrison's incorporating his narrative of being a male rape victim specifically "foregrounds race, rather than gender, as the category determining domination or subjection to rape" (419), as well as Sitter's reading of masculinity in the novel.

2. Compare Homans' discussion of *Beloved* with remarks made about gender and narrative by Sally Robinson, quoted in both the Introduction and in Chapter Three of this book. See also Schopp's analysis of Morrison's treatment of narrative; Schopp observes that although patriarchal narratives about slavery prove oppressive, nevertheless, the characters within *Beloved* must rely on the tools of narrative.

3. Several critics analyze the complexities of designating *Beloved* as a postmodern novel, given that it is so far removed from what D'Haen terms "central postmodernism," associated with self-referential language play of American male metafictionists, for example. Rimmon-Kenan identifies *Beloved* as belonging to "a counter-tendency within postmodernism, incorporating doubt yet going beyond it" (109). See also Spalding's insightful discussion of African American postmodernism and *Beloved* (12–17), as well as Kimberly Chabot Davis's thoughtful examination of the complexities of "black postmodernism." According to Davis, Morrison on the one hand adopts "the poststructuralist view that reality is a function of discourse," while on the other hand, she embraces "the idea that new representations can change our perceptions of historical reality" (82). Lanser also addresses the issue in a helpful manner in her chapter on Morrison's novels, "Unspeakable Voice: Toni Morrison's Postmodern Authority" (*Fictions of Authority* 120–138), as does Perez-Torres, who finds that "*Beloved* and other novels that emerge from multicultural histories diverge from classically postmodern texts [...] in their relation to sociohistorical realities" (92). These critics provide compelling arguments for interpreting *Beloved* through the lens of postmodern theory, with the recognition that postmodernism itself has many manifestations, not all of which are relevant to—indeed some run counter to—Morrison's project in *Beloved*.

4. The same semiotic modes of communication and attention to the imaginary bond between mother and child that characterize *Housekeeping* and *The Stone Diaries* likewise characterize Morrison's novel, especially in the sections narrated in Sethe's and Beloved's first-person voices. Nearly all critics approaching *Beloved* from a psychoanalytic perspective suggest something similar to Jackson's claim about psychoanalysis as a methodology for interpreting the socially subversive function of the fantastic: social norms "are reproduced and sustained" in the unconscious (6); thus their approach diverges from an essentialist psychoanalytic approach and is always historicized, given that the historical conditions that foster slavery are what give rise to Sethe's and Beloved's need to bond in the powerful and ultimately destructive manner that they do. Morrison, too, as Wyatt and Moglen point out, insists on characters' access to socially symbolic discourse, exposing the limits of the semiotic (cf. Homans 12). In order to move beyond paralyzing historical forces, all the characters must engage with them in symbolic terms, or as Wyatt puts it, in "relation to other subjects" (475). Wyatt concentrates on Denver's situation at the end of the novel, while Moglen traces as well Baby Suggs's movement from semiotic to symbolic expression. Other critics who analyze the mother-daughter bond between Beloved and Sethe within a psychoanalytic framework, but often emphasizing the need to historicize, include Anderson (137), Cummings, Koenen (119–120), Liscio (33–37), and Waxman (74–82). For an alternate approach to explaining the unconventional language and punctuation of Beloved's first-person narration, see Lawrence, who argues that "in *Beloved*, the question of authority over one's own body is consistently related to that of authority over discourse; bodily and linguistic disempowerment frequently intersect" (190).

5. The list of critics who address the novel as a ghost story is too long to include here, but those critics who view the novel as belonging specifically to the mode of the fantastic include Armitt, Christol, Cornwell, Cutter, Daily, Dubey, Jessee, Koenen, Malmgren, Moglen, Rimmon-Kenan, and Trussler. Like Cornwell and Cutter, Jessee draws explicitly on Todorov, concluding that *Beloved* is both marvelous and uncanny, situated on the border between the two insofar as Beloved is both a ghost and a psy-

chological "illusion" of the characters (203). Rimmon-Kenan makes a similar point, emphasizing the novel's "insoluble ambiguity" and arguing against a "univocal" reading of the text as either uncanny or supernatural (118–119). Christol, who also frames her reading in terms of Todorov's work, tends to conflate the terms "fantastic" and "supernatural" in an essay that does not explore *Beloved*'s borderline status or the concept of hesitation but which does make numerous insightful points about the function of the fantastic, explored in more detail in the discussion below of the fantastic's relationship to an African world view. The notable exception among critics with regard to the supernatural element is House, whose article offers a completely naturalistic explanation for the mysterious young woman called Beloved. The essay has come under attack for ignoring or failing to account for much evidence that supports the supernatural reading, but nonetheless, many of House's insights about the naturalistic explanation for Beloved have important bearing on the novel's fantastic dimension insofar as the evidence House presents casts doubt on the simple acceptance of the supernatural status of Beloved and hence renders the novel fantastic in Todorov's terms, though House herself does not adopt this view, since she dismisses the supernatural reading altogether. A few early reviewers dismiss the novel precisely because of its fantastic dimension: see, for example, reviews by Bayles, Crouch, and Reumens, who complain that the presence of a ghost undermines the social realism (see Bayles 40). But as I explore below, and as most critics of the novel agree, the presence of the ghost actually invites deeper historical analysis than would be possible without the device.

6. Cutter discusses focalization at length in her discussion of the novel as an example of the pure fantastic, arguing that readers tend to overlook cues for naturalistic explanations or at least allow cues for a supernatural reading of the character Beloved to overshadow the naturalistic ones because the novel makes it difficult for the reader to stake out a position about Beloved's status that differs from the position adopted by Sethe and Denver: Beloved is indeed the embodied ghost of the dead baby (63). Cutter even goes so far as to suggest that this phenomenon constitutes a flaw in the narration or a "mistake" on Morrison's part because the text then becomes closed, because readers can then settle on a final meaning (66). However, the extent to which the text simply invites the reader to share the point of view of Denver and Sethe (whose views are not, as Cutter implies, identical), is likely overstated. While it is true that many readers of this novel do resolve the moment of hesitation by accepting the presence of the supernatural, nonetheless a number of elements in the text resist final closure. Far from being fixed, Beloved's meanings remain multiple and indeterminate, and the narration in fact specifically invites analysis along these lines. For insightful arguments about the novel's ambiguity concerning Beloved, see articles by Rimmon-Kenan and Phelan. See also Rimmon-Kenan's commentary on narrative technique and the importance of the lack of internal focalization in the chapter in which the young woman Beloved appears at 124 (112–114).

7. Other critics who identify *Beloved* as a magic realist novel include Armitt, Cornwell, Faris, Hegerfeldt, Schroeder, Spalding, and Zamora. While Cornwell is clear about his terms in discussing the novel as both fantastic and magic realist, Armitt is not, simply using the terms interchangeably. Cornwell's observation that the novel incorporates both magic realism and the fantastic can be expanded with careful attention to how the narrative point of view shapes the reader's hesitation in his or her attempt to account for seemingly impossible events. Morrison herself, who objects to the term "magic realist," locates her novel's fantastic dimension in African spirituality. See Morrison's interview with Christina Davis (especially 144–145) where Morrison explains her objections or "indifference" to the term magic realist. In brief, she expresses fears that "magic," used in conjunction with the writing of "discredited people," has connotations of exoticism or Orientalism (145); she is concerned that literary critics label works magic realist as "a convenient way to skip again what was the truth in the art of certain writers" (144). Certain formulations of magic realism as escapism or as a privileged construction of reality, the manner in which critic Lori Chamberlain, for example, construes the mode (7) bear out Morrison's fears. Yet more recent developments in magic realist theory over the past thirty years, which have evolved in conjunction with postcolonial theory and which expand considerations of magic realism beyond Latin America, would seem to beset the fears that Morrison expressed to Davis.

8. Other critics remark upon Morrison's combining seemingly incompatible genres. See Malmgren's consideration of the tensions between the ghost story and the historical novel in *Beloved*. Horvitz, who comments on the novel's use of realist conventions within the ghost story, writes that "the text is so grounded in historical reality that it could be used to teach American history classes" (157); Moglen notes that Morrison employs conventions of both "realism and fantasy," which "constitut[e] each other as fictive modes while appearing to be mutually exclusive" (201); but "by reconcep-

utalizing the relation of the genres that she writes within, Morrison radicalizes both realism and the fantastic" (205). Ferguson writes that in *Beloved*, "what is commonly called the supernatural is also the manifestation of history" (113). And Armitt argues against House's reading of the novel as "pure social mimesis": rather, "the supernatural carries the socio-historical along with it" (122–123).

9. Morrison herself comments in an interview about her earlier novel *Song of Solomon* that she wants to reclaim the history of African American people, to "debate" versions of history written by those who write from the "conqueror's" perspective (Davis 142).

10. I am not suggesting that Cutter herself overlooks evidence for a naturalized reading of Beloved's presence, merely that she exaggerates the manner in which the novel's narrative point of view invites readers to overlook ways of viewing the character of Beloved other than as the incarnation of Sethe's murdered daughter.

11. Horvitz is the first to advance this view (see especially 162–163.) Holden-Kirwan argues that Beloved is the ghost only of Sethe's mother, not the ghost of the dead baby.

12. Cf. Anderson, who writes that "there is no authoritative version of history, no single 'truth.' The narrative voice does not offer a transcendent level of knowledge—a position from which the reader can 'understand'—but blends instead with the other voices in the novel" (138). This point has bearing as well on the discussion below of how Morrison revises traditional historiography. For a somewhat different view, see Lanser's analysis of the authorial narrator in *Beloved*; she argues that the narrator never confirms the characters' views of Beloved's identity until the very last word of the novel, where the authorial voice signals the narrator's belief that Beloved is indeed Sethe's murdered daughter (135).

13. Morrison's treatment of identity is, like her novel's relationship to postmodern theory, complex; the novel bridges the traditional concept of identity inherent in identity politics and a postmodern concept of identity, identity thereby constituting yet another middle ground in which critics locate the novel. As Keizer states the matter, "the novel intervenes in current debates about black subjectivity, helping to define a position for the black subject between essentialism and postmodern fragmentation" (105), a sentiment echoed by numerous other critics. Keizer, drawing on Althusser's theory of interpellation, analyzes the ways in which the novel's characters resist interpellation and achieve agency when African aspects of their identity come into conflict with aspects of the dominant culture's attempts to define them in its terms. For other insightful discussion of the issues at stake, see Mohanty's essay and Spalding's discussion of African American postmodernism (12–23). While Morrison suggests that characters in *Beloved* must struggle to "gather their pieces...in all the right order (271–2), Beloved herself "explode[s]" (263) or "erupts into her separate parts" (274), her disremembered status at the novel's end troubling the notion of wholeness or stable identity.

14. At the novel's end, Beloved remains a being "whose multiplicity transcends any story that can be told about her" (Phelan 239). See also Krumholz's "The Ghosts of Slavery: Historical Recovery in *Beloved*," where Krumholz notes the dual nature of Beloved's role in the novel, concluding that "Beloved, as a trickster figure, participates in the healing function of the novel, but by refusing to be fixed by a unitary meaning she also remains unhealed—a rift in the attempt to close meaning and thereby close off the past from the present" (402). Similarly, Spearey writes that after the exorcism, "in her ensuing '(dis)incarnation,' Beloved [...] refuses—in spite of her persistent demands to be named and claimed—to become static or unitary, or to identify herself according to the terms of any single discourse" (175). While many critics thus see a positive function in Beloved's refusing to be named at the novel's end, readers should consider, too, that the baby ghost's very namelessness during her short lifetime—she is called only the "crawling already? baby," and her tombstone contains no name, just the word "Beloved" that Sethe recalls from the funeral service and purchases from the engraver in exchange for ten minutes of sex (5)—is deeply problematic in the African ancestor tradition, since in order for the departed to appear to family members after death, in the state of living death, "recognition by name is extremely important" (Mbiti, *African Religions and Philosophy* 25).

15. Cornwell also notes the importance of the different focalizations and the use of Schoolteacher's point of view in these several pages that contrast with Sethe's own account (201–2).

16. In an analysis of Schoolteacher's discourse, Heller makes a similar point, writing that "Schoolteacher represents an extreme embodiment of the logocentric assumptions of the written word as constitutive of the domain of knowledge and truth" ("Reconstructing Kin" 222).

17. See Henderson's article in its entirety, especially pages 75–83, for an insightful discussion of Sethe as feminist historiographer.

18. See also O'Reilly's thorough account of Morrison's treatment of African-American motherhood, its alternative not only to patriarchy, but also to "dominant [white] ideologies of motherhood" (137).

19. See also Atkinson's analysis of the oral tradition in *Beloved*: stories "are not locked into a static position, but rather they have a flexibility that allows for, and validates, a number of tellings and retellings" (24). In addition to storytelling and the oral tradition, one means by which critics explore the recursive narrative patterns of *Beloved*, readers should also consider the influence on the novel of African American musical forms. See, for example, Rodriguez's analysis of the blues aesthetic in *Beloved*.

20. Many of Morrison's critics draw on Mbiti to explicate African concepts embodied in *Beloved*. See, for example, Waxman (79–80); Jessee (200–201); Keizer (110ff); and Christian (367–370). Christian's essay, titled "Fixing Methodologies," argues explicitly for an Africanist reading of *Beloved* and is designed to serve as a corrective to readings based on Western literary theories. Christol, however, who also uses Mbiti's work, makes a convincing case for analyzing *Beloved* both through the lens of theories of the fantastic as they have been applied to Western writing and through the lens of African culture, since the former in effect calls attention to the reader's cultural blinders and invites consideration of the latter. Handley draws on Jahn's study *Muntu* (1961) in his reading of *Beloved*'s African philosophical concept *nommo*, "the magic power of the word to call things into being" (677), which constitutes a key means for his understanding of Beloved and the presence of ancestors who have passed in Morrison's novel. See also Washington's article, which employs other sources on African culture to provide an Africanist reading of *Beloved*.

21. As Mbiti points out, the relative lack of emphasis upon future events in African conceptions of time influences understanding of history and also precludes a Judeo-Christian religious perspective, with its emphasis on the "world to come" (*African Religions and Philosophy* 23). Morrison's subsequent novel, *Paradise*, explores much more explicitly the dynamic that results when a group of African Americans adopt American foundational myths couched in Puritan Jeremiad rhetoric, and it employs elements of African religion to counter this "progressive" tendency. While I want to emphasize here the importance of the fact that *Beloved*'s fantastic dimension incorporates an African world-view as one of the means by which it counters Western constructions of reality and positions the reader in an alternate reality, I develop in Chapter Seven a more detailed reading of Morrison's treatment of patriarchal Christianity and her use of African and Afro-Christian belief systems in her novel *Paradise*.

22. Cf. Hegerfeldt's discussion of the magic realist strategy of literalizing metaphors (56–59). Morrison also adopts a strategy that Hegerfeldt identifies as a characteristic effect of magic realism: destabilizing or defamiliarizing reality. That is, when information is presented through ex-centric focalizers, as is the case in most of *Beloved*'s narration since the majority of the novel is focalized through the ex-slaves' perspectives, that which seems strange or impossible to the Western reader is presented as an accepted reality (like the baby ghost early in the novel or some characters' assumption later in the novel that Beloved is the incarnation of Sethe's dead daughter), while that which is more familiar to readers (like the institution of slavery in America) is presented as strange or unbelievable (Hegerfeldt 203–204). As a result, "the contrast between the two triggers a reinterpretation of received assumptions" (204). Several of Morrison's critics observe a similar phenomenon. Waxman notes that Morrison's employing the "magical context of reincarnation" constitutes "an effective strategy for encouraging reinterpretation of a reality about which we have some preconceptions, that is, the history of slavery" (70). According to Spalding, "in *Beloved*, Morrison creates an alternative representation of slavery that mines the formal dimensions of the gothic novel but forces readers to shift their focus away from the fantastic elements like the haunted house and the ghost toward the 'real' gothic elements of the text: slavery itself and those who systematically perpetuated it" (63). And Schmudde hypothesizes that "*Beloved* may be unique in using the ghost story to shock its readers into locating the source of horror not in mysteries beyond this world, but rather in the repressed and unclaimed realities of the factual, historical past" (415). In fact this is a common strategy of texts that employ both magic realist and fantastic conventions and is not unique to *Beloved*. See also Redding, who comments on the way that *Beloved*'s use of the fantastic calls attention to the "fantasized 'America' [that] has been staked out" (176).

23. Many critics have analyzed Morrison's revisions to the slave narrative. See, for example, Travis's essay on how Morrison complicates this genre, with attention to the ways that the narrative positions the reading audience. Lovalerie King explores in detail an important exchange between Schoolteacher and Sixo that for her constitutes a key element of the novel's revisions to the slave narrative. Weissberg comments on *Beloved*'s combining the slave narrative and the Gothic novel (112–114). Hamilton provides a concise overview of slave narrative conventions (436) and subsequent analysis of how the gothic elements of *Beloved* challenge these conventions (440–441). Mobley makes a similar point in writing that "Morrison's novel exposes the unsaid of the narratives, the psy-

chic subtexts that lie within and beneath the historical facts" by emphasizing more than the "material conditions of slavery" (192–193), as does Dubey, writing about the novel's "generic excess that destabilizes the reasonable, literate discourse of the slave narratives (195). Koolish (421), Waxman (58–60), and Koenen (115) also comment on how the form of Morrison's novel and its fantastic dimension create a new way of recounting the history of slavery, revising historiography. Robbins's article presents the case that critics need to attend to gender issues, not just issues of race, when analyzing the slave narrative genre. See also Spalding's recent book on postmodern slave narratives, which provides a very thorough account of nineteenth-century slave narratives. Spalding generally views Morrison, among the other authors that he treats, as recuperating many elements of these narratives in addition to revising them, identifying more continuity between the older narratives and *Beloved* than do many other critics. Morrison herself comments on her revisions to the genre in "The Site of Memory."

24. The gothic elements of *Beloved* are explored by Britton, Booher, Bryant, and Weissberg among others, but *Beloved*'s intersection with the twentieth-century female gothic in particular has been a neglected aspect of the novel.

25. See Sitter's article for a thorough examination of the contrast between Garner's white patriarchal view and Sixo's African definition of manhood, and Paul D's position with regard to these competing definitions. See also Schopp's comments on Paul's manhood, 221–223. Though these critics do not do so, it is useful to locate the novel's treatment of masculinity within its critique of classic gothic conventions.

26. Of the novel's gothic elements, Koenen writes that "the haunted house does not symbolize a gendered conflict between female powerlessness and male violence in the nuclear family, but a racial conflict between black powerlessness and white violence that disastrously affects the black family" (119). I maintain that gender, too, is important; Sitter's analysis of the novel allows readers to see the intersection of issues of race and gender. Brogan also notes that in ethnic ghost stories or the genre that she identifies as "cultural hauntings," of which *Beloved* is one central example, "as an absence made present, the ghost can give expression to the ways in which women are rendered invisible in the public sphere" (25).

27. See Morrison's "Unspeakable Things, Unspoken," in which she comments on how she chose the designation for 124 and the "thrilling prospect" for slaves of having an address (31).

CHAPTER 7

1. *Homily on Luke 1, Homilies on Luke: Fragments on Luke* 5–6, cited in Ehrman 13.

2. For excellent readings of the novel's critique of patriarchal Christianity that do not comment on the novel's relationship to Gnosticism, see articles by Romero, Sweeney, Burr, and Terry. While several other critics identify the source of the epigraph, few explore the implications of Morrison's choice to use a portion of "The Thunder, Perfect Mind" from the Nag Hammadi texts. David briefly comments on the significance to *Paradise* of the female divine figure who is the speaker of the poem (180–182). Bouson, who likewise identifies the source, notes that the novel's moment of "closure [...] presents the healing and redemptive gesture foreshadowed in the novel's epigraph," (*Quiet As It's Kept* 215), while Aguiar points out that the epigraph "establishes 'death' as one of the central ideas of the novel" (514). Wood also notes the source of the epigraph (124). Grewal, in a discussion of *Jazz*, cites lines from the Gnostic text not used in the epigraph to either *Jazz* or *Paradise*, pointing out that the poem's speaker "who declares, 'I am peace,/ and war has come because of me/ And I am an alien and a citizen' becomes a perfect correlative of the narrator of post–Civil War, post-reconstruction mayhem" in *Jazz* (121); certainly this observation applies equally well to the situation of *Paradise*. Jessee treats more thoroughly than other critics the novel's intersections with aspects of Gnosticism (see "The 'Female Revealer' in *Beloved*, *Jazz*, and *Paradise:* Syncretic Spirituality in Toni Morrison's Trilogy" 151–155.) Stave argues against the importance of Gnosticism to the text (215–216). Many critics identify the town's conception of God as an Old Testament one, while the Convent women practice a version of Christianity that coincides with a New Testament conception of God. See, for example, Gail Fox, Gauthier, and Page. But critics overlook that the novel invokes as well early Christian texts excluded from the Biblical canon; knowledge of these alternative Christianities is necessary for the reader to understand Morrison's critique of the very process of canonization and emergence of orthodoxy.

3. Galbreath makes a case for the fantastic as a type of gnosis based on the fact that both present alternative kinds of knowledge from "consensus reality" (Hume's term). He ultimately identifies this knowledge as transcendent, but I would argue that while the alternative knowledge or insight that Morrison presents in *Paradise* contains elements of the transcendent, her vision and the uses to which she puts the fantastic are predominantly socio-historical.

4. Morrison is insistent in this interview and

others that ghosts constitute a reality for many African American peoples. The conception of reality obviously differs from one culture to another. Hegerfeldt (52–53) and Koenen (43–44) both offer critiques of Hume's term "consensus reality" on the grounds that it erases cultural differences and has a Eurocentric bias.

5. Compare Hegerfeldt's comments on the nature of magic as a challenge "two prominent Western paradigms of knowledge: science and empirical historiography" (162). Hegerfeldt comments on Angela Carter's use of magic not to promote faith in the supernatural but to "demythologize" "material human practice," as Carter states in an interview ("Notes from the Front Line" [1983], in *Shaking a Leg: Journalism and Writing*, ed. Jenny Uglow, London, 1997, p. 38, cited in Hegerfeldt 161.) It might well be that Morrison holds beliefs that Carter does not share, but nonetheless, she employs the fantastic in *Paradise* very much to demythologize the Ruby citizens' myths about their past, among other myths.

6. Sweeney's references are to Adam Mars-Jones's "Ruby's a Strange Town. And the People There Aim to Keep It That Way." Rev. of *Paradise*, by Toni Morrison. In *The Observer* [database online] Mar 29, 1998 [cited October 4, 2001]. <http.//www.books.guardian.co.uk/Printo, 2858,3924442,00.html>; and to Michiko Kakutani's "'Paradise': Worthy Women, Unredeemable Men." Rev. of *Paradise*, by Toni Morrison. *Books of the Times*, Jan 6.

7. Other arguments, like Sweeney's, counter critics' complaints about the escapism of Morrison's ending. For example, Dalke writes that Morrison's *Beloved*—and the same is surely true of *Paradise* as well—unites "political protest and religious illumination" (13). Similarly, Judylyn Ryan notes the coincidence of women's "spiritual and sociopolitical leadership" ("Spirituality and/as Ideology" 268). Karen King argues that in the vision offered in *The Gospel of Mary*, "social criticism and spiritual development were irrevocably linked together" (79), dismissing arguments that "religious teaching" must be viewed "not only as apolitical, but as anti-political—an escapist ideology that serves only to distract people from effective political engagement by focusing on interior spiritual development and flight from the material world" (77). Flint's reading, less spiritually oriented than some others, nonetheless reads the spiritual dimensions of the novel's ending as politically engaged; in the after-life realm in which they appear, the Convent women enact a new "type of cultural citizenship' (606).

8. See Leonard's review of Morrison's *Jazz*. Leonard points out this fact to account for Morrison's employing part of *The Thunder, Perfect Mind* as her epigraph for that novel. I am indebted to the work of Ron David for first calling my attention to Morrison's connection with Pagels (180). David's book, a student guide to Morrison's novels, is fraught with problems; nonetheless, he offers an interesting reading of *Paradise* as a novel about deconstructing myths (153–192).

9. In addition to Ehrman's *Lost Christianities* (2003), books published recently on this topic include Pagels's *Beyond Belief* (2003); King's *The Gospel of Mary of Magdala* (2003), *Images of the Feminine in Gnosticism* (2000), and *What is Gnoticism* (2003). The publication of Dan Brown's *The DaVinci Code* in 2003 also sparked numerous responses to its portrayal of the sacred feminine.

10. Morrison's epigraph matches the translation provided in Robinson's *The Nag Hammadi Library*, though her line breaks are slightly different.

11. For. a clear and succinct history and summary of major tenets of many Christian texts called Gnostic, see Ehrman, chapter 6, "Christians 'In the Know': The Worlds of Early Christian Gnosticism," 113–134, as well his chapter on *The Gospel of Thomas*, 47–65.

12. Interested readers should see books by Pagels and Ehrman, as well as the final chapter of King's *The Gospel of Mary of Magdala*, for thorough and highly readable accounts of these matters.

13. It is important to note that Morrison doesn't simply fall into the binary logic that she opposes: while the town and the convent may seem to stand in binary opposition to one another in the novel, in fact the two exist along a continuum, with women figures from the town being aligned more with the convent than with Ruby, and with a male figure like Reverend Misner, and in certain respects Deacon Morgan, opposing the narrow thinking of their male counterparts and being aligned with the women rather than with the town patriarchs. Several of the novel's critics make this observation. Peach points out that "the sense of female collectivity [...] extends and interrogates the initial impression we have of the Convent as a separate community from Ruby" (154). Krumholz notes that "the greater insight of Misner and Deacon Morgan by the end of the novel indicates these gender divisions are not biologically determined" (25). Romero points out that characters move freely between the two spaces in such a way that the novel avoids replicating the hierarchies of traditional Christianity (419); Fraile-Marcos makes a similar point about the Convent as a "crossroads" (23). See also Aguiar 514–516.

14. Drawing on *The Gospel of Truth*, another Gnostic text found at Nag Hammadi, Ehrman writes that "'Orthodox' Christianity claimed

that Christ died for the sins of the world and that his death and resurrection are what brings salvation. This Gospel, however, maintains that Jesus brought salvation by delivering the truth that could set the soul free. Moreover, it was out of anger for his deliverance of this knowledge that the ignorant rulers of this world erroneously put him to death [...]. 'Orthodox' Christianity insisted that people are made right with God by faith in Jesus' death and resurrection. This Gospel maintains that people are saved by receiving the correct knowledge of who they really are" (128). As we see in the next section of this chapter, Morrison is interested in the idea of salvation and the attaining of paradise through receiving correct knowledge, though the nature of this knowledge differs from the Gnostic conception of it. That the Convent women's is a gospel of wisdom and knowledge rather than a gospel of the cross is further evidenced by the fact that the Convent women have apparently removed the figure of Christ from the cross (12). For a different reading of the relationship of the cross to alternative Christianities represented in *Paradise*, see Bassard, who argues that the novel, in addition to other African American texts that engage with Christianity, "evidences a shift in the figuration of the Cross from a more orthodox African American Protestantism to a displacement of meanings out into the African American (woman's) community itself" (98).

15. Yukins, in a feminist reading of the novel that focuses especially on the Patricia Best chapter, argues that the treatment of Patricia's mother, who is of mixed-race heritage and who was left by the community men to die in childbirth, represents a third, patriarchal version of the Disallowing, a repetition of the original Disallowing perpetrated by those who were originally "disallowed' and unrecognized by them as a repetition of that which they claim to oppose. (241).

16. See also David's extensive commentary on the incongruities in the opening passage and throughout the novel (170–174).

17. Morrison writes of the Haven group's lack of resources early in the novel (see page 13). For interesting commentaries on the similarities between Morrison's imagined Exoduster town of Haven and the historical Exoduster experience, see Romero (422–423) and also Bouson, who both suggest that Norman Crockett's *The Black Towns* (Lawrence: Regents Press of Kansas, 1979) is a source for Morrison's depiction of Haven. Crockett's work details oppression of lighter-skinned blacks by those with darker skin. Flint suggests that Big Papa has an historical counterpart in Benjamin 'Pap' Singleton, who considered himself to be "the 'father' of the Exoduster movement." Since *Paradise* offers a critique of "patriarchal leadership," Flint continues, it might well be "that Morrison fictionally represents an often overlooked chapter of American history so that she may reexamine the issue of black patriarchy and its relationship to (white) American society [...]" (587).

18. DuPlessis discusses women's science fiction in her chapter on "Speculative Consciousness and Collective Protagonists" (178–197). Her comments are relevant to *Paradise* as well: "social and political transformation may be depicted through realistic projections of contemporary life and through uncanny spiritual realms. These female authors seem especially interested in portraying changes of consciousness that call into play the spiritual and unverifiable" (179–80). Lanser, as was noted in the chapter on *The Poisonwood Bible*, observes that the collective protagonist coincides with a new formal, narrative possibility: the communal voice. *Paradise* does not constitute a communal narrative since it is told in third-person authorial and figural voice rather than in either of the two forms of first-person communal narration that Lanser identifies. Nonetheless, Morrison's liberal use in *Paradise* of figural narration focalized through the various women characters approaches the ideological effects of the sequential, communal narrative, in which women retain important individual identities while still forming a community. Morrison's narrative voice thus fully allows for the "democracy of narrative participation" that Judylyn Ryan theorizes and avoids the potential "hegemony" that Lanser cautions might attend the authorial voice (278). In addition, when the narrative is focalized through the town patriarchs, the "male voices, when they speak at all, are usually unreliable voices present [...] to be criticized and ironized," as Lanser observes of the male voices in the communal narrative in Ntozake Shange's *for colored girls who have considered suicide when the rainbow is enuf* (Lanser 263). Reverend Misner is the exception in *Paradise*, since his perspective more closely resembles that of the women characters than that of the town patriarchs.

19. For more information about these particular types of writing from the ancient world, see Layton's introduction to "Thunder, Perfect Intellect" in *The Gnostic Scriptures*, 77–78, and his "The Riddle of the Thunder."

20. For excellent readings of the novel's engagement with Puritan jeremiad rhetoric and American exceptionalism, readers should also see articles by Dalsgärd, Flint, and Fraile-Marcos.

21. This gospel is a fragmentary Coptic translation of a text found not at Nag Hammadi in 1945 but earlier, in the late nineteenth century. It is widely considered 'gnostic,'

though King herself disagrees with this classification.

22. Scholars disagree about the meaning of the phrase "living Jesus." King speculates that the phrase is "a way of acknowledging his resurrection as well as his continuing presence" (164). Ehrman points out that some strains of Gnosticism denied Christ's humanity at all (225), and the proto-orthodox Church reacted against this docetic view. Morrison's use of the term seems more in keeping with Meyer's and Pagels' comments on the Gnostic living Jesus, emphasizing his humanity even more than did the Orthodox Church. For example, as Meyer points out in his recent translation of various Gnostic gospels, "Jesus in the Gospel of Thomas is not designated the Christ or the messiah, he is not acclaimed master or lord [...]. Jesus [...] is not presented as the unique incarnate son of God, and nothing is said of a cross with saving significance or an empty tomb. Jesus is named the living Jesus [...]" (5).

23. The Convent building itself blends the sensual and the spiritual: in its stage as the embezzler's mansion, it contains erotic bathroom fixtures and other *objets d'art* that offend Mary Magna; in its incarnation as a convent school, the building becomes more ascetic since the nuns attempt to strip it of its sensual features. But as the descriptions of it in the 1976 frame of the novel indicate, the two traditions coexist within its walls in an odd tension, a tension that Connie eventually resolves in the syncretistic religious ethos that she expresses later, celebrating both flesh and spirit.

24. Fraile-Marcos, one of the few critics who treats in any detail the strange passages that recount Connie's affair with Deacon (see 25–29), interprets Connie's language and actions here as evidence that "she is clearly reading her relationship with Deacon and her love for him through the prism of Catholic faith and rituals"; she interprets Deacon's rejection of Consolata at this particular moment as evidence of his "Protestant animadversion against Catholicism and the Pope" (25). It is true that all the churches in Ruby are Protestant and that the elders bear suspicion of Catholics (see *Paradise* 7). But as we have seen, Connie views her relationship with Deacon as a challenge to her Catholic beliefs; reading her discourse on the affair through the lens of Gnosticism, with its differences from organized, orthodox religion, suggests a different understanding of Morrison's difficult and elliptical account of the affair and its effects on Connie.

25. See *Paradise* 252; *The Gospel of Thomas* 43 (Robinson 131) and 91–92 (Robinson 136); see also Pagels, *Gnostic Gospels*, 131.

26. Fraile-Marcos notes the resemblance of this figure, whom she calls "a sort of apparition," to Connie (27), as does Sweeney, who calls the figure "a god" (58). Bouson likewise makes the observation that the tea-colored hair and green eyes recall descriptions of Connie herself. He interprets this mysterious man as a "guardian deity or ancestral guide" who "represents the core part of Consolata's identity—the deity within or beloved part of the self" (209). Bouson links this figure, though, solely with an African-Brazilian religion, Candomblé, as does Terry. Though they make a convincing case, Morrison's work resonates equally well with elements of Gnosticism. See, for example, Filoramo's description of the gnostic's encounter with the Revealer (40).

27. Connie's statement about her identity and her mission recall statements made in Gnostic scriptures by various soteriological figures. Filoramo points out that the substance of such texts is essentially the same: a "Revealer-Saviour [is] called upon [...] to illuminate that part of the spiritual substance fallen into the world of darkness." The examples he cites begin with an identifying statement—"I am [...]"—and conclude with a statement about what that figure will teach (115). At the same time, as is typical in *Paradise*'s blending of Gnostic Christian and African religious beliefs, Connie's physical as well as internal transformation in this passage recalls Pilate's *legba* abilities in *Song of Solomon*. Pilate is able to alter her physical appearance when she plays the role of an Aunt Jemima in order to free Milkman and Guitar from prison *(Song of Solomon* 205–207).

28. Ruether comments on Mary Daly's work *Gyn/Ecology*, pointing out its "remarkable duplication of ancient Gnostic patterns, but now built on the dualism of a transcendent spirit world of femaleness over against the deceitful anticosmos of masculinity" (229–230), ultimately arguing against its separatism as a viable feminist spirituality. Likewise Morrison would oppose Daly's vision since it embraces a paradise defined by exclusion; in spite of several reviewers' complaints about easy gender divisions in the novel and the portrait of all men as evil, Morrison does create sympathetic male characters, especially in the figures of Deacon Morgan, with his transformation at the novel's end, and Richard Misner. Her version of paradise by no means excludes men. Nor are men the only perpetrators of sexual violence—Seneca has been abused by a female character, Norma Fox, and Pallas has been scarred by her mother's sexual behavior.

29. Ehrman, while pointing out that there is no evidence that Gnostics were intolerant of others like proto-Orthodox Christians were (256), nonetheless identifies the Gnostics as elitist (132–133). In contrast, Filoramo suggests that all humans could potentially achieve gno-

sis: the mysteries "are not the inheritance of a restricted elite." But he does note that only for a limited time can one achieve salvation, and at some point the number of the saved will be "complete" and "the gates of the Kingdom of Light will finally be closed" (137), something that is certainly anathema to Morrison's vision.

30. According to Fiorenza, in Gnosticism, "the female principle is secondary, since it stands for the part of the divine that became involved in the created world and history. Gnostic dualism shares in the patriarchal paradigm of Western culture. It makes the first principle male, and defines femaleness relative to maleness. [...] Gnostic dualism reflects the chasm between the world and the divine, the body and the spiritual self" (274–275). In addition, various passages in Ruether's work point out how Gnosticism reinforces an androcentric world view by castigating female carnality (e.g. 36–37; 100; 128; 196; 248).

31. These spiritual ways of knowing oppose "the ways of knowing which have developed in the West [that] betray an obsession with rational thought; an inability to connect body, mind and spirit" (Barbara Omolade, *The Rising Song of African American Women*. New York and London: Routledge, 1994, p. 106, quoted in Ryan, *Spirituality as Ideology* 25.) In *Paradise*, this is precisely the type of knowledge that Consolata and Lone possess, a kind of knowledge opposed to Pat Best's history and genealogy of the town which pretends to be an objective, rational form of knowledge that proves ultimately futile since Pat burns her work; Pat's rational methods of knowing, although her chapter provides crucial information for the reader, are supplanted in the novel's organization, being followed immediately by the "Consolata" and "Lone" chapters. Morrison herself speaks in an interview of her use of "enchantment" or spiritual knowledge as a form of knowledge discredited in the West and hence denigrated as "magic" (Davis 144–145). Similarly, Gnostics set knowledge against blind faith, but the knowledge of which they speak is supranatural; Hans Jonas offers a lucid explanation of the nature of Gnostic knowledge, differentiating it from rational thought (34–37).

32. Paris's work *The Spirituality of African Peoples* (Minneapolis: Fortress Press, 1995, p. 35) is cited in Ryan's *Spirituality as Ideology* 33. Readers should also see the work of William Andrews on nineteenth-century African-American authors of spiritual autobiography: "women implicitly identify themselves with an inchoate community of the spirit that transcends normal social distinctions in the name of a radical egalitarianism. [...] We find this spirit manifested socially in the communities of women that formed around" various of the nineteenth-century authors that Andrews includes in his study (20). These comments closely resemble the community of women in the Morrison's Convent, organized around Consolata's spiritual leadership and comprising a group of women who transcend all the class, national, racial, and religious oppositions that certain members of the town of Ruby want to preserve. The portrayal of Consolata also recalls Rebecca Jackson, author of a nineteenth-century spiritual autobiography, who possessed healing powers like Connie's and who used food as "spiritual sustenance" to draw her listeners (Dalke 5–6), just as Consolata prepares a ritual feast just prior to her transformation and her offering spiritual guidance to the convent women. (Dalke's reference is to Rebecca Johnson's *Gifts of Power*, written between 1830 and 1864 and published as a spiritual autobiography by Jean Humez in 1981.)

33. Readers should also see Morrison's oft-cited interview with Marcus and her Nobel lecture (270) for comments about the need to find paradise on earth.

34. Tally's reference is to Judylyn Ryan's "Contested Visions/Double-Vision in *Tar Baby*" in Peterson, 63–87, p. 70.

35. See Bouson, 214–216, and notes 5–7, 238–241, for an insightful discussion of the ways in which the spiritual practices at the Convent resemble elements of Candomblé, as well as other Brazilian religious traditions. Coale also connects Connie's later practices with Candomblé (178, 186–7), but neither Coale nor Bouson considers Gnostic texts as other sources for understanding Consolata's spirituality. Bouson does note, however, with reference to Ean Begg's *The Cult of the Black Virgin* (London: Arkana/Routledge 1985) that the Black Madonna has "Gnostic Christian origins" (Bouson 241, note 6).

36. See also Robolin's account of the multiple versions of the stories that resist "reduction into a single strand" (313). In addition, Morrison's ending invokes the dilemma tale, an open-ended, West African form of narrative that involves the reader/listener in active interpretation (Wilentz 148 and 158).

Bibliography

Aguiar, Sarah Appleton. "'Passing on' Death: Stealing Life in Toni Morrison's *Paradise*." *African American Review* 38.3 (Fall 2004): 513–519.

Aldrich, Marcia. "The Poetics of Transience: Marilynne Robinson's *Housekeeping*." *Essays in Literature* 16.1 (Spring 1989): 127–140.

Anderson, Linda. "The "Re-Imagining of History in Contemporary Women's Fiction." *Plotting Change: Contemporary Women's Fiction*. Ed Linda Anderson. London: Edward Arnold, 1990. 128–141.

Andrews, William. *Sisters of the Spirit: Three Black Women's Autobiographies of the Nineteenth Century*. Bloomington: Indiana University Press, 1986.

Anghel, Corina. "Reconfiguring Female Characters of the American West: Marilynne Robinson's *Housekeeping*." *How Far Is American from Here?* Eds. Theo D'Haen et al. Amsterdam, Netherlands: Rodopi, 2005. 415–440.

Armitt, Lucie. *Contemporary Women's Fiction and the Fantastic*. London: Macmillan, 2000.

———. *Theorising the Fantastic*. London: Arnold, 1996.

Atkinson, Yvonne. "Language That Bears Witness: The Black English Oral Tradition in the Works of Toni Morrison." *The Aesthetics of Toni Morrison: Speaking the Unspeakable*. Ed. Marc C. Connor. Jackson: University Press of Mississippi, 2000. 12–30.

Atwood, Margaret. "Great Unexpectations: An Autobiographical Foreword." *Margaret Atwood: Visions and Forms*. Eds. Kathryn VanSpanckeren and Jan Garden Castro. Carbondale and Edwardsville: Southern Illinois University Press, 1988. xiii-xvi.

———. *Lady Oracle*. New York: Simon and Schuster, 1976.

Bachhilega, Cristina. *Postmodern Fairy Tales: Gender and Narrative Strategies*. Philadelphia: University of Pennsylvania Press, 1997.

Bak, Hans. "Between the Flower and the Stone: The Novel as Biography/ The Biography as Novel—Carol Shields' *The Stone Diaries*." *European Perspectives on English-Canadian Literature*. Eds. Charles Forceville and Hillig van't Land. Amsterdam: Free University Press, 1995. 11–22.

Barnett, Pamela E. "Figurations of Rape and the Supernatural in *Beloved*." *PMLA: Publications of the Modern Language Association of America* 112.3 (May 1997): 418–427.

Barr, Marleen. "Afterword." *Women's Studies: An Interdisciplinary Journal* 14.2 (1987): 187–191.

Barzilai, Shuli. "The Bluebeard Syndrome in Atwood's *Lady Oracle*: Fear and Femininity." *Marvels & Tales: Journal of Fairy-Tale Studies* 19.2 (2005): 249–273.

———. "'Say That I had a Lovely Face': The Grimms' 'Rapunzel,' Tennyson's 'Lady of Shalott,' and Atwood's *Lady Oracle*." *Tulsa Studies in Women's Literature* 19.2 (Fall 2000): 231–254.

Bassard, Katherine Clay. "The Race for Faith: Mercy and the Sign of the Cross in African American Literature." *Religion and Literature* 38.1 (Spring 2006): 95–114.

Bayles, Martha. "Special Effects, Special Pleading." Rev. of *Beloved*. *The New Criterion* 6.5 (January 1988): 34–40.

Becker, Susanne. *Gothic Forms of Feminine Fictions*. Mancheste, UK: Manchester University Press, 1999.

Benson, Stephen. "Stories of Love and Death: Reading and Writing the Fairy Tale Romance." *Image and Power: Women in Fiction in the Twentieth Century*. Eds.

Sarah Sceats and Gail Cunningham. London: Longman, 1996. 103–113.
Bent, Jeffrey. "Less Than Divine: Toni Morrison's *Paradise*." *Southern Review* 35.1 (Winter 1999): 145–9.
Beran, Carol. "'At Least Its Voice Isn't Mine': The Concept of Voice in Margaret Atwood's *Lady Oracle*." *Weber Studies: An Interdisciplinary Humanities Journal* 8.1 (Spring 1991): 54–71.
Billingham, Susan. "Fragile Tissue: The Fiction of Carol Shields." *British Journal of Canadian Studies* 13.2 (1998): 276–287.
Bohannan, Heather. "Questioning Tradition: Spiritual Transformation Images in Women's Narratives and *Housekeeping*, by Marilynne Robinson." *Western Folklore* 51.1 (January 1992): 65–79.
Bok, Christian. "Sybils: Echoes of French Feminism in *The Diviners* and *Lady Oracle*." *Canadian Literature* 125 (Winter 1992): 80–93.
Booher, Mischelle, "'It's Not the House': *Beloved* as Gothic Novel. *Readerly-Writerly Texts: Essays on Literature, Literary/Textual Criticism, and Pedagogy* 9.1–2 (Winter–Spring 2000): 117–131.
Bouson, J. Brooks. *Brutal Choreographies: Oppositional Strategies and Narrative Design in the Novels of Margaret Atwood.* Amherst: University of Massachusetts Press, 1993.
_____. *Quiet As It's Kept: Shame, Trauma, and Race in the Novels of Toni Morrison.* Albany: State University of New York Press, 2000.
Boynton, Victoria. "The Sex-Cited Body in Margaret Atwood." *Studies in Canadian Literature/Etudes en Littérature Canadienne* 27.2 (2002): 51–70.
Briganti, Chiara. "Fat, Nail Clippings, Body Parts, or the Story of Where I Have Been: Carol Shields and Auto/biography." Eden, Edward and Dee Goertz, eds. *Carol Shields, Narrative Hunger, and the Possibilities of Fiction.* Toronto: University of Toronto Press, 2003. 175–200.
Britton, Wesley. "The Puritan Past and Black Gothic: The Haunting of Toni Morrison's *Beloved* in Light of Hawthorne's *The House of the Seven Gables*." *Nathaniel Hawthorne Review* 21:2 (Fall 1995): 7–23.
Brodzki, Bella and Celeste Schenck. "Introduction." *Life/Lines: Theorizing Women's Autobiography.* Eds. Bella Brodzki and Celeste Schenck. Ithaca, NY: Cornell University Press, 1988. 1–15.
Brogan, Kathleen. *Cultural Hauntings: Ghosts and Ethnicity in Recent American Literature.* Charlottesville, VA: University Press of Virginia, 1998.
Bromberg, Pamela S. "The Two Faces in the Mirror in *The Edible Woman* and *Lady Oracle*." *Margaret Atwood: Visions and Forms.* Eds. Kathryn VanSpanckeren and Jan Garden Castro. Carbondale and Edwardsville: Southern Illinois University Press, 1988. 12–23.
Brontë, Charlotte. *Jane Eyre: Case Studies in Contemporary Criticism.* Ed. Beth Newman. Boston: Bedford, 1996.
Brontë, Emily. *Wuthering Heights.* New York: Signet, 1959.
Brooke-Rose, Christine. *A Rhetoric of the Unreal: Studies of Narrative and Structure, Especially of the Fantastic.* Cambridge: Cambridge University Press, 1981.
Bryant, Cedric Gael. "'The Soul Has Bandaged Moments': Reading the African American Gothic in Wright's 'Big Boy Leaves Home,' Morrison's *Beloved*, and Gomez's *Gilda*." *African American Review* 39.4 (Winter 2005): 541–553.
Burke, William. "Border Crossings in Marilynne Robinson's *Housekeeping*." *Modern Fiction Studies* 37.4 (Winter 1991): 716–724.
Burr, Benjamin. "Mythopoetic Syncretism in *Paradise* and the Deconstruction of Hospitality in *Love*." Stave 159–174.
Busia, Albena P.B. "Words Whispered over Voids: A Context for Black Women's Rebellious Voices in the Novel of the African Diaspora." *Studies in Black American Literature III: Black Feminist Criticism and Critical Theory.* Eds. Joe Weixlmann and Houston A. Baker, Jr. Greenwood, FL: Penkevill, 1988. 1–41.
Buss, Helen M. "Reading for the Doubled Discourse of American Women's Autobiography." *a/b: Autobiography Studies* 6.1 (Spring 1991): 95–108.
Capitani, Diane N. "Ideas of the Good: Iris Murdoch's *The Sea, the Sea*." *Christianity and Literature* 53.1 (Autumn 2003): 99–108.
Carpenter, Lynette, and Wendy Kolmar, eds. *Haunting the House of Fiction.* Knoxville: University of Tennessee Press, 1991.
Caver, Christine. "Nothing Left to Lose: *Housekeeping*'s Strange Freedoms."

American Literature 68.1 (March 1996): 111–137.

Chamberlain. Lori. "Magicking the Real: Paradoxes of Postmodern Writing." *Postmodernism: A Bio-Bibliographic Guide.* Ed. Larry McCaffery. New York: Greenwood, 1986. 5–21

Champagne, Rosaria. "Women's History and *Housekeeping*: Memory, Representation and Reinscription." *Women's Studies* 20.3–4 (1992): 321–329.

Chanady, Amaryll Beatrice. *Magical Realism and The Fantastic: Resolved Versus Unresolved Antinomy.* New York: Garland, 1985.

Christian, Barbara. "Fixing Methodologies: *Beloved.*" *Female Subjects in Black and White: Race, Psychoanalysis, Feminism.* Eds. Elizabeth Abel, Barbara Christian, and Helene Moglen. Berkeley: University of California Press, 1997. 363–370.

Christol, Helene. "The African American Concept of the Fantastic as Middle Passage." *Black Imagination and the Middle Passage.* Eds. Maria Diedrich, Henry Louis Gates, Jr., and Carl Pedersen. New York: Oxford University Press, 1999. 164–173.

Clark, Maria B. "Usurping Difference in the Feminine Fantastic from the Riverplate." *Studies in Twentieth Century Literature* 20.1 (Winter 1996): 235–249.

Clayton, Laura Van Tuyl. Rev. of *The Stone Diaries. The Christian Science Monitor.* March 30, 1994: 19.

Coale, Samuel. *Paradigms of Paranoia: The Culture of Conspiracy in Contemporary American Fiction.* Tuscaloosa: University of Alabama Press, 2005.

Cohan, Steven. "From Subtext to Dreamtext: The Brutal Egoism of Iris Murdoch's Male Narrators." *Women and Literature* 2 (1982): 222–242.

Coontz, Stephanie. *The Way We Never Were: American Families and the Nostalgia Trap.* New York: Basic, 1992.

Cornwell, Neil. *The Literary Fantastic: From Gothic to Postmodernism.* New York: Harvester Wheatsheaf, 1990.

Cranny-Francis, Anne. *Feminist Fiction: Feminist Uses of Generic Fiction.* New York: St. Martin's, 1990.

Crouch, Stanley. *Beloved.* Rev. of *Beloved. New Republic* 194 (October 19, 1987): 38–43.

Cummings, Katherine. "Reclaiming the Mother('s) Tongue: *Beloved, Ceremony, Mothers and Shadows.*" *College English* 52 (September 1990): 552–69.

Cutter, Martha. "The Story Must Go On: The Fantastic, Narration, and Intertextuality in Toni Morrison's *Beloved* and *Jazz.*" *African American Review* 34.1 (Spring 2000): 61–75.

D'Haen, Theo. "Magic Realism and Postmodernism: Decentering Privileged Centers." In Zamara and Faris, 191–208.

———. "Postmodernisms: From Fantastic to Magic Realist." *International Postmodernism: Theory and Literary Practice.* Eds. Hans Bertens and Douwe Fokkema. Amsterdam: John Benjamins, 1997. 283–293.

Daily, Gary W. "Toni Morrison's *Beloved*: Rememory, History, and the Fantastic." *The Celebration of the Fantastic: Selected Papers from the Tenth Anniversary International Conference on the Fantastic in the Arts.* Eds. Donald E. Morse, Marshall B. Tymn, and Csilla Bertha. Westport, CT: Greenwood, 1992. 141–147.

Dalke, Anne. "Spirit Matters: Re-Possessing the African-American Women's Literary Tradition." *Legacy: A Journal of American Women Writers* 12.1 (1995): 1–16.

Dalsgärd, Katrine. "The One All-Black Town Worth the Pain: (African) American Exceptionalism, Historical Narration, and the Critique of Nationhood in Toni Morrison's *Paradise.*" *African American Review* 35.2 (Summer 2001): 233–248.

Davey, Frank. "Lady Oracle's Secret: Atwood's Comic Novels." *Studies in Canadian Literature* 5 (1980): 209–221.

David, Ron. *Toni Morrison Explained.* New York: Random House, 2000.

Davidson, Arnold E. and Cathy N. "Margaret Atwood's *Lady Oracle*: The Artist as Escapist and Seer." *Studies in Canadian Literature* 3 (1978): 166–177.

Davidson, Lale. "Daughters of Eurydice in Absentia: The Feminine Heroic Quest for Presence in *Housekeeping.*" *Journal of the Fantastic in the Arts* 4.4 (1991): 19–36.

Davidson, Rob. "Racial Stock and 8-Rocks: Communal Historiography in Toni Morrison's *Paradise.*" *Twentieth Century Literature: A Scholarly and Critical Journal* 47.3 (Fall 2001): 355–73.

Davies, Madeleine. "Margaret Atwood's Female Bodies." *The Cambridge Companion to Margaret Atwood.* Ed. Coral Ann

Howells. Cambridge: Cambridge University Press, 2006. 58–71.

Davis, Christina. "Interview with Toni Morrison." *Presence Africaine*. 145 (1988): 141–156.

Davis, Kimberly Chabot. "'Postmodern Blackness:' Toni Morrison's *Beloved* and the End of History." *Productive Postmodernism: Consuming Histories and Cultural Studies*, John N. Duvall, ed. Albany: State University of New York Press, 2000. 75–92.

Day, William Patrick. *In the Circles of Fear and Desire: A Study of Gothic Fantasy*. Chicago: University of Chicago Press, 1985.

DeMarr, Mary Jean. *Barbara Kingsolver: A Critical Companion*. Westport, CT: Greenwood, 1999.

Demory, Pamela H. "Into the Heart of Lightness: Barbara Kingsolver rereads *Heart of Darkness*." *Conradiana* 34.3 (2002): 181–193.

Diengott, Nilli. "Narratology and Feminism." *Style* 22.1 (Spring 1988): 42–51.

Dipple, Elizabeth. *Iris Murdoch: Work for the Spirit*. London: Methuen, 1982.

Du Plessis, Rachel Blau. *Writing Beyond the Ending: Narrative Strategies of Twentieth-Century Women Writers*. Bloomington: Indiana University Press, 1985.

Dubey, Madhu. "The Politics of Genre in *Beloved*." *Novel: A Forum on Fiction* 32.3 (Spring 1999): 187–206.

Duncan, Cynthia. "An Eye for an 'I': Women Writers and the Fantastic as a Challenge to Patriarchal Authority." *Inti: Revista de Literatura Hispanica* 40–41 (Fall 1994–Spring 1995): 233–246.

Durix, Jean-Pierre. *Mimesis, Genres, and Post-Colonial Discourse: Deconstructing Magic Realism*. New York: St. Martin's, 1998.

Eden, Edward and Dee Goertz, eds. *Carol Shields, Narrative Hunger, and the Possibilities of Fiction*. Toronto: University of Toronto Press, 2003.

Ehrman, Bart. *Lost Christianities: The Battles for Scripture and the Faith We Never Knew*. New York: Oxford University Press, 2003.

Estes, David. "'Hoodoo? God Do': African American Women and Contested Spirituality in the Spiritual Churches of New Orleans." *Spellbound: Women and Witchcraft in America*. Ed. Elizabeth Reis. Wilmington, DE: Scholarly Resources, 1998. 157–82.

Faris, Wendy. *Ordinary Enchantments: Magical Realism and the Remystification of Narrative*. Nashville: Vanderbilt University Press, 2004.

_____. "Scheherazade's Children: Magical Realism and Postmodern Fiction." In Zamora and Faris. 163–190.

Fee, Margery. "Auto/biographical Fictions." Rev. of *The Stone Diaries*. *Canadian Literature* 144 (Spring 1995): 173–174.

_____. *The Fat Lady Dances: Margaret Atwood's Lady Oracle*. Toronto: ECW, 1993.

Ferguson, Rebecca. "History, Memory and Language in Toni Morrison's *Beloved*." *Feminist Criticism: Theory and Practice*. Ed. Susan Sellers. Toronto: University of Toronto Press, 1991. 109–127.

Filoramo, Giovanni. *A History of Gnosticism*. Trans. Anthony Alcock. Oxford, England: Basil Blackwell, 1990.

Fiorenza, Elisabeth Schussler. *In Memory of Her: A Feminist Theological Reconstruction of Christian Origins*. New York: Crossroad, 1983.

Fitzgerald, Penelope. "Sunny Side Up." Rev. of *The Stone Diaries*. *London Review of Books* September 9, 1993: 19.

Flint, Holly. "Toni Morrison's *Paradise*: Black Cultural Citizenship in the American Empire." *American Literature* 78.3 (September 2006): 585–612.

Foster, Thomas. "History, Critical Theory, and Women's Social Practices: 'Women's Time' and Housekeeping." *Signs* 14.1 (1988): 73–99.

Fox, Gail. "Biblical Connections in Toni Morrison's *Paradise*." *Notes on Contemporary Literature* 34.3 (May 2004): 7–8.

Fox, Stephen. "Barbara Kingsolver and Keri Hulme: Disability, Family, and Culture." *Critique: Studies in Contemporary Fiction* 45.4 (Summer 2004): 405–417.

Fraile-Marcos, Ann Maria. "Hybridizing the 'City upon a Hill' in Toni Morrison's *Paradise*." *MELUS: The Journal of the Society for the Study of the Multi-Ethnic Literature of the United States* 28.4 (Winter 2003): 3–33.

Freibert, Lucy M. "The Artist as Picaro: The Revelation of Margaret Atwood's *Lady Oracle*." *Canadian Literature* 92 (Spring 1982): 22–33.

Friedan, Betty. *The Feminine Mystique*. New York: Dell, 1964.

Friedman, Susan Stanford. "Women's Autobiographical Selves: Theory and Practice." *The Private Self: Theory and Practice of Women's Autobiographical Writings*. Ed. Shari Benstock. Chapel Hill: University of North Carolina Press, 1988. 34–62.

Frye, Joanne. *Living Stories, Telling Lives: Women and the Novel in Contemporary Experience*. Ann Arbor: University of Michigan Press, 1986.

Galbreath, Robert. "Fantastic Literature as Gnosis." *Extrapolation* 29.4 (1988): 330–337.

Galehouse, Maggie. "Their Own Private Idaho: Transience in Marilynne Robinson's *Housekeeping*." *Contemporary Literature* 41.1 (Spring 2000): 117–137.

Gates, Henry Louis, Jr. *The Signifying Monkey: A Theory of Afro-American Literary Criticism*. New York: Oxford University Press, 1988.

Gauthier, Marni. "The Other Side of Paradise; Toni Morrison's (Un)Making of Mythic History." *African American Review* 39.3 (Fall 2005): 395–414.

Gernes, Sonia. "Transcendent Women: Uses of the Mystical in Margaret Atwood's *Cat's Eye* and Marilynne Robinson's *Housekeeping*." *Religion and Literature* 23.3 (Autumn 1991): 143–165.

Geyh, Paula E. "Burning Down the House? Domestic Space and Feminine Subjectivity in Marilynne Robinson's *Housekeeping*." *Contemporary Literature* 34.1 (Spring 1993): 103–122.

Gilbert, Sandra M. "Plain Jane's Progress." *Jane Eyre: Case Studies in Contemporary Criticism*. Ed. Beth Newman. Boston and New York: Bedford, 1996. 475–501.

Gilbert, Sandra M. and Susan Gubar. *The Madwoman in the Attic: The Woman Writer and the Nineteenth-Century Literary Imagination*. New Haven, CT: Yale University Press, 1979.

Givner, Jessie. "Mirror Images in Margaret Atwood's *Lady Oracle*." *Studies in Canadian Literature/Etudes en Littérature Canadienne* 14.1 (1989): 139–146.

Godard, Barbara, "My (m)Other, My Self: Strategies for Subversion in Atwood and Hébert. *Essays on Canadian Writing* 26 (Summer 1983): 13–44.

Goldblatt, Patricia. "The Implausibility of Marriage." *Multicultural Review* 10.3 (September 2001): 42–48, 73.

Gordon, David J. *Iris Murdoch's Fables of Unselfing*. Columbia, MO: University of Missouri Press, 1995.

Goshgarian, Gary. "Feminist Values in the Novels of Iris Murdoch." *Revue des Langues Vivantes* 40 (1974): 519–527.

Grace, Sherrill. "Gender as Genre: Atwood's Autobiographical 'I.'" *Margaret Atwood: Writing and Subjectivity*. Ed. Colin Nicholson. New York: St. Martin's, 1994. 189–203.

Greene, Gayle. *Changing the Story: Feminist Fiction and the Tradition*. Bloomington: Indiana University Press, 1991.

Grewal, Gurleen. *Circles of Sorrow, Lines of Struggle: The Novels of Toni Morrison*. Baton Rouge: Louisiana State University Press, 1998.

Grimshaw, Tammy. *Sexuality, Gender, and Power in Iris Murdoch's Fiction*. Madison, NJ: Farleigh Dickinson University Press, 2005.

Hamilton, Cynthia. "Revisions, Rememories, and Exorcisms: Toni Morrison and the Slave Narrative." *Journal of American Studies* 30.3 (December 1996): 429–445.

Handley, William R. "The House a Ghost Built: *Nommo*, Allegory, and the Ethics of Reading in Toni Morrison's *Beloved*." *Contemporary Literature* 36.4 (Winter 1995): 676–701.

Hansen-Pauly, Marie-Anne. "Carol Shields: A (De)Constructivist Approach to Identity in Auto/Biography Writing." *Latitude 63° North: Proceedings of the 8th International Region and Nation Literature Conference, Östersund, Sweden 2–6 August 2000*. Ed. David Bell. Östersund, Sweden: Mid-Sweden University College, 2002. 295–315.

Harris, Trudier. "Woman Thy Name is Demon." *Critical Essays on Toni Morrison's Beloved*. Ed. Barbara H. Solomon. New York: G.K. Hall, 1998. 127–137.

Hegerfeldt, Anne. *Lies that Tell the Truth: Magic Realism seen through Contemporary Fiction from Britain*. Amsterdam: Rodopi, 2005.

Heinz, Denise. *The Dilemma of Double-Consciousness in Toni Morrison's Novels*. Athens: University of Georgia Press, 1993.

Heller, Dana. *The Feminization of Quest-Romance: Radical Departures*. Austin: University of Texas Press, 1990.

_____. "Reconstructing Kin: Family, History, and Narrative in Toni Morrison's *Beloved*. *Race-ing Representation: Voice, History, and Sexuality*. Lanham, MD: Rowman & Littlefield, 1998. 213–227.

Henderson, Mae. "Remembering the Body as Historical Text." *Comparative American Identities: Race, Sex and Nationality in Modern Texts*. Ed. Hortense J. Spillers. New York: Routledge, 1991. 62–86.

Herman, David. "Introduction: Narratologies." *Narratologies: New Perspectives on Narrative Analysis*. Ed. David Herman. Columbus: Ohio State University Press, 1999. 1–30.

Heusel, Barbara Stevens. *Iris Murdoch's Paradoxical Novels: Thirty Years of Critical Reception*. Rochester, NY: Camden House, 2001.

Hite, Molly. *The Other Side of the Story: Structures and Strategies of Contemporary Feminist Narrative*. Ithaca, NY: Cornell University Press, 1989.

Hoffman, Gerhard. "The Fantastic in Fiction: Its 'Reality' Status, its Historical Development, and its Transformation in Postmodern Narration." *Yearbook of Research in English and American Literature* 1 (1982): 267- 364.

_____. *From Modernism to Postmodernism: Concepts and Strategies of Postmodern American Fiction*. Amsterdam: Rodopi, 2005.

Hogan, Patrick Colm. *Colonialism and Cultural Identity: Crises of Tradition in the Anglophone Literatures of India, Africa, and the Caribbean*. Albany, NY: State University of New York Press, 2000.

Holden-Kirwan, Jennifer. "Looking into the Self That Is No Self: An Examination of Subjectivity in *Beloved*." *African American Review* 32.3 (Fall 1998): 415–426.

Hollenberg, Donna Krolik. "An Interview with Carol Shields." *Contemporary Literature* 39.3 (Fall 1998): 339–355.

Homans, Margaret. "Feminist Fiction and Feminist Theories of Narrative." *Narrative* 2.1 (January 1994): 3–16.

Horstkotte, Martin. *The Postmodern Fantastic in Contemporary British Fiction*. Trier, Germany: Wissenschaftlicher, 2004.

Horvitz, Deborah. "Nameless Ghosts: Possession and Dispossession in *Beloved*." *Studies in American Fiction* 17.2 (Autumn 1989): 157–167.

House, Elizabeth. "Toni Morrison's Ghost: The Beloved Who Is Not Beloved." *Studies in American Fiction* 18.1 (Spring 1990): 17–26.

Howells, Coral Ann. *Contemporary Canadian Women's Fiction: Refiguring Identities*. New York: Palgrave, 2003.

_____. *Margaret Atwood*. 2nd edition. Basingstroke, Hampshire, UK: Palgrave Macmillan, 2005.

Hume, Kathryn. *Fantasy and Mimesis: Responses to Reality in Western Literature*. New York: Methuen, 1984.

Hutcheon, Linda. *A Poetics of Postmodernism: History, Theory, and Fiction*. London: Routledge, 1988.

_____. *The Politics of Postmodernism*. London: Routledge, 1989.

Ingersoll, Earl G, ed. *Conversations with Margaret Atwood*. London: Virago, 1992.

Irigaray, Luce. *This Sex Which is Not One*. Trans. Catherine Porter. Ithaca, NY: Cornell University Press, 1985.

Jackson, Rosemary. *Fantasy: The Literature of Subversion*. London: Methuen, 1981.

_____. "Introduction." *What Did Miss Darrington See? An Anthology of Feminist Supernatural Fiction*. Ed. Jessica Amanada Salmonson. New York: The Feminist Press at the City University of New York, 1989. xv-xxxv.

Jacobs, J.U. "Translating the 'Heart of Darkness': Cross-Cultural Discourse in the Contemporary Congo Book." *Current Writing* 14.2 (2002): 104–117.

Jacobson, Kristin J. "The Neodomestic American Novel: The Politics of Home in Barbara Kingsolver's *The Poisonwood Bible*." *Tulsa Studies in Women's Literature*. 24.1 (Spring 2005): 105–127.

Jahn, Janheinz. *Muntu: The New African Culture*. Trans. Marjorie Grene. New York: Grove, 1961.

Jameson, Frederic. *The Political Unconscious: Literature as a Socially Symbolic Act*. Ithaca, NY: Cornell University Press, 1981.

Jay, Elizabeth. "Why 'Remember Lot's Wife'? Religious Identity and the Literary Canon." In *Literary Canons and Religious Identity*. Eds. Erik Borgman, Bart Philipson, and Lea Verstricht. Hants, England: Ashgate, 2000. 33–50.

Jessee, Sharon. "The 'Female Revealer' in *Beloved*, *Jazz*, and *Paradise*: Syncretic Spirituality in Toni Morrison's Trilogy." Stave 129–158.

———. " 'Tell me Your Earrings: Time and the Marvelous in Toni Morrison's *Beloved*." *Memory, Narrative, and Identity: New Essays in Ethnic American Literatures.* Eds. Amritjit Singh, Joseph T. Skerrett, Jr., and Robert E. Hogan. Boston: Northeastern University Press, 1994. 198–211.

Johnson, Deborah. *Iris Murdoch.* Sussex, England: Harvester, 1987.

Johnson, Lisa. "She Enlarges on the Available Materials: a Postmodernism of Resistance in *The Stone Diaries*." Eden and Goertz 201–229.

Jonas, Hans. *The Gnostic Religion.* Boston: Beacon Press, 1958.

Kahane, Claire. "The Gothic Mirror." *The (M)other Tongue: Essays in Feminist Psychoanalytic Interpretation.* Eds. Shirley Nelson Garner, Claire Kahane, and Madelon Strengnether. Ithaca, NY: Cornell University Press, 1985.

Kaivola, Karen. "The Pleasures and Perils of Merging: Female Subjectivity in Marilynne Robinson's *Housekeeping*." *Contemporary Literature* 34.4 (Winter 1993): 670–690.

Keizer, Arlene R. "*Beloved*: Ideologies in Conflict, Improvised Subjects." *African American Review* 33.1 (Spring 1999): 105–123.

King, Karen. "Afterword: Voices of the Spirit." *Women Preachers and Prophets through two Millennia of Christianity*." Eds. Beverly Mayne Kienzle and Pamela J. Walker. Berkeley: University of California Press, 1998. 335–343.

———. *The Gospel of Mary of Magdala: Jesus and the First Woman Apostle.* Santa Rosa, CA: Polebridge, 2003.

King, Kristin. "Resurfacings of *The Deeps*: Semiotic Balance in Marilynne Robinson's *Housekeeping*." *Studies in the Novel* 28.4 (Winter 1996): 565–580.

King, Lovalerie. "The Disruption of Formulaic Discourse: Writing Resistance and Truth in *Beloved*." *Critical Essay on Toni Morrison's Beloved.* Ed. Barbara H. Solomon. New York: G.K. Hall, 1998. 272–283.

Kingsolver, Barbara. *The Poisonwood Bible.* New York: HarperCollins, 1998.

Kirkby, Joan. "Is there Life after Art? The Metaphysics of Marilynne Robinson's *Housekeeping*." *Tulsa Studies in Women's Literature* 5 (1986): 91–109.

Koenen, Anne. *Visions of Doom, Plots of Power: The Fantastic in Anglo-American Women's Literature.* Frankfurt, Germany: Vervuert Verlag, 1999.

Koolish, Lynda. "Fictive Strategies and Cinematic Representations in Toni Morrison's *Beloved*: Postcolonial Theory/Postcolonial Text." *African American Review* 29.3 (Fall 1995): 421–438.

Koza, Kimberly A. "The Africa of Two Western Women Writers: Barbara Kingsolver and Margaret Laurence." *Critique: Studies in Contemporary Fiction* 44.3 (Spring 2003): 284–294.

Kristeva, Julia. "About Chinese Women." *The Kristeva Reader.* Ed. Toril Moi. New York: Columbia University Press, 1986. 153–155.

Krumholz, Linda J. "The Ghosts of Slavery in *Beloved*." *African American Review* 26:3 (Fall 1992): 395–408.

———. "Reading and Insight in Toni Morrison's *Paradise*." *African American Review* 36.1 (Spring 2001): 21–34.

Kunz, Diane. "White Men in Africa: On Barbara Kingsolver's *The Poisonwood Bible*." *Novel History: Historians and Novelists Confront America's Past (and Each Other).* Ed. Mark C. Carnes. New York: Simon and Schuster, 2001. 285–297.

Laennec, Christine Moneera. "Christine Antygrafe: Authorial Ambivalence in the Works of Christine de Pizan." *Anxious Power: Reading, Writing and Ambivalence in Narrative by Women.* Ed. Carol J. Singley and Susan Elizabeth Sweeney. Albany: State University of New York Press, 1993. 35–50.

Lanser, Susan Snaider. *Fictions of Authority: Women Writers and Narrative Voice.* Ithaca, NY: Cornell University Press, 1992.

———. "Shifting the Paradigm: Feminism and Narratology." *Style* 22.1 (Spring 1988): 52–60.

———. "Toward A Feminist Narratology." *Essentials of the Theory of Fiction,* 2nd ed. Michael Hoffman and Patrick D. Murphy, eds. Durham, NC: Duke University Press, 1996. 453–472. Reprinted from *Style* 20 (1986): 341–363.

Lassner, Phyllis. "Escaping the Mirror of Sameness: Marilynne Robinson's *Housekeeping*." *Mother Puzzles: Daughters and Mothers in Contemporary American Literature.* Ed. Mickey Pearlman. Contributions in Women's Studies 110. New York: Greenwood, 1989. 49–58.

Lawrence, David. "Fleshly Ghosts and Ghostly Flesh: The Word and the Body in Beloved. *Studies in American Fiction* 19.2 (Autumn 1991): 189–201.

Layton, Bentley, ed. *The Gnostic Scriptures: Ancient Wisdom for the New Age.* New York: Doubleday, 1987, 1995.

_____. "The Riddle of the Thunder (NHC Vi, 2): The Function of Paradox in a Gnostic Text from Nag Hammadi." *Nag Hammadi, Gnosticism, and Early Christianity.* Eds. Charles W. Hedrick and Robert Hodgson, Jr. Peabody, MA: Hendrickson, 1986. 37–54.

Leavis, L. R. "The Anti-Artist: The Case of Iris Murdoch." *Neophilogus* 72 (1988): 136–154.

Lecker, Robert. "Janus through the Looking Glass: Atwood's First Three Novels. *The Art of Margaret Atwood: Essays in Criticism.* Eds. Arnold E. and Cathy N. Davidson. Toronto: House of Anansi, 1981. 177–203.

Leonard, John. "Her Soul's High Song." Rev. of *Jazz*. *The Nation*. May 25, 1992.

Lin, Su-ying. "Loss and Desire: Mother-Daughter Relations in Marilynne Robinson's *Housekeeping*." *Studies in Language and Literature* 9 (June 2000): 203–226.

Lionnet, Francoise. *Postcolonial Representations: Women, Literature, Identity.* Ithaca, NY: Cornell University Press, 1995.

Liscio, Lorraine. "Beloved's Narrative: Writing Mother's Milk." *Tulsa Studies in Women's Literature* 11.1 (Spring 1992): 31–46.

Macpherson, Heidi Slettedahl. "Women's Travel Writing and the Politics of Location: Somewhere In-Between." *Gender, Genre, and Identity in Women's Travel Writing.* Ed. Kristi Siegel. New York: Peter Lang, 2004. 193–208.

Malekin, Peter. "Knowing about Knowing: Paradigms of Knowledge in the Postmodern Fantastic." *The State of the Fantastic: Studies in the Theory and Practice of Fantastic Literature and Film.* Ed. Nicholas Ruddick. Westport, CT: Greenwood, 1990. 41–48.

Mallon, Anne-Marie. "Sojourning Women: Homelessness and Transcendence in *Housekeeping*." *Critique: Studies in Contemporary Fiction* 30.2 (Winter 1989): 95–105.

Malmgren, Carl D. "Mixed Genres and the Logic of Slavery in Toni Morrison's *Beloved*." *Critique: Studies in Contemporary Fiction* 36.2 (Winter 1995): 96–106.

Marcus, James. "This Side of Paradise." Interview with Toni Morrison. 1998. Amazon.*http://www.amazon.com/exec/obidos/tg/feature/-/7651/104-8595730-1497527.*

Massé, Michelle A. *In the Name of Love: Women, Masochism, and the Gothic.* Ithaca, NY: Cornell University Press, 1992.

Mbiti, John S. *African Religions and Philosophy.* New York: Praeger, 1969.

_____. "Flowers in the Garden: The Role of Women in African Religion." *African Traditional Religions in Contemporary Society.* Ed. Jacob K. Olupona. New York: Paragon House, 1991. 59–72.

_____. *Introduction to African Religion.* 2nd ed. Oxford: Heinemann International Literature, 1991.

McDermott, Sinead. "Future-Perfect: Gender, Nostalgia, and the Not Yet Presented in Marilynne Robinson's *Housekeeping*." *Journal of Gender Studies* 13.1 (November 2004): 259–270.

McGill, Allyson F. "A Tangle of Underground Streams." Rev. of *The Stone Diaries*. *Belles Lettres: A Review of Books by Women* 10.1 (Fall 1994): 32, 34.

McGowan, John. *Postmodernism and Its Critics.* Ithaca, NY: Cornell, 1991.

McHale, Brian. *Postmodernist Fiction.* London: Methuen, 1987.

McKinstry, Susan Jaret. "Living Literally by the Pen: The Self-Conceived and Self-Deceiving Heroine-Author in Margaret Atwood's *Lady Oracle*." *Margaret Atwood: Reflection and Reality.* Ed. Beatrice Mendez-Egle. Ediburg, TX: Pan American University Press, 1987. 58–70.

McMillan, Ann. "The Transforming Eye: *Lady Oracle* and the Gothic Tradition." *Margaret Atwood: Visions and Forms.* Eds. Kathryn VanSpanckeren and Jan Garden Castro. Carbondale: Southern Illinois University Press, 1988. 48–64.

Meese, Elizabeth. *Crossing the Double Cross: the Practice of Feminist Criticism.* Chapel Hill: University of North Carolina Press, 1986.

Mellor, Winifred M. "'The Simple Container of Our Existence': Narrative Ambiguity in Carol Shields's *The Stone Diaries*." *Studies in Canadian Literature* 20. 2 (1995): 96–110.

Meyer, Marvin. *The Gnostic Gospels of Jesus: The Definitive Collection of Mystical Gospels and Secret Books about Jesus of Nazareth.* New York: HarperCollins, 2005.

Michael, Magali Cornier. "Re-Imagining Agency: Toni Morrison's *Paradise.*" *African American Review* 36.4 (Winter 2002): 643–61.

Mile, Sian. "Femme Foetal: The Construction/Destruction of Female Subjectivity in *Housekeeping*, or Nothing Gained." *Genders* 8 (Summer 1990): 129–136.

Miller, D.A. *Narrative and Its Discontents: Problems of Closure in the Traditional Novel.* Princeton, NJ: Princeton University Press, 1981.

Mobley, Marilyn Sanders. "A Different Remembering: Memory, History, and Meaning in Toni Morrison's *Beloved.*" *Toni Morrison: Modern Critical Views.* Ed. Harold Bloom. New York: Chelsea House, 1990. 189–200.

Moglen, Helene. "Redeeming History: Toni Morrison's *Beloved.*" *Female Subjects in Black and White: Race, Psychoanalysis, Feminism.* Eds. Elizabeth Abel, Barbara Christian, and Helene Moglen. Berkeley: University of California Press, 1997. 201–220.

Mohanty, Satya P. "The Epistemic Status of Cultural Identity: On *Beloved* and the Postcolonial Condition." *Reclaiming Identity: Realist Theory and the Predicament of Postmodernism.* Paula M.L. Moya and Michael R. Harmes-Garcia, eds. Berkeley: University of California Press, 2000. 29–66.

Moi, Toril. *Sexual/Textual Politics: Feminist Literary Theory.* London: Routledge, 1985.

Morrison, Toni. *Beloved.* New York: Alfred Knopf, 1988.

_____. *Jazz.* New York: Alfred Knopf, 1992

_____. "Memory, Creation, Writing." *Thought* 59 (1984): 385–390.

_____. Nobel Lecture, 1993. *Toni Morrison: Critical and Theoretical Approaches.* Nancy J. Peterson, ed. Baltimore, MD: Johns Hopkins University Press, 1997. 267–273.

_____. *Paradise.* New York: Alfred Knopf, 1998.

_____. *Playing in the Dark: Whiteness and the Literary Imagination.* Cambridge, MA: Harvard University Press, 1992.

_____. "The Site of Memory." *Out There: Marginalization and Contemporary Cultures.* Ed Russell Ferguson, et al. Cambridge, MA: MIT Press, 1990. 299–305.

_____. *Song of Solomon.* New York: Alfred Knopf, 1977.

_____. "Unspeakable Things, Unspoken: The Afro-American Presence in American Literature." *Michigan Quarterly Review* (Winter 1989): 1–34.

Murdoch, Iris. "Against Dryness." 1961. *The Novel Today: Contemporary Writers on Modern Fiction.* Ed. Malcolm Bradbury. Glasgow, Scotland: Fontana, 1976. 23–31.

_____. *The Fire and the Sun: Why Plato Banished the Artists.* Oxford: Oxford University Press, 1977.

_____. *Sartre, Romantic Rationalist.* 1953. New Haven, CT: Yale University Press, 1967.

_____. *The Sea, the Sea.* New York: Viking, 1978.

_____. "The Sublime and the Beautiful Revisited." *Yale Review* 49.2 (Winter 1960): 247–271.

Murphy, Patrick D. "Introduction: Feminism Faces the Fantastic." *Women's Studies: An Interdisciplinary Journal* 14.2 (1987): 81–90.

Neuman, Shirley. "Autobiography and Questions of Gender: An Introduction." *Autobiography and Questions of Gender.* Ed. Shirley Neuman. London: Frank Cass, 1991. 1–11.

Nicol, Bran. *Iris Murdoch: The Retrospective Fiction.* New York: St. Martin's, 1999.

O'Brien, Sheila Ruzycki. "*Housekeeping* in the Western Tradition: Remodeling Tales of Western Travelers." *Women and the Journey: The Female Travel Experience.* Eds. Bonnie Frederick and Susan McLeod. Pullman, WA: Washington State University Press, 1993. 217–234.

O'Reilly, Andrea. *Toni Morrison and Motherhood: A Politics of the Heart.* Albany: State University of New York Press, 2004.

Ognibene, Elaine R. "The Missionary Position: Barbara Kingsolver's *The Poisonwood Bible.*" *College Literature* 30.3 (Summer 2003): 19–36.

Olsen, Lance. *Ellipse of Uncertainty: An Introduction to Postmodern Fantasy.* London: Greenwood, 1987.

Omoyajowo, Joseph Akinyele. "The Role of

Women in African Traditional Religion and Among the Yoruba." *African Traditional Religions in Contemporary Society.* Ed. Jacob K. Olupona. New York: Paragon House, 1991. 73–80.

Osland, Diane. *"The Stone Diaries, Jane Eyre* and the Burden of Romance." Eden and Goertz. 84–112.

Othow, Helen Chavis. "Comedy in Morrison's Terrestrial Paradise." *CLA Journal* 47.2 (March 2004): 366–73.

Page, Philip. "Furrowing all the Brows: Interpretation and the Transcendent in Toni Morrison's *Paradise. African American Review* 35.4 (Winter 2004): 637–664.

Pagels, Elaine. *Beyond Belief: The Secret Gospel of Thomas.* New York: Random House, 2005.

———. *The Gnostic Gospels.* New York: Random House, 1979.

Parini, Jay. "Men and Women: Forever Misaligned." Rev. of *The Stone Diaries. The New York Times Book Review* March 27, 1994: 3, 14.

Parsons, Anne. "The Self-Inventing Self: Women Who Lie and Pose in the Fiction of Margaret Atwood." *Gender Studies: New Directions in Feminist Criticism.* Ed. Judith Spector. Bowling Green, OH: Popular, 1986. 97–109.

Peach, Linden. *Toni Morrison.* 2nd ed. New York: St. Martin's, 2000.

Perez-Torres, Rafael. "Knitting and Knotting the Narrative Thread—*Beloved* as Postmodern Novel." *Toni Morrison: Critical and Theoretical Approaches.* Ed. Nancy J. Peterson. Baltimore, MD: Johns Hopkins University Press, 1997. 91–110.

Phelan, James. "Toward a Rhetorical Reader-Response Criticism: The Difficult, The Stubborn, and the Ending of *Beloved.*" *Toni Morrison: Critical and Theoretical Approaches.* Ed. Nancy J. Peterson. Baltimore, MD: Johns Hopkins University Press, 1997. 225–244.

Pratt, Mary Louise. *Imperial Eyes: Travel Writing and Transculturation.* London: Routledge, 1992.

Punja, Prem Parkash. *The Novels of Iris Murdoch: A Critical Study.* Jalandhar, India: ABS, 1993.

Rao, Eleanora. "Margaret Atwood's *Lady Oracle*: Writing against Notions of Unity." *Margaret Atwood: Writing and Subjectivity.* Ed. Colin Nicholson. New York: St. Martin's, 1994. 133–152.

Ravits, Martha. "Extending the American Range: Marilynne Robinson's *Housekeeping.*" *American Literature* 61.4 (Winter 1989): 644–666.

Raynaud, Claudia. "The Poetics of Abjection in *Beloved.*" *Black Imagination and the Middle Passage.* Eds. Maria Diedrich, Henry Louis Gates, Jr., and Carl Pedersen. New York: Oxford University Press, 1999. 70–85.

Redding, Arthur. "'Haints': American Ghosts, Ethnic Memory, and Contemporary Fiction." *Mosaic: A Journal for the Interdisciplinary Study of Literature* 34.3 (December 2001): 163–182.

Reumens, Carol. "Shades of the Prison House." Rev. of *Beloved. The Times Literary Supplement* (October 16–22, 1987): 1135.

Richards, Dona. "Let the Circle Be Unbroken: The Implications of African-American Spirituality." *Presence Africaine: Revue Culturelle du Monde Noir/Cultural Review of the Negro World*: 117–118 (1981): 247–292.

Rigney, Barbara Hill. *Margaret Atwood.* Totawa, NJ: Barnes & Noble, 1987.

Rimmon-Kenan, Shlomith. "Narration, Doubt, Retrieval: Toni Morrison's *Beloved.*" *Narrative* 4.2 (May 1996): 109–123.

Robbins, Sarah. "Gendering the History of the Antislavery Narrative: Juxtaposing *Uncle Tom's Cabin* and *Benito Cereno*, *Beloved*, and *Middle Passage.*" *American Quarterly* 49.3 (September 1997): 531–573.

Robinson, James M., gen. ed. *The Nag Hammadi Library In English*, Revised Edition. Translated and Introduced by Members of the Coptic Gnostic Library Project of the Institute For Antiquity and Christianity, Claremont, California. New York: HarperCollins, 1990.

Robinson, Marilynne. *Housekeeping.* New York: Farrar, Straus & Giroux, 1981.

Robinson, Sally. *Engendering the Subject: Gender and Self-Representation In Contemporary Women's Fiction.* Albany: State University of New York Press, 1991.

Robolin, Stephane Pierre Raymond. "Loose Memory in Toni Morrison's *Paradise* and Zoe Wicomb's *David's Story.*" *Modern Fiction Studies* 52.2 (Summer 2006): 289–320.

Rodriguez, Eusebio L. "The Telling of *Beloved.*" *The Journal of Narrative Technique* 22.1 (Spring 1991): 153–169.

Romero, Channette. "Creating the Beloved Community: Religion, Race, and Nation in Toni Morrison's *Paradise*." *African American Review* 39.3 (Fall 2005): 415–430.

Rose, William K. "Iris Murdoch, Informally." Interview with Murdoch. *London Magazine* 8 (June 1968): 59–73.

Rosenstone, Robert R. "Experiments in Writing the Past—Is Anybody Interested?" *Perspectives: American Historical Association Newsletter* 30.9 (December 1992): 10, 12, 20.

Rosowski, Susan. *Birthing a Nation: Gender, Creativity, and the West in American Literature*. Lincoln: University of Nebraska Press, 1999.

———. "Margaret Atwood's *Lady Oracle*: Social Mythology and the Gothic Novel." *Research Studies* 49.2 (June 1981): 87–98.

Ross, Catherine Sheldrick. "'Banished to this Other Place': Atwood's *Lady Oracle*." *English Studies in Canada* 6 (1980): 460–474.

Roy, Wendy. "Autobiography as Critical Practice in *The Stone Diaries*." Eden and Goertz 113–146.

Rubenstein, Roberta. *Boundaries of the Self: Gender, Culture, Fiction*. Urbana: University of Illinois Press, 1987.

Rudolph, Kurt. *Gnosis*. Translated by Robert Wilson (translation editor), P.W. Coxon, and K.H. Kuhn. San Francisco: Harper and Row, 1983.

Ruether, Rosemary Radford. *Sexism and God-Talk: Toward a Feminist Theology*. Boston: Beacon, 1983.

Ryan, Judylyn. "Spirituality and/as Ideology in Black Women's Literature: The Preaching of Maria W. Steward and Baby Suggs, Holy." *Women Preachers and Prophets through Two Millennia of Christianity*. Eds. Beverly Mayne Kienzle and Pamela L. Walker. Berkeley: University of California Press, 1998. 267–287.

———. *Spirituality as Ideology in Black Women's Film and Literature*. Charlottesville: University of Virginia Press, 2005.

Ryan, Maureen. "Marilynne Robinson's *Housekeeping*: The Subversive Narrative and the New American Eve." *South Atlantic Review* 56.1 (January 1991): 79–86.

Sale, Maggie. "Call and Response as Critical Method: African-American Oral Tradition and *Beloved*." *African American Review* 26:1 (Spring 1992): 41-50.

Sanders, Julie. *Novel Shakespeares: Twentieth-Century Women Novelists and Appropriation*. Manchester, UK: Manchester University Press, 2001.

Sandler, Linda. "A Question of Metamorphosis." In Ingersoll, 40–57.

Schmudde, Carol E. "The Haunting of 124." *African American Review* 26.3 (Fall 1992): 409–416.

Schopp, Andrew. "Narrative Control and Subjectivity: Dismantling Safety in Toni Morrison's *Beloved*." *The Centennial Review* 39.2 (Spring 1995): 355–379.

Schroeder, Shannin. *Rediscovering Magical Realism in the Americas*. Westport, CT: Praeger, 2004.

Sherman, Geraldine. "Straining to Fulfill Ambitions." Rev. of *The Stone Diaries*. *The Globe and Mail* October 2, 1993: C23.

Shields, Carol. *The Stone Diaries*. New York: Penguin, 1993.

Showalter, Elaine. "Feminist Criticism in the Wilderness." *The New Feminist Criticism: Essays on Women, Literature and Theory*. Ed. Elaine Showalter. New York: Pantheon, 1985. 243–270.

Silverman, Kaja. *The Acoustic Mirror: The Female Voice in Psychoanalysis and Cinema*. Bloomington: Indiana University Press, 1988.

Sitter, Deborah Ayer. "The Making of a Man: Dialogic Meaning in *Beloved*." *African American Review* 26.1 (Spring 1992): 17–29.

Slethaug, Gordon E. "'The Coded Dots of Life': Carol Shields's Diaries and Stones." *Canadian Literature* 156 (Spring 1998): 59–81.

Smith, Richard. "Afterword: The Modern Relevance of Gnosticism." In James Robinson, 532–549.

Smith, Sidonie. "Construing Truths in Lying Mouths: Truthtelling in Women's Autobiography." *Studies in the Literary Imagination* 23.3 (Fall 1990): 145–163.

———. *Moving Lives: Twentieth-Century Women's Travel Writing*. Minneapolis: University of Minnesota Press, 2001.

———. *A Poetics of Women's Autobiography: Marginality and the Fictions of Self-Representation*. Bloomington: Indiana University Press, 1987.

Smyth, Jacqui. "Sheltered Vagrancy in Marilynne Robinson's *Housekeeping.*" *Critique: Studies in Contemporary Fiction* 40.3 (Spring 1999): 281–291.

Spalding, A. Timothy. *Reforming the Past: History, the Fantastic, and the Postmodern Slave Narrative.* Columbus: Ohio State University Press, 2005.

Spearey, Susan. "Substantiation Discourses of Emergence: Corporeality, Spectrality and Postmodern Historiography in Toni Morrison's *Beloved.*" *Body Matters: Feminism, Textuality, Corporeality.* Eds. Avril Horner and Angela Keane. Manchester, UK: Manchester University Press, 2000. 170–182.

Spector, Judith A. "The Fatal Lady in Margaret Atwood's *Lady Oracle.*" *Studies in Literature* (West Hartford, CT) 19.3 (1985): 33–44.

Staels, Hilde. *Margaret Atwood's Novels: A Study of Narrative Discourse.* Tübingen and Basel: A. Francke Verlag, 1995.

Stave, Shirley A. "The Master's Tools: Morrison's *Paradise* and the Problem of Christianity." Stave 215–231.

_____. *Toni Morrison and the Bible: Contested Intertextualities.* New York: Peter Lang, 2006.

Stein, Karen. *Margaret Atwood Revisited.* New York: Twayne, 1999.

_____. "Monsters and Madwomen: Changing Female Gothic." *The Female Gothic.* Ed. Juliann E. Fleenor. Montreal, Canada: Eden, 1983. 123–137.

Stephens, Autumn. "Twists of Fate within an Ordinary Life." Rev. of *The Stone Diaries. San Francisco Chronicle* March 20, 1994: 3.

Struthers, J.R. "Playing Around." In Ingersoll, 58–68.

Sullivan, Zohreh T. "Women Novelists and Variations on the Uses of Obscurity." *South Carolina Review* 16.1 (Fall 1983): 51–58.

Sweeney, Megan. "Racial House, Big House, Home: Contemporary Abolitionism in Toni Morrison's *Paradise.*" *Meridians: Feminisms, Race, Transnationalism* 42.2 (Summer 2004): 40–67.

Tally, Justine. *Paradise Reconsidered: Toni Morrison's (Hi)stories and truths. FORECAAST (Forum for European Contributions to African American Studies)* Vol. 3. Hamburg, Germany: Lit Verlag, 1999.

Taylor-Guthrie, Danille. "Who are the Beloved? Old and New Testaments, Old and New Communities of Faith." *Religion and Literature* 27.1 (Spring 1995): 119–129.

Terry, Jennifer. "A New World Religion? Creolisation and Candomblé in Toni Morrison's *Paradise.*" Stave 192–214.

Thomas, Clara. "Carol Shields's *The Republic of Love* and *The Stone Diaries*: 'Swerves of Destiny' and 'Rings of Light.'" '*Union in Partition': Essays in Honour of Jeanne Delbaere.* Eds. Gilbert Debusscher and Marc Maufort. Liege, Belgium: L3-Liege Language and Literature, 1997. 53–160.

_____. "*Lady Oracle*: The Narrative of a Fool-Heroine." *The Art of Margaret Atwood: Essays in Criticism.* Eds. Arnold E. and Cathy N. Davidson. Toronto: House of Anansi Press, 1981. 159–176.

Thomas, Joan. "'The Golden Book': An Interview with Carol Shields." *Prairie Fire* (Winter 1993–4): 54–62.

Todorov, Tzvetan. *The Fantastic: A Structural Approach to a Literary Genre.* Trans. Richard Howard. Ithaca, NY: Cornell University Press, 1975.

Traill, Nancy. *Possible Worlds of the Fantastic: The Rise of the Paranormal in Fiction.* Toronto: University of Toronto Press, 1996.

Travis, Molly Abel. "Race and Rhetoric in *Beloved* and *Middle Passage.*" *Narrative* 2.3 (October 1994): 179–200.

Trussler, Michael. "Spectral Witnesses: The Doubled Voice in Martin Amis's *Time's Arrow*, Toni Morrison's *Beloved*, and Wim Wenders' *Wings of Desire.*" *Journal of the Fantastic in the Arts* 14.1 (Spring 2003): 28–50.

Tucker, Lindsey. "Released from Bonds: Iris Murdoch's Two Prosperos in *The Sea, the Sea.*" *Contemporary Literature* 27.3 (Fall 1986): 378–395.

_____. *Textual Escap(e)ades; Mobility, Maternity, and Textuality in Contemporary Fiction by Women.* Westport, CT: Greenwood, 1994.

Turner, Nick. "Saint Iris? Murdoch's Place in the Modern Canon." *Iris Murdoch: A Reassessment.* Ed. Anne Rowe. Basingstoke, Hampshire, UK: Palgrave Macmillan, 2007. 115–123.

Vauthier, Simone. "Ruptures in Carol Shields's *The Stone Diaries.*" *Anglophonia: French Journal of English Studies* 1 (1997): 177–192.

Vincent, Sybil Korff. "The Mirror and the Cameo: Margaret Atwood's Comic/Gothic Novel, *Lady Oracle*." *The Female Gothic*. Ed. Julian E. Fleenor. Montreal: Eden, 1983. 153–163.

Walker, Nancy A. *The Disobedient Writer: Women and Narrative Tradition*. Austin: University of Texas Press, 1995.

Warhol, Robyn. "Guilty Cravings: What Feminist Narratology Can Do for Cultural Studies." In Herman, *Narratologies*: 340–355.

Washington, Teresa N. "The Mother-Daughter Ájé Relationship in Toni Morrison's *Beloved*." *African American Review* 39.1–2 (Spring 2005): 171–188.

Wasmeier, Marie-Louise. "Fictional Fossils: Life and Death Writing in Carol Shields's *The Stone Diaries*." *Forum of Modern Language Studies* 41.4 (October 2005): 439–448.

Watson, Greer. "Assumptions of Reality: Low Fantasy, Magical Realism, and the Fantastic." *Journal of the Fantastic in the Arts* 11.2 (2000): 164–172.

Waxman, Barbara Frey. "Changing History Through a Gendered Perspective: A Postmodern Feminist Reading of Morrison's *Beloved*." *Multicultural Literatures through Feminist/Poststructuralist Lenses*. Barbara Frey Waxman, ed. Knoxville: University of Tennessee Press, 1993. 57–83.

Weissberg, Liliane. "Gothic Spaces: The Political Aesthetics of Toni Morrison's *Beloved*." *Modern Gothic: A Reader*. Eds. Victor Sage and Allan Lloy Smith. Manchester, England: Manchester University Press, 1996. 104–120.

Whibley, M.E.L. "The Redemption of Art." *British Journal of Aesthetics* 38.4 (October 1998): 375–83.

White, Hayden. *The Content of Form: Narrative Discourse and Historical Representation*. Baltimore, MD: Johns Hopkins University Press, 1987.

Wilentz, Gay. "Civilizations Underneath: African Heritage as Cultural Discourse in Toni Morrison's *Song of Solomon*." *Toni Morrison's Song of Solomon: A Casebook*. Ed. Jan Furman. New York: Oxford University Press, 2003. 137–163.

Williams, David. "Making Stories, Making Selves: 'Alternate Versions' in *The Stone Diaries*." *Canadian Literature* 186 (Autumn 2005): 10–28.

_____. "Re-imagining a Stone Angel: The Absent Autobiographer of *The Stone Diaries*." *O Canada: Essays on Canadian Literature and Culture*. Ed. Jorn Carlsen. Aarhus, Denmark: Aarhus University Press, 1995. 126–141.

Wilson, Rawdon. "The Metamorphoses of Fictional Space: Magical Realism." In Zamora and Faris, 209–234.

Wilson, Sharon R. "The Fragmented Self in *Lady Oracle*." *Commonwealth Novel in English* 1.1 (January 1982): 50–85.

_____. *Margaret Atwood's Fairy-Tale Sexual Politics*. Jackson: University Press of Mississippi, 1993.

Winsbro, Bonnie. *Supernatural Forces: Belief, Difference, and Power in Contemporary Works by Ethnic Women*. Amherst: University of Massachusetts Press, 1993.

Wood, Michael. "Sensations of Loss." *The Aesthetics of Toni Morrison: Speaking the Unspeakable*. Ed. Marc. C. Conner. Jackson: University of Mississippi Press, 2000. 113–124.

Wyatt, Jean. "Giving Body to the Word: The Maternal Symbolic in Toni Morrison's *Beloved*." *PMLA* 108.3 (May 1993): 474–488.

_____. *Reconstructing Desire: The Role of the Unconscious in Women's Reading and Writing*. Chapel Hill: University of North Carolina Press, 1990.

York, R.A. *The Extension of Life: Fiction and History in the American Novel*. Madison, NJ: Farleigh Dickinson University Press, 2003.

Yukins, Elizabeth. "Bastard Daughters and the Possession of History in *Corregidora* and *Paradise*." *Signs* 28.1 (Fall 2002): 221–247.

Zamora, Lois P. "Magical Romance/Magical Realism: Ghosts in U.S. and Latin American Fiction." In Zamora and Faris. 497–550.

Zamora, Lois Parkinson, and Wendy B. Faris, eds. *Magical Realism: Theory, History, Community*. Durham, NC: Duke University Press, 1995.

Index

African language 114–116, 118, 120–121, 124, 196n20
African religion 28, 114–116, 118–124, 135–136, 138–139, 147, 151, 157, 160, 165–170, 173, 196n21, 200n27
African spiritual beliefs 17–18, 20, 110, 192n7, 192n9, 194n7
Aguiar, Sarah 197n2, 198n13
Aldrich, Marcia 187n9
Althusser, Louis 195n13
Anderson, Linda 195n
Andrews, William 201n31
Anghel, Corina 186n2, 187n6, 188n13
Anzaldua, Gloria 178n16
Armitt, Lucie 7, 175n1 179n22, 183n4, 193n5, 194n7, 195n8
Atkinson, Yvonne 196n19
Atwood, Margaret 24; "Great Expectations" 182n1; *Lady Oracle* 1, 5, 16, 17, 23, 25, 43, 47, 48–68, 71, 7, 140, 143, 180n4, 186n3
Autobiography 25–26, 89–93, 95, 97–98, 101, 103–104, 184n12, 201n32

Bachhilega, Cristina 175n1
Bak, Hans 189n4, 190n6
Barnett, Pamela 193n1
Barr, Marleen 1, 2 3, 176n6
Barth, John 12
Barthelme, Donald 12
Barzilai, Shuli 66, 185n16, 185n22, 185n26
Bassard, Katherine 199n14
Bayles, Martha 194n5
Becker, Susanne 76, 183n9, 184n15
Begg, Ean 201n35
Behn, Afra 190n15
Benson, Stephen 63, 182n3
Bhabha, Homi 177n12, 191n3
Billingham, Susan 189n4, 190n18
Blanchot, Maurice 13
Bohannon, Heather 186n2 187n10
Bok, Christian 184–185n15
Booher, Mischelle 197n24

The Book of Thomas 162
Borges, Jorge Louis 13
Bouson, J. Brooks 171–172, 185n23, 197n2, 199n17, 200n26, 201n35
Boynton, Victorian 183n8
Britton, Wesley 197n24
Brodski, Bella 104
Brogan, Kathleen 125, 133, 78n16, 197n26
Bromberg, Pamela 183–184n9
Brontë, Charlotte 186n5, 189n5
Brontë, Emily 100
Brooke-Rose, Christine 12, 177n11, 178n15
Brown, Dan 198n9
Bryant, Cedric 197n24
Burke, William 186n2, 186n3
Burr, Benjamin 197n2
Busia, Albena 137
Buss, Helen 191n17

Calvino, Italo 13
Candomblé 171, 200n26, 201n35
Capitani, Diane 182n19
Carpenter, Lynette 178n16
Carter, Angela 17, 22, 23, 179n26, 198n5
Caver, Christine 74–75, 76, 186n2, 187n12
Chamberlain, Lori 194n7
Champagne, Rosaria 85, 188n13
Chanady, Amaryll 9–10, 15, 17–18, 176n6, 176n8, 177n11, 179n21
Chodorow, Nancy 97
Chopin, Kate 74
Christian, Barbara 196n20
Christol, Helen 138, 193n5, 196n20
Cixous, Helen 184n15
Clark, Maria 6, 21, 175n1, 2, 176n3
Coale, Samuel 201n35
Cohan, Steven 36
Coontz, Stephanie 48–49
Coover, Robert 12
Cornwell, Neil 131, 176n4, 176n6, 177n11, 178n14, 193n5, 194n6, 195n15
Cranny-Francis, Anne 14, 176n8
Crockett, Norman 199n17

217

Crouch, Stanley 194*n*5
Cummings, Katherine 193*n*5
Cutter, Martha 130, 193*n*5, 194*n*6, 195*n*10

Daily, Gary 193*n*5
Dalke, Anne 198*n*7, 201*n*33
Dalsgärd, Katrine 199*n*20
Daly, Mary 200*n*28
Davey, Frank 183*n*6
David, Ron 197*n*2, 198*n*8, 199*n*16
Davies, Madeleine 184*n*15
Davis, Christina 144, 148, 194*n*7, 195*n*9, 201*n*31
Davis, Kimberly Chabot 193*n*3
Day, William Patrick 31, 34, 65
DeMarr, Mary Jean 117–118, 122, 192*n*11
Demory, Pamela 101, 191*n*3
Derrida, Jaques 44
D'Haen, Theo 18, 21–22, 26, 104, 173, 177*n*12, 178*n*14, 179–280*n*28, 193*n*3
Dickinson, Emily 118, 186*n*2
Diengott, Nilli 175
Dipple, Elizabeth 32, 36, 44, 46, 62, 180*n*1, 182*n*19
Doane, Mary Ann 6, 175*n*2
Dubey, Madha 143, 193*n*5, 197*n*23
Duncan, Cynthia 175*n*1
DuPlessis, Rachel 23, 44, 57, 74, 78, 87, 95, 155–157, 179*n*25, 186*n*4, 199*n*18
Durix, Jean-Pierre 178*n*17

Ehrman, Bart 149, 151, 155, 173, 197*n*1, 198–199*n*9, 199*n*10, 199*n*11, 199*n*12, 199*n*14, 200*n*22, 200*n*29
Eliot, George 190*n*15
Erdrich, Louise 192*n*12
Estes, David 168

Fantastic: classic or traditional 11, 15, 16, 43, 73, 128, 178*n*17; displaced 12, 178*n*18; generalized 11–15, 33, 128, 175*n*3, 178*n*17; pure 9, 12, 16, 17, 25, 31–32, 72, 127, 132
Fantasy 7, 8, 9–10, 19, 175*n*1, 176*n*8
Faris, Wendy 15, 18, 27, 109, 111, 112–113, 115, 119, 121, 122, 123, 179*n*23, 194*n*7
Fee, Marjorie 73, 87, 185*n*24, 189*n*3, 189*n*4
Feminist narrative theory 1–3, 6–8, 10, 16, 19–24, 25, 26, 32, 78–80, 88–105, 111, 122, 126, 170*n*30, 183*n*4
Ferguson, Rebecca 195*n*8
Filoramo, Giovanni 162, 200*n*26, 200*n*27, 200–201*n*29
Fiorenza, Elisabeth 201*n*30
Fitzgerald, Penelope 189*n*4

Flint, Holly 198*n*7, 199*n*17, 199*n*20
Flores, Angel 177*n*10
Foster, Thomas 186*n*2, 187*n*9, 187*n*10
Fox, Gail 197*n*2
Fox, Stephen 110, 191*l*n*1
Fraille-Marcos, Ann Marie 198*n*13, 199*n*20, 200*n*24, 200*n*25
Freibert, Lucy 183*n*5
Freud, Sigmund 38, 176*n*3
Friedan, Betty 48, 54
Friedman, Susan Stanford 97–98
Frye, Joanne 21, 26, 79–80, 93, 96, 99–101, 126, 187*n*13

Galbreath, Robert 197*n*3
Galehouse, Maggie 83, 185*n*1, 186*n*2, 186*n*4, 188*n*21
Garcia Marquez, Gabriel 17
Garner, Margaret 132, 134, 139
Gass, William 13
Gates, Henry Louis 150
Gauthier, Marni 197*n*2
Genette, Gerard 79, 199*n*14
Gernes, Sonia 187*n*10
Geyh, Paula 186*n*2, 186*n*3, 187*n*10, 188*n*19, 188*n*21
Gilbert, Susan 84, 186*n*5, 187*n*7
Gilman, Charlotte Perkins 74
Givner, Jessie 183*n*9, 184*n*15
Gnosticism 28, 146–174 *passim*
Godard, Barbara 183*n*9, 184*n*12
Goldblatt, Patricia 116, 191*n*6
Gordon, David 182*n*19
Goshgarian, Gary 33, 180*n*2
Gospel of Mary 159, 168, 173–174, 198*n*7
Gospel of Philip 165
Gospel of Thomas 147, 161, 162–165 *passim*, 169, 200*n*25
Gothic 8, 23, 24–25, 27, 31–68 *passim*, 76, 139, 140–143; comic gothic 56; female gothic 37–38, 41, 52, 197*n*23
Grace, Sherrill 183*n*6, 184*n*12
Graff, Gerald 21
Greene, Gayle 21, 23, 32, 57, 59, 61–62, 63, 67, 126, 175*n*25, 179*n*27, 184*n*9, 184*n*12, 184*n*15, 185*n*20
Grewel, Gurleen 197*n*2
Grimshaw, Tammy 180*n*2
Gubar, Sandra 84, 187*n*7

Hamilton, Cynthia 139, 140, 196*n*23
Handley, William 196*n*20
Hansen-Pauly, Marie 189*n*4, 190*n*6
Hawkes, John 12
Hegerfeldt, Anne 2, 3, 8, 15, 18, 50, 58, 113, 122, 128, 135, 155, 176*n*8, 177*n*11,

178–179*n*19, 179*n*24, 179*n*28, 184*n*14, 194*n*7, 196*n*22, 198*n*4, 198*n*5
Heinz, Denise 129
Heller, Dana 186*n*2, 187*n*6, 188*n*18, 195*n*16
Henderson, Mae 134–135, 136–137, 195*n*17
Herman, David 7–8
Hesitation 3, 8, 9–13, 15–17, 23, 28, 31–32, 36, 40, 51–52, 54, 55, 58, 62, 72–73, 85, 88, 105, 110, 125, 127–132, 138, 173–174, 177*n*11, 178*n*18, 180*n*1, 182*n*18, 184*n*11, 194*n*5, 194*n*6
Heusel, Barbara 189*n*1
Hite Molly 21, 23, 48, 49–52, 54, 55, 56, 57, 65, 67, 126, 179*n*25, 183*n*6, 183*n*7, 183*n*8, 183*n*9, 184*n*15, 185*n*19, 185*n*20, 185*n*26
Hoffman, Gerhard 12–13, 177*n*12
Holdern-Kirwan, Jennifer 195*n*11
Hollenberg, Donna 90
Homans, Margaret 20–21, 126, 137, 139, 179*n*25, 193*n*5
Horstkotte, Martin 8, 10, 13, 175*n*3, 176*n*6, 176*n*8, 179*n*26
Horvitz, Deborah 194*n*8, 195*n*11
House, Elizabeth 194*n*5, 195*n*8
Howells, Coral Ann 67, 182*n*3 184*n*13, 185*n*26, 190*n*9
Hulme, Peter 191*n*6
Hume, Kathryn 176*n*8, 179*n*23, 197*n*3, 198*n*4
Hutcheon, Linda 177*n*14, 191*n*18

Irigaray, Luce 40, 64, 65, 87, 89, 95–96, 98, 104, 182*n*15, 184*n*9

Jackson, Rebecca 201*n*32
Jackson, Rosemary 7, 40–41, 43, 76, 155–156, 175–176*n*3, 176*n*6, 176*n*8, 193*n*4
Jacobson, Kristin 110, 191*n*1
Jahn, Janheinz 114, 115–116, 118, 120, 196*n*20
James, Henry 9
Jameson, Frederic 132
Jay, Elisabeth 148
Jessee, Sharon 193*n*5, 196*n*20, 197*n*2
Johnson, Deborah 40, 180*n*2, 182*n*16
Johnson, Lisa 102, 190*n*14, 190*n*16
Jonas, Hans 201*n*31
Jones, Gayle 22

Kafka, Franz (*The Metamorphosis*) 11, 14, 15, 177*n*10, 177*n*11, 177*n*13
Kahane, Claire 182*n*13
Kaivola, Karen 186*n*2, 188*n*16
Kakatani, Michiko 148
Keizer, Arlene 109, 195*n*13, 196*n*20

King, Karen 154, 159, 174, 198*n*7, 198*n*9, 198*n*12, 200*n*21, 200*n*22
King, Kristin 72, 78, 80, 188*n*15, 188*n*17, 190*n*7
King, Lovalerie 196*n*23
Kingsolver, Barbara 18; *The Poisonwood Bible* 1, 5, 17, 23, 24, 27, 109–124, 125, 148, 179*n*20, 197*n*25
Kirkby, Joan 186*n*2
Koenen, Anne 2, 5, 6, 7, 14, 43, 50, 60, 85, 144, 157, 175*n*1, 175–176*n*4, 176*n*5, 176*n*6, 176*n*8, 178*n*14, 180*n*29, 182–183*n*4, 186*n*2, 187*n*8, 188*n*14, 193*n*5, 197*n*23, 197*n*26, 198*n*4
Kolmar, Wendy 178*n*16
Koolish, Lynda 137, 197*n*23
Koza, Kimberly 115, 116, 191*n*1, 191*n*3
Kristeva, Julia 40, 77, 94, 184*n*15, 187*n*9, 190*n*8
Krumholz, Linda 169, 195*n*14, 198*n*13
Kunz, Diana 110, 191*n*1

Lacan, Jaques 40, 41, 72, 76, 176*n*3
Laennec, Christine 98
Lanser, Susan Snaider 2, 3, 20–21, 23, 24, 26, 72, 79–80, 91, 92, 94, 98, 99, 101–103, 111, 122–124, 128, 157, 175*n*1, 179*n*25, 188*n*14, 18*n*15, 190*n*15, 192*n*12, 192–193*n*14, 193*n*3, 195*n*12, 199*n*18
Lassner, Phyllis 187*n*6, 10, 11
Lawrence, David 193*n*5
Layton, Bentley 150, 158, 199*n*19
Leavis, L.R. 180*n*2
Lecker, Robert 185*n*22
Leonard, John 198*n*8
Lessing, Doris 22
Lin, Su-Ying 76, 78, 187*n*8
Lionnet, Francoise 112
Liscio, Lorraine 193*n*5

MacMillan, Ann 183*n*5
Macpherson, Heidi 83, 186*n*2, 187*n*6
Magic Realism 2, 8, 9, 10–11, 15, 16, 17, 18, 19, 27, 28, 49, 55, 58, 88, 72–72, 104, 109–111, 112–113, 114, 119, 122–124, 127–132 *passim*, 135, 138, 155 177*n*10, 177*n*12, 178*n*14, 178–179*n*19, 179*n*21, 179*n*23, 179*n*24, 179–180*n*28, 180*n*1, 184*n*14, 194*n*7, 196*n*22
Malekin, Peter 174, 178*n*14
Mallon, Anne-Marie 187*n*10
Malmgren, Carl 193*n*5, 194*n*8
Marcus, James 201*n*33
Mars-Jones, Adam 148, 198*n*6
Mason, Mary 97
Massé, Michelle 35, 39–40, 41, 43, 52, 54,

220   Index

57, 65, 180–181*n*4, 181*n*6, 183*n*5, 184*n*10, 184*n*15, 185*n*20
Mbiti, John 135, 137, 166–168, 171, 195*n*14, 196*n*20, 196*n*21
McDermott, Sinead 186*n*2, 188*n*19
McGill, Allyson 189*n*4
McGowan, John 45
McHale, Brian 13, 177*n*13, 178*n*18
Mckinstry, Susan 66, 184*n*12, 184*n*15, 188*n*29
Meese, Elizabeth 71, 187*n*10
Mellor, Winifred 90, 190*n*16
Metafiction 12–14, 22–23, 32–33
Metamorphosis, and the fantastic 42–43, 115, 117, 118, 119–121
Meyer, Marvin 200*n*22
Micahel, Magali 165, 197*n*2
Mile Sian 75
Miller, D.A. 74
Mimicry 95–96, 98
Mobley, Marilyn 196–197*n*23
Moglen, Helen 193*n*4, 193*n*5, 194–195*n*8
Mohanty, Satya 195*n*13
Morejon, Nancy 114
Morrison, Toni 17, 23, 24; *Beloved* 1, 5, 16, 17, 24, 27, 123, 125–145, 147–148, 166, 192*n*10; *Jazz* 166; "Memory, Creation, Writing" 138; Nobel lecture 201*n*33; *Paradise* 1, 5, 6, 16, 17, 18, 23, 28, 145, 146–174, 196*n*21; "Site of Memory" 197*n*23; *Song of Solomon* 195*n*9, 200*n*27; "Unspeakable Things, Unspoken" 130, 139, 197*n*27
Murdoch, Iris 23, 24, 50, 65; "Against Dryness" 180*n*3; *The Black Prince* 32, 39; *The Fire and the Sun* 33, 42; *Sartre, Romantic Rationalist* 31; *The Sea, the Sea* 1, 5, 16, 17, 25, 31–47, 49, 52, 62, 66, 133, 143, 140; "The Sublime and the Beautiful Revisited" 180*n*3, 181*n*7, 184*n*11
Murphy, Patrick 1, 2, 3, 176*n*6

Nag Hammadi 146, 147, 151, 158, 198*n*14, 199*n*21
Narrative self-consciousness 8, 21 24–25, 32–36, 40, 47, 50, 56, 61–62, 64–68, 78–81, 88–89, 90–91, 93–94, 98–99, 101–104, 124, 126, 185*n*22
Narrative strategy: feminist 18, 40, 126, 137, 147, 149, 155, 173–174, 188*n*13, 188*n*17; semiotic 26, 75–78, 94–98, 101, 103, 104, 127, 184–185*n*15, 190*n*12, 193*n*4
Narrative voice: authorial 24, 78–81, 86, 91, 92, 98, 101–104, 111, 123–124, 131, 192*n*12, 199*n*18; autodiegetic 102; communal 24, 27, 111, 122–124, 192*n*12,

192*n*14, 199*n*18; ex-centric focalization 122, 196*n*22; externally focalized 131; extradiegetic 15, 89; extrarepresentational 91, 92, 101–103, 123; figural 24, 103, 131, 199*n*18; first-person 6, 16–17, 24, 25, 26, 47, 66–68, 72, 79–81, 85–86, 87, 90, 96, 98, 99–103, 122, 123–124, 127, 131, 184*n*12 188*n*13, 188*n*14; 192*n*12, 199*n*18; heterodiegetic 102, 188*n*14; homodiegetic 17, 90, 102, 188*n*14; internally focalized 80, 89, 131, 134, 139; omniscient 72, 79–81, 86, 88–89, 98, 101, 103, 123, 127, 130, 188*n*17, 198*n*4, 198*n*5; overt authoriality 94, 101–102; personal 24, 79–80, 98–99, 101–103, 111, 123–124; representational 91–94, 99, 101–102; third-person 26, 80, 87, 89–93, 99, 100–103, 123–124, 127, 184*n*12, 188*n*14, 188*n*17, 189*n*4, 189*n*5
Naylor Gloria (*Linden Hills*) 180
Neuman, Shirley 190–191*n*17

O'Brien, Sheila 186*n*4
Oedipal narratives 75–76, 95
Ognibene, Elaine 122, 191*n*4, 193*n*15
Olsen, Lance 13
Omolade, Barbara 201*n*31
Omoyajowo, Joseph 166
O'Reilly, Andrea 144, 195*n*18
Origen of Alexandria 146
Ortiz, Fernando 191*n*2
Osland, Diane 189*n*5
Othow, Helen 168

Page, Philip 197*n*2
Pagels, Elaine 146, 148–149, 159, 160, 161–165 *passim*, 198*n*8, 198*n*9, 198*n*12, 200*n*22, 200*n*25
Parini, Jay 189*n*4
Paris, Peter 168, 201*n*32
Parsons, Anne 185*n*22
Peach, Linden 198*n*13
Perez-Torres, Rafael 193*n*3
Phelan, James 131–132, 194*n*6 195*n*14
Plath, Sylvia 49, 60, 185*n*18
Plato 33–34, 180*n*3
Postcolonial fiction and theory 2, 17–18, 27, 109–124 *passim*, 178*n*14, 178*n*17, 184*n*20, 194*n*7
Postmodernism 2, 7, 12–14, 21–22, 26, 33, 43, 45, 65, 103–104, 126–128, 132, 149, 158, 171*n*1, 177*n*11, 177–178*n*14, 179*n*26, 179–180*n*28, 190*n*16, 191*n*18, 193*n*3, 195*n*13
Pratt, Mary Louise 27, 112, 113, 124, 116–117, 191*n*2, 191*n*6

Punja, Prem Parkash 182*n*18
Pynchon, Thomas 12, 176*n*7

Rabinowitz, Peter 128
Rama, Angel 191*n*2
Rao, Eleanor 59, 64–65, 183*n*5, 184*n*15
Ravitz, Martha 187*n*6
Redding, Arthur 71, 83, 85, 86, 188*n*20, 196*n*22
Reumens, Carol 194*n*5
Richards, Dona 116, 120, 166, 171
Robbe-Grillet, Alain 21
Robbins, Sarah 197*n*23
Robinson, Marilynne 18, 24, 110, 127; *Housekeeping* 1, 5, 17, 25, 41, 47, 68, 71–86, 88, 94, 101, 104, 124, 125, 141, 143, 179*n*20, 185*n*15, 190*n*7, 190*n*10, 193*n*4
Robinson, Sally 20, 22–23, 57, 78, 92, 93, 126, 179*n*25
Robolin, Stephane 201*n*36
Rodriguez, Eusebio 196*n*19
Romero, Chanette 158–159, 172, 197*n*2, 198*n*13, 199*n*17
Rommon-Kenan, Shlomith 127, 139, 193*n*3, 193–194*n*5, 194*n*6
Rose, William 180*n*9
Rosenstone, Robert 133
Ross, Catherine 183*n*6
Roswoski, Susan 48, 52, 184*n*15, 185*n*20, 186*n*2
Roy, Wendy 189*n*6, 190*n*8, 190*n*9
Rubenstein, Roberta 186*n*2, 187*n*9
Rudolph, Kurt 149, 151, 158, 173
Ruether, Rosemary 146, 159, 166, 172, 200*n*28, 201*n*30
Rushdie, Salman 17
Ryan, Judylyn 157, 166–167, 171, 198*n*7, 199*n*18, 201*n*31, 32, 34
Ryan, Maureen 186*n*2, 187*n*6, 188*n*13

Sale, Maggie 134
Sanders, Julie 182*n*20
Sandler, Linda 182*n*2
Schenck, Celeste 104
Schmudde, Carol 196*n*22
Schopp, Andres 197*n*25
Schroeder, Shannin 194*n*7
Sexton, Anne 49
Shakespeare, William 34, 46, 182*n*20
Shange, Ntozke 199*n*18
Sherman, Geraldine 189*n*4
Shields, Carol 110, 127; *The Stone Diaries* 1, 5, 6, 17–18, 23, 24, 26, 41, 47, 68, 81, 87–105, 124, 135, 179*n*20, 184*n*12, 185*n*15, 188*n*14, 193*n*4
Showlater, Elaine 76, 78, 187*n*8

Silverman, Kaja 187*n*12
Sitter, Deborah 141, 193*n*1, 197*n*23, 197*n*26
Slethaug, Gordon 104, 190*n*16
Smith, Richard 146, 152
Smith, Sidonie 90–91, 92, 94, 95, 113, 190*n*12, 190*n*17, 191*n*6, 191–192*n*7
Smyth, Jaqui 83, 185*n*1
Spalding, Timothy 125, 140, 193*n*3, 194*n*7, 195*n*13, 196*n*22, 197*n*23
Spearey, Susan 137, 195*n*14
Spector, Judith 185*n*17, 185*n*18
Staele, Hilde 185*n*22
Stanzel, Franz 103, 190*n*15
Stave, Shirley 197*n*2
Stein, Karen 37, 67, 180*n*4, 185*n*25
Stephens, Autumn 103
Struthers, J.R. 185*n*25
Sullivan, Zohreh 180*n*2
Sweeney, Megan 148, 165, 169, 197*n*2, 198*n*6, 198*n*7, 200*n*26

Tally, Justine 166, 171–172, 201*n*34
Tan, Amy 192*n*12
Taylor-Gurthrie, Danille 128
Tennyson, Alfred ("The Lady of Shalott") 59–61, 184*n*15, 185*n*16
Terry, Jennifer 197*n*2, 200*n*2
Tertullian 146
Thomas, Clara 183*n*6, 189*n*4
Thomas, Joan 88
"Thunder, Perfect Mind" 147, 149–151, 158, 160, 162, 172, 197*n*2
Todorov, Tzvetan 2, 3, 7–15, 16, 19–20, 22–23, 24, 25, 28, 31–33, 36, 51–52, 58, 72, 127–129, 132, 138, 175*n*1, 176*n*3, 176*n*6, 176*n*7, 177*n*9, 177*n*10, 177*n*11, 177*n*12, 177*n*13, 178*n*17, 178*n*18, 179*n*20, 179*n*23, 180*n*1, 184*n*11, 193–194*n*5
Tolkien, J.R.R. 178*n*14
Traill, Nancy 176–177*n*9, 179*n*22
Transculturation 17, 109–124 *passim*, 191*n*1, 191*n*2, 192*n*9
Travis, Molly 128, 196*n*23
Trussler, Michael 193*n*5
Tucker, Lindsey 41, 42, 182*n*19, 182*n*20, 184*n*15, 185*n*18
Turner, Nick 180*n*2

Vauthier, Simone 89–90, 102, 189*n*5, 190*n*13, 190*n*16
Vincent Sybil 184*n*11

Walker, Nancy 73, 186*n*2, 187*n*10, 187*n*11, 188*n*17, 188*n*19
Warhol, Robyn 3
Washington, Teresa 136, 196*n*20

Wasmeier, Marie-Louise 188–189n2, 189n4
Watson, Greer 176n8
Waxman, Barbara 133, 193n51, 196n20, 196n22
Weissberg, Lilaine 196n23, 197n24
Whibley, M.E.L. 180n3
White, Hayden 44, 133, 181n5
Wilentz, Gay 201n36
Williams, David 88, 189n3, 189n5
Wilson, Rawdon 18
Wilson, Sharon 185n16, 183n6

Winsbro, Bonnie 178n16
Winterson, Jeanette 179n26
Wood, Micahel 197n2
Woolf, Virginia 156
Wyatt, Jean 77, 86, 137, 187n9, 187n10, 190n10, 193n4, 193n5

York, R.A. 110
Yukins, Elizabeth 199n15

Zamora, Lois 194n7

www.ingramcontent.com/pod-product-compliance
Ingram Content Group UK Ltd.
Pitfield, Milton Keynes, MK11 3LW, UK
UKHW021845140426
5217IPUK00022B/1594